KT-215-680

C016173003

CHARLES
THE HEART OF A KING

CATHERINE MAYER

WH
ALLEN

1 3 5 7 9 10 8 6 4 2

WH Allen, an imprint of Ebury Publishing,

20 Vauxhall Bridge Road,

London SW1V 2SA

WH Allen is part of the Penguin Random House group of companies whose addresses can be found
at global.penguinrandomhouse.com

Copyright © Catherine Mayer 2015

Catherine Mayer has asserted her right to be identified as the
author of this Work in accordance with the Copyright,
Designs and Patents Act 1988

'Always Look On The Bright Side Of Life' Words and Music by
Eric Idle © Copyright 1990 Python (Monty) Pictures Limited.
Universal Music Publishing Limited. All Rights Reserved.
International Copyright Secured. Used by permission of Music Sales limited.

'These Hands' words and music © Dave Gunning. Used by permission.

First published by WH Allen in 2015

This edition published by WH Allen in 2016

www.eburypublishing.co.uk

A CIP catalogue record for this book
is available from the British Library

ISBN 9780753555958

Printed and bound by CPI Group (UK) Ltd, Croydon, CR0 4YY

Picture Credits:

Section 1

1. Top: Getty Images /Keystone-France/Gamma-Keystone, bottom: Rex Features/Reginals Davis 2. Top: Corbis/© Adam Woolfitt, bottom: Corbis/ © Hulton-Deutsch Collection 3. Top: Rex Features/Clive Limpkin/Associated Newspapers, centre: Getty Images/Hulton Archive, bottom: Rex Features 4. Top: Corbis/© Douglas Kirkland, bottom: Getty Images/Tim Graham 5. Top: Rex Features/News Group, bottom: Getty Images/Odd Andersen/AFP 6. Top: Rex Features/Reginald Davis, bottom left: Getty Images/Lisa Sheridan/Studio Lisa, bottom right: Getty Images/Arthur Edwards 7. Top left: Press Association Images/Sean Dempsey, top right: Alamy/© WENN UK, bottom: Press Association Images/ PA News 8. Top: Rex Features/Thomas Abrahams/Associated Newspapers, centre left: Getty Images/ David Cairns/Express, centre right: Rex Features/Eddie Boldizsar, bottom: Rex Features/Kent Gavin

Section 2

1. Top: Getty/Tim Graham, bottom left: Alamy/© Arcaid Images, bottom right: Alamy/© Duncan Shaw 2. Top: Getty Images/Chris Jackson, bottom: Getty Images/Helena Smith 3. Top: Getty Images/ Katie Garrod, bottom: courtesy of Mark Malloch Brown 4. Top left: Topfoto/© PA Photos, top right: Getty Images/Gareth Cattermole/AFP, bottom: Press Association/Dylan Martinez/AP 5. Top: Getty Images/John Stillwell, bottom: Getty Images/Mark Cuthbert/UKPress 6. Top: Getty Images/Chris Jackson, bottom left: Getty Images/Fayez Nureldine/AFP, bottom right: Getty Images/Max Mumby/ Indigo 7. Top: Getty Images/John Stillwell, bottom: Getty Images/Anwar Hussein Collection/ROTA/ WireImage 8. Top: Corbis/© Jason Bell/epa, bottom: Corbis/© Pool Photograph

MIX
Paper from
responsible sources
FSC
www.fsc.org   FSC® C018179

Penguin Random House is committed to a sustainable future for our
business, our readers and our planet. This book is made from Forest
Stewardship Council® certified paper.

To Andy, perennially

Contents

Author's Note

The year since publication of *Charles: The Heart of a King* has been eventful for Prince Charles. The Duchess of Cambridge delivered his first granddaughter. The UK's supreme court delivered a tranche of his so-called 'black spider memos' to public view. The Scottish government published more of his private correspondence. In updating this book to incorporate these and other significant news events, it would be perverse to ignore a story that kept Charles in the headlines for the best part of a month: the hullabaloo generated by and around this book.

The Prince may have read it; his wife planned to take it on their March 2015 trip to the US. If he has skimmed these pages, he's unlikely to have relished the experience. It is never easy to read about yourself, and a lifetime in the public eye rather than thickening the princely skin has instead worn it to the thinnest parchment. This is by no means a hatchet job but I set out to understand rather than to flatter. Many sources, including insiders in the royal households and denizens of Charles's inner circle, have been kind enough to tell me I captured my subject well and with humanity. At least one member of the Prince's family has gifted copies to friends. A contact with close knowledge of Charles and his strange world emailed to commend the book for 'balance and accuracy … though I did snort tea out of my nose several times while reading it.'

Aides at Clarence House – the Prince's London home and the collective name for his staff – by contrast suffered something of a humour failure. In February 2015 the *Times* ran pre-publication extracts from the biography and the *Daily Mail* – which had earlier published a gossip item reporting, wrongly, that I was claiming the Prince had authorised the book – concocted its own imaginative serialisation. (At my book party, I thanked both newspapers for their serialisations, adding, tongue firmly in cheek, 'and they say I don't know the difference between authorised and unauthorised'.) In response to the coverage, an anonymous Clarence House staffer allegedly briefed journalists that lawyers would study the full text with a view to possible prosecution. Newspapers quoted the staffer insisting against a wealth of evidence that I had spent only a total of 'about nine minutes' with the Prince in the course of my research.[1] In a spiky phone call, an aide denied the smear emanated from Clarence House, but there was no move to set the record straight. Instead William Nye, then Principal Private Secretary to Charles and Camilla, ratcheted up the furor with a letter to the *Times* protesting 'ill-informed speculation … in your columns and elsewhere'.[2]

There had indeed been ill-informed speculation. Nobody at Clarence House at this stage had actually read the book.

When aides finally did so, they of course found revelations that they, and their employer, might have preferred to keep quiet. There is also a detailed assessment of the Prince's substantial contribution to public life, and more than that, a rounded picture of a man who more frequently appears in one-dimensional caricature. The novelist Will Self, a lifelong republican, in his review wrote that the book had prompted him to an unexpected realisation: 'On the whole – and certainly by contrast with the rest of his family – I rather liked [the Prince].'[3]

Many readers reacted in a similar vein. The media barrage eventually subsided. Concerned friends and more than a few of Charles's associates invited me for stiffening drinks, expressing relief to find me in good spirits. This wasn't a pose. For one thing, the controversy propelled the biography straight into the bestseller lists. For another I had anticipated the rumpus if not its intensity and had anatomised in the book exactly the mechanisms that again came into play: a mischief-making media and courtiers so eager to defend the Prince and their own positions that they react on a hair-trigger. One insider had described Clarence House to me as 'Wolf Hall'. In the weeks after this biography first appeared, Wolf Hall bared its teeth and lived up to its billing.

I had also expected legitimate questions about the amount of time I spent with the Prince and the terms of that special access and had used my original author's note to set out detailed answers. Here is that note, updated and shortened but otherwise untouched – and more relevant than ever.

In October 2013, a short 'teaser' on *TIME*'s website generated headlines across the world. These headlines quickly described a narrative arc of their own, from the factual 'PRINCE CHARLES IN NO HURRY TO BECOME KING'[4] to the sexed-up 'PRINCE CHARLES FEARS BECOMING KING WILL BE LIKE "PRISON"'[5] and through a U-turn: 'PRINCE CHARLES "PRISON" CLAIM DENIED'[6]. I had posted the teaser to draw attention to the newly published issue of *TIME* magazine, which carried my cover profile of the Prince.[7] The teaser pointed to some of the main conclusions of that longer piece: that Charles is a passionate philanthropist, one of the world's most prolific charitable entrepreneurs. He does not have the leisure to sit about waiting to be king and is driven by a sense of urgency to get as much done as possible before that day arrives. I wrote: 'Much of what you think you know about the Prince is wrong … I found a man not, as caricatured, itching to ascend the throne, but impatient to get as much done as possible before, in the words of one member of his household, "the prison shades" close. The Queen, at 87, is scaling back her work, and the

Prince is taking up the slack, to the potential detriment of his network of charities, initiatives and causes.'[8]

Teased or not, the cover story was always bound to draw attention, and not just because Charles emerged as a bit of a charmer, who inspired his close friend, the actor Emma Thompson, to the tongue-in-cheek observation that dancing with him was 'better than sex'. (The quote in my *TIME* profile, which launched a first set of lurid headlines, had in fact been truncated for space. Who knows what the tabloids would have made of Thompson's unexpurgated tribute: 'He's a great, great dancer. He's the best dancer. Not disco-dancing. Proper dancing. I've never danced with anyone who can actually lead me and I can just relax and go, this is great, this is better than sex. He's a very charismatic, virile dancer.')[9]

I had been given remarkable access by the standards of royal press management, which is to say, nowhere near as much as a *TIME* journalist might expect from a President or Prime Minister, but enough to get a strong sense of my quarry and for him to get a sense of me. Before the project could be green-lit, he met me and spoke to me off the record. For six months, I trailed him, came close to learning to remember to curtsey every time we met, listened to his speeches – and his jokes – visited his homes, struggled to keep up with him as he strode across muddy fields, attended a private concert at his Welsh bolthole, mingled at multiple events to promote his charities and initiatives, on one occasion in 2013 I dined with him at the Scottish mansion Dumfries House, listened in on one of his private meetings (and inevitably became drawn into the discussion that took place), interviewed a substantial number of people close to him and eventually sat down in his living room in Birkhall to an on-the-record conversation with him.

His aides at Clarence House agreed to the Prince speaking on condition that this would not be billed as an 'interview' and that he could review his quotes pre-publication. A few of the most revealing things he said ended up on the cutting-room floor; so did some utterly innocuous remarks. Monarchy moves in mysterious ways. I did not use any rewritten quotes that changed the meaning of the original. About half of the interviewees, particularly those working for the royal households or Charles's charities and initiatives, insisted that I send their comments about 'HRH' or 'the Boss' for prior approval, and like the Prince excised the anodyne as well as the controversial. Other sources opted to remain anonymous.

Similar preconditions were necessary to secure some of the many additional interviews conducted for this book. These did not include a second recorded conversation with Charles. In January 2014, I travelled back to Dumfries House to research a second piece and accompanied Charles on a long march around the estate, lasting about five hours. I seized many additional opportunities to observe him at close quarters, for example in May of the same year accompanying him and the Duchess of Cornwall on their official visit to Canada, interacting with both of them and watching them interact with others.

There is a convention that private conversations with royals are not to be quoted directly. The definition of a private conversation is less than crystalline. One such conversation, between the Prince and a volunteer guide at the Canadian Museum of Immigration at Pier 21 in Nova Scotia, found its way into the *Daily Mail*, prompting a diplomatic spat with Russia. The *Mail* explained its decision to publish on the basis that the volunteer had been standing in the official line-up at the museum.[10] I decided in this book to quote from a few conversations that Clarence House would class as private – for example, between Charles and a collective of Welsh butchers – to give a flavour of the way he speaks and how he engages with people, but I have steered clear of repeating any remarks that would lend themselves to headlines either because they misrepresented his true views or revealed them all too clearly but without context.

In other circumstances, a biographer could rely on previously published work to fill in the gaps. With Charles, for reasons set out in greater detail in the pages that follow, that would be problematic. Many secondary printed sources are unreliable. So my voluminous reading has been supplemented by multiple interviews with people who know Charles well. I hope so. I have also drawn on a large body of research about the royals amassed over three decades, most recently as the author of four *TIME* cover stories and co-author of a *TIME* book and also as the editor and behind-the-scenes point person for a *TIME* cover story on the Queen in 2006 for which I also interviewed Prince Andrew. Two years before that I had shadowed Andrew on one of his trade missions to China and interviewed him in Beijing. I've been delving into the royals since the Diana years. Every encounter with Prince Charles, his family, staff and friends, quotable or not, has deepened my understanding. Controlled access is better than the only alternative open to the vast majority of biographers: no access.

The Queen has never given an interview, by that name or any other; her children and grandchildren rarely do so. The Freedom of Information Act in England, Wales and Northern Ireland exempts communications with the Queen, Prince Charles and the second in line to the throne, William, from public scrutiny. Palace staff sign confidentiality agreements. Royal press secretaries almost never comment on stories deemed to stray into the ever-narrowing sphere of the purely personal. That policy means some journalists inevitably make honest mistakes based on faulty information from trusted sources cultivated to supplement the meagre fare provided by close-lipped royal aides. More unscrupulous reporters see in such reticence a licence to fabricate or embroider stories that they calculate the palace will find too trivial or intrusive to rebut. There's an assumption, too, that the royals will not sue. So the world is awash with royal nonsense. Inaccuracies and inventions, left unchallenged, are repeated. Repetition gives credence. Once a sufficient number of news organisations has repeated a fiction, it becomes a multi-sourced fact. News-gathering in the age of aggregation is a giant game of Chinese whispers, in which stories become, like the Prince's eggs, more scrambled with each retelling.

In 2012, Clarence House took the unusual step of publishing on its website a list of 'frequently asked questions' about Charles and rubbishing the answers generously provided by the press. 'Does the Prince of Wales have seven boiled eggs cooked for his breakfast but eat only one, as claimed in Jeremy Paxman's book *On Royalty*?' the website wondered. 'No, he doesn't and never has done, at breakfast or any other time.' Paxman, a distinguished BBC broadcaster, had told a story relayed to him by a friend of Charles. After a day's hunting, staff would put out boiled eggs 'in an ascending row of numbers. If the Prince felt that number five was too runny, he could knock the top off number six or seven.' The story, Paxman added, 'seems so preposterously extravagant as to be unbelievable'.[11]

Yet it may well have been rooted in fact. Wendy Berry, a former housekeeper at Highgrove, published a memoir of her time in service to Charles in which she described, with pride, serving perfectly cooked boiled eggs to the Prince after he returned from hunting. She put a first batch of eggs on to cook when Charles arrived but realising that a member of his party had been delayed, discarded the first batch and started again. There is no suggestion that Charles asked her to do so or knew of the waste, which he would as likely have reprimanded as applauded. His lifestyle, as with much else about him, is riven with contradictions. He lives high on the hog by just about any standard, but combines the showiness of royal life – the banquets, the acreage of cut flowers, retinues larger than most other family members employ – with a frugality absorbed from his parents and from austere schooling at the Scottish public school Gordonstoun, and more consciously informed by his environmental concerns. He keeps his homes at frigid temperatures, sometimes wears clothes that are more patch than original material, and for several parched months of a hot summer funnelled his used bathwater through a blue plastic pipe from his tub at St James's Palace into the garden below. 'Here is a man who, when you're having tea with him, gets any leftovers wrapped up and brought back for his next meal and the next one,' said Clive Alderton, who got to know the Prince during a secondment to Clarence House from the Foreign Office, and at the time of speaking to me had rejoined the FCO, serving as Her Majesty's Ambassador to Morocco. Alderton returned to Clarence House in August 2015 as Principal Private Secretary. 'I've rarely met someone who is so frugal: not in the sense of meanness but an absolute allergy to waste and in particular waste of food', Alderton concluded.[12]

Nevertheless, the eggs, repurposed as Charles's breakfast-time whim and served as proof of his profligacy, began doing the rounds, joining other half-myths of the spoiled princeling: that a valet squeezes his toothpaste for him and that he ordered his servant to hold the specimen bottle as he deposited a princely urine sample. Neither of these stories is without a kernel of truth. Michael Fawcett, one of the most compelling and ambiguous members of the Prince's inner coterie, worked for many years as his valet, and when an accident put Charles's arm in a sling, he assisted with tasks that would have been difficult with only one hand free. Before and after that brief interlude, Charles has managed such functions, as it were, single-handed. 'It's very difficult to fight back,' says Elizabeth Buchanan, a former Private Secretary to the Prince. 'Because you can fight back [but] how demeaning to have to say the Prince of Wales does not have his toothpaste squeezed. Guess what, if you break your arm funnily enough there are some things you can't do.'[13]

The distortions seem harmless, but combine to create a reputation for dissipation that is hard to dispel. Most people believe at least some of the falsehoods in circulation about the royals, not least because some fictions slide into fact. For nineteen months after her wedding, the Duchess of Cambridge found herself declared pregnant on a weekly basis. Then reality caught up with invention (though the twins, heralded on the cover of at least three separate magazines, failed to materialise).

In the absence of news, editors try to change the narrative to retain interest. For Kate, most often depicted as a blissed-out madonna, a paragon of young motherhood, that meant her March 2014 trip to the Maldives with William – and the couple's decision to travel without George, then seven months old – provided the *Daily Mail* with an opportunity to test out an alternative storyline. 'ROYALS JET OFF INTO A STORM OF PROTEST' declared its print and online editions; 'the [couple's] decision sparked a storm on social networking sites Mumsnet, Netmums and Twitter'.[14]

It was a manufactured tempest in a child's teacup. Netmums posted an item inviting comment on the royal jolly only at the request of the *Mail*. There had been no discussion before that and the thread generated little reaction among the website's 1.2 million members. Of forty-two comments in total, only two could be construed as negative. After Netmums protested that the story was inaccurate, the *Mail* deleted the reference to the site from the online article. Had there been outrage on Mumsnet? Not according to Katie O'Donovan, Mumsnet's head of communications, who emails that there were 'just over 300 responses, which isn't really a "storm" by Mumsnet's standards. Not at all unanimous in criticism of the couple and it's worth noting that about one third of the thread comes after (and so in response to) the *Mail* piece being published.'[15] The swell of Twitter reaction also appears to have been triggered by the *Mail* piece that purported to describe it.

This isn't just a function of cynical journalism. The problem for and with the monarchy is that much of what it does, when things are going right, has little news value. Yet the royals need to publicise their work, such as it is, for fear of being accused of laziness and also because much of that work involves drawing publicity to worthy causes or flying the flag for the nations they represent. As a result, there is a constant low-level struggle between the palace press teams, which vainly hope to satisfy reporters with a thin gruel of visits and speeches and photo opportunities, and the media organisations, which have to find something newsworthy in the soup.

Amongst the British national press, only the lofty *Financial Times* takes the obvious option not to report these events at all. The *Independent*'s Editor Amol Rajan has returned the newspaper to its founding principles which happen to dovetail neatly with its tight editorial budgets, only running royal stories that are 'of constitutional significance' and 'done in a proportionate manner'.[16] Baby George's christening, the front-page splash for many papers, was thus relegated to the news-in-brief column.

Organisations that deploy costly teams to cover the royals must always conjure up a result. In 1985, the *Guardian* dispatched a young reporter to Australia to cover a visit to the country by the Prince and Princess of Wales. Alan Rusbridger, who went on to edit the *Guardian* for 20 years, remembers the assignment as 'the most awful job I've ever done … It was just sort of humiliating as a journalist. You were bussed from place to place and stood behind a table and something would happen, there would be a ribbon and a pair of scissors and then you would be bussed back and then there would be thirty of you on the bus and your job was to try and concoct something at the end of the day that was not as banal as I've just described it. And it was everything you hated about them and our fascination with them so I just ended up writing four pieces from Australia which were all about what it was like to cover them.'[17]

Before Diana came on the scene, most broadsheet journalists were spared such ignominy; their editors abandoned royal coverage to the red-tops whose intrusions were minor by later standards. 'Did you get a picture of my left earhole?' Prince Philip, sailing in Scotland, shouted at a dogged photographer in 1962.[18] Some of the popular press chose to publish a photograph of Philip's left ear with his commentary.

Higher-minded media disdained such trivia. When Anthony Holden, a journalist for the broadsheet *Sunday Times*, decided the Prince's 1977 trip to Canada might make good fodder for a piece, the startled subject of his interest asked: 'What on earth are *you* doing here?'[19] As the only writer trailing Charles, Holden enjoyed near-unfettered access. It was the same story later the same year on a sweep through South America. He went on to write three biographies of Charles, at ten-year intervals, each chronicling his increasing disenchantment with the Prince and his media handlers. The feelings were mutual after Holden's second biography revealed strains in the royal marriage that remained largely concealed until the convulsive events of 1992. But Holden's books also charted the changing challenges of royal media management. No longer might a journalist hope for the ad-hoc dinners and head-to-heads with Charles that Holden enjoyed on the 1977 trips. Instead, after Charles's marriage to Diana made royal coverage a commercial imperative for most organisations, the author found himself 'in Australia for the bicentennial celebrations of 1988 ... one of 200 writers and photographers, as many as 70 of whom had flown out from Britain, permitted only to observe the couple from behind ropes, at a safe distance.'[20] More than 450 journalists were accredited for William and Kate's 2014 tour of the Antipodes.

Distance has bred distance, of the wrong kind. Monarchy matters but only the republican press consistently acknowledges that fact. Much royal coverage is lobotomised fluff that understands the Windsors only as the cast of a long-running reality TV show – showbiz but not necessarily even showbiz royalty – or conceals an edge of resentment common to all celebrity reporting. Stories are spun from the thinnest of materials.

Relations between royals and reporters haven't always been this fraught. For a period in the 1990s, the Prince opened up to his biographer Jonathan Dimbleby, whose book and film have remained a key resource for researchers as a result but have never been updated. Now Charles is a born-again virgin – hence his concerns about giving 'interviews'. It took a sustained campaign to persuade Clarence House, and the Prince himself, that allowing me access to profile him for *TIME* might, from their perspective, do more good than harm. I wasn't promising puffery but substance and balance – and that inevitably meant there would be elements in the story they didn't like. My counter-argument was that puff pieces don't move the dial on public opinion.

That opinion still owes a good deal to Diana. She understood the power of imagery and the wounds that a well-placed leak could inflict. She, too, cultivated special relationships among the ranks of the media. Her friends, old and new, spread the word about her husband's derelictions. His camp fought back, but without the same skills and hampered by a principal who could never match Diana's lustre or her bloodlust. A substantial minority of Britons still supports an idea she boosted in her magnificently dissident 1995 interview for the BBC's *Panorama*: that the succession should skip Charles and pass directly to their son William. Her estranged husband might not actually want to be king, she suggested: 'Being Prince of Wales produces more freedom now, and being king would be a little bit more suffocating.' 'Would it be your wish that when Prince William comes of age that he were to succeed the Queen rather than the current Prince of Wales?' asked interviewer Martin Bashir. 'My wish is that my husband finds peace of mind, and from that follows other things, yes,' answered the Princess, permitting herself a small smile as she delivered a line that would haunt her husband for ever more.

Eighteen years later, I forgot that smile as I attempted to skewer another widespread myth: that Charles is frustrated by his mother's refusal to die or stand down and let him take what Diana called 'the top job'. Multiple conversations with insiders – his friends, house-holders, people working for his charities – had led me to the understanding that the opposite was true. For one thing, the Prince doesn't deal well with death. Despite the comfort his religious and philosophical beliefs should presumably provide, he still mourns, with a startlingly raw grief, his grandmother, his great-uncle Louis Mountbatten, and mentors such as Laurens van der Post – a man of many self-descriptions including explorer and anthropologist and too loose a relationship with the truth to trust his self-descriptions – and Kathleen Raine, a poet. Charles dreads the deaths of his parents.

The Queen's grand age is not only a source of anxiety for the Prince but, before the start of my research for the *TIME* piece, had set in train a difficult process behind the scenes at Clarence House, to make space for Charles to shoulder more of the traditional duties of kingship. He was looking at rationalising his existing commitments and reining in his impulse to intervene. Instead of extending his hand to fresh beneficiaries and new causes, he was under pressure to cut some existing liegemen adrift. This ran counter to his usual instincts and also generated considerable bad blood as courtiers turned on each other in the fight for survival. In all of this, Charles put duty before passion. That was why a member of his household compared the Prince to the growing boy in William Wordsworth's 'Intimations of Immortality' for whom 'shades of the prison-house begin to close' as adulthood nears.

So it was a fair point well made by my informant, but I had reck-oned without the acute neuralgia the spirit of Diana still triggers within palace walls. Clarence House swiftly issued a denial of some-thing my piece had not implied because it wasn't true: that Charles was my unnamed source. 'This is not the Prince of Wales's view and should not be attributed to him as he did not say these words,' said the statement. 'The Prince has dutifully supported the Queen all his life and his official duties and charitable work have always run in parallel.'

The denial inadvertently gave the story fresh legs and these days resides in the ether along with all the earlier 'Charles doesn't want to be king' stories, inevitably to be recycled at various points in the future, shorn of context.

Charles does want to be king. But, as I discovered, that's the least of his ambitions.

Introduction

If thou pretend'st to be a prince like me,
Blame not an act, which should thy pattern be.
I saw the oppressed, and thought it did belong
To a king's office to redress the wrong:
I brought that succour, which thou ought'st to bring,
And so, in nature, am thy subjects' king.

John Dryden, *Almanzor and Almahide*

The Prince is a polished host. Years of putting strangers at ease have endowed him with a repertoire of useful tricks. His bright eyes never glaze. He listens attentively and squirrels away nuggets of information to nourish future conversations. He matches subject and tone to each person with perfect pitch and repays confidences with glimpses into his own life – nothing too intimate, just amusing anecdotes or wry tales of the tribulations of parenting or latterly heartfelt paeans to the joys of grandparenting – to create a sense of connection, of shared experience.

On this particular September evening in 2013, shared experiences threaten to be in short supply. His twenty-four guests hail from France,

Poland, Russia, Spain, South Africa, Taiwan, the US, Uzbekistan and different corners and conditions of Britain, with little in common apart from the basic fact of humanity and that around half of the people sipping aperitifs in the Tapestry Room at Dumfries House own, between them, an astonishing slice of global wealth. Mischievous members of Charles's staff have coined a collective term for the moneyed classes that he regularly lures to such dinners: 'Bond villains'.

His aides are adamant that all potential donors are subjected to careful background checks and this contingent certainly appears more inclined to philanthropy than villainy, aiming not to dominate the world but to help it. Guests turn out to be sponsors of worthy causes; backers of foundations; patrons of music and the visual arts. One man describes himself as an art collector. 'Any particular kind of art?' 'Yes,' he says airily, 'art that I like.'

At Dumfries House, artworks by old masters hang alongside water-colours by the oldest ever heir to the British throne. In 2007, Charles scrambled a consortium to buy this Palladian mansion in Scotland, sparing the building a future that might have seen it sprout ungainly wings as a resort hotel, and staying an auction that would have dispersed an unparalleled collection of Thomas Chippendale furniture. Under his auspices, the house has become a heritage attraction and the estate is a seedbed for his charities and initiatives, all of which gobble up money.

So there is no such thing as a free lunch with the Prince, much less a free dinner at Dumfries House, for all that scenes of careless revelry provide the backdrop for pre-dinner cocktails. The mansion's original Flemish tapestries, stitched in the early eighteenth century in the Brussels workshop of Leyniers-Reydams, have been sent away for restoration; in their place hang near-perfect replicas across which Bacchus and various maidens and minions cavort with the sort of happy abandon that the previous year landed Prince Harry in the tabloids. ('HEIR IT IS,' announced the *Sun*'s headline above a grainy image of a naked Harry, cupping his 'crown jewels' during a game of strip poker in a Las Vegas hotel.) A few of this evening's guests have already opened their wallets to the Prince's charities. They have been invited to bind them more closely into these organisations. Charles hopes to persuade the rest to follow suit over a visit that includes the dinner, a tour of the house and, the following day, a vigorous march around the grounds that he leads himself.

Over cocktails he entertains his 'villains' with tamer episodes from Harry's youth. He speaks with obvious pride and affection, and a touch of wonderment. For all his bonhomie, his jokes and a delight in the absurd that saw him at Harry's thirteenth birthday party laughing uproariously while competing with Emma Thompson in a game in which players donned hats covered in Velcro to try to catch felt-covered balls, Charles is fundamentally serious. His younger son lives in the moment. It is hard enough to master that trick when the future is mapped out far in advance and in hourly increments, harder still for someone of Charles's temperament and experiences.

There's a revealing joke the Prince tells so often that it has acquired a patina of use, like his two favourite pairs of day shoes, buffed and polished and trotted out over the decades. His comic timing has always been good, and his constricted elocution lends itself at least as easily to humour as to solemnity. (Friends and staff can't help themselves but mimic his voice and the rictus that pulls down the left corner of his mouth when he is at his most emphatic.) In a parallel universe he might have made a decent stand-up, the funny-looking teenager, his face too narrow a base for the Windsor beak and wing-like ears, growing up to exploit the natural comedy in being a man out of joint with ordinary life and turning his bafflement into an amusing routine. Instead, the man who expects one day to reign over the United Kingdom and fifteen other Commonwealth Realms deploys wit to leaven speeches on weighty issues or simply to entertain guests at private functions. These days he is a confident performer, easy in a skin that has come with age to suit him – he turned sixty-seven on 14 November 2015. He is dextrous with words, quick with a riposte, and can deliver zingers. But time and again, he returns to this same tired gag.

'If ever you're afraid of being somehow marooned on a desert island – perhaps you're flying a light aeroplane over the South Seas – always make sure you have in your knapsack a cocktail shaker, one of those collapsible goblets such as they used to issue in the army, a small jar of olives, some cocktail sticks, a phial of vermouth and a hip flask of gin or vodka,' he counsels his audience. 'If, by misfortune, you do find yourself stranded, like Robinson Crusoe, all alone on a desert island, have no fear. All you have to do is unpack your martini paraphernalia and start to mix the drink.'

He pauses, signalling the imminent arrival of a punchline. 'I can guarantee that within a minute, someone will jump out of a tree and say, "That's not the proper way to mix a martini!"'

The joke reliably earns a big laugh, a bigger pay-off than it would seem to deserve, but then that's the really funny thing about royalty: its members seldom experience the world as the rest of us do because their presence changes it. The Prince knows humanity on its best behaviour and at its worst – sycophantic, shallow, sharp-elbowed. He's used to people applauding his every pronouncement and responding to his jokes with great, grating guffaws.

Yet there's a reverse side to the coinage that carries his mother's head. There always seems to be someone poised to leap out of the shrubbery to declare he doesn't know how to mix a martini. Commentary and criticism have attended him throughout his life like resentful valets. He has never enjoyed the luxury of trying and failing privately. As soon as he began to express opinions, he discovered he was speaking through a loudhailer. As the frail struts of his first marriage corroded, he found himself widely miscast. He had famously semaphored his unease after the engagement was announced, when an interviewer ventured that he and Lady Diana Spencer were 'in love'. 'Of course,' said Diana. 'Whatever "in love" means,' added her fiancé, his face frozen.

In failing to love the 'queen of people's hearts', as Diana would later accurately characterise her public role, Charles appeared a knave as well as a joker.[1] In avoiding the pitfalls of doing little of substance during an apprenticeship to be sovereign that his mother's longevity has stretched over more than half a century, he instead earns censure for doing too much. He's a dabbler, straying into areas of expertise that are not his own. He's a meddler, ignoring constitutional proprieties to intervene in the political process. If he finally accedes to the throne – which he is gnawingly impatient to do – Charles III promises to be as memorable a king as Charles I.

The last point may well prove true, if for different reasons. United with the woman he loves and fondly observing his sons establishing a Camelot of their own, with his charitable empire in full swing and a host of initiatives and campaigns under his stewardship, the Prince is probably more contented than he's ever been. He enjoys life, sometimes. He can be excellent company, in spite, or even because of, the jokes. He has a talent for telling them. A man often mimicked, he is an expert mimic of others. 'He's a sort of Rory Bremner,' says his godson and cousin, Tim Knatchbull. 'He's got the thing where he'll change his face; it's a studied little move. He's got the knack for imitating. You've either got the knack or you don't. The Queen's the same and he's clearly inherited the gene from her.'[2]

The Prince is a multilingual polymath, a decent watercolourist and expert gardener. The royals are popularly assumed to be horse-mad. Charles, however, has a passion for sheep. Emma Sparham, helped by his charity the Prince's Trust to start her own business, met him at a St James's Palace reception and mentioned the rare breed which she keeps. 'If I was to say the word "Soay" to a hundred people, maybe five of them might know what it is,' she said afterwards.

'He knew exactly what it was, what island they come from and he knows the nature of the animal. He asked if I could catch them because they are renowned for being uncatchable.'[3] The Prince keeps flocks of sheep at several of his homes, has devised campaigns to promote wool and mutton, and scooped the 2012 George Hedley Memorial Award presented by Britain's National Sheep Association in recognition for his outstanding contribution to the ovine sector.

He is kind. He keeps track of the personal circumstances of the people around him, asks after their loved ones, makes an effort to attend events that are important to them. As family members gathered for the funeral of his brother-in-law Mark Shand in May 2014, it was Charles, warm and 'extraordinarily tactile', who brewed tea and dispensed sympathy, says Ben Elliot, co-founder of the Quintessentially Group and the Prince's nephew by marriage.[4] Charles organises surprises and treats for friends and for people he admires, such as a joint eightieth birthday celebration at Clarence House for the playwright Ronald Harwood and the actor Maggie Smith. He inspires devotion, sometimes more than is good for him. He is loyal to a fault, sometimes to the point of fault. 'He's a very human person, incredibly emotionally alert. The radar is very powerful, and he picks up on things,' says Ian Skelly, a BBC broadcaster who often helps the Prince to write speeches and has also collaborated with him on a startling book. 'Because of his background he's spent his entire life trying to work out who's true and who's full of flannel.'[5] Unlike the rest of his family, when Charles asks: 'And what do you do?' he's keenly interested in hearing the answer.

A compulsive philanthropist, he has founded more than twenty-five charities. 'Every one of them is a little pilot project that lights a candle in a dark space,' says Lord Sacks, Britain's former Chief Rabbi. Sacks goes so far as to speak of the Prince's 'greatness'. 'I do not go around using that word liberally, I really don't,' he adds. 'You know why the world doesn't see him for what he is? Because we have very little room for greatness. We're interested in celebrity.'[6]

But after a lifetime of being found wanting – the proverbial prophet without honour in his own country – Charles rarely recognises his own achievements. He is 'a glass-half-empty man' in the words of one member of his inner circle, a Prince of Wails. Another person close to him says he has a short fuse. 'The royal rage, I call it. Here comes the royal rage.' At the darkest points of his life, his despondency has been profound. Even now, in his late-blooming prime, he recites litanies of injustice and in rare on-the-record conversations cannot prevent plaintive notes from sounding. 'Each thing I did, you had to meet another lot of people who have all sorts of views of you beforehand, all sorts of prejudices,' he confides.[7]

This biography aims to puncture those prejudices in order to close in on the far more interesting truth. As good a starting place as any must be to identify the mechanisms which occlude that truth. The Prince often blames a toxic press, and he is not wrong. But that toxicity has fermented into a complex jelly, amid social change and global strains, at the intersection of republicanism and an avid celebrity culture, in a Britain facing new battles with identity and old struggles with class. Stifling deference has given way to a prevailing mistrust of institutions and public figures. Palace structures have struggled to manage a mainstream media itself in transition and, latterly, in existential crisis. As newspaper revenues have declined, the pressure to produce stories, by hook or by crookery, has increased. Legitimate inquiries must navigate a miasma of half-fact and fiction surrounding the royal households, often without reliable guides and frequently bumping up against official secrecy. The Internet promised a new age of transparency and has instead added to the miasma.

At the centre of this confusion, hand in pocket, stands Charles, a man who would in any circumstances prove hard to decode. He is fascinating, flawed as we all are, yet not as we are: a product of an upbringing set apart, conditioned to be different and to believe that difference must be maintained, a native of Planet Windsor. 'He identifies with other people's precariousness. In many ways I feel that he's a strange figure in that set-up, precisely because he seems to have all of these passions and concerns about issues and people,' says Lucia Santa Cruz, his friend since university days. 'I think he's one of the most misunderstood figures in history.'[8] She may well be right. Charles is hard to understand because we cannot measure him against our own experiences and expectations. For the same reasons he does not always understand us and that can complicate communications.

He seeks intimacy yet continues with the alienating custom under which many of his friends and all of his staff call him 'sir'. (He sometimes signs personal notes 'Carrick', a name taken from one of his earldoms.) 'There's a competition at Clarence House to see how deep you can curtsey without falling over,' says a member of his household. A conspicuous beneficiary of entrenched inequality, the Prince works hard, through his charities, to redress inequality. He shuttles between stately homes and palaces in a swirl of retainers, yet has installed a wide range of eco-friendly, energy-saving technologies at Highgrove and his other homes. In his search for wisdom, he has sometimes done stupid things and listened to poor advice. He's easier to criticise than to comprehend. 'Quite possibly the most creative initiator of charitable projects in the world', as Sacks describes him, he is more frequently depicted as someone without purpose or motivation.[9] A thought leader on the environment, he is caricatured as a man who talks to plants. He works from early morning into the night, combining an increasing burden of royal duty with the voluminous role he has carved out for himself, but is widely assumed to be underemployed.

Born to be king, he actually aims much higher. For himself, he seeks meaning, enlightenment, happiness. For everyone else he is more zealous still. He has set his sights on nothing less than improving the human condition and fixing a battered world. 'I only take on the most difficult challenges. Because I want to raise aspirations and recreate hope from hopelessness and health from deprivation,' he told me, sitting in his comfortable study at Birkhall on the Balmoral estate.[10] 'We talk a lot about the guilt of privilege. Sometimes I think he's driven by guilt,' muses Emma Thompson.[11]

It's easy to see why that might be. Birkhall is one of four residences listed on his website and he also has use of other homes in Scotland and Romania as well as access to the family palaces. His publicly declared income in 2014–15 comprised £19.8 million from the Duchy of Cornwall, the landed estate founded in 1337 to fund heirs to the throne, plus a further £2.2 million from the Sovereign Grant, the money provided by the government to support the Queen, and in some cases her family, in the execution of duties as head of state. The Prince's Annual Review and the accounts of the Duchy of Cornwall lack fine detail but in the same year revealed official expenditure for his own household of £11.6 million, another chunk for maintaining sons and daughter-in-law in style, expenditure on capital projects and a tax bill of £4.5 million, leaving a net cash surplus of £342,000 on top of any private investment income.

So he's rich – maybe not as stonkingly rich as his 'Bond villains' – but more than comfortable. Some of his critics suggest this means he should fund his own charities. 'All the charities are governed and run independently. Whilst HRH is the figurehead, he does not have the funds to keep them all going and it wouldn't be helpful for him to do so,' says an aide. 'Whilst fund-raising is essential to any charity, engaging with businesses, government and the public is of equal importance. If HRH were funding all of these charities privately they would lack credibility and essential buy-in from other sectors.'

Clarence House doesn't publish information on Charles's private wealth or the tax he pays on such income. At a briefing about his 2013–14 Annual Review, his then Principal Private Secretary William

Nye batted away a question. 'Let's be clear,' said Nye, proceeding to give an answer that fell some way short of that premise. 'If [the Prince] had other private income it would be private, so I wouldn't tell you about it. But, to be clear, any income that he has, he pays tax on. There's certainly no income on which he doesn't pay tax.'[12]

A similar fog hangs around the monarchy. Buckingham Palace used to say that the annual bill to every Briton for the Queen was no more than the price of a cup of coffee, but that was before affluent urbanites became used to shelling out £2.85 for a venti cappuccino, far more than the 56 pence per head the Palace now reckons the Queen costs. The Palace's calculation seems to be based on dividing her taxpayer funding, the Sovereign Grant of £37.9 million in 2014–15, amongst the entire UK populace instead of just the taxpayers who shoulder the expenditure. Their annual per capita outlay must be well over a pound or significantly higher if an estimate for policing is included – the sum for guarding VIPs including the royals is thought to be around £128 million a year.

She's not cheap but the Queen isn't the most expensive head of state either (a distinction one university study awarded to the French; the purely ceremonial German Presidency turned out to be only marginally less dear than the UK royals).[13] A British President and his or her apparatus may not prove any more economical. But a President would preside over citizens, not subjects. The real issue about privilege – the reason some people will never accept the monarchy and the essential injustice that could well induce twinges of guilt in a thoughtful heir apparent – is that the role of head of state is inherited, not earned. The monarchy relies, like Bertrand Russell's teapot, on mass acceptance of a ridiculous idea. Russell compared religious dogma to an invented china teapot orbiting in space. 'Nobody would be able to disprove my assertion provided I were careful to add that the teapot is too small to be revealed even by our most powerful telescopes,' he argued. 'But if I were to go on to say that, since my assertion cannot be disproved, it is intolerable presumption on the part of human reason to doubt it, I should rightly be thought to be talking nonsense. If however the existence of such a teapot were affirmed in ancient books, taught as the sacred truth every Sunday, and instilled into the minds of children at school, hesitation to believe in its existence would become a mark of eccentricity.'[14] In the UK and the Realms, allegiance to the sovereign and a system that distributes rights and responsibilities – and wealth – unevenly, through birth rather than democratic mandate, is promoted from pulpits and nurtured in schools.

Nor is the monarch just a figurehead. The Queen holds a constitutional role that is surprisingly substantial. She is the so-called Fount of Justice, Head of the Armed Forces and Supreme Governor of the Church of England; she signs off on legislation and has the power to prorogue Parliament. She advises the Prime Minister of the day and has twice been forced to choose a new premier when the governing party failed to replace its leader. She has mostly adhered to the convention that sovereigns should remain disengaged from politics. Her eldest son does not do so.

Charles seeks to perform the most delicate of manoeuvres, 'highlight[ing] issues which are of concern to himself and to others in the aim of opening up a public debate ... over what he sees as vital issues to the health of the nation while avoiding party political issues'.[15] His position simultaneously gives him a platform for his views and deafens a swathe of his audience to messages they might applaud from other sources. Nevertheless, with his idealism untempered by the limitations that confront most campaigners, his vision unclouded by the need to seek election or carry board members with him, he has developed into a formidable operator with potent convening powers who has exerted a significant impact across a wide range of fields – indeed, far more significant than many of his supporters or his critics recognise. His thinking, similarly unfettered, leads him to wilder philosophical territories than most people beyond his inner circle realise.

The book which the Prince co-authored with Ian Skelly and British environmentalist Tony Juniper, published in 2010, opens with a startling sentence: 'This is a call to revolution.'[16] *Harmony: A New Way of Looking at Our World* is his manifesto. Worried aides did as little as possible to promote the text, because of its unsettling content. Charles had already caused consternation in some corners of Anglicanism in 1994 by suggesting that he alter the monarch's title of 'Defender of the Faith' to 'Defender of Faith', a comment misconstrued to mean he subscribed equally to all religions.[17] *Harmony* reveals the personal creed that underpins and links his activism in areas as apparently disparate as architecture, integrated medicine, ecology, education, promoting inter-faith understanding and a determination to get Britons eating mutton again. His philosophy blends perennialism with its core belief in ancient wisdoms, holism which insists on the interconnectedness of all natural systems, and other mystically inclined ideas with the narrower faith of the Church he expects one day to represent. An edition of the book rewritten for children and published only in the United States concludes with another eye-catching phrase: 'I intend to be the Defender of Nature. Will you come and help me?'[18]

A closer read reveals a fundamental and counterintuitive key to its author. His Royal Highness Prince Charles Philip Arthur George, Prince of Wales, KG, KT, GCB, OM, AK, QSO, PC, ADC, Earl of Chester, Duke of Cornwall, Duke of Rothesay, Earl of Carrick, Baron of Renfrew, Lord of the Isles and Prince and Great Steward of Scotland – monarch-in-waiting, symbol of entitlement, avatar of the Establishment – sees himself as a renegade.

For years he has lobbed opinions into the public discourse and watched debates ignite. 'Because of his position he can be an amplifier of messages and a conductor of ideas,' says his friend Patrick Holden, an organic farmer and the founding director of the Sustainable Food Trust (and no relation to Anthony Holden, *Sunday Times* journalist and Charles's biographer). 'This sense of service goes right to the heart of the man.'[19] The amplification sometimes enables important ideas to be heard; at other times proves devastatingly loud. Monarchists and republicans alike argue that the Prince should be more like his mother, distant and largely silent, a screen to reflect projected ideals of unity and public service. But Charles will never, in that respect, be like his mother. He has more in common with his opinionated, idiosyncratic, foot-in-mouth father, despite documented strains between them. And, in a keen and overlooked irony, he shares many defining characteristics with Diana, Princess of Wales, whose life – and 1997 death in a car crash in Paris – would do so much to define public attitudes to him.

'Diana explained to me once that it was her innermost feelings of suffering that made it possible for her to connect with her constituency of the rejected,' said her brother Earl Spencer in his famous funeral oration. Intuitive, compassionate and volatile, the Prince, like his former wife, has turned his own pain outwards, trying, in helping others, to make himself whole. Like her, he is capable of building things up or tearing them down. By instinct and practice, Charles is a king of hearts, compelled to reach out, to try to make a difference. He has recently come to believe that doing so stands not in opposition to his hereditary role – current and future – but offers a way to invest the monarchy with new relevance.

Yet as he increasingly shares his mother's duties as head of state, he is coming under pressure to sublimate these impulses and passions, to protect the monarchy by joining the forces that deliberately or by accident obscure the scope and scale of his activities and influence. This biography is written in the belief that concealment neither benefits the institution whose future relies on him nor serves the needs of the democracies of which it is a constitutional pillar. If the narrative often reads like comedy, that is because Charles's life serves up comedy at many turns, from the way people behave around him to the way he himself sometimes behaves. He makes jokes and occasionally the joke is on him. As Emma Thompson observes, 'there is a deeply absurd aspect to it all, and he's a very intelligent man who's perfectly capable of seeing that'.[20]

But this book also has a serious intent. Informed debate around the purpose and future of the monarchy is essential for the health of the democracies in which it is embedded. Counter-arguments in support of the monarchy – and unlike Russell's teapot, they glow bright enough if you know where to look – require an understanding of the role of the head of state; the gravitational pull of Planet Windsor; and how the destruction of that celestial body might play out back on Earth. This book attempts to bring clarity to both sides of the debate.

As for the Prince, he deserves to be understood.

On 4 March 2014 the occupants of Kensington Palace – 'KP' – forced themselves to act against the grain: they held a soirée for journalists, and not just any journalists, but royal correspondents, benighted souls contracted to spend their days scratching for stories about the House of Windsor. Princes William and Harry, whose dislike of the profession is visceral, looked uncomfortable. William made stilted small talk and escaped as quickly as possible. His younger brother, a flush spreading up from his collar, took a more combative line, interrogating staffers from the *Daily Mail* about the news organisation's quick-fire online operation and in particular its paparazzi-driven gallery of short news items, the so-called 'sidebar of shame'. Kate, baby George on hip, mingled easily.

It was an odd event, the grudging quality of the hospitality reflected in its location – a corridor linking some of the administrative offices dealing with the young royals' affairs – and in the meagre supply of wine in screw-top bottles. Some of the guests perceived in these arrangements not a potential insult but a positive: that the Duke and Duchess of Cambridge, as William and Kate have been known since their 2011 marriage, and Prince Harry, who in a plot device worthy of a sitcom lives alongside them at KP, are determined to break away from the formality of their grandmother's and father's courts. They are more in tune with the times, so this analysis goes, and thus closer to the people.

Officials explicitly articulated this message before the trio appeared. The young princes had now reached adulthood, William's military career was over, Harry had swapped his helicoptering for an army desk job, and together with Kate they were embarking on lives as working royals. Their aides could not yet be quite sure what form this would take or which causes the Cambridges and Harry might espouse, but the object of the reception was to position their charges as separate brands, integral to the overarching family firm yet distinct from its longer established leading marques, Queen Elizabeth II and the Prince of Wales. Harry, preparing that week to launch one of his first big solo projects, the Invictus Games, a sporting competition for injured members of the armed forces, made one thing abundantly clear to those of us with whom, in a soldierly manner, he later engaged: he doesn't want to build up a sprawling charitable empire – or large staff – like his dad's. He intends to do things his way.

The problem Harry now faces is one that has defined Charles's life: how to turn an accident of birth into a meaningful vocation. Three generations of Britain's monarchy are all out and about performing the royal job – that's eighteen people in total, including the Queen and Prince Philip; Camilla, Charles, his sons and daughter-in-law; plus Princes Andrew and Edward and Edward's spouse Sophie, Countess of Wessex; Princess Anne and a raft of names and faces even royal-watchers would be hard put to identify: the Duke of Gloucester, the Duchess of Gloucester, the Duke of Kent, the Duchess of Kent, Princess Alexandra, and Prince and Princess Michael of Kent – all fulfilling an amorphous form of public service defined largely in the doing of it. There are no manuals and, for those loitering in the lengthening line of succession, few predetermined duties. 'To be heir to the throne is not a position. It is a predicament,' observed Alan Bennett, and it's a line Charles often inserts into his speeches, with feeling.[21] His productivity can't be measured by the number of engagements he performs. The Queen still romps through multiple short meetings and events in a day, while her eldest tends to devote larger chunks of time to each occasion. His value is even harder to gauge, like his mum's entangled in wispy sentiments about national pride and identity, but lacking the core function that gives her substance: being head of state. The success of the royals, collectively and individually, is however more easily tested: through public opinion.

On that basis the monarchy is doing quite well. The Queen is also Head of the Commonwealth, a voluntary association of fifty-three countries, most but not all former British colonies, and reigns as head of state over sixteen of them: the Realms of Antigua and Barbuda, Australia, the Bahamas, Barbados, Belize, Canada, Grenada, Jamaica, New Zealand, Papua New Guinea, St Kitts and Nevis, Saint Lucia, Saint Vincent and the Grenadines, the Solomon Islands, Tuvalu and the United Kingdom. (She is also head of state of the Crown Dependencies of Jersey, Guernsey and the Isle of Man, which are not part of the UK, and of twelve Overseas Territories, remnants of Empire: Anguilla, Bermuda, British Antarctic Territory, the British Indian Ocean Territory, the British Virgin Islands, the Cayman Islands, the Falkland Islands, Gibraltar, Montserrat, the Pitcairn Group of Islands, St Helena, Ascension Island and Tristan da Cunha, South Georgia and the South Sandwich Islands, the Sovereign Base Areas of Akrotiri and Dhekelia on Cyprus, and Turks and Caicos Islands.)

Jamaica's premier Portia Simpson Miller returned to power in January 2012 promising to make the country a republic; a poll later the same year suggested that her compatriots are narrowly against such a move.[22] 'This issue still remains the subject of ongoing discussion in Jamaica and no final decision regarding the exact course to be pursued has yet been taken,' wrote Diedre Mills, Jamaica's Deputy High Commissioner in London, in response to an emailed query in April 2014 about concrete plans to realise Simpson Miller's pledge.

Australians were given an opportunity to break from the Crown in 1999. In a referendum 54.87 per cent opted to keep the hereditary head of state compared to 45.13 per cent who voted to replace the monarch with an elected President. The monarchists still appear to be winning. A Nielsen poll released in April 2014, as William and Kate arrived in Sydney, saw republican sentiment plummet to thirty-five-year lows. Australia's then Prime Minister Tony Abbott, a former executive director of the pressure group Australians for a Constitutional Monarchy, reintroduced a British-style honours system of knighthoods and damehoods. His successor revoked it.

New Zealand's Prime Minister John Key instituted a debate about redesigning the national flag as part of a wider discussion about ditching the monarchy, an outcome he believes inevitable if not necessarily desirable. The New Zealand flag has incorporated Britain's union flag since colonisation in the nineteenth century. In 2014 came a new invasion. William and Kate arrived on New Zealand shores, the streets filled with excited throngs eager to wrap themselves in the flags of Britain and New Zealand, and Key revised his assessment. 'I think in my heart of hearts it probably is inevitable [a republic] will happen, but the time frame has moved considerably further out.'[23]

In Britain, that prospect looks more distant still. In 1969, when pollsters first began to ask treasonous questions about whether the country might be better off without the Windsors, about 20 per cent of respondents answered yes. That number for years held remarkably steady, apart from a few small surges in republicanism fuelled by royal missteps and mishaps and skirmishes in the Wars of the Waleses, the bitter conflict that consumed Charles and Diana. In the immediate aftershock of Diana's death, anti-monarchy feelings, which might have been expected to swell, instead plunged sharply. If republicanism failed to flourish, the monarchy lost active support too. The British Social Attitudes survey (BSA) tracked these developments from 1983, when 86 per cent of Britons said it was important to retain the monarchy, through royal doldrums in 2006, when that figure declined to 59 per cent. Yet by 2012 the picture had changed again, and dramatically. An Ipsos-MORI poll ahead of the Queen's Diamond Jubilee registered another precipitous fall in republican sentiment, but this time against a corresponding and protracted resurgence in royal popularity.[24] By 2013, a full 75 per cent of respondents to the BSA survey believed the monarchy indispensable.[25]

That recovery is remarkable if you consider its context. Politics is in bad odour. Banking and journalism smell worse. Faith in the police and in that most benign of fireside companions, the BBC, is dented. Churches, mired in scandal, their pews sparsely populated, have struggled to adjust to social change. It is the same everywhere you look. Across the globe, trust in big institutions is eroding. Strong government has become an oxymoron in most democratic nations. In the messy aftermath of the Arab spring and amid the globalisation of anti-globalisation movements, anger rather than pride more reliably brings people onto the streets.

In Spain that rage burned bright against a monarch who had been revered for his role in returning the country to democracy after the death of dictator Francisco Franco. King Juan Carlos might have been forgiven for holidaying in Botswana with a female companion who was not his Queen, and whilst on safari shooting elephant despite his honorary presidency of the Spanish branch of conservation charity WWF. But his timing was awful, in the maul of an economic crisis that stripped a quarter of the Spanish workforce and a full half of the country's youth of jobs. The King had claimed sympathy; the situation gave him sleepless nights, he said. In June 2014, with his daughter Princess Cristina embroiled as a witness in a corruption investigation into her husband's business dealings and support for Spain's monarchy languishing below 50 per cent for the first time since its restoration, Juan Carlos abdicated in favour of his son Felipe. (Cristina was subsequently charged with tax fraud; through lawyers both she and her husband Inaki Urdangarin denied wrongdoing.) The institution of monarchy is no more proof against the spirit of the age than any other.

Yet crowds still turn out to cheer the Windsors. A million pressed into central London for the 2011 wedding of William and Kate. Tens of thousands squeezed into Wellington's Civic Square and tens of thousands more gathered at Sydney Opera House to glimpse the pair during their 2014 tour of New Zealand and Australia. 'I'm a royalist from way back,' said an onlooker called Caroline Mumford, waiting outside the opera house. 'It's really in my blood, it's about actually seeing Kate, her beauty and her radiance – she's a breath of fresh air. And William, we mustn't forget him.'[26]

So often did Kate's photograph grace front pages during the trip that a reader felt moved to write to the editor of *The Times* on the day his newspaper failed to carry her image: 'Sir, Wednesday's paper did not have a photo of the Duchess of Cambridge. I do hope she is all right.'[27] Like the mother-in-law she never met, Kate contributes a glamour not matched by the Windsor genes, and that means that, like Diana, she sometimes seems to absorb the light rather than refracting it.

The Queen, however, is rarely occluded, whether by shining youth or rain clouds. Sodden throngs huddled along the Thames for her Diamond Jubilee pageant to witness the monarch, then eighty-six, brave a two-hour sail standing and waving from the prow of a barge, in a numbing downpour that sent six people aboard the accompanying flotilla to hospital with hypothermia. 'I have to be seen to be believed,' she has said.[28]

In that spirit, the Windsors range widely, touring factories and stores, schools and hospitals, attending events, cutting ribbons, unveiling plaques, working rope lines and rooms full of people, being seen and fostering belief. As the Queen and her consort wind down with age, opting for shorter-haul trips and taking on a lighter palette of public duties, the two generations below them are stepping up to the mark. In October 2013, after tutelage from his father in the intricacies of conducting investitures, including a practice session with a sword specially transported to Birkhall, William for the first time stood in for the Queen at a Buckingham Palace ceremony to confer honours. The following month, Charles made his debut presiding in place of his mother at the biennial Commonwealth Heads of Government Meeting.

This was a particularly delicate assignment, part of the extended choreography designed to accustom Commonwealth members to acceptance of the Prince as the next head of the organisation – an outcome that is not automatic, but will be decided by Commonwealth leaders when his mother dies. The voluntary association of independent countries faces its own challenges if it is to endure much beyond the second Elizabethan age. A reworking of vestiges of Empire as a vehicle for empowerment rather than subjugation, its members are bound by a charter committing them to democracy, open government and the rule of law. Yet as palace officials watched from behind spread fingers, the Prince found himself conducting the ceremonial opening of a leaders' summit hosted by Sri Lanka, amid international protests against the country's bloody human-rights abuses and a state crack-down on the media trying to cover the meeting. It was, says a Clarence House insider drily, 'one of the friskier CHOGMs of recent years'.

This book will give new insight into Charles's foreign missions and the deployment of royal soft power not just to promote British interests and maintain the Commonwealth, but to tread where government does not dare. To the Dalai Lama and his supporters, the Prince is a champion. He is venerated in Armenia. Romanians embrace him as their own and not just because Charles claims descent from Vlad the Impaler, the fifteenth-century ruler on whom Bram Stoker based his fanged fictional character Dracula. 'I do have a bit of a stake in the country,' jokes the Prince, not infrequently. He owns two properties in Transylvania and lobbies for the preservation of the region's traditional villages.

Middle Eastern royals, unimpressed by the usual ranks of diplomats, open to Charles as an equal: 'He's there doing something nobody else can do,' says a source during the Prince's February 2014 trip to Saudi Arabia. Charles has been widely pictured stepping his way through a sword dance – 'He loves dressing up and dancing,' says a friend – but this is not what the source means. The Prince has been a great supporter of the UK intelligence services. He volunteered to be their first royal patron and came up with the idea of their internal awards scheme, offering a way to recognise good work among professionals whose job means they must hide their lights. Britain's domestic and international intelligence agencies – the Security Service (MI5), the Secret Intelligence Service (MI6) and the electronic intelligence agency GCHQ – provided a statement for this biography: 'His Royal Highness's engagement with the intelligence services is hugely appreciated by the members of the three agencies and warmly welcome.' Later in this book I will give exclusive insights into the nature and scope of that engagement. 'He's incredible – he's a huge asset,' says an official from Britain's Foreign and Commonwealth Office.

Given such rave reviews and his family's buoyant fortunes, you might think the Prince would sit high in public affections, and he is gaining in approval as he performs more head-of-state duties. Yet polls still show him as a weak link, squeezed between his unassailable mother and the younger generation's allure. He may not be hated, but he's not much loved either, except in republican circles where he is hailed as a walking, talking argument for an elected head of state. So is Charles really a liability to the monarchy, to democracy, to himself?

Over the following pages, I aim to answer those questions and to look forward to a future more likely than not to see him enthroned. To do so means revealing the Prince in all his complexity, the humanitarian urges that drive him and the caprices and compulsions that imperil his record. I will highlight his extraordinary achievements and sometimes equally extraordinary mistakes, explain the culture and influences that produced someone capable of such extremes, and try to delineate the scale of ambitions that mean he will never be content as just a figurehead. And to answer one question immediately: one reason the mature meat of this story, like the mutton he champions, remains undervalued is that he can be, and not infrequently is, his own worst enemy.

Charles looks like the ultimate insider, born with a whole canteen of silver spoons in his mouth and since the death of his grandfather in 1952 only one rung below the very apex of the Establishment. Yet that privilege – or life sentence – has doomed him never to feel part of the commonality, but always at a distance, watched and watching. His sense of alienation is palpable. 'I try to put myself in other people's position and because I drive about the country endlessly, I've often thought about the lives of people in the places I pass, the streets,' he told me.[29] Other members of his family seem more easily to accept their lot. 'People say to me: "Would you like to swap your life with me for twenty-four hours? Your life must be very strange,"' says his bluff brother Prince Andrew. 'But of course I have not experienced any other life. It's not strange to me. The same way with the Queen. She has never experienced anything else.'[30]

If offered a life swap for twenty-four hours, Charles would jump at the chance. Instead, he seeks out guides to the planet he can never fully inhabit. Thus it was that in 1985 he arrived at my then place of work, the *Economist*, for a lunch with 'people of his age'. His request – or command – excluded me. I was too junior, and like him, alien. I wouldn't have breathed easy in the thin air of the fourteenth-floor executive dining room. An American educated in Britain, for the most part at a grammar school and then a redbrick university, I believed in meritocracy – not just that it was a good idea but that we were living it. The scales fell from my eyes after I joined the *Economist*, working alongside men and a handful of women, all but a few of whom seemed to have emerged from the same cosy nest of elite schools and Oxbridge colleges. Three decades later, class still mottles British life. The nation's quality press like many other key institutions remains overwhelmingly white, male and privileged, its workforce simultaneously exemplifying and helping to perpetuate structural and cultural impediments to social mobility. One of the most potent arguments against the monarchy is that it acts as guarantor of the dysfunctional status quo. You have only to watch the political elite groping for connection to ordinary voters and outsourcing their communications to tabloid editors, or spend time around British troops and observe the frequency with which ranks and accents tally, to understand how profound the dysfunction is.

The *Economist* has always been even posher than the rest of the quality press. Back then quite a few of the writers had country piles and owned smoking jackets, sufficiently old money to look down on the royal family as German arrivistes. Our glass-and-concrete ivory tower – a piece of new brutalist architecture the Prince surely abhorred – hardly seemed the place to look for clues to the real world. Yet this was in most respects a benign and civilised environment. My colleagues were brilliant, the best of British – and Charles urgently needed to tap their wisdom.

Four years earlier, a series of events had changed the course of his life: his marriage to Lady Diana Spencer on 29 July 1981, and before that inner-city rioting in England – in April in Brixton, south London, and, just weeks ahead of his wedding, in the Handsworth area of Birmingham, Leeds' Chapeltown district, Toxteth in Liverpool and in Sheffield. 'I remember when there were these appalling riots, I just felt how can we find ways of giving these characters more opportunity because the whole thing is based on frustration and alienation,' he said later.[31] (He often refers to people as 'characters', an unfortunate phrase that reflects his own alienation.)

That impulse started the process that would transform his rudderless Prince's Trust into an effective interventionist organisation that proudly claims to help more than 55,000 young people every year to set up businesses, or move into education, training or employment. The charity has evolved into the least controversial element of his astonishingly broad and idiosyncratic portfolio of works. In the 1980s, in tandem with its founder, the Trust was figuring out its role in a highly politicised context. This wasn't easy, not least because of the convention that the sovereign – and by extension her heirs – should remain above politics.

In one important respect, the Prince's Trust and Margaret Thatcher's government sang from the same hymn sheet. Both lauded the spirit of enterprise. Still, the state had clearly and comprehensively failed the young people the Trust scooped up and gave practical assistance to develop that spirit. Thatcherites ascribed the failure to a welfare system that cosseted and infantilised; the Left ascribed the failure to Thatcherism, which was busily dismantling parts of the welfare system and restructuring nationalised industries that were no longer fit to compete. Britain's manufacturing base shrank while the country's first and as yet only female Prime Minister held power, from 17.62 per cent of GDP in 1979 to 15.18 per cent when she left office eleven years later. In the same period, the ranks of the UK population deemed officially poor swelled from 13.4 per cent to 22.2 per cent.[32]

'I was just trying to find ways of reacting to the situation so as unemployment grew – and it was three million or something – and as these traditional industries were shut down, what on earth are we going to find to replace these forms of employment for so many people? It was all taking so long for anything else to spring up so I just thought whatever we could do in a small way would be better than nothing,' said Charles.[33] What he could do for others in a small way began to solve in a big way the conundrum that had tormented him for years: how to put his non-job of apprentice monarch to good use. Yet this course was fraught with difficulty for a man literally not of the world, a fact that quickly became apparent to his hosts at the *Economist*.

Michael Elliott, then the *Economist*'s political correspondent (and one of its rare grammar-educated staffers), now president and CEO of the campaigning organisation ONE, recalls a discussion that foundered before the coffee for lack of common reference points. 'Most of the conversation was taken up with an agonised appraisal of the Prince's proper role, together with much royal muttering (conventional wisdom in 1985) that Britain had lost the dynamism for which it once was famous. I begged to differ, and implored the Prince to consider the new, entrepreneurial, street-cred economy being created at that very moment in the clubs and streets, the fashion houses and TV studios and advertising agencies of Soho and Covent Garden. I remember to this day the look of utter incomprehension on the Prince's face as I made my case. Only later did a colleague point out the obvious; that with the exception of visits to the Royal Opera House, it was highly unlikely that the Prince had ever visited Soho and Covent Garden, much less wandered its streets picking up the vital signs of the new Britain.'[34]

As Elliott points out, there was only one royal capable of recognising that new Britain and speaking its demotic language: Diana. The Princess might have helped connect her husband to that reality. Instead, as their relationship festered, she used her gifts to undermine him.

For all that he is among the most exposed figures in the world – his progress relentlessly charted from birth through his first day at school, his first drink at a bar, his first girlfriends, his first marriage, the first signs of discord, the first signs that this discord would disfigure lives – Charles remains obscure. 'It bothers me that people don't get him, but in the broad sweep of history he absolutely will be seen for who he is,' says Elizabeth Buchanan.[35]

She is right, but the Prince and all the apparatus around him have long put faith not in transparency but control. 'Its mystery is its life. We must not let in daylight upon magic,' observed Walter Bagehot, the great Victorian essayist and *Economist* editor, in his analysis of monarchy.[36] Bagehot, who remains a touchstone for constitutional historians – and for palace press managers – defined the role of the monarch in relationship to the government as a series of rights: to be consulted, to encourage and to warn. The monarch-in-training has always felt impelled to exercise the last of these rights with exceptional vigour.

As a teenager looking down from Planet Windsor, Charles saw what man had made and, behold, it was very bad, at least some of it. 'I couldn't bear the physical aspect of destroying town centres and historical places, digging up all the hedgerows, cutting down trees, making terrifying prairies covered in chemicals. All that stuff. I thought this was insanity,' he says of his young self.[37]

Even now he is driven by alienation and urgency. Travelling more widely and meeting a greater range of people than most Ministers, he routinely shares with those Ministers insights gleaned from his encounters via handwritten letters, dubbed 'black spider memos' by Julia Cleverdon, a long-time member of his team, most recently vice president of his charity Business in the Community and special adviser to his charities on responsible business practice. Charles writes prodigiously, sometimes dispatching as many as ten memos after dinner, often to staff or ad-hoc advisers, and he also keeps journals of his travels. Accustomed to the protection of confidentiality agreements signed by all palace staff, used to layers of official secrecy – and with the physical protection, says a former Cabinet Minister who received such missives regularly, of three envelopes, each marked 'strictly confidential' – the Prince expresses himself freely. 'I've never had a problem with him,' says that former Minister. 'He is entitled to opinions.'

By no means everyone agrees. The reasons, explored in this book, relate both to the constitutional role of the monarchy and, even more so, to the often controversial nature of the Prince's ideas.

Because Charles is a man of the strongest convictions. He now needs the courage of them in a world that has become too porous to rely on secrecy. Half-truths and orphan facts seep almost daily into the public domain. Revelations appear without context. The *Guardian*, under Alan Rusbridger, explored legal avenues to bring greater scrutiny to bear on the Prince and dragged some of his memos into the open.

Most republicans assume, as Rusbridger does, that familiarity with royalty, and especially with Charles, will breed contempt – that his mystery is his life. Exposed for who and what he is, this royal joker will break the consensus that sustains the Crown. They may be right. To know the Prince is not necessarily to love him, whatever love means. He has admirable qualities, an arsenal of jokes and a cupboard full of vulnerabilities that explain much of what he does, while not giving him a free pass. He means well. He cares. He spends his life trying to contact the world in order to save it. He is 'a man who has no ambition but to make a difference for the better and to do good', in Buchanan's view.[38] He is also complex, difficult, more than occasionally intemperate, not infrequently wrong-headed, and on some issues plain wrong. This biography attempts to draw a balance among those flaws – and the flawed outcomes they sometimes produce – and the closely woven skeins of positive influence and good works that, like Charles's letters, remain routinely hidden. There is murk around our understanding of the role of the head of state, the meaning of neutrality and whether Britain's king of charitable endeavour is suited to become Britain's King. Let daylight in.

Chapter 1

His Life in a Day

Every one of the 6,000-plus residents of Treharris in South Wales appears to have decanted onto the pavements lining either side of the narrow street outside the butcher's shop, Cig Mynydd Cymru. Inside the small premises, an officer from the Metropolitan Police Service's special protection unit SO14 completes his inspection. Despite the potential security risk, he asks the proprietors to leave the back door gaping wide. 'Keep it cool,' advises the officer. 'He likes it as cool as possible.'

Eight-year-olds Ben and Ryan, swinging from the crowd barriers, wonder what other demands the Very Important Person about to arrive in their midst may make. They are aware that the visitor has special powers. 'He bosses people around,' says Ben. Ryan – 'fully Welsh, no English whatsoever' as he proudly declares – expands on the theme. The VIP 'tells people what to do and if they don't, he'll behead them'. When the Prince's car pulls into view, both boys holler and whoop and the whole crowd, young and old, applauds and waves Welsh flags, demonstrating the sense of local ownership that has always underpinned the strength of the Windsors' global brand. The last Welsh Prince of Wales, Llywelyn ap Gruffudd, died in 1282. Sentiment against the English Crown still flares in some parts of the country, but Treharris lays on a royal welcome.

This is a typical day for Charles, which is to say, it bears little detailed resemblance to the day before or the day after, but in outline appears numbingly similar, a production line of public engagements and sidebar meetings, small talk, the brief sanctuary of the car, then out again to wave and smile and entertain.

On this particular date, 3 July 2013, the third day of his annual summer visit to Wales – 'Wales Week' – he has risen early at his whitewashed farmhouse Llwynywermod. ('"Llwyn" rhymes with ruin,' a helpful member of his household emails. The double L, technically known as a 'voiceless alveolar lateral fricative', sounds 'like throat clearing'. Y is pronounced 'uh', 'werm' and 'od' are as you'd expect.) Most mornings Charles undertakes a series of exercises originally devised to keep the pilots of the Royal Canadian Air Force in fine fettle and which he uses to alleviate his bad back. 'Occasionally,' says Julia Cleverdon, 'in the royal train you hear a frightful bump.'[1]

He will have consumed a small breakfast, likely 'a few grains', according to a staff member, and not a boiled egg culled from a long row of boiled eggs. This will keep him going until dinner. He never eats lunch if he can help it and the people who work with him quickly learn to carry hidden food supplies for themselves. He'll also have drunk enough water to sustain him but not so much as to require unscheduled pit stops. 'He knows exactly how to hydrate his body to just the right degree,' says his godson Tim Knatchbull. 'It's an incredible talent. As it is to be most of the time – not all of the time, but most of it – an incredibly affable human, happy to listen, talk and be interested. Everyone's always telling him you've got to move along here but he'll get interested and find someone to talk to and do everything at a leisurely pace.'[2]

During the first engagement, the Prince has chatted with other alien species, Ood and Sontaran, and been persuaded to use a voice modulator to address a Dalek in a Dalek voice. 'Exterminate!' he called out, laughing. 'Exterminate!' Much of the conversation, however, revolved around the succession. The reigning Time Lord, actor Matt Smith, is preparing to make way for a new Doctor Who, and Charles, touring the set at the BBC's Roath Lock studios in Cardiff with wife Camilla, seemed keenly interested in the choreography of the handover. Smith won over doubters after taking on the role in 2010 from popular predecessor David Tennant. His successor has big shoes to fill.

It's a predicament familiar to the Prince, who has spent more than sixty years preparing to take over from a popular predecessor. The Queen has lumbered her son with two huge problems. In reigning so successfully for so long, she has fixed public expectations about what sovereignty means. If Charles outlives his mother – and the 'if' is not inconsequential; the Queen appears in robust health again after a brief illness in 2013 and her own mother lasted to 101 – he will inevitably attract criticism simply for not being her. If he does become king, he'll only have at most one or two decades in which to make the role his own.

In the eternity of the meantime, the Queen has consigned her son to a destiny that is both inescapable and nebulous, like a Sontaran force field. Most jobs come with descriptions and clear parameters. Being heir to the throne has none of these attributes. It is an open-ended contract and, like everything about Britain's unwritten, fluid constitution, is defined by conventions and precedents and how the incumbent decides to play it.

'A few people are lucky enough to know exactly what they want to do. They've got the talent or whatever it is. There's no problem,' says Charles. 'But there's a hell of a lot of others who don't really know and may not be obviously academic, who suffer from low self-esteem. I see it absolutely everywhere.' His shoulders rise and fall. This isn't a shrug of acceptance but an involuntary shudder. 'That's one of the reasons I wanted to make a difference to people's lives,' he concludes.[3]

The Prince whom the people of Treharris are about to meet appears confident to the point of smoothness. He seems to know exactly who he is and why he's on this planet. Yet his youth was scarred by self-doubt and lack of direction and he still grapples with big existential questions. Like many philanthropists, in helping others, Charles has found a way to help himself.

Many years ago he embarked on a chivalric quest of his own devising, seeking meaning, enlightenment and happiness. Capturing any of these grails – and he's still trying, though happiness is finally in his grasp – depends on his ability to reimagine the possibilities of princedom. In attempting to do so, he has roused fire-breathing dragons and has more than once breathed fire himself, scorching instead of debating. He has appeared at times a heroic King Arthur, defending core values, at other moments a figure of fun, Don Quixote tilting at wind turbines which he once called 'a horrendous blot on the landscape'[4] only later to recommend their use in *Harmony* (though he still prefers the offshore variety).

A late developer, as a young man Charles often appeared to have little more idea than Ben or Ryan what being a Prince of Wales might actually entail, but his instincts were always to push at the limitations of his position. Just as his own sons are intent on estab-lishing their own styles and specialities, he yearned to do things differently from his parents.

'I want to consider ways in which I can escape from the ceaseless round of official engagements and meet people in less artificial circum-stances. In other words, I want to look at the possibility of spending, say, 1. three days in one factory to find out what happens; 2. three days, perhaps, in a trawler (instead of one rapid visit); 3. three or four days on a farm,' the thirty-year-old Charles wrote to his Assistant Private Secretary in 1978. He tends to be emphatic in written commu-nications, underlining key phrases and drizzling exclamation points throughout his texts. 'I would also like to consider 4. more visits to immigrant areas in order to help these people to feel that they are not ignored or neglected and that we are concerned about them as individuals.'[5]

He never did escape the ceaseless round, and although he spends more time on average at each engagement than the Queen, he packs several appointments into every grinding day. His dream of immersion in real-world experiences remains mostly that, a dream, though he has dipped briefly into other lives. 'He's lived in a croft on the outer Hebrides,' says Elizabeth Buchanan. 'He's been on hill farms, he's been on trawlers, he's been on fishing rigs down in Cornwall. He's been in the inner cities all over the country, inner cities everywhere.'[6]

Charles also does quite a lot of things that his mother does, conducting around half of all investitures, supporting the armed forces and the charitable sector by holding honorary positions and patronages, officiating at events, listening politely to speeches, secretly scrunching his toes in his shoes to stay awake during languorous passages, or ranging across the United Kingdom and the Realms to meet as many people as possible, to be seen and believed. He defines this royal role as supporting his mother in acting 'as the focal point for national pride, unity and allegiance and bringing people together across all sections of society, representing stability and continuity, highlighting achievement, and emphasising the importance of service and the voluntary sector by encouragement and example'.[7] Yet there are fundamental differences from his mother in approach and content. The aspirations of his 1978 memo foreshadowed the way he has used his position not as the Queen uses hers, to maintain the status quo, but to campaign for change.

More recently, he has accepted that encroaching kingship must necessarily curtail his activism. His charities and causes would take a back seat once and if he ascended the throne or in the case of regency, if his mother grew too infirm to continue as acting head of state. One of his former Principal Private Secretaries, Michael Peat, set out the nature of that change as part of a response issued in March 2007 to the makers of a hostile documentary about the Prince: 'It hardly needs saying that the Prince of Wales, of all people, knows that the role and duties of the heir to the throne are different to those of the sovereign and that his role and the way he contributes to national life will change when he becomes king. In other words it is misconceived and entirely hypothetical to suggest that problems will result if the Prince of Wales fulfils his role in the same way when king. He will not.'[8]

Charles has already started to cut back commitments in order to take on more of his mother's work. That process started with an attempt at closer integration with Buckingham Palace, inserting some of his staff into its structures in anticipation of that transition. None of this has been easy for Charles. His independence is hard won. The mounting pressures emanating from Buckingham Palace have therefore helped to spur him to a reappraisal: perhaps becoming king might in some respects enhance his role as a change-maker rather than bringing it to a close. This is not only because the convening power of a king is surely greater than the convening power of a prince. The most thoughtful member of the royal family, Charles has been pondering long and hard about how the monarchy can best serve its subjects.

This royal train of thought has deposited him in uncharted terrain. Throughout his adult life, people (and most woundingly his father) have dismissed the things he has chosen to do – whether trying to help the socially excluded or save rainforests or preserve dying skills – as time-fillers, eccentricities, indulgences. He has come to believe that such activities are not only compatible with his status, but could be integral to royal duty, to reasserting the relevance of the Crown.

All royal visits within the UK are planned by palace aides in conjunction with local officials. In the Commonwealth Realms, each government takes the lead. On foreign soil, British diplomats negotiate itineraries with the national authorities. But no matter how the details have been finessed, each schedule for Prince Charles is designed in his distinctive image.

So in a single day, Wales will get to see how multifaceted its Prince is, from the joker-royal, game for a laugh on the *Doctor Who* set, through more serious – and controversial – incarnations as the day progresses until evening when he transforms again, this time into a generous host. All of these Princes are more confident and comfortable than the troubled spirit who first visited these parts after being made Prince of Wales at the age of nine and returned here as a lonely student and later as a lonelier husband and later still as a widower. This is the Charles of Charles-and-Camilla, finally settled with the woman he calls 'my dearest wife' – and that epithet is clearly true in both senses. When they are together, they are solicitous of each other, exchanging secret smiles, fleeting touches of the arm and waist. When they are apart, her influence is still tangible to those who knew him before. He has close relationships with his sons and has grown fond of his daughter-in-law and she of him. His grandchildren delight him. The royal barometer is more often set to fair than rain.

At the end of the Cardiff studios tour, he and the Duchess part company better to distribute the largesse of their time. He heads to the nearby Prince's Trust Cymru headquarters, newly opened with the aim of helping at least some of the rising ranks of young unemployed – in Wales standing at more than one in four – into training or work. Camilla, who has been developing her own spread of campaigning interests, departs for Porthcawl in Bridgend, to meet a group of activists working to establish an outpost of the homelessness charity Emmaus in the seaside resort hit by sagging visitor numbers and the impact of the economic downturn on an area that never recovered from the closure of the South Wales coalfield in the 1980s.

Such destinations impart a flavour that some palates define as dangerously political. To ask teenagers about their experience of seeking employment in a jobs drought or men and women sleeping rough about how they came to live on the streets is to discuss policy failures as well as personal turbulence. A 1986 documentary followed Charles on a visit to a Prince's Trust project at a holiday camp in Great Yarmouth. As the camera watches him watching a group of kids perform a version of the Pink Floyd track 'Another Brick in the Wall', they unexpectedly insert a lyric aimed at the Thatcherite credo of the time: 'We don't need no jobs creation / We don't want a fascist nation.' The voiceover is deadpan: 'Where a politician might have decided this was an appropriate moment to move on, the Prince chose to stay and talk to them.'[9]

In visiting the butcher's shop in Treharris, the Prince pursues another of his agendas. All the Windsors are more 'country' than 'town', brought up to enjoy rural pursuits such as stalking and shooting, to take a hand in estate management, and most at ease when the glow of sodium lamps recedes into the distance. 'I'm a countryman – I can't stand cities,' Charles once said.[10] In a commentary which the Queen provided for the 1992 documentary *Elizabeth R* – the closest she has ever come to giving an interview – she talked about her involvement with the Sandringham estate and stud farm: 'I like farming. I like animals. I wouldn't be happy if I just had arable farming. I think that's very boring.'[11] She lives and breathes – and breeds – horses, as her mother did before her and her daughter now does.

Charles also used to take an interest in horse flesh (though it was never as keen as his fascination with sheep). He gave up polo, the sport he described as his 'one great extravagance', aged fifty-seven, only after almost as many injuries. He stopped riding out with his local hunt in Gloucestershire after fox hunting with dogs was banned in 2004. But there is much else that binds him into rural life on a daily basis, not least the Duchy of Cornwall which under his stewardship has diversified and expanded, buying more than 12,000 hectares of agricultural land from the Prudential insurance company in 2000 to take its total footprint to around 53,000 hectares in twenty-three counties and increasing its capital account from £408 million in 2004 to £871 million in the financial year ending April 2015.

The Duchy is Charles's golden goose – and an albatross. Any male who is first in line to the throne automatically becomes Duke of Cornwall. The Duchy operates to generate profits for such heirs and though it now does so in a thoroughly modern way, as a property developer and landlord, it retains original period features. It is exempt from capital gains tax and it is not subject to corporation tax because it is not legally a corporation. The income enables the Prince to maintain a laboratory for his ideas; the anomalous status of the Duchy fosters resentment against antique privilege.

It is yet another factor that sets Charles apart from most people yet it also created his connection to constituencies that feel themselves ill represented by metropolitan politicians: foresters, gamekeepers, hedge layers, small farmers such as the founders of Cig Mynydd Cymru. In securing his own rural base – the Duchy purchased Highgrove House in Gloucestershire and the nearby Duchy Home Farm in 1980 – the Prince consummated his love affair with the land. At Highgrove he redesigned the gardens, telling a documentary team in 1986: 'I love coming here. And I potter about and sit and read or I just come and talk to the plants.'[12] It was one of his jokes but it lumbered him with the label of plant-whisperer, especially after the satirical television show *Spitting Image* depicted his latex alter ego inviting a potted fern to his fortieth birthday party.

Duchy Home Farm under the Prince's direction became a model of organic husbandry. Modern agriculture tends to produce repetitive vistas pocked by ugly buildings. At Duchy Home Farm improbably glossy rare-breed cattle graze certified organic fields demarcated by verdant hedgerows. Barley and wheat grow upright, the unmodified strains unlike higher-yield varieties strong enough to support their crowns of grain. Mixed varieties of cabbages flourish in beds laid out almost as prettily as the gardens at Highgrove, fronds of cavalo nero mimicking the three feathers of the Prince of Wales's heraldic badge.

It's a working farm, but also a showcase for sustainable methods that it's hard to imagine anyone else would have found the time or resources to establish, especially more than thirty years ago. 'He was in the vanguard of [environmental thinking] but he came at it from his unique perspective,' says the Sustainable Food Trust's Patrick Holden. 'Given that no person on the planet has travelled more widely, he's been a witness to the destructive impact of humanity on the environment at first hand and feels obliged to do something about it.'[13]

In 1990 the Prince again moved ahead of the pack, founding one of Britain's first organic brands, Duchy Originals, under the aegis of his charitable foundation. His farm supplied some of the oats for the brand's first product: oaten biscuits. The line expanded to encompass more than 200 organic brands sold by a variety of retailers, swelling the coffers of the foundation until economic downturn and strategic weakness turned the tables, making Duchy Originals dependent on financial sustenance from the foundation. But the Prince isn't a man who easily relinquishes his initiatives. When trouble brews, his favoured response has been to regroup and rebrand, sometimes sustaining enterprises that would never survive without his involvement, at other times producing stronger organisations. In 2009, an exclusive licensing and distribution deal with Waitrose effectively outsourced the management of the brand to the supermarket. 'You know Waitrose aren't in some way bailing out or rescuing Duchy Originals because we are not staying as we are,' said Michael Peat. 'We're fine as we are. They are helping us to move to the next level.'[14] Accounts for the previous two financial years suggested a different story, but under the stewardship of Waitrose, Duchy Originals has indeed moved to another level, worth over £72 million according to figures released in 2013, and contributing an annual cash flow to the Prince's charities, £3 million in 2014. This serves a double function, Elizabeth Buchanan explains, not only generating funds but helping to popularise sustainably produced foods by putting them into supermarkets. 'There's no point fiddling around in a corner. I mean, great for those who are artisan, and that's wonderful. The Prince is their biggest supporter. But equally he wants more people to eat organically.'[15]

Three years after the launch of Duchy Originals, Charles took pleasure in seeing ground broken on another project: Poundbury, often described as his model village but actually an extension to the town of Dorchester in Dorset, on Duchy land and like Duchy Home Farm and Duchy Originals both prototype and platform, in this case for community architecture, traditional crafts and walkable, mixed-use, mixed income, low-carbon development. Its quaint streets are explored in a later chapter.

'The difference between the Prince and an elected politician is the time horizon,' says Fiona Reynolds, the former Director-General of the National Trust – the Prince is its Patron – who also worked with him during her stints at the Council for National Parks and the Council for the Protection of Rural England. 'An elected politician is always thinking about the next three to five years; tomorrow afternoon can be a long way off in politics. Whereas he is unashamedly thinking about the long term, and in fact it's his duty as heir to the throne to think about the long term. Although what he's often said has been controversial, he has been positioning things precisely where politicians are very unlikely to be ... He has moved the debate forward in a number of ways; he has made respectable the very notion of climate change which twenty years ago was seen as an extraordinarily distant and contentious issue.'[16]

Charles made his first public speech on the environment at

twenty-one, warning of the need to 'discipline ourselves to restrictions and regulations ... for our own good'.[17] In the intervening years, his ambitions, and his rhetoric, have ripened. 'My greatest fear is that we're busily wrecking the chances for future generations at a rapid rate of knots by not recognising the damage we're doing to the natural environment, bearing in mind that this is the only planet that we know has any life on it,' the Prince says, urgent and unblinking. 'It is insanity in my humble opinion to destroy this miraculous entity floating around in space that is linked with the extraordinary harmony of the universe.'[18]

His profound environmental concerns twine with a determination to preserve and safeguard traditional rural life and these, in turn, connect to his other causes and activities, all of which find expression not only in patronages of existing causes – which number more than 400 in total – but in charities and initiatives that he sets up.

Much of this activity takes place below the radar, to the frustration of the Prince and his aides. 'When I was Private Secretary, people would say to me: "What has the Prince done for us?" And I'd say: "Well, there's the Prince's Trust." And they'd say: "Oh yes, that has helped a lot of people to get off the unemployment queue and realise their potential,"' recalls Clive Alderton. 'Then they'd say: "He doesn't really do very much," and I'd say: "He did hundreds of royal engagements last year," and it would be 500 or more, and they'd say: "Oh, that's really very good." And I'd see that *Monty Python* scene about "What have the Romans done for us?" playing out in my mind.'[19]

There are many Pythonesque notes to the Prince's existence. At times he could be one of the prophets from *Life of Brian*, addressing a slack-jawed crowd, or Brian himself, thrust into a public role he never sought. (By coincidence, the satirical magazine *Private Eye* has long dubbed him 'Brian', a name its editors thought more appropriate than Charles for a soap opera character.) His quest and the jostling of the knights around him recall *Monty Python and the Holy Grail*. Though the Prince employs some professionals of a high calibre, the underlying structure of Clarence House is of a court, with all the intrigues and rivalries that entails. What little organisational logic there is to the Prince's portfolio has been applied after the fact. For more than forty years, he has spotted what he sees as gaps in the voluntary sector, often on the basis of single conversations, and sought to plug them, grafting onto the creaking structures of his court the massive apparatus of Britain's widest-ranging professional charitable empire.

The Prince has no hesitation in exporting his ideas and obsessions abroad, to Commonwealth countries or places like Romania for which he simply feels an affinity. At home, he also sees it as his job to 'promote and protect the country's enduring traditions, virtues and excellence' whether through inter-faith work or patronages or a focus on rural Britain that he feels is otherwise lacking. Cig Mynydd Cymru (the name translates as 'Welsh mountain meat'), the little butcher's shop in Treharris's Perrott Street, is the kind of enterprise he wants to see thrive, a cooperative formed in 2006 when local farming families came together to work out if they could market quality meats at affordable prices. Only John and Celia Thomas from Penrihw have followed the Prince's lead to take their herds organic – and risk the price premium which that entails in a low-income region – but all of the meat on sale is traceable and distances are short between pastures, slaughterhouses and customers.

Waiting for the Prince's arrival amid the hum of chiller cabinets full of beef, chicken, duck, lamb, pork and, of course, mutton, and a tempting display of crusty pies and Welsh Scotch eggs, John Thomas expresses gratitude for the Prince's advocacy on behalf of small-scale and traditional farming. 'He has promoted mutton which has been a neglected meat for many years. He has done a great deal for farming, and recently for wool, which is a neglected byproduct of the farming industry,' says Thomas. The Prince in his estimation is doing a good job, whatever the job might be. 'Rather than struggling to find a role, he's found a very practical role and he's to be admired for it.'

Finally the royal visitor arrives, pushing into the butcher's shop through a pandemonium of cheers. He's wearing the suit with the patched pocket and one of his ancient pairs of shoes. He still affects the severe parting of his hair, low above his left ear, which he's maintained since childhood. 'I've fought him tooth and nail for years. I just want him to move it, up or bloody down, somewhere, because it's always been in the same place,' says Emma Thompson.[20] The bald patch that had already started to show by the time of his first marriage has now expanded to a tonsure. He looks more like a monk than the figure he has become: the knight errant of the Realms. Camilla calls her husband a 'workaholic' and not just because of the hours he keeps. At this moment, using his position to do something he believes in – something he believes is doing good – he is giving in to an apparently benign addiction. Although he quickly buckles down to business, such as it is, he will overrun the time allotted in his schedule for this stop because he is fascinated.

He can talk to anyone but feels most at home with country people such as his hosts at the shop and with the teenagers he met earlier at the Prince's Trust in Cardiff. He quizzes Thomas and other members of the collective about marketing and pricing, and tells them about a training scheme for butchers at Dumfries House, teaching them how to cook the products they sell. Graduates of the course are reporting a 20 per cent sales increase, says the Prince, because they are able to suggest recipes to their customers and tempt them into trying different meats and cuts. 'You need to know exactly what the constellation of the animal should be.' Then he's off on another tack, about whether there's any demand for the flesh of old ewes and talking about his 'mutton renaissance' again. 'I'm trying to tell everyone just how marvellous mutton really is.'

The Prince plays the old ham at the butcher's, entertaining his audience and mugging for the camera produced to immortalise the occasion. 'If the photographers weren't interested, that would be the time to start worrying,' the Prince said in 1982.[21] This was a brave declaration from someone who had always disliked media attention, even before that attention soured. Aged fourteen, he walked into a bar and ordered a cherry brandy. It was the sort of escapade that for other teenagers would have brought few if any consequences, and he only did so to take shelter from crowds who had recognised him. Unfortunately for Charles, a journalist inside the bar recognised him too and filed a story. The incident made headlines, the licensee and the barmaid who served him faced charges, later dropped, the Prince had privileges at school revoked, and, worst of all, saw his royal protection officer sacked from the squad for allowing the princely misdemeanour.

But the Prince endures, and even encourages, press coverage about his official and charity work because he understands its utility. 'One must grimace and bear it,' he says.[22] When the Welsh butchers offer him a plate of faggots, he adopts an expression of comical alarm: 'Which bit of the animal is this? Don't tell me it's the bits nobody else wanted.' Asked to bite into a beefburger by the photographer, he declines, laughing. 'Forgive me, I'm not going to do my wide-mouthed frog for you.'

For most working royals, there are two main aims to such visits, at home or abroad: to provide a boost to their hosts, in terms of positive reinforcement and publicity; and to promote the monarchy, by being seen and believed. Like most things the Windsors do, there's little hard information available to measure impacts scientifically by balancing business or funding generated against the disruption and costs incurred. The Prince's Duchy of Cornwall income covers his and Camilla's official activities and those of his sons and daughter-in-law, but not the bill for the upkeep of Clarence House or for official travel, which amounted in total to £1.73 million in the year to April 2015, drawn from public funds. Wales Week in 2012 incurred two transport bills of over £10,000 each. In 2013 none of the individual journeys breached this threshold so they were not itemised. They included a variety of different methods of transport including a helicopter journey for Camilla to Porthcawl. There's an additional cost to taxpayers for security. A request to the local Merthyr Tydfil County Borough Council about the expense of policing the Prince's visit to Treharris produces only the figure for the road closures (£15) and the installation of the crash barriers (£150).

Without a complete rundown, it's tough to judge value for money, and even then many of the benefits are intangibles. Celia Thomas of Cig Mynydd Cymru emails later: 'We all thoroughly enjoyed the visit and meeting the Prince of Wales, and everyone is still talking about it. We have made a poster with some of the lovely photographs taken on the day, which is proudly displayed on the wall of the shop. We found the Prince so easy to chat to and he showed a genuine interest in what we are doing. He even asked about our shop refurbishment when he was talking to Dai Havard, our MP, the other day. There certainly was a huge benefit to the shop and a huge boost to morale.'

At the time, the wider populace of Treharris also appears delighted. Ben and Ryan, who get to meet the Prince when he goes on a short walkabout, pronounce him 'a-mazin'', and he departs with various spoils: a styrofoam box of choice cuts, a raft of fresh information about farming in Wales and a set of questions and follow-up actions arising from the conversation, all immediately entrusted to an aide. But the publicity will disappoint. Only local newspapers pick up the story.

By contrast, William and Kate's trip to Australia and New Zealand the following year will generate worldwide saturation coverage, including daily transmission of images of beauty spots. The bill for the nine-day New Zealand leg tots up to some NZ$1 million, and is met by taxpayers at the destination, like most official travel by royals to the Realms. Tourism chiefs in Australia and New Zealand proclaim the publicity beyond price. For the monarchy it certainly is. 'I'm officially no longer a republican,' tweeted Patrick Gower, the political editor of the Wellington-based television station 3 News. The journalist may not have been entirely serious but his compatriots, like their Australian counterparts, succumbed to the charm offensive in droves.

The Prince cannot hope to match the poster children of the monarchy, and not just because of his greater age. Charles knew what it was to be overshadowed from the moment he married Diana. On the couple's 1983 perambulations around Australia, he ran his wife a poor second. 'So infatuated was the crowd at every walkabout that as [the royal couple] got out to work the crowd, an involuntary moan would rise from that part of the crowd which turned out to be nearest to the Prince and furthest from the Princess,' recounts Jonathan Dimbleby.[23] It is an experience already familiar to his son William, cast in the shade by Kate's dazzle, but there the similarity ends. William is proud of Kate as Charles never was of Diana and the Cambridges work as a team in a way the Waleses never managed. William is more easily photogenic than his dad, too. 'Never forget that William is a Spencer,' says a Buckingham Palace official. 'William and Harry are rock stars around the world,' says former Prime Minister John Major, who became the boys' financial guardian after Diana's death.[24] The Princess lives on in her sons.

'I hope this isn't an anticlimax. I can only imagine it must be,' says the Prince as he arrives at Ebbw Fawr Learning Community to find that some of the people gathered outside the new state school have been waiting since early morning for a glimpse of royalty. It's a refrain familiar to anyone who has heard him give speeches. 'I am immensely grateful to you all for taking the time to be here this afternoon – even if it's only out of curiosity!' he has said more than once.[25] 'Ladies and gentlemen, I am enormously impressed to find so many of you here this evening prepared to consider the role of investors and, in particular, pension funds, in the move to a sustainable economy. I can only take it as a compliment to four of my charities which operate in this area – unless, of course, you are all here out of curiosity as to what I might say next!' he tells another gathering.[26] 'Well, ladies and gentlemen,' he greets another group, 'I'm so glad I've got this opportunity to join you all this afternoon. I had this dreadful thought that all I had done was to stop you doing all sorts of other things you'd much rather be doing!'[27]

Self-deprecation may be a good ice-breaker but the Prince's insecurities are real. Excitement and affection greet him wherever he walks a rope line or works a room, yet for the glass-half-empty Prince, the crowds might always be bigger and the coverage better. Though he observes William and Harry with intense paternal pride, the emotion is marbled with a little jealousy and a wider vein of frustration, not because he begrudges their popularity but because of what he could do with such backing. Unlike his more charismatic sons and glistening daughter-in-law, over and above being a royal, he is a missionary with urgent messages to impart. There are bigger issues at stake than just the survival of the monarchy.

His visit to the butcher's shop Cig Mynydd Cymru has been slotted into the schedule to flag up the dangers of industrialised farming, the imbalances created by ill-thought-out subsidies, the perception he sets out in *Harmony* that 'modern high-tech agriculture' risks turning 'farming into an arms race against Nature, excluding everything from the land except the highly bred crops designed to be resistant to powerful pesticides and grown using industrial production methods'. (The Prince invariably refers to nature with a capital N, and as 'she' or 'her', in conscious opposition to mainstream culture. The Enlightenment 'objectified' nature, he complains. '"She",' he writes sadly in *Harmony*, 'became "it".')[28]

At his next stop he zeroes in on another preoccupation: inequality. He has come to Ebbw Fawr to launch the first Wales-based programme run by the education charity Teach First. In partnership with the Welsh government, Teach First plans to recruit highly skilled graduates to work in schools located in impoverished areas, giving additional assistance to 6,000 disadvantaged pupils each year. The Prince strolls through the school connecting easily with the dignitaries who have turned out in Sunday finery to meet him and more easily still with the pupils. After a quick private meeting with representatives of the charity, local government and the teaching profession, the Prince gives a (self-deprecating) speech and sits patiently through several more. 'We are incredibly proud that the Prince of Wales visited us,' emails Ebbw Fawr director Graeme Harkness later. 'Given that we had only been open as a school a few months this was a great fillip for the students and staff. The visit also had an impact on the local area which is not seen as an attractive place, has high levels of deprivation and unemployment ... Our students certainly still remember the visit and we have marketed his picture in items such as newsletters and digital signage.'

Teach First defines its mission as ending inequality in education. 'How much you achieve in life should not be determined by how much your parents earn,' declares its website. 'Yet in the UK, it usually is.' The Prince is the charity's patron. He sees no contradiction between its mission and his position. Indeed the phrase resonates. He believes that who your parents are should not restrict how much you can achieve – even if you're the Prince of Wales.

Back at Llwynywermod, it's not much of a stretch for Charles to imagine himself in a parallel universe, living out his days as a gentleman farmer. His residence in Carmarthenshire is large but by no means palatial, rustic rather than grand, with lime-plaster walls and slate roofing. Like increasing numbers of rural landowners, he even rents out rooms – when he's not in residence – to paying guests.

Like them, the Prince is transient, arriving for at most a few consecutive days. To simulate homeliness, he always brings with him certain essentials: framed photographs of Camilla and his children, his canvases and paints, and a cushion, more than once paraded by the British press as a symbol of indulgence but better understood as a support for the Prince's troublesome spine if not as his version of a security blanket. As a schoolboy sent away to board from the age of eight, he poignantly wrote of missing his 'homes'.[29] As an adult, he has accepted a life of permanent homesickness, shuttling between houses which he inhabits but apart from two cottages in Romania doesn't strictly speaking own. His regular haunts include Llwynywermod, Tamarisk in the Scilly Isles and Highgrove (all property of the Duchy of Cornwall); Dumfries House (owned by a trust); family residences such as Birkhall (which he rents from his mother) and the other mansions on the Balmoral estate as well as Sandringham; and Crown properties such as the complex on the Mall that incorporates the Prince's London operational base, since 1988 St James's Palace and, from 2002 onwards, expanded to encompass neighbouring Clarence House.

Until Queen Victoria moved to the larger, uglier Buckingham Palace just down the Mall, sovereigns resided at St James's Palace. These days the elegant Tudor building, commissioned by Henry VIII and once home to Anne Boleyn, is a frequent setting for conferences, meetings and receptions. Prince Charles may not command front pages as younger family members do or bring out crowds in anything like equivalent numbers, but what he lacks in mass appeal, he makes up in convening power. He has received – and bent the ears of – a startlingly diverse range of guests, from the Dalai Lama and Aung San Suu Kyi to Kylie Minogue, from people at the top of their game to figures whose moment in the public gaze, unlike their host's, has since passed or shaded into notoriety. The Prince welcomed Jimmy Savile as a frequent visitor, unaware of his habit of touching up the palace secretarial staff, and in 2002 glad-handed Bashar al Assad.

Few people reject an invitation from a future king. If this means the Prince has sometimes kept dubious company, it also grants him extraordinary access and a platform. He used his 2013 Advent reception, attended by the Archbishop of Canterbury and other prominent religious leaders, to highlight the suffering of Syrian Christians in the civil conflict that Assad's brutality triggered. He holds regular powwows with business and industry, pushing his interlinked agendas of sustainability and community engagement. He recalls, with gratitude, the advice of the politician and diplomat Sir Christopher Soames – the father of one of his close friends, MP Sir Nicholas Soames – who first alerted him to the ease with which he might expect to bring high-level participants together. 'That is a piece of advice I have never forgotten and I've developed and pursued and I've found over and over again,' says the Prince. 'And right, there may be advantages in my case because I haven't got a particular axe to grind and people notice that, I suppose, when you get people round a table you discover that frequently it's the first time they've all sat round a table. You think, this can't be possible. They must've sat and talked. These are people you'd think would form a sensible integrated approach. Not a bit of it.' He takes pride in his ability at 'getting business people, government and agencies to sit down with NGOs, who normally they might never have talked to, except they shout across a huge chasm'.[30]

In 2009, a clutch of world leaders and prominent figures pulled up gilt chairs around one of his capacious tables for a summit of his Prince's Rainforest Project (PRP): eight elected premiers – Australia's Kevin Rudd, France's Nicolas Sarkozy, Germany's Angela Merkel, Guyana's Samuel Hinds, Indonesia's Susilo Bambang Yudhoyono, Italy's Silvio Berlusconi, Japan's Tarō Asō and Norway's Jens

Stoltenberg – plus then US Secretary of State Hillary Clinton, four British Cabinet Ministers (Secretary of State for Energy and Climate Change Ed Miliband; Secretary of State for Environment, Food and Rural Affairs Hilary Benn; Secretary of State for International Development Douglas Alexander; and Foreign Secretary David Miliband), the President of the European Commission José Manuel Barroso, Canada's Minister of Finance Jim Flaherty, the Secretary-General of the United Nations Ban Ki-moon, Gabon's Defence Minister Ali Bongo Ondimba, Saudi Arabian Foreign Minister Prince Saud Al Faisal, and World Bank President Robert Zoellick.

The Prince had established the PRP two years earlier, focusing its efforts on identifying the economic drivers of deforestation and suggesting possible alternatives. The international community was mulling a market mechanism akin to carbon credits to make trees more valuable alive than dead but the Prince worried that the scheme would arrive too late and do too little. He used the 2009 summit to float the idea of an emergency bridge. His intervention led to the formation of a secretariat by the Norwegian and British governments that in turn kicked off an intergovernmental process. The following May in Oslo thirty-five donor countries agreed an investment of US $4 billion over three years into projects to reduce carbon emissions.

The Prince continues to drive his environmental campaign, presiding over further summits at St James's Palace and taking the podium at high-level conferences. His PRP lives on, renamed the International Sustainability Unit, and entrusted with a broader remit that looks at bringing agriculture and forestry in harmony, rather than competition, as well as at sustainable fishing and resilience, particularly food and water security. Few of the summit attendees retain the same portfolios or even hold office. Merkel is the only elected leader who attended the summit to remain in power. The Prince's constancy comes at a price. He has no democratic mandate, nor is there a mechanism for voting him out. It is one of his greatest strengths as a campaigner and the reason why some people will never accept his right to campaign.

At a pub in the market town of Llandovery, another group of people convened around a table by the Prince embark on a game without fixed end. The players include off-duty protection officers, drivers and aides, members of the retinue that accompanies Charles on most of his travels, road-weary veterans whose devotion to the Prince can be measured in the numbers of days they spend away from home and the breadth of their knowledge of pub games. This particular contest sees each player alternately exclaim 'fuzzy duck' or 'ducky fuzz', or at least try to. If someone fumbles the phrase, often producing an obscenity and a double measure of amusement, he or she takes a deep drink and the direction of the game reverses.

The entertainment earlier in the evening at nearby Llwynywermod has also provoked hilarity, if not so predictably. The Prince and his Duchess conclude their day in Wales by hosting people from the locality and further afield to an evening of Welsh folk songs and dances. The guests who take their seats in Llwynywermod's converted barn reflect different strands of the couple's interests: cultural figures, assorted flavours of civic worthiness, business leaders who may prove good for donations to the Prince's charities, and a few real friends – like Patrick Holden, who farms in the area, and his wife. At first everyone is transported by the music of the truest of voices harmonising a cappella, sometimes accompanied by harp and fiddle – and blackbirds nesting in the eaves, late in fledging, that fill every interlude in the programme with more singing. After two summer carols comes the first clog dance, then four more carols and a harp solo.

At the second clog dance, '*Pedwarawd clocsio*' – a clogging quartet – Camilla's shoulders begin to shake. The royal hosts sit in the front row, backs to most guests, who perhaps assume the beauty of the music has moved her. As she struggles to conceal her tears, it becomes apparent that the dancing display, as athletic as aesthetic, has indeed made her cry, with suppressed laughter. The Prince touches her hand, restraining or comforting, and his shoulders shake too. Her tears – and mascara – continue to flow.

It isn't the most regal of behaviour, not something you can imagine the Queen doing. For the public, this is proving a positive and, for the Prince, it has undoubtedly always been part of Camilla's attraction. From his earliest years, warmth, spontaneity and humour have been scarce commodities in his life.

He is at his most serene in her company, yet on this evening in Wales, as most nights, he will not follow her straight to bed, but instead sits down to his paperwork. It's what he does. 'I keep trying to get him to have more than one gin,' says Emma Thompson. 'Have another, I keep screeching.'[31] But there are always letters to read and more to write. The black ink scuttles across the virgin sheets, urgent and insistent.

Any understanding of the Prince must flow from an understanding of the institution that created him and which he serves. Concern about his questing extends beyond republican circles and the tea tables of staunch traditionalists. In the corridors and back rooms and private apartments of Buckingham Palace there is mounting anxiety as the Queen's reign enters what an insider calls 'its inevitable twilight'. In defining his role as heir apparent, the Prince has signalled a redefinition of the monarchy. Some courtiers – and the sovereign herself – fear that neither the Crown nor its subjects will tolerate the shock of the new.

The Queen set the terms by which her son is judged – and so often found wanting. Yet her reign speaks to the importance not of staying still but of maintaining the illusion of unbroken tradition, perfect continuity. The next chapter examines that reign and her role and the private person so rarely glimpsed. The biggest test of her change management will come with her passing, determined by decisions beyond her control yet still bearing her stamp. How the Prince inhabits kingship – and how firmly – will owe much to the Queen, not just as a role model but as a mother, and to Prince Philip, the father he fears and whose approval he still seeks. His parents schooled Charles in duty and tried to give him a grounding in the real world, recognising that the monarchy must mirror the experiences of its peoples. His upbringing of lonely privilege and public-school privations left him flailing. The roots of his activism and awkwardness, his urgent need to make sense of the world and to improve it – the drivers for his princely quest – lie deep in the strangest of childhoods.

Chapter 2

Mother Load

You know she's near because like the Wicked Queen in a fairy tale, she's preceded through palace corridors by slavering hounds. There are four of them – Holly and Willow, Candy and Vulcan – two corgis and two dorgis, the offspring of a morganatic union between a corgi and a dachshund. One of the dorgis seems fond of the salt naturally secreted by human skin and sets with rough tongue to licking any ankles left uncovered, growling if interrupted. Her owner proves at least as intimidating: tiny, flinty and near impossible to read. Elizabeth II has spent more than eight decades perfecting her poker face.

In the course of her life, the world has convulsed and shuddered like a werewolf under a full moon, pushing out a new coat and fangs, the old familiar lines disappearing under a mass of phenomena that to many of her generation seem monstrous. When Princess Elizabeth was born in 1926, the British Empire extended across a quarter of the globe. By the time she ascended the throne, the relics of Empire were crumbling, leaving a difficult legacy in the former colonies and at home in a nation that no longer felt sure of its identity, place or purpose. Britain had won a war but risked losing itself.

The new head of state handled these transitions with the inscrutability she had cultivated from the moment her uncle's traumatic abdication pushed her to the top of the line of succession. With this same lack of expression she has presided over social and cultural revolutions harnessed to new technologies that have shrunk the physical world while amplifying its tumult and confusion. She watches, apparently impassive, as the peoples of her Realms adopt peregrine ways of speaking, dressing, thinking and behaving, native to their age groups and globalised cultures or imported as populations diversify. At the time of her accession just over 4 per cent of the British population was foreign born; that total now stands northwards of 12 per cent, a figure that does little to reflect the thrilling heterogeneity of British cities or the tensions accompanying that transformation. In 1952, most women married, like the Queen, at twenty-one and like her quickly popped out a first child. Only 35 per cent of them worked, as she did (and none of those working worked as she did). Female participation in the UK labour force has risen to 74.5 per cent. When she took the driving seat of the family business, just a quarter of households owned cars. Now only a fifth do not. During her reign churchgoing has sharply declined. The average age of congregations has risen heavenwards, mirroring changes to the wider population as fewer people marry or stay married or raise large families or have any children at all during lifespans that have lengthened by thirty years since the beginning of the twentieth century. Britons, like their Queen, are becoming grizzled.

Hers are the grey hairs of unique experience. She has held weekly audiences with twelve Prime Ministers and accepted the resignations of eleven of them, starting with Winston Churchill. She discussed the Suez Crisis with Anthony Eden; the Falklands War with Margaret Thatcher; the first Gulf War with John Major; Kosovo, Sierra Leone, Afghanistan, Iraq and the War on Terror with interventionist Tony Blair; and with David Cameron Libya and the decision forced on him by a rebellious Parliament to stay plans for military action against Syria. Major, who served as Prime Minister from 1990 to 1997, describes the audiences as 'a hugely valuable resource ... In politics you have to be careful what you say, however close the person is to you. But with the Queen there need be no such inhibition.' The weekly discussions, he says, 'are like a confessional with a particularly trusted priest'.[1]

The Queen has twice been forced to use her prerogative to choose Prime Ministers, in 1957 and again in 1963 before the Conservative party instituted a formalised process of selecting a leader, both times passing over a prominent candidate, Richard Austin (Rab) Butler, to appoint respectively Harold Macmillan and then Alec Douglas-Home who renounced an earldom and lesser peerages to serve as plain Sir from the benches of the House of Commons. Butler had pioneered Britain's free school system and supported the post-war Labour government's introduction of the welfare state; he referred to some of his own Tory colleagues as 'Colonel Blimps'. In appointing Macmillan, the Queen overrode the advice of her outgoing Prime Minister, Anthony Eden, but conformed to the urgings of his predecessor Winston Churchill and other Conservative grandees. By selecting Douglas-Home, she appeared to favour a man not only of the unambiguous Right but of the aristocracy over the more charismatic, Left-leaning Butler. Constitutional historian Vernon Bogdanor argues she had little real choice and that the decision 'cannot be said seriously to have misrepresented Conservative opinion at the time'.[2] 'Prime Ministers who've seen the Queen at close quarters often for many years would not be able to tell you with any certainty what her party political views are,' says John Major.[3]

If the Queen conceals her political instincts like a hand of cards, her personal likes and dislikes, played almost as close to her chest, are ecumenical. Her favourite Prime Ministers both rose from the lower middle classes: Labour's Harold Wilson and Major, a Tory. There was no love lost between her and Thatcher or real connection between her and Blair. These views have filtered through the accounts of palace observers and the Prime Ministers themselves. The Queen has never again been forced to make her preferences public. The Conservative party adopted a mechanism for choosing its leaders without the need for royal intervention and Britain's first-past-the-post electoral system until 2010 reliably produced emphatic outcomes that the monarch simply affirmed when the pre-selected leader of whichever party emerged with the largest number of parliamentary seats and made his – or, in 1979, 1983 and 1987, her – way to Buckingham Palace.

Ahead of the May 2010 general election with polls predicting electoral stalemate, there was speculation that the Queen might be forced once more to intervene in the selection of a Prime Minister. 'We're told the monarchy is "value for money",' wrote Graham Smith, director of the anti-monarchist group Republic. 'Well now's the time for the monarch to earn her crust. If she ducks the responsibility she confirms once and for all that she is constitutionally pointless, a political eunuch stranded by the tide of modern democratic principles our leaders try to apply to a feudal system.' He added: 'If the Queen has written herself out of the script for fear of making the wrong decision what we're left with are shadowy deals and secret memos that will shape the way in which our next Prime Minister is chosen without the benefit of public scrutiny. Whatever the outcome of this election, we need the appointment of the Prime Minister to be conducted in the open.'[4]

The Queen did not, in Smith's terms, earn her crust. For five days the incumbent Prime Minister Gordon Brown hung on in the hopes of forming a coalition with the Liberal Democrats until they opted to enter government with David Cameron's Conservatives. The Queen remained aloof from all the negotiations. A palace source suggests this represented not the abdication of her constitutional role but its practice, steadying nerves through the fact of her existence during the transition from one political reality to another that occurred without unrest on the streets or jitters in the financial markets.

Graham Smith did see one wish partially fulfilled. Within months, the new coalition had published a draft of the Cabinet Manual, a document setting out the guidelines that had been used in formation of the government. In his introduction to the finalised text, Cameron cited a 'desire for a political system that is looked at with admiration around the world and is more transparent and accountable … For the first time the conventions determining how the Government operates are transparently set out in one place. Codifying and publishing these sheds welcome light on how the Government interacts with the other parts of our democratic system.'[5] Downing Street officials warned that the manual should not be mistaken for the beginnings of a written constitution but it remains the only official publication of the modern era to attempt to define in writing the role of the monarch.

It does so in one pithy sentence, that doesn't so much prescribe what a monarch should do as describe what the Queen has done: 'The Sovereign is the head of state of the UK, providing stability, continuity and a national focus,' the document declares. That is the job the Prince expects to inherit. Supporters of a republic would prefer to replace the hereditary system with elected heads of state, each poll pitting different visions of Britain against each other. That might prove bracing. It would not be comforting. 'You don't have an election and a dispute as to who the next monarch is, with half the country thinking the wrong person has been elected, as you do with a republic,' says John Major.[6]

In remaining on show, apparently immutable, as everything changed around her, the Queen may have provided a waypost in unfamiliar landscapes and a nucleus of unity at a time when most impulses favour disintegration. The European project is fracturing. The concept of Britishness has stretched thin. Both ideas are coming under increasing strain as nationalist and populist movements gain strength in befuddled response to globalisation. While Scotland contemplated a rupture with the rest of the United Kingdom, leaders of the campaign for independence assured voters that shuffling off the yoke of Westminster need not mean losing the Queen or the reassurance of stability the Crown provides. Though the monarch devoutly hoped Scots would opt to stay in the union, and despite the urgings of a member of her close family to intervene, she kept her views guarded, going no further than to express the wish that Scots would 'think very carefully about the future.' Her aides went to 'great lengths to communicate the Queen's own unimpeachable position,' says a palace insider. After the September 2014 referendum, in which 55 per cent of voters opted to retain Scotland's place within the sovereign's still United Kingdom, Buckingham Palace released a statement by the Queen. 'As we move forward, we should remember that despite the range of views that have been expressed, we have in common an enduring love of Scotland, which is one of the things that helps to unite us all,' she said.

Such gestures of reconciliation come naturally. Sources say she found it harder to accept the apologies of the Prime Minister who was caught by film crews during a trip to the UN General Assembly in New York later the same month boasting about calling the Queen to convey the referendum result. 'The definition of relief is being the Prime Minister of the United Kingdom and ringing the Queen and saying, "It's all right, it's OK,"' Cameron told former New York Mayor Michael Bloomberg ahead of a business meeting. 'That was something. She purred down the line.' While nobody in the palace rejected the idea that the result secretly pleased the Queen, officials were irritated by the breach of protocol that revealed her private thoughts. John Major cannot recall a similar lapse, he says. 'However far back you go, Prime Ministers will talk generically but they will not talk specifically. If they did then you lose the value of the private audiences with the monarch.'[7]

Cameron's description of the Queen purring drew snorts not only of anger but of incredulity. Around Prince Philip she is sometimes, disconcertingly, kittenish, but to most people – and certainly Cameron – she remains unyielding and literally and figuratively unstrokeable. To touch the Queen is an act of lese-majesty.

In commanding respect, she has also gained public affection. She may be owed a debt of gratitude too. Far Right parties have been making significant gains in some countries, as voters lash out at mainstream politicians they don't trust and immigrant populations they find convenient to scapegoat for economic hardships. The French National Front won almost a quarter of the vote, more than any other party, in the May 2014 European elections. Its close equivalent in the UK, the British National Party, lost the one seat it held in the European Parliament, as another anti-immigration, eurosceptic party, the United Kingdom Independence Party – UKIP – surged to claim twenty-four seats. UKIP shares many hallmarks of far Right parties and gives succour to the central mythology that foreigners and outsiders threaten national cultures and prosperity. Its leader, Nigel Farage, drew fire – and, presumably, hard Right votes – by suggesting Britons would be right to be concerned if Romanians moved in next door to them.[8] But his party has also made a show of expelling or disciplining representatives for expressing 'unacceptable' views, such as the Henley-on-Thames councillor David Silvester who perceived in severe flooding in England God's response to the same-sex marriage bill. Such views may play well with a narrow band of the electorate, but are seen by the UKIP leadership and less partial observers to mitigate against the party's chances of continuing to capture a wider vote and solidifying its position as an electoral force.

There are many reasons why Britons may be less susceptible than some other Europeans to an unvarnished far Right, not least its lucky habit of producing incompetent far Right leaders. Richard Chartres, Bishop of London and close to the Prince since they attended Cambridge University together, believes that Britain's constitutional monarchy and its staunch Queen have also helped to immunise the population against far Right populism. 'One of the things that the monarchy has done in this country very much is keep the right wing respectable,' he says. 'If you look at all those countries where the monarchies collapsed after the First World War, one of the consequences was a visceral street rightism, which has flourished in a vacuum of iconic figures who could sum up national pride. One of the things that the Queen has done is she's occupied that space. She's also offered the kind of reassurance and continuity at a time when our place in the world is dramatically reduced.'[9]

A nagging question for those who see the Queen as a bulwark against extremism and disintegration is this: will her son be able to fulfil that role?

If the man of God's argument for saving the Queen is unprovable, the fact of her steady presence in public life is undeniable. 'Apart from my sister, she is the only other person who has been a total constant in my life ever since I came to consciousness. The Queen was there and that's an incredible rock I think to have in your life,' says Helen Mirren.[10] After a career spanning four decades, stage, television and film, the avant garde and Hollywood mainstream, Mirren accepted the role that would snag her an Oscar in 2007 and lodge her almost as indelibly in the public imagination as the character she played. The movie *The Queen* dramatised and sought to explain in human terms Elizabeth II's greatest misstep: her failure to read the national – and global – mood in the wake of Princess Diana's death. As the sovereign grieved in private, anger against the Windsors built like suppressed sobs. Finally the Queen let herself be persuaded to display her sorrow on television. 'We have all been trying in our different ways to cope. It is not easy to express a sense of loss, since the initial shock is often succeeded by a mixture of other feelings: disbelief, incomprehension, anger – and concern for those who remain. We have all felt those emotions in these last few days,' she said.

It was enough but only just. Such mistakes have been few and far between, and they have always been similar to each other in nature. The Queen appeared austere and uncaring in 1966 when she waited six days before visiting Aberfan in South Wales after a landslide of coal waste buried its school, killing 116 children and 28 adults. She missed the funeral in Lockerbie of a ten-year-old victim of the terror attack on Pan Am Flight 103 over the Scottish town. 'At a time of national mourning, we rightly and naturally turn to the Queen for our lead,' wrote columnist Jean Rook in the *Daily Express*. 'Broken-hearted Britain watching TV needed to see their equally grieving monarch.' Buckingham Palace provided a frigid explanation: the Queen does not attend memorial services or funerals.[11]

The Queen scrapped that convention and adjusted as far as she is temperamentally able to a world that needs to see her grief to believe it. She also relaxed into motherhood, enveloping her second batch of children, Andrew and Edward, with a warmth denied to Charles and Anne. She loved her first- and second-born but in the early years of her reign focused on her duty as sovereign to the exclusion of much else.

Charles, in particular, learned early in life to equate duty with denial and denial with his destiny. That he was born to assume the crown, the Prince said, 'dawned on me with a ghastly inexorability'.[12] When he was just one year old, his mother spent six weeks away, and on her return took four days to catch up with administrative affairs − slipping in a quick trip to the races − before rejoining her son. After she acceded to the throne, such separations became more protracted. In 1953, she toured the Commonwealth with Prince Philip for six months. When Charles boarded the royal yacht, excited finally to see his parents after their long absence, he tried to join the dignitaries lined up to greet them. 'No, not you, dear,' said the Queen.'[13]

This book explores a character shaped by nature and nurture and perhaps just as much by the absence of nurture. Charles was born into a unique set of circumstances and an odd environment. He was also the product of an age that still warned against showing children too much tenderness for fear of spoiling them. His mother may appear changeless but she has always reflected the times – and moved with them.

The Windsors would like you to believe that the things they do are things that have always been done, but that is just a case of smoke and gilded mirrors. The dynasty rebrands and refreshes itself constantly and carefully and sometimes weathers more radical re-inventions too. The premier symbols of Britishness refer to themselves as 'European mongrels' in Prince Andrew's words, and that's about right, though the most concentrated element of the Windsor line is German, with a leavening of Danish blood.[14] In 1917, as European powers slid towards war and British antipathies to all things German deepened, King George V quietly exchanged his family name Saxe-Coburg-Gotha for Windsor, the reassuringly English-sounding name of their castle in Berkshire. He urged Prince Louis of Battenberg, his cousin and married to one of Queen Victoria's granddaughters, to anglicise his surname too. Battenberg, who had carved out a high-flying career in the Royal Navy, rising to First Sea Lord by the time war with Germany appeared inevitable, complied. It wasn't enough to save his job, but spared royal embarrassment, not least when in 1947 his grandson Prince Philip of Greece and Denmark took British citizenship and adopted the clunky new family name, Mountbatten, just before marrying the future Elizabeth II and gaining a new title, Duke of Edinburgh.

Most changes to the institution of monarchy during the Queen's reign have barely rippled the surface, 'imperceptible' in the words of one courtier; yet in their totality they've been profound and trans-formative. Everything is the product of instinct, not analysis or training. 'I didn't have an apprenticeship,' she once said. 'My father died much too young and so it was all a very sudden kind of taking on and making the best job you can. It's a question of maturing into something that one's got used to doing and accepting the fact that here you are and it's your fate. Because I think continuity is very important.'[15]

Unlike her long-serving heir, she benefited from only a few years of formal preparation for assuming the throne after her father's unexpected elevation to kingship; on-the-job experience and lessons from Henry Marten, the Vice Provost of Eton College, who instructed her in constitutional history including the works of Walter Bagehot.

A more vivid history lesson came courtesy of the Luftwaffe. In September 1940, a German bomber scored a direct hit on Buckingham Palace. 'We heard the unmistakable whirr-whirr of a German plane. We said "ah a German" and before anything else could be said there was the noise of aircraft diving at great speed, and then the scream of a bomb,' wrote Elizabeth's doughty mother, Queen Elizabeth. 'It all happened so quickly that we had only time to look foolishly at each other, when the scream hurtled past us, and exploded with a tremendous crash in the quadrangle.' The letter ends with a postscript, key words underlined in the family tradition. 'Dear old BP is still standing and that is the main thing.'[16] Her daughter understands that no edifice, however famous or solid looking, is invulnerable. She has dedicated her life to keeping the monarchy standing.

In 1947 the Princess celebrated her twenty-first birthday in South Africa, during a royal tour that failed in its objective of revitalising support for the pro-British General Jan Smuts, but launched the young Elizabeth as a future sovereign and gave a foretaste of the high solemnity with which she would approach the role. In a broadcast from Cape Town, she said: 'This is a happy day for me; but it is also one that brings serious thoughts, thoughts of life looming ahead with all its challenges and with all its opportunity.' She spoke of the 'terrible and glorious years of the Second World War' and looked forward with others of her age group to being 'able to take some of the burden off the shoulders of our elders who have fought and worked and suffered to protect our childhood'.

'There is a motto,' she said, 'which has been borne by many of my ancestors – a noble motto, "I serve". Those words were an inspiration to many bygone heirs to the throne when they made their knightly dedication as they came to manhood. I cannot do quite as they did. But through the inventions of science I can do what was not possible for any of them. I can make my solemn act of dedication with a whole Empire listening. I should like to make that dedication now. It is very simple. I declare before you all that my whole life whether it be long or short shall be devoted to your service and the service of our great imperial family to which we all belong.'

In 1952 that earnest service started in earnest with her father's death. Elizabeth was just twenty-five. Her daughter, Anne, not yet three years old, was deemed too young to attend the coronation. Charles, aged four, his hair already severely parted, rested a weary head on his hand as he watched his mother crowned. Ahead of the ceremony, she had undertaken practice sessions wearing sheets pinned together to give her a sense of the robes she must manoeuvre into Westminster Abbey and wore the imperial state crown around Buckingham Palace to try to accustom herself to its weight. 'It goes on, the ceremony, for quite a long time, so you can end up with a terrible headache,' the Prince explained. 'So I remember my mother coming up, when we were being bathed as children, wearing the crown. It was quite funny. That's a vivid memory, I must say.'[17]

The new Queen found herself in charge of a palace system stocked with courtiers, who occupied positions as she did, by dint of heredity. She preserved some of the picturesque pomp and the florid job titles – she still employs a Mistress of the Robes; the Master of the Horse rides alongside her carriage at ceremonial occasions; she is serenaded every morning at 9 a.m. by the Queen's Piper, though she once confessed that the sound of bagpipes had long since palled – but she has stocked key roles with professionals. The Keeper of the Privy Purse may sound ceremonial, but the title incorporates management of both the private and public revenues of the Queen, responsible for intricate budgets and for defending them to parliamentary committees. The incumbent since 2002, Sir Alan Reid, used to be a senior partner at KPMG. Sir Christopher Geidt, the eighth Private Secretary of her reign, served in the military, at a think tank and as a diplomat in Sarajevo, Geneva and Brussels before joining the royal household.

In 1957, a television crew came to Sandringham to film, for the first time, the Queen's Christmas message. 'I very much hope that this new medium will make my Christmas message more personal and direct,' she said. 'It is inevitable that I should seem a rather remote figure to many of you, a successor to the kings and queens of history; someone whose face may be familiar in newspapers and films but who never really touches your personal lives. But now at least for a few minutes I welcome you to the peace of my own home.' She has continued to look for ways to bridge the gap between herself and her subjects. In 1958, at the urging of the Duke of Edinburgh, she quietly retired the custom for debutantes to be presented at court, opening her doors instead to a wider range of guests, often nominated by external organisations such as charities or selected as representatives of identity groups: women in business, Irish living in Britain, the Asian community. She holds multiple audiences, not just with Prime Ministers but with other senior figures of the British Establishment, and travels around meeting as many people as can be filed past her. The number of bedecked and behatted guests turning up to her garden parties tops 30,000 per year. 'She likes a rapid throughput,' says an aide.

In the years before Diana's death the Queen signed off on significant changes in the way the monarchy interfaced with the rest of the state, advised by the so-called Way Ahead Group, a body of senior aides and royals that formed in recognition that the monarchy urgently needed to do some strategic thinking. On 20 November

1992, towards the end of a dismal twelve-month run that saw the Morton book published and the marriages of three of the Queen's four children collapse, flames gutted Windsor Castle, causing £36.5 million worth of damage and burning away the notion that Britons would unquestioningly shell out to maintain the trappings of their monarchy. John Major's government, wrestling unsuccessfully with recession and the aftermath of a currency crisis that had just tipped sterling out of the European Exchange Rate Mechanism, announced that it would foot the repair bill, provoking outrage. 'It was a bump in the road,' says Major now. 'Even in the most difficult moments of the 1990s, there wasn't a millisecond when the monarchy was in any real danger from the point of view of the people up and down the country. It is deeply rooted … You don't dig it up quickly.'[18]

The senior royals feared that growing numbers of Britons might go in search of shovels. Four days after the fire, the Queen made a speech at Guildhall to mark the fortieth anniversary of her accession. 'There can be no doubt,' she said, 'that criticism is good for people and institutions that are part of public life. No institution – city, monarchy, whatever – should expect to be free from the scrutiny of those who give it their loyalty and support, not to mention those who don't.'[19]

Yet the mechanisms for funding royalty had been kept deliberately opaque. A 1972 amendment to the Civil List Act for the first time inserted a requirement for the Treasury to review the Queen's spending, but set the reviews at ten-year intervals. More frequent scrutiny, the law stated, would not be 'consistent with the honour and dignity of the Crown'; daylight is dangerous. MPs were forbidden from asking questions about the royal finances except during the review period.

Monarchs from George III onwards surrendered the assets of the Crown Estates to government in return for official expenses and annuities through the Civil List, later augmented by grants from various government departments. In addition, the monarch enjoyed a substantial – and tax-exempt – private income from the Privy Purse, mostly generated by the Duchy of Lancaster, an estate held in trust for the monarch and constituted along similar lines to the Duchy of Cornwall. Before the Windsor fire, the Queen had already held discussions about making voluntary tax payments, as Prince Charles already did, giving the Treasury 50 per cent of his Duchy of Cornwall income in advance of his first marriage and 25 per cent after that happy day.

Each review of the Civil List invariably drew headlines about 'pay rises' for the Queen. The Prince had tried in the 1980s to head off criticism by exploring ways of fundamentally altering the financial arrangements between government and the royal households. His imagination was caught by a proposal to retire the Civil List and return the Crown Estates, and their income, to royal care. The idea wouldn't fly and not only because the costs of the monarchy by now exceeded the revenues from its hereditary lands. A self-financing monarchy would no longer be beholden to Parliament, becoming more remote, more royal, in effect more powerful.

The Windsor fire precipitated a compromise. The government announced that the Queen intended to pay income tax and capital gains tax on her private income and also to slash the numbers of royals living on handouts from the state by financing them herself. Charles echoed the move, opting to pay the maximum rate of income tax on his Duchy revenues. The Queen also implemented a cost-cutting programme, agreeing that her court would live on a static budget for the next two decades. Still protests against the plan for a taxpayer-funded restoration of Windsor Castle smouldered. 'Is there not something brutally unfair about the fact that it is estimated that at least £60 million will be paid out by taxpayers to the richest woman in Britain to repair one of her homes without any contribution from herself, when only 400 yards away from another of her homes,

Buckingham Palace, people have to live in cardboard boxes and pensioners will die this winter from hypothermia?' asked Labour's Dennis Skinner in a House of Commons debate and though he over-stated the cost of repairs, for once a significant slice of people across the chamber agreed with him in principle.[20] After the failure of a private fund-raising initiative for Windsor Castle that attracted only £25,000 in donations, the Queen found the money for repairs by opening Buckingham Palace to tourists. Around half a million visitors from across the Realms and beyond tramp through the state rooms every summer, producing a useful revenue stream and opening up a narrow strip of royal life to public view.

The Way Ahead Group eventually disbanded, but only after the practice of strategic thinking had been incorporated into the fibre of palace organisation. That has meant continuing small-scale reform and a few more eye-catching measures. In 2011 the Queen signed off on a new system for financing herself and future heads of state to a formula agreed by the coalition government whose birth pains she had observed the previous year. The Sovereign Grant consolidated the grants and sources of income previously paid to the monarch via the Civil List and government departments, making the arrangements a tad less impen-etrable, rendering its custodians a touch more accountable and giving the Queen a smidgeon more of the independence the Prince had sought.

The formula is still complicated – the Grant is calculated as the greater of either the funding received in the previous year or the agreed rate of 15 per cent of the Crown Estate's net surplus two years earlier – but reviews now take place every five years by the Prime Minister, Chancellor of the Exchequer and Keeper of the Privy Purse, with annual accounts audited by the National Audit Office and examined by the parliamentary Public Accounts Committee. The sum handed to the Queen in the first year of the arrangement, 2012–13, amounted to £31 million, a nice whack but insufficient to cover her household's net expenditure of £33 million. The booming value of the Crown Estate's portfolio has controversially seen that grant rise to a projected £42.7 million in 2016. Officials say this is needed to pay for a backlog in maintenance works to royal palaces including Buckingham Palace, St James's Palace and Clarence House, as well as Windsor Castle, built up during the twenty-year freeze in the Queen's public income.

Guests and the tourists paying to visit Buckingham Palace enter a stage set, constructed and maintained to project majesty. A one-star review in the 2000 *Which? Guide to Tourist Attractions* dismissed the palace tour as 'inhuman and sterile', eliciting a contemptuous response from a palace official. 'There must be a misunderstanding in the mind of the inspector to produce this report about what the state apartments in a palace are. To say that they are inhuman is using a 21st-century criticism of a building that was put up 200 years ago,' said Hugh Roberts, director, until his 2010 retirement, of the Royal Collection, the body responsible for organising the tours.[21]

Look closer, and you'll find cracks in the edifice of monarchy, not so much metaphorical fissures as palpable decay that in 2007 sent masonry crashing from the roof, narrowly missing Princess Anne as she got into her car, and two years later dislodged a chunk of stone that came close to felling a police officer on duty. In March 2012 the Public Accounts Committee flagged up the statistic that 39 per cent of royal properties stood, precariously, in need of remedial work. The committee's then chairwoman MP Margaret Hodge criticised the Queen's household. 'I expected to see a better performance,' she said. 'They've got to get a bit real.'[22]

Nobody who has seen them would call the back corridors of Buckingham Palace sterile or assume the royal household to lack a sense of harsher realities. Away from the public areas, thick carpeting gives way to worn runners along corridors that branch into a series of domains: working offices, working kitchens, the engine rooms of an international corporation, and beyond those, staff bedrooms, guest suites and royal apartments. The geography of the palace reflects the topology of the Queen's life. Nobody can say for sure where the sovereign's public duty ends and her private sphere begins. Paperwork and retainers trail the Queen like corgis. No royal home ever feels truly homely but Buckingham Palace is the bleakest. Surrounded by more than 800 employees and a clutter of unwanted gifts and excess furniture, stacked wellington boots and dog hair, the Queen, Prince Philip, and a shifting population that at times includes their children Anne, Andrew and Edward and cousin Princess Alexandra, carry out their odd sort of work and their odder form of living.

'Most people have a job and then they go home and in this existence the job and the life go on together,' the matter-of-fact Queen tells viewers of *Elizabeth R.* 'Because you can't really divide it up; the boxes and the communications just keep on coming and of course in modern communications they come even quicker. Luckily I'm a quick reader so I can get through a lot of reading in quite a short time ... I do rather begrudge some of the hours that I have to do instead of being outdoors.'[23]

That is a rare complaint. Mostly the Queen just gets on with the business of being Queen, accepting the lack of freedom and restriction of personal space which that entails and expecting her children to knuckle down to their fate with similar resignation. She planned to invite the Home Secretary of the day to attend the birth of Prince Charles just as an earlier Home Secretary in 1926 had paced the halls of her parents' house in Bruton Street during her own difficult delivery. She had grown up understanding that such invitations were part of a tradition dating back to 1688 when opponents of James II circulated a rumour that he had substituted an imposter child, smuggled in a warming pan into the palace, for his stillborn heir. Sir Alan Lascelles, her father's Private Secretary, brought her the welcome news that the custom, like so many royal traditions, had been fabricated, in this instance spun to permit officials to cluster 'in the private apartments of royalty daily, and particularly at moments of special significance such as births, marriages and deaths'.[24]

So on 14 November 1948 baby Charles drew his first breath in Buckingham Palace without a Home Secretary present to attest to his bona fides. He often seems like a cuckoo in the royal nest – superficially more at odds with his parents than like them – but nobody has ever challenged his heritage: it's clearly visible in his features, his expressions, his habit of clasping his hands behind his back just like his father.

What he never learned to do is wear a mask, as his mother does. If you cannot hide, you can at least hide your feelings. The impassivity that defines the Queen's public image is not feigned, but it is assumed. Even in the compromised privacy of her family circle, she gives little away and with her husband has created a family culture that prizes restraint and approves of stoicism. Friends remember that her corgis once got into a fight with Princess Anne's dogs. A dog died. Neither the Queen nor Princess Anne mentioned the incident, to each other or the rest of the family.

Her staff learns to look for fractional signs of displeasure: is the Queen's mouth a little more downturned, the presence a degree more glacial? From behind the mask, she misses very little. Her micromanagement is legendary. She knows things about palace life – about what members of the household have been up to – that can only come from bat-like hearing and preternatural powers of observation. She pays attention to the smallest details. A 2014 trial into allegations of bribery and phone hacking by employees of Rupert Murdoch's *News of the World* heard that the monarch had reprimanded police on guard at Buckingham Palace for eating snacks put out for guests; a witness claimed she had drawn lines in the bowls to monitor levels.[25] Praise – and her transfiguring smiles – fall like desert rain.

Her foil and consort, support and centre of the most hidden of public private worlds, the Duke of Edinburgh, is their most frequent recipient. He still brings out a softer side to the Queen. He has never publicly commented on rumours of his infidelity, though he once inquired of a relative: 'How could I be unfaithful to the Queen? There is no way that she could possibly retaliate.'[26] Whatever the royal couple's arrangement, the marriage works, as a loving relationship and a professional partnership. 'Regardless of whether my grandfather seems to be doing his own thing, sort of wandering off like a fish down a river, the fact that he's there – personally, I don't think [the Queen] could do it without him, especially when they're both at this age,' said Prince Harry in 2011.[27]

Penniless and stateless, Philip wasn't an obvious choice to marry the future head of a reigning royal house, though his candidacy was buoyed, or burdened, by support from his uncle Louis 'Dickie' Mountbatten. 'I have come to the conclusion that we are going too fast,' King George VI, father of the prospective bride, warned Mountbatten in response to the latter's unrestrained enthusiasm for the project.[28] Mountbatten's ardour burned so bright that Philip wrote to his uncle pleading for a little space: 'Please, I beg of you, not too much advice in an affair of the heart, or I shall be forced to do the wooing by proxy.'[29] Elizabeth needed no encouragement. It may have been the only time in her life that she allowed heart to rule head, putting her own desires before duty. Courtiers thought she was making a mistake. Philip seemed to them uncouth, lacking in polish. Her suitor might speak the King's English but he lacked a filter between brain and mouth. He still does.

His gaffes have become legend. 'Are you running away from something?' the Duke asked expatriate Brits in Abu Dhabi. He compared schoolgirls in red uniforms to 'Dracula's daughters' and suggested Nigerian President Olusegun Obasanjo, in national dress, looked 'ready for bed'. 'Damn fool question!' he told a journalist who asked if the Queen was enjoying an official trip. To another solicitous enquiry – 'How was your flight?' – he responded: 'Have you ever flown? It was just like that.' He has racked up as many sexist and racist comments as a rogue UKIP candidate. 'You're not wearing mink knickers, are you?' he asked a female fashion writer. He warned a British student in China: 'If you stay here much longer, you'll go home with slitty eyes.' His popularity may owe something to the misplaced notion that statements that offend against political correctness are a sign of authenticity. Yet he is authentic, in the sense that he never seeks favour by falsifying his views, though he often conceals them in public. A moderniser – at least by the standards of the family he married into – his most significant role has unfolded behind the scenes, supporting and encouraging his unflappable wife, and overseeing the raising of their children.

Philip grew up with a surfeit of surnames, Schleswig-Holstein-Sonderburg-Glücksburg, and a paucity of security. A year after his birth, on 10 June 1921 on Corfu, his uncle Constantine of Greece was forced for a second time to vacate his throne. Losses in a war with Turkey hardened sentiment against the royals, who had been imported from Denmark a generation earlier. Military rebels executed the general of the Greek army and came close to meting out the same punishment to the King's brother, Prince Andrew, who had commanded troops in the disastrous conflict. Instead they dispatched him into exile with his fragile wife, Princess Alice, their four daughters and only son Philip. Their youngest daughter, Sophie, married first, in 1930, to a German aristocrat who died as a high-ranking SS officer in an air crash in Italy in 1943. The three elder girls wed within months of each other in 1931, all making alliances with German nobles. The matrimonial flurry coincided with a deterioration in their mother's mental state. Consigned to a sanatorium, Princess Alice moved in and out of institutions, diagnosed at one point with schizophrenia, but eventually recovering sufficiently to found an order of nuns. Her husband washed up in the South of France, beached first by the pleasures of the region and then by the outbreak of the Second World War, which erected political and logistical barriers between members of a family already divided by emotional conflict.

From the age of nine, Philip commuted between far-flung relatives and schools in Paris, England, Germany and Scotland, the last two institutions shaped by Kurt Hahn, a visionary – and eccentric – educator. Philip arrived at Salem in southern Germany just as Hahn, a Jew who spoke out against the Nazis, departed for the safety of Britain, where he swiftly found in a vacant eighteenth-century estate called Gordonstoun a more secure plantation for his ideas. Philip followed him there in 1934.

The school in the far north-east of Scotland imposed a spartan physical regimen on pupils – a later alumnus, novelist William Boyd, wrote that 'if Borstals or remand homes were maintained in similar conditions, there would be a public outcry' – but looked for its educational ethos to Athens and Plato's *Republic* rather than to Sparta.[30] 'Hahn followed Plato in defining virtue in the individual as a harmony or balance between the various faculties of the psyche, more simply expressed in public-school jargon as the ideal of the "all-rounder",' noted Robert Skidelsky. '"What do you do with the extrovert?" Hahn was asked. "I turn him outside in," was the reply. "And with the introvert?" "I turn him inside out."'[31] Hahn's regime failed to turn the outer-directed Philip inward but confirmed the future husband of the Queen in the belief that the best way to transform boys into men is to set them challenges. That idea underpins the Duke of Edinburgh awards scheme which he founded in 1956 at Hahn's behest and informed the educational route Philip charted for all three sons.

The Duke has always relished challenges and has a record of rising to them. He became 'Guardian' or head boy at Gordonstoun and captained the school cricket and rugby teams. At Dartmouth naval college, he won distinction as an outstanding cadet. Serving aboard the HMS *Valiant* as a midshipman during the Second World War, he earned a mention in dispatches for his part in the Battle of Matapan, a 1941 skirmish off the coast of Greece that sank five Italian vessels.

By the end of the war, he had transferred to the British Pacific Fleet, participating in the landings on Iwo Jima and aboard one of the escort ships that accompanied the USS *Missouri* and HMS *Duke of York* to accept the Japanese surrender.

His wife's sudden elevation scotched his promising career and landed him, like all Windsors apart from the Queen, with the predicament of prominence without predefined purpose. At Matapan he wielded the spotlight, turning it on enemy ships. As the royal consort he is caught in it, always at the edge of its circle, trailing two steps behind the woman on whom it is trained. She learned to give away nothing in its full beam. In Philip she found a mate whom experience had taught to deny his feelings even to himself.

Two people short on self-doubt and long on composure, the Queen and Prince Philip have always been self-sufficient, sustained largely by each other and the odd martini. (The Duke's preferred way to mix the drink is inevitably at odds with Charles's; Philip likes the 'lemon mixed with the drink, only a little bit of vermouth, triple the gin steeped on the ice and left for ten minutes'.[32])

Their eldest son remembers his childhood as a series of tests, upsets and discomforts. He was shaped as much by adversity as by positive example: through the absence of his parents but also friction with his father. As the Queen grappled with her new role as head of state, the Duke of Edinburgh had taken charge of child-rearing, approaching the problem – and Charles in his father's estimation has always been a problem – with his usual directness. The Duke noted that Charles was a sensitive child – so unlike his robust little sister Anne – and drew the conclusion that the best, and kindest, course of action would be to toughen him up. The toughening-up process sometimes looked like mockery. When the child flinched, it provoked the father to poke harder.

The dynamics of the relationship have barely altered. In much of what Prince Charles does – his passionate conservationism, his commitment to helping young people, even in his hobby of painting – he emulates the Duke of Edinburgh and reflects their common heritage as products of Kurt Hahn's schooling. Yet communications between them are congested and the approval he craves is rarely bestowed. Brickbats fly when he least expects them. In a 2008 television interview, his father took a sideswipe unprovoked by any line of questioning. 'Organic,' he said. 'It's not an unmixed blessing and it's not an absolute certainty that it's quite as useful as it sounds ... You've got to be emotionally committed to it but if you stand back and try to be open-minded about it, it is quite difficult to really find where it's been a real benefit.'[33] Viewers would have known that Charles has been banging the drum for organic farming since the 1980s. Less obvious was that in the mouth of the irascible Duke, 'emotionally committed' is a scathing criticism. It also describes the way his son approaches every project and cause he espouses.

After the death of Sir Christopher Soames, the Prince sent a letter of condolence to his bereaved friend Nicholas. 'I have minded so much for you and thought so much of you during these last few days while you had to watch your father gradually slip away before your eyes,' he wrote. 'I kept thinking that it might have been my father and I can imagine all the thoughts and feelings that you were probably experiencing, both before and after he died. Relationships with fathers can be such complex ones – I remember we often talked about our own relationships with our own respective fathers and how they've not been easy always ... So often, I supposed, one must long to have got on better or to have been able to talk freely about the things that matter deeply, but one was too inhibited to discuss.'[34]

That inhibition has always been two-sided, generational. The Queen and her consort are the products not only of their own demanding upbringings but of the wider spirit of the post-war period. 'These professional naval officers and military officers trooped home having watched their buddies have heads blown off and limbs blown off and tried to settle back into civvy street,' says Tim Knatchbull.[35] The survivors' impulse was to put a brave face on things, whatever the cost.

Knatchbull knows the Queen not as a distant head of state but a dear and supportive cousin and friend of the family. His father Lord Brabourne grew close to the Queen and the Duke of Edinburgh after marriage to Mountbatten's eldest daughter Patricia, now Countess Mountbatten of Burma. Both couples produced their first children in the late 1940s, bringing them up, says Knatchbull, according to 'a prototype of childhood and parenting from the previous generation, from the Empire and India'.[36] By the time the couples turned their attention to their youngest children – Prince Edward, Timothy Nicholas and his identical twin Nicholas Timothy, all born in 1964 – the sensibility applied to the process had changed. In place of the earlier parenting that Knatchbull equates with the regimented 'Preobrazhensky March', a piece of music that often accompanies displays of Russian military muscle, Knatchbull says he and his twin and their cousin Edward were nurtured to the more relaxed rhythms of the Beatles era. 'The Queen and Prince Philip and my parents were very clever, hip, savvy, intelligent, interested, forward-looking people, interested in young people, interested in the revolutions going on across Europe, the cultural revolutions, the social revolutions and rather in sympathy with them and regarded by their peers as being avant garde because of how quickly they adopted some of the new ideas of the Swinging Sixties, including new ideas of parenting, which is that you spend masses of time with your kid. Which is what Prince Edward got. Which is what I got.'[37] Which is what Charles did not get.

In 1979, Irish republicans detonated gelignite they had concealed on the fishing boat Knatchbull's family used when staying at Classiebawn Castle, Mountbatten's Irish holiday home. Knatchbull was gravely injured. His parents defied doctors' predictions to pull through but remained hospitalised for months. Everyone else aboard died: Knatchbull's grandfather Mountbatten, his grandmother Lady Brabourne, a fifteen-year-old local boy called Paul Maxwell and Nicholas, Knatchbull's twin.

During Knatchbull's long convalescence, the Queen invited him and one of his sisters, Amanda, to stay at Balmoral. They found her in 'almost unstoppable mothering mode'.[38] 'The Queen is extraordinarily animated when it comes to care and detail and motherliness and economy and domestic matters and that isn't understood,' says Knatchbull, sitting in his west London office, shrapnel scars faint but visible. 'People assume she's a lofty figure and head of state but no, actually she's first and foremost a homemaker and therefore a caregiver to the people in the home.'[39]

Her youngest sons Andrew and Edward benefited from that well-concealed motherliness. She has easy connections with her grandchildren and other family members such as Knatchbull. Princess Anne, her father's favourite, has always been at least as stalwart as her parents. Charles, the first child and the neediest, just three when his mother ascended the throne, drew a shorter straw. He suffered another misfortune too. Instead of growing up in the palace, tended by private tutors and shielded from curious eyes, Charles became a royal guinea pig, the first heir to the throne to attend school. The change, like most of the careful recalibrations of Elizabeth II's reign, made perfect sense. The monarchy must evolve, stay in touch with the people. The strategy produced a Prince of Wales avid to understand his future subjects and to be understood, but only partially equipped to succeed in either endeavour.

Nor has he ever developed the thicker skin his father hoped for him, especially where Philip himself is concerned. In 2012, when the Diamond Jubilee tour brought the Queen and the Duke of Edinburgh to Burnley, Charles seized the moment to lay before them some of the fruits of his labour. Six of his charities had been working to regenerate Weaver's Triangle, a derelict area in a town that has frayed with the decline of the cotton industry. 'No other group of charities could have played the same role or achieved as much as the Prince's Charities,' enthused a 2011 evaluation report, published by the Cass Business School, at City University London. As the royal trio travelled by barge to Weaver's Triangle, Philip's voice cut through the excitement. 'I can't think why you want to save all these terrible old places,' he said. Of all people, the Duke really should have known the answer.

Chapter 3

A Prince Among Men

Charles is a passionate gardener, of ideas and initiatives as well as gardens. 'These things have grown like topsy over the years, as I've seen what I feel needs to be done,' he says of his charities. 'I couldn't do it all at once. I couldn't at Highgrove just do the whole garden in one or two years. Bit by bit you go round.'[1]

The landscapes he creates, whether figurative or physical, bear marked similarities. Though he recognises the necessity for pruning to maintain healthy plants and sustainable organisations, he shies from too stark an approach. 'We ask before we cut anything,' said Suzie Graham, one of two head gardeners at Birkhall.[2] Charles's impulse is to create refuges, for other people and for himself. 'All my life I have wanted to heal things, whether it's been the soil, the landscape or the soul,' he explained in the introduction to one of seven books about Highgrove that have sprung up as a result of his green fingers.[3]

His gardens are full of hiding places, paths that twist unexpectedly and rustic shelters. 'The eye should be led; you want to think "I wonder what's around that corner?" Little follies are terribly important, too, as they give a focus to reach or sit in once you get there,' he once ruminated.[4] Most of the follies encircle seats just large enough for a Prince and his cushion. At Highgrove he also installed a larger sanctuary of stone, clay and barley straw, equipped with a wood-burning stove and built to geometric principles which he considers sacred. The phrase inscribed above the wooden door in Pictish – the language of a tribe of ancient British farmers, ruled by kings – means 'Lighten our darkness we beseech thee, o Lord'. His old friend Richard Chartres, Bishop of London, who consecrated the structure in 2000, says it is a hermitage where the Prince reads the *Philokalia*, texts written for contemplation by the monks of Mount Athos between the fourth and fifth centuries and collected for publication in the eighteenth century.[5] Charles has made several private visits to Mount Athos, staying at the monastery of Vatopedi, exciting speculation that he may have secretly converted to Christian orthodoxy and criticism for spending time on a peninsula that is forbidden territory for women. To Charles, raised in palaces without privacy, often most alone when surrounded by people, Mount Athos seemed to offer respite and solitude. Instead his visits generated noise.

For his sixtieth birthday he took delighted possession of a new folly, a thatched summer house nestling on an island in the Muick, the tributary of the River Dee that cuts a path through Birkhall's grounds. On a sparkling September day in 2013, he should really be enjoying its seclusion or indulging in another experience his youth too seldom provided, the opportunity to spend quality time with close family. He has come to Birkhall for a short break. William and Kate have brought baby George to visit. Camilla is pottering upstairs. But here is the Prince, closeted in his sitting room with a journalist, while aides paw the carpet outside, impatient to bend his ear ahead of a lengthy meeting scheduled the next day with the heads of his charities. He continues to respond just as Gordonstoun programmed him to do: the more stressful his own life, the more hemmed in by duties and deadlines, the more he volunteers to take on additional responsibilities. It's a debt to Kurt Hahn – or a curse – that Charles freely acknowledges.

School taught him that sitting back wasn't an option, he says. 'I always feel that reflection and discussion should lead to practical action.' He leans forward. 'I also feel more than anything else it's my duty to worry about everybody and their lives in this country, to try to find a way of improving things if I possibly can.'[6]

'*Plus est en vous*' – more is in you: Gordonstoun's motto reflects the school's abiding ambition to mould students into individuals who aren't simply academically proficient but socially engaged. Its founder took guidance from Plato, who wrote that 'the whole of education should be directed to the acquisition of such a knowledge as will teach a man to refuse the evil and choose the good', and sketched out a map towards achieving that end that started with physical exercise or 'gymnastic'.[7] Gordonstoun pupils did a lot of gymnastic during the Prince's incarceration at the school – cold runs, cold baths clouded with the effluvia of previous occupants – but their academic lessons didn't look much different from those taught at other British public schools of the time. The heir to the throne studied literature and Classics, wrestled with algebra and marvelled at the burst of radiance created by holding magnesium strips in the flame of a Bunsen burner. There were few other sources of brightness. 'It's such hell here, especially at night,' he scrawled in a private letter. 'I don't get any sleep practically at all nowadays … The people in my dormitory are foul. Goodness they are horrid. I don't know how anyone could be so foul. They throw slippers all night long or hit me with pillows or rush across the room and hit me as hard as they can, waking up everyone else in the dormitory at the same time.'[8]

Many former pupils of Britain's elite boarding schools recall similar experiences. The changes in attitude to parenting that redefined family relationships in the 1960s – the transition to a more nurturing culture that Tim Knatchbull describes – took far longer to percolate into the public-school system. Children as young as seven were routinely dispatched into the care of institutions that, like the parents who sent them, believed a little adversity built character. By daylight the teaching staff imposed discipline, but at night and in unseen corners of the schools a second layer of enforcement kicked in as fellow pupils acted out their own difficult assimilation by picking on those yet more vulnerable than themselves.

Charles was an obvious target. 'It was a point of honour to make physical contact with the Prince of Wales [during school games],' remembered one of his contemporaries at Gordonstoun. 'And the more violently the better.'[9] That wasn't the sharpest source of his misery. At Charles's first school, Hill House in London, a brief ferment of press coverage, stemmed by obliging editors at the request of Buckingham Palace, marked him as an outsider. He carried the embarrassment and discomfort to his next schools, boarding from the age of eight, first at Cheam, an English prep school his father had briefly attended. His attempts to blend in, never entirely convincing to himself or his supposed peers, bit the dust at the end of his first year when they sat together to watch the closing ceremony of the Empire and Commonwealth Games. With no prior warning to her son, the Queen announced that she had elevated him to his hereditary title: Prince of Wales. Soon afterwards, paraded in his new principality for the public, he found himself mobbed by crowds who in an excess of patriotic zeal broke through barriers. The same status that threatened to overwhelm him with mass attention ensured he remained profoundly isolated. Classmates shunned his company for fear of being accused of sycophancy.

Cheam introduced its emissary from Planet Windsor to the business end of another British institution: corporal punishment. Palace officials had insisted he should be treated as other boys. The school authorities may not have been able to force other children to follow this instruction but they took it seriously enough to twice administer beatings to the heir to the throne for his part in dormitory fights. At Gordonstoun, the regime of punishment reflected Hahn's unusual educational vision. The cane was part of the headmaster's arsenal – by the time Charles arrived in 1962, Hahn had retired leaving a man called Robert Chew at the helm – but symbolic and ritual sanctions played a larger role. Boys earned promotion through stages defined by uniforms and so-called training plans detailing their non-academic tasks and activities. After the Prince's infamous cherry brandy incident, Chew demoted his royal charge to 'new boy', stripping him of the rank he had painstakingly earned and adding to Charles's anguish.

The school aimed to instil a sense of personal responsibility in each student. Pupils filled in forms every night to assess themselves against a series of goals they helped to identify. Hahn had devised his teaching methods to counteract social ills he feared risked squandering the promise of younger generations in listless self-indulgence. He listed these 'diseases' in a treatise written the year Charles came to Gordonstoun: 'decline of fitness and physical health: in particular due to the modern methods of motion, e.g., car, train, and elevator; decline of initiative and the spirit of adventure: easily to be recognised as "spectatoritis", an "illness" brought about by the new media, e.g., radio, film, and television; decline of imagination and recollection: especially fostered by the restlessness of modern people and their increasing fear of silence, loneliness, and seclusion; decline of carefulness and thoroughness: primarily caused by the dwindling importance of the crafts and by the increasing inclination to look for quick results and easy solutions; decline of self-discipline and renunciation: chiefly furthered by material affluence and the easy access to alcohol, cigarettes, and pills; decline of compassion and mercy: in particular encouraged by the diminished community life and the expanding subjectivism, individualism, and egoism.'[10]

Long before the rise – and slump – of the couch potato, Hahn had spotted in the Weimar Republic signs that the social and technological change that too much of the world appeared to regard as progress might carry downsides. Graduates emerged from his schools in

Germany and Scotland sharing his scepticism about modernity. They were also wedded to the value of public service. 'There are three ways of trying to win the young,' said Hahn. 'There is persuasion, there is compulsion and there is attraction. You can preach at them, that is a hook without a worm; you can say "You must volunteer", that is of the devil; and you can tell them, "You are needed." That appeal hardly ever fails. I am quite certain that the young of today respond better to the service which is demanded from them in the interest of others than to the service which is offered them for their overt benefit and improvement.'[11] Gordonstoun today is a markedly kinder institution than when Charles was a pupil, co-educational and closely attentive to student welfare, but the school still demonstrates commitment to its founding ideals by maintaining the student-run fire brigade, mountain rescue team, lifesavers and coastguard watch that provided rare glints of enjoyment in the young royal's gloomy days.

As the boy clutched his bedcover against the onslaught of bullies, so the adult clings to the positives retrieved from Gordonstoun. He did not send his own sons to the school – William and Harry experienced the softer climes of Eton – but in his charitable endeavours, in the ceaseless campaigning, the relentless fund-raising, Charles continues to put into practice the central tenet of the education his parents chose for him. 'At the end of the day it was very good for you. It wasn't a holiday camp. But on the other hand it did build a character,' he says. 'And I do think character-building is vital. It's another reason I've been trying for years to try and ensure this is still possible within the education system and as part of the extra-curricular aspect of education.'[12]

The Queen and Prince Philip are not infrequently discomfited by the child produced by their genes, parenting and educational choices. 'He always says if they didn't want me to do things and have ideas, they shouldn't have sent me to a Kurt Hahn school,' says an aide.

There was one magnesium burst of light towards the end of his schooldays: six months at Timbertop, a school in the middle of the Australian bush run to Hahnian principles. Though at least as rugged as Gordonstoun, baking hot rather than icy, the culture suited Charles; and distance from many of the things that troubled him, not least his own parents, enabled him to develop a veneer of assurance. Back at Gordonstoun, to his own surprise as well as his father's, he became head boy. Charles also was the first royal to take A-levels.

His B in History and C in French might not have suggested an academic bent, much less recommended that he study among the eggheads and bluestockings of Cambridge University, but in this, as in other key decisions, the Prince had no say and the Queen expressed no view. She sat silent at a Buckingham Palace dinner in 1965 as guests including the Prime Minister of the day, Harold Wilson, the Archbishop of Canterbury and senior members of the military and academia, but excluding Charles, hashed out a plan that saw him head to Trinity College, Cambridge, and then, just as he threatened to settle, to University College of Wales at Aberystwyth for a term to learn Welsh ahead of his investiture as Prince of Wales. The idea was to mollify Welsh nationalists; the Prince's own desires took a back seat.

To a BBC interviewer he said: 'As long as I don't get covered in too much egg and tomato, I'll be all right.'[13] He joked, nervously, in a first televised interview with David Frost: 'I don't think I can sort of rush in and declare the whole place a republic or Home Rule for everybody, you know.' Did the Prince consider his childhood an advantage or a disadvantage, Frost asked. 'Well, it's a disadvantage I suppose in the sense that one is trying to lead as normal a life as possible at school and at Cambridge,' replied Charles, steepling his hands. 'But it's not a disadvantage because it's not ... If you're leading a more sheltered life, you know, because obviously one's been brought up ...' He tailed off, spread his hands, tried again. 'It's a very ... It's a sort of dual upbringing that one has to try to do, and I think that perhaps that I've gone to school and university and everything in a much more normal way than any of my predecessors did has been an experiment in royal education. And of course it has been slightly difficult and there have been disadvantages at moments when I've regretted it but I think one gets over this.'[14]

It would take him half a lifetime to do so. He fitted into university a little better than school but he always felt conspicuous, never at ease. 'He was immensely distracted by the fact that he had to go off and be invested and so it was a very difficult life,' says Richard Chartres, a fellow undergraduate. 'He's a person of high intelligence which I think is often denied by people. He got a really very good degree when you realise the distractions that he had to cope with. [Charles graduated with a lower second.] But he was a bit young for his age, perhaps. Not so knowing.' He adds: 'I was struck by things that continue to be the case with him. Elaborate courtesy, the real desire to put people at their ease and a sense of humour and memory of what you said. We had great conversations about witchcraft I remember ... Very very agreeable, courteous person who never threw his weight around or presumed. He was very good news, very good news indeed.'

Lucia Santa Cruz, the daughter of the Chilean Ambassador, met the Prince at a Cambridge dinner party thrown by Rab Butler for whom she worked as a research assistant. The Conservative politician, twice passed over as Prime Minister, had by now become a Lord and the Master of Trinity. 'Charles was very mature intellectually in so far as his interests and his curiosity, and maybe not so mature emotionally which is understandable because he had been submitted to very few experiences personally in terms of friends and relationships,' she says.[15] That duality would endure for years.

Never certain of his father's approval or his mother's affection, Charles has tended to form bonds with older men and women, and even in friendships with people closer to his own age, the child prince is still visible. He looks up to the preternaturally confident Richard Chartres, unfolds in the serene presence of Patrick Holden, relaxes with the buoyant Nicholas Soames, blossoms around the vibrancy of Emma Thompson or, indeed, his dearest wife Camilla, and has employed more than a few warm, enveloping women over the years: his long-time adviser Julia Cleverdon, Martina Milburn who runs the Prince's Trust and his former Private Secretary Elizabeth Buchanan, for example. He enjoys the company of people who respect his position but don't stand on ceremony. In return, he has learned to overcome the reserve that was the legacy of his parents' genera-tion and class even before its magnification in palace culture. 'The fact that Prince Charles is such a kissy man is brilliant, because how the hell does he stand up to all the pressure on him not to be kissing his sons or even his cousins or godchildren. But I grew up with that relationship with him and it continued,' says Tim Knatchbull.[16]

Two older family members provided the young Prince with much-needed measures of surrogate parenting and a range of formative influences. The Queen Mother was the most nurturing presence in royal circles, gladly looking after her grandson when her daughter travelled and becoming one of his mainstays as he grew older. The Prince credits his grandmother with inspiring his love of the arts and music. She supported him through turbulences, but rarely gave sharp advice. 'That was not her style,' explained the Queen Mother's official biographer William Shawcross. 'She never liked to acknow-ledge, let alone confront, disagreeableness within the family. It was a characteristic which had earned her the nickname "imperial ostrich" among some members of the [royal] household. She thought her role was not to try and change people's courses but to be an anchor.'[17]

Nevertheless, her disapproval could be as palpable as her daughter's and she imbued her grandson with a 'tremendous sense of duty', according to Nicholas Soames. As a boy, Soames aspired to be a stee-plechase jockey and worked for horse trainer Peter Cazalet. 'My father had horses [at Cazalet's stables] and the Queen Mother had lots of horses there and I looked after two of the Queen Mother's horses,' Soames recalls. 'She came down after church on Sunday to see her horses and they were all paraded for her and I remember seeing her coming down the hill with Peter Cazalet and his wife, strolling, and suddenly she saw – I've never forgotten this, it's been with me all my life – she suddenly saw a group of people from the local village who'd come to applaud her and they started clapping as she walked down the hill and suddenly she just went from walking to being ramrod. She picked herself up like a showhorse. Terrific. A completely different animal. When you're on parade, you're on parade.'[18]

In his great-uncle Louis Mountbatten, Charles found a father figure who closely resembled his real father. Mountbatten had dash, raffish charm and a compelling backstory as a statesman, war hero, the last Viceroy of India and its first Governor-General when it became an independent dominion. Unlike Philip, he rarely crackled with contempt, spoken or unvoiced, towards Charles. And unlike the Queen Mother, he doled out advice – vigorously. The mentoring started in earnest in 1972, when Charles's naval career stationed him in Portsmouth and he became a frequent visitor to Mountbatten's Hampshire house, Broadlands. Mountbatten's advice on women and marriage would prove disastrous, but he gave better counsel on being a royal, frequently warning Charles against any behaviour that recalled another of the Prince's great-uncles, the feckless Edward VIII, known to the family as David, whose self-indulgence led to 'his disgraceful abdication and his futile life ever after'.[19] He ticked the Prince off for proposing a sudden change in his travel plans that would have inconvenienced other people. This was 'unkind and thoughtless – so typical of how your Uncle David started'.[20] This useful reprimand came in April 1979, just a few months before Mounbatten's assassination.

The loss of Mountbatten made him want to die too, Charles wrote in his diary: 'In some extraordinary way he combined grandfather, great-uncle, father, brother and friend.'[21] The fates were kinder in respect of the Queen Mother, who lived to the age of 101. Yet when she died in 2002, just a few weeks after the death of her daughter, Princess Margaret, the Prince fell into despair. Despite his belief in an afterlife, the comfort his faith should bring and a wider philosophy that sees death as a necessary part of the ecosystem, Charles never quite relinquishes his grief. He fills his domains with little shrines and memorials; he goes into his gardens to talk not to the plants but to the deceased. He tries to keep the Queen Mother, Mountbatten, Laurens van der Post and a host of other departed spirits alive in his heart even if there is one persistent, shape-shifting ghost called Diana he would sometimes prefer to forget.

A 1998 movie centres on Truman Burbank, a salesman who turns twenty-nine before he discovers his life is a fiction spun for a reality-television programme *The Truman Show*. He reacts by rebelling against the unseen director and then opting out of the show. Charles has lived a version of that story, always observed, but unlike Burbank painfully aware of the fact. He never walked off the set, despite the temptation, nor did he rebel consciously. Yet by embracing duty and simultaneously redefining it in terms provided by his parents and his education, he created a narrative strand for the Windsor Show that its directors didn't anticipate and couldn't control.

To be fair, there weren't many other options available to the young royal. Worthy precedents and inspirational role models were in short supply. Since the eighteenth century, male heirs to the throne had welcomed their fate not as a challenge, but as an invitation to make hay while the sun still shone on their predecessors. 'There's a long history of relationships between Princes of Wales and actors,' says Emma Thompson. 'Not just actresses, not just the rude relationships as HRH would say, though,' she jokes. 'God knows I've tried, I've tried – he wasn't having any of it.'[22]

It's a familiar theme among friends and members of the Prince's household. 'If he had been more frivolous and less hard-working he may well have been more popular,' muses Richard Chartres. 'But actually when you think of the possibilities of frivolling in such a position they're considerable.'[23] 'He could do what most of his predecessors did – he could be sitting on a beach in the Caribbean with fast cars and fast women and fast horses and fast boats and everything else and living off the money of the Duchy of Cornwall, and be very comfortable,' says Elizabeth Buchanan.[24] 'HRH has every right to sack all of us and go round the world on a yacht,' says Andrew Wright, Treasurer to the Household of the Prince and Duchess and also Executive Director of the Prince of Wales Charitable Foundation. 'Over the last forty years he could have said, "I'll spend all of that money on myself and do the odd engagement just to keep my profile up."'[25] 'He works like a Trojan,' says his Principal Private Secretary Clive Alderton. 'That's one of the reasons people close to him buy into him. If you have nineteen million pounds a year, you could choose to have quite an easy time of it. I think the UK and other Realms are fortunate to have someone who didn't choose the easy road.'[26]

Would press and public look any more kindly on a Playboy Prince than they do on the Perturbed Prince who inhabits the space? George, Prince of Wales, later Prince Regent and King George IV, became the butt, almost literally, of gloriously savage caricatures that mocked his rotund backside and pilloried his extravagant lifestyle. A century later, Queen Victoria's eldest son Edward, known as Bertie, earned a similar treatment and the malicious nicknames 'fat Edward' and 'Edward the caresser' during his fifty-nine years as heir apparent, the longest such apprenticeship before Charles's.

Bertie's many mistresses included theatre stars Lillie Langtry and Sarah Bernhardt, the aristocratic Lady Randolph Churchill (great-grandmother to Nicholas Soames) and Alice Keppel, who endured a second, post-mortem bout of notoriety during the break-up of the Waleses' marriage as Camilla's great-great-grandmother. His accession as Edward VII, far from intensifying the criticism, helped to dissipate it. After Victoria's long and increasingly sombre reign, his evident enjoyment of life represented permission to wider society to loosen up a bit.

Yet the louche conduct of a Prince of Wales has also accurately predicted failure as King. Mountbatten was right to hold up Charles's great-uncle David as an example to avoid. 'For some years after I joined his staff, in 1920, I had a great affection and admiration for the Prince of Wales,' wrote Sir Alan Lascelles, former Private Secretary to the man who would reign as Edward VIII for only 325 days. 'In the following eight years I saw him day in and day out. I saw him sober, and often as near drunk as doesn't matter; I travelled twice across Canada with him; I camped and tramped with him through Central Africa; in fact, I probably knew him as well as any man did. But, by 1927, my idol had feet, and more than feet, of clay.

'Before the end of our Canadian trip that year, I felt in such despair about him that I told Stanley Baldwin (then Prime Minister, and one of our party in Canada) that the heir apparent, in his unbridled pursuit of wine and women, and of whatever selfish whim occupied him at the moment, was going rapidly to the devil and would soon become no fit wearer of the British Crown. I expected to get my head bitten off, but he agreed with every word. I went on: "You know, sometimes when I am waiting to get the result of some point-to point in which he is riding, I can't help thinking that the best thing that could happen to him, and to the country, would be for him to break his neck." "God forgive me," said SB. "I have often thought the same."'[27]

Edward VIII didn't fulfil their wishes and tumble from a horse. He fell further than that, abdicating the kingship and responsibility.

His marriage to a divorcee meant he could not remain on the throne; his admiration for Hitler and support for appeasement may have caused a different set of problems if he had stayed. His spectre still haunts palace thinking, and not without reason. He showed up the danger to the institution from members who put desire before duty. Some of Prince Charles's harshest critics within the palace (his father tops the list, says a well-placed source) accuse the current heir to the throne of similarly selfish behaviour. It's not that they blame him for choosing Camilla over Diana. They feel he puts his more cerebral passions – his activism – before his royal job. They are a long way from being persuaded of Charles's evolving view: that campaigning and kingship can be synthesised.

Yet if a Prince with a purpose inevitably creates controversies, purposeless royals are often liabilities. Charles not only grew up schooled on stories of his great-uncle's disastrous reign and more disastrous departure but grew older watching his younger brothers flounder. Despite the similarities between the siblings, the shared genes, their Planet Windsor sensibilities and Gordonstoun education, the alchemy that created in Charles a compulsion to make a difference seems absent in Andrew and Edward.

Military service tends to suit royals; institutionalised from birth, they are comfortable inside a system in which everybody knows their rank. The comparative anonymity of uniform also affords them their best chance at blending in, and even then it's only a partial pass to real-world experience. 'For me [being stationed at Camp Bastion] is not that normal because I go into the cookhouse and everyone has a good old gawp, and that's one thing that I dislike about being here,' said Prince Harry, during one of two deployments to Afghanistan as Captain Wales of the Blues and Royals. 'Because there's plenty of guys in there that have never met me, therefore look at me as Prince Harry and not as Captain Wales, which is frustrating.' The remarkable dysfunction of a war zone offered Harry a simulacrum of the commonplace.

In choosing to serve Queen and country, he and his older brother William followed a well-trodden path. Their father and Windsor uncles all spent time in uniform. Only Prince Edward failed to qualify, reportedly to the implacable fury of his father dropping out in 1987 after only a few months' training to be a Royal Marine. 'Edward has been put through a terrible ordeal and has no one to speak for him,' said Romy Adlington, who had apparently got to know the Queen's youngest and most tender son during his undistinguished studies at Cambridge and has been described in the press as a former girlfriend. 'As one of his closest friends, I want the public to know he is a normal human being who has to make an important decision. He doesn't have the same responsibility as his brothers, yet he still can't go off and do what he wants. He has often asked me: "What's it like to go for a walk alone in the park? How does it feel to be able to walk into a shop without everyone staring at you?" That's all he wants to be able to do.'[28]

Charles's naval career lasted longer – five years – but despite the action-man tag defence chiefs never risked putting him in the line of danger. 'I had a yearning for some sort of action – some sort of constructive, <u>useful</u> naval operation where perhaps a medal could be won,' he confided in a letter.[29] That wish would not be satisfied and though he earned pilot wings, he could not fully spread them, being restricted to the safest craft and deployments. He proved a proficient pilot but an indifferent seaman, and was eventually promoted to captain a minesweeper. His officers appreciated his command, less because of his naval skills than because of his kindness. They also marvelled at his lack of confidence.

Prince Andrew has never appeared troubled by questions about his abilities, or by many questions at all, though he describes himself as insatiably curious. With no small irony, insiders say he owes his self-assurance to the mothering of the Queen who indulged her second son as she never did her older children and continues to shield him. He took easily to the Navy and benefited from greater leeway to serve than his big brother, as the 'spare' rather than the 'heir'. Returning from the Falklands War, he found himself greeted more like a pop star than a veteran. 'Is it his cheerful charm, his natural-ness, his exploits as a helicopter pilot in the Falkands or his roguish reputation with beautiful girls? Or a combination of these that go to make Andrew the most charismatic of the young royals?' This was Andrew Morton in 1983, nine years before the journalist produced a more substantial piece of writing. 'His arrival on the scene has given a new meaning to the initials HRH. With Andrew they stand for His Royal Heart-throb.'[30] The only direction for His Royal Heart-throb after such adulation was down. Consigned to a desk job in 1997 and from 2001 out of the Navy as a 'full-time working member of the royal family' as Buckingham Palace describes him, he soon acquired a less flattering nickname, 'Air Miles Andy', reflecting the widespread perception that he was rather more skilled than his elder brother at frivolling – and spending taxpayers' money to do so.

For nearly a decade after leaving the military, Andrew performed a role of sorts, as Britain's Special Representative for Trade and Investment, dispatched on missions by the British government to foster business links abroad. On one such trip in 2004 the Duke of York – Andrew has worn the title since marriage to Sarah Ferguson – arrived in Beijing to find a banner festooned across the entrance to the hotel: 'WELCOME TO THE DUCK OF YORK'. He roared with laughter. He approached everything in China with similar good cheer, putting in long hours and apparently achieving results for a number of British enterprises, not least in 'the agricultural sector where we want to be able to produce a lot of genetic semen and stock for the [Chinese] pig trade', as he said at the time.[31] Royal life has never been as glam-orous, but to be royal in the twenty-first century is to operate as a salesperson for all manner of products and concepts.

The Duke made a number of comments revealing a gulf between the Windsor species and his hosts that could not be explained by geography or language alone. He told Chinese students they shouldn't worry about Chinese culture being diluted by globalisation on the basis that British culture showed no signs of US influence; he later asked the journalist who laughed to hear him say that (me) what she had found funny, wrinkling his brow in puzzlement rather than pique. In 2008, the US Ambassador to Kyrgyzstan, Tatiana Gfoeller, sent a cable describing a two-hour briefing brunch with Andrew during another of his trade missions as 'astonishingly candid; the discussion at times verged on the rude'. During the same brunch, he apparently took a pop at journalists from the *Guardian* 'who poke their noses everywhere'. The newspaper duly published the cable after receiving it from Wikileaks.[32]

The candour that disturbed the US Ambassador to Kyrgyzstan played well with British business people as Gfoeller observed. That was also true in China and, perhaps more significantly, the Duke's royal status opened doors in the People's Republic that might not have yielded to mere ministers. Whether his advocacy for Britain can secure deals worth more than the considerable cost of his travel is a moot point, not least since he stood down as trade envoy in 2011, explaining on his website that he wanted to 'evolve the role that I perform with the Government and business, resulting in a more diverse portfolio of activities that reflects these changes'. In reality, it had become difficult to deploy him as an official standard-bearer for Britain after press revelations about his links with Jeffrey Epstein, a US financier with whom Andrew continued to frivol after Epstein had served a jail sentence for soliciting prostitution with a minor. The friendship between the royal and Epstein came under the spotlight in the wake of a 2010 scandal that saw Sarah Ferguson fall for the wiles of Mazher Mahmood, an undercover journalist posing as a Middle Eastern businessman. Reportedly some £5 million in the red, the Duchess of York offered to facilitate access to her ex-husband for a fee. Further digging exposed the Yorks' ties to Epstein, who had given the Duchess money towards clearing her debt mountain and introduced the Duke to young women, including Virginia Roberts who alleged that Epstein had paid her for sex when she was just fifteen. A photograph taken when Roberts was seventeen shows Andrew with his arm around her. He denied any impropriety, a denial reported 'emphatically' by Buckingham Palace in January 2015 after an anonymous litigant pursuing a civil case related to Epstein lodged papers at a Florida court alleging she had been coerced into sexual relations with the royal. An interview with Roberts in the *Mail on Sunday* alleged three encounters with Andrew.

The Duke had long since retreated to a lower profile role and though he still undertakes official engagements and operates a small charitable trust, palace insiders admit that the range of possible meaningful deployments for him have narrowed still further. 'It was his tragedy that they didn't let him stay in the Navy,' says the source. Nicholas Soames chimes with that opinion: 'Where he was really happy was in the Navy and he should never have left it because he was jolly good at it.'[33]

Yet Andrew had probably given as much as he could to the military. He was good at the practical side of the job but no strategist; his value as a recruiting sergeant – and young royals are among the forces' best recruiters – had expired. When he left the Navy, he once said wistfully, he would have liked to have learned a trade, perhaps become a plumber, but he wasn't allowed to do so.

The dream of real-world experience often crops up on Planet Windsor but the prospect of a royal arriving to fix your leaking closet flange or rod your drains remains remote. Where there's muck there's brass and where there's brass there's the possibility of being spattered with accusations of exploiting royal connections for profit.

When Sophie, Countess of Wessex, married into the royal family, she sought to continue her career in public relations. A 2001 exposé by Mazher Mahmood in the *News of the World* brought her time in the commercial world to a close. She and her business partner had been lured by the false prospect of business in the Middle East into touting the advantages of hiring a member of the royal family. 'When people find we're working for you, the chances are you'll get people interested: Oh gosh, they've employed the Countess of Wessex's PR company,' Sophie told Mahmood, whom she believed to be a prospective client.[34]

Her husband, Prince Edward, the youngest of the Queen's sons, also stumbled in the commercial world. Since royalty is sometimes viewed as a branch of show business, he saw no reason he could not reinvent himself as showbiz royalty. By the time he stepped down as joint managing editor of Ardent Productions in 2002, the television company had certainly made an impact, turning out few programmes and no critical or popular successes, but forced to apologise after apparently breaching an agreement by the rest of the British media to avoid dogging Prince William during his studies at St Andrew's University. 'They're a sad joke in the industry, really,' an anonymous television executive told the *Guardian*. 'As time has gone on, their incompetence has become more and more obvious. There have been very small examples of vanity TV companies before, but not on this scale. Any company, in any industry, that had burned through that much share capital without making a profit would've been closed down by its investors years ago.'[35]

The limits of Edward's instincts for light entertainment had been laid bare mere months after he left the Marines, by the most bizarre public-relations sally in the Windsors' history. He cooked up *The Grand Knockout Tournament*, a celebrity revival of a game show called *It's a Knockout*, held in front of a plywood castle at Alton Towers theme park, pitting four teams against each other headed by himself, the Yorks and Princess Anne. It was, unfortunately, the only show he ever masterminded that drew a mass audience, 18 million in the UK and eventually some 400 million worldwide. Though it was compered by one of Charles's friends, the comic actor Rowan Atkinson, the Prince of Wales and then wife Diana gave proceedings a wise, wide berth. Stuart Hall, the presenter of the original game show and co-conspirator with Edward in devising the tournament, set the contestants to slapstick challenges and periodically thrust his microphone at the team captains for sound bites. 'What are we going for? Gold, gold, gold!' bellowed Edward, but his team only scraped into third place. His sister, by contrast, described her tactics as 'cool, calm and collected'. 'All this quasi-excitement doesn't matter a damn to you then,' said Hall. 'No, we're the strong, silent types,' replied Anne.[36]

Not so her little brother, who walked out of the press conference after journalists had failed to praise the spectacle, with a parting complaint: 'Thanks for sounding so bloody enthusiastic!' Hall later hit out at critics who said the tournament damaged the royal brand. 'We are a giant theme park and they are the main attraction,' he said. 'We didn't bring them into disrepute.'[37] (His own career would end in deepest disrepute; he pleaded guilty in 2014 to assaulting fourteen young girls, one only nine years old, during the two decades leading up to the tournament.)

Princess Anne's team – and Save the Children, the charity whose standard she has carried as its president since 1970 – emerged the winners. Of the Queen's children, she is the only one to have tasted success on a regular basis and managed the awkward straddle between Planet Windsor and planet earth with anything approaching ease. Her participation in the tournament marked a rare lapse in her strong and largely silent dealings with the world that saw her cap her career as an equestrian competitor by earning a gold medal at the 1971 European Eventing Championships and two silvers at the same contest in 1975, as well as competing at the 1976 Olympic Games in Montreal. 'If it doesn't fart or eat hay, she isn't interested,' her father quipped, but having a particular skill and an unremitting focus has helped Anne to find and maintain direction where her brothers could not. She continues to work with horses, breeding them at her Gatcombe Park estate and holding several horse trials there including the annual Festival of British Eventing. She designs eventing courses, for external clients as well as Gatcombe Park, and runs the estate as a working farm, all the while managing her royal engagements and charitable patronages with brusque efficiency.

Her children have been spared a similar balancing act. Anne declined royal titles for them, enabling son Peter and daughter Zara to live as subjects of the Crown, rather than its representatives. Peter is a banker; Zara an equestrian who has at least equalled if not surpassed her mother's considerable achievements. There are already signs that the royal first cousins have been handed a rougher deal. Andrew's daughters are patrons of charities; his website states that his eldest Princess Beatrice 'works full time in business' but after she left an internship at Sony Pictures in January 2015, the tabloids tailed her to a series of luxury holiday destinations. Younger daughter Princess Eugenie is described as 'pursuing a career in the art world.' Lady Louise Windsor and James, Viscount Severn, born in 2003 and 2007 respectively to Edward and Sophie, are likely to face similar difficulties and dilemmas.

William and Harry, meanwhile, must make choices that long ago set a previous heir and spare on divergent courses. William knows how limited his options are, but is essaying a compromise as an air-ambulance pilot for a charity based in East Anglia. Harry, bumped by his niece Charlotte to fifth in line to the throne, left the military in 2015 and has been doing charity work. Both brothers understand that traditional royal duties – cutting ribbons, supporting Grandmum by keeping mum – may not be enough to sustain popularity or their own sanity. Today's Royal Heart-throb is potentially tomorrow's hapless royal headache. Their father has carved out another option, but after watching His Royal Humanitarian struggle with his critics and his own self-doubt, the boys are seeking a third way.

In this they are also guided by their mother's example, both in terms of what they would hope to achieve and the remorseless attention they are determined to escape. They were too young when she died to grasp the true dynamics of their parents' relationship, the dysfunction each brought to the marriage or the ways in which its collapse played out in private and in the media. She has been dead for more than seventeen years, but her influence still pervades every corner of royal life.

Chapter 4

The Knave of Hearts

They are both naturals; they have rhythm, posture, neat footwork. He mastered the moves at an early age – everyone in his family learns ballroom dancing and Highland reels. On the dance floor he has discovered one of the few environments where he can express himself freely. His wife studied ballet, harboured fleeting ambitions to continue to professional level. She's taller than her husband, even in her stockinged feet, but the difference isn't jarring. Once buttery, with plump cheeks and ample décolletage, she has become, like him, spare. Her asymmetrical turquoise-coloured evening gown exposes one fleshless shoulder and a jutting collarbone. As the band strikes up Stevie Wonder's paen of wonder 'Isn't She Lovely?', the pair begins to whirl. Fellow guests at the Southern Cross Hotel in Melbourne stay seated, applauding the display and cheering small flourishes that see the man spin his partner like a ballerina. It's a polished performance but also a strange, strained one. The couple wrestles around the room, the sum of two graceful presences oddly graceless. There's no chemistry. Charles and Diana may be in step, but they are not in harmony.

They first danced for the cameras two years earlier, also in Australia. Then there was a spark in the marriage and the Prince grinned as he steered Diana through arc turns. By the time of their 1985 tour, the Waleses find themselves acting out cheery storylines for their gullible audiences. Their union has already met its dynastic goal, producing an heir, William, and a spare, Harry. The Prince and Princess dote on their sons but barely tolerate each other. They live separately for much of the time. Within a year, both of them will have committed adultery. Diana believes Charles has already done so, from the outset of their marriage. This detail and other claims and counterclaims will become the subjects of countless studies: articles, books – fact, fiction and genres in between – plus documentaries, films and art projects, as well as diverse legal investigations. The Internet will provide a platform for everything from solemn tribute sites to the wackiest of conspiracies. Interest gutters but always flares again.

If it seems extraordinary that a relationship severed by decree nisi in 1996 and more permanently by death the following year should still mean something to so many people, that is because the union intended as a symbol and guarantor of tradition became, in its unravelling, an agent of change. The nuptials had done more than provide light relief from the fractious reality of recession and a government determined to push through harsh reforms; 21.7 million Britons and as many as 850 million viewers worldwide sat glued to their sets to watch what the Archbishop of Canterbury Robert Runcie with unintended acuity termed a 'fairy tale' in his address to the congregation. This was an event of significance not only to its principals and to the interlocking institutions of the Establishment they represented, but to a global constituency that found in their story a unifying ideal. The failure of that ideal is still playing out.

The Prince is an activist and provocateur. His greatest ambition is to drive change, but he certainly never imagined or hoped that his first marriage would contribute towards a more sceptical society or encourage a fiercer media. These changes appal him and impact him. Diana haunts him.

So although it is old history, this period of his life remains active history, the prism through which much of the world perceives him. He was born in 1948 but his most enduring public persona emerged during his mother's *annus horribilis*, 1992, with the publication of Andrew Morton's portrait of Diana in June and the formal announcement of the Waleses' separation by Prime Minister John Major to the House of Commons in December.

The Prince on show today, the one closely observed for and in this book, has developed a veneer of assurance and below it the stirrings of real confidence. It is easy in the company of this Charles to accept the most firmly rooted interpretation of his first marriage: of a substantially older man who chose a child bride for dynastic rather than romantic reasons, who recoiled as she cracked under the strain of public and palace life, and who betrayed her. Many aspects of the tale hold true yet there is a missing piece that when slotted into the image subtly alters it. This doesn't excuse the pain the Prince caused Diana but it helps to make sense of what happened. Twelve years and seven months in age separated the couple, a gulf between their generations. But Planet Windsor operates on a different calendar from earth. In human years Diana's bridegroom was almost as unformed as she was herself, barely out of his teens.

As Nicholas Soames shakes with laughter, the towers of paperwork on his desk threaten to topple. The idea tickling him is that he and his childhood friend might have been more sophisticated than their contemporaries because they had the run of palaces. 'We were not experienced men of the world. Absolute balls, that is. It's just so funny all that. It's an absolutely preposterous idea. Charles was at Gordonstoun, which he hated, and I was at Eton, and we saw each other in the holidays and we lived an incredibly simple, straightforward – OK, we were very lucky – but we lived a very simple life,' he says. 'The idea that this was wonderfully glamorous …'[1] When the Conservative Member of Parliament for Mid Sussex grimaces, which he does frequently during a long and discursive conversation at his Portcullis House offices, his resemblance to his maternal grandfather Winston Churchill is inescapable.

Soames has remained close to the Prince since they met as twelve-year-olds, apart from a period of exile when Charles tried to mollify Diana by cutting ties with old friends. 'I'm sixty-six tomorrow,' Soames says. 'I'm sixty-six years old. It's a lifetime. And for two years in the middle of that lifetime I didn't see him at all. For two years he was married to Princess Diana. He was kept under lock and key.'

The slip about the length of the royal marriage – which in legal terms endured for more than fifteen years and in public perception from wedding day to disintegration, achieving a stretch of at least a decade – is revealing. It was during the first years of the marriage that the Prince made consistent efforts to please his wife and find equilibrium within the relationship. During that period, says Soames, the Prince 'was just trying desperately, in my judgement. He was desperately trying to make it work and was trying quite rightly to make every concession to make that happen.'

Diana always viewed Soames as an enemy, and she had reason to do so. He was one of only a handful of friends of the Prince to question the wisdom of their engagement and to remain immune to her charm offensive. His loyalty to the Prince is boundless and a touch bromantic. 'He's absolutely amazing,' says Soames at one point. 'I'm not just holding a candle for him. He just is.' To supporters of Diana – and after all these years, the world and royal circles still divide into Diana and Charles camps – Soames's testimony is too partial to be valuable. Yet his fervour tells its own story about how the Prince has lived much of his life, surrounded by people who feel moved to fight his cause. More than that, Soames is a mirror image of Charles, the sort of person the Prince's background and breeding might have been expected to produce, hearty and largely uncomplicated. 'His pleasures were those of the countryside,' says Soames. 'I didn't go to university; I went straight into the Army; but the Prince went off to Cambridge and I should think Cambridge was a very sophisticated life for him. He wasn't sophisticated in the sense you understand it. His manners were sophisticated and he had sophisticated tastes, I suppose, but he wasn't sophisticated in the way of the world in any sense at all.'

Soames illustrates his point with an anecdote. In 1970, he became Equerry to the twenty-one-year-old Prince, and the two young men travelled together. 'We went to the most marvellous places. We stayed with this woman. She was a very famous actress called – Jesus Christ!' Soames strikes his forehead. 'I can't remember what her name was. I've never laughed so much in my life. We stayed in rooms in her house. She was a friend of Lord Louis [Mountbatten] and Prince Philip's. Would it be Merle Oberon? We stayed in her house and everything was electronic. You'd never seen anything like it. You pressed a button and the curtains opened. I remember thinking: "This is way above our pay grade." It was like playing with a dodgem set.'[2]

The Prince who found electric curtains exciting also found pretty young women electric, though there would always be rumours about his sexual preferences not least because dating him turned out to be a chaste experience. It was hard enough for him to meet potential girlfriends, much less "sow his wild oats and have as many affairs as he can", as Mountbatten urged the Prince in a letter to do.[3] A bleak childhood that simultaneously entrenched the idea of his social superiority and instilled a sense of deep inferiority had left Charles ill equipped for a relationship of equals. His position gave him almost no chance of learning unobserved.

Girls expecting to meet the Prince of press reports – a dashing action man, 'fearless, full-of-fun Charlie' as one alliteration-loving hack dubbed him, the world's most eligible bachelor – discovered a starkly different reality.[4] As a student and later a naval officer, the Prince possessed freedom neither of spirit nor of movement. The isolation that had dogged his schooldays endured. Lucia Santa Cruz, one of few close friends forged at university – and never, she says crisply, a girlfriend, despite misleading reports – recalls that when the Prince returned from a six-month deployment in the Navy, he wrote to ask her to meet him when his ship docked. He had nobody else to welcome him home. 'Everybody was being met by somebody and I felt so sorry,' she says. 'I was already engaged and it was quite difficult because of what the press were saying [about their relationship] but I thought, I can't let him down. That was an instance of how precarious his emotional support was, really.'[5]

Diaries and bleak letters written during that period chart a series of encounters more comical than romantic. At a nightclub in Acapulco, he sat rooted to his chair, eventually summoning up the nerve to ask 'a lonely-looking girl' to dance, only for her to turn him down 'in a terrifying American accent'.[6] According to Jonathan Dimbleby's biography, when the Prince's ship arrived in Hawaii, he tremulously accepted an invitation to accompany two women to their apartment only to realise that the naughtiness they had in mind consisted in persuading him to smoke a joint. His protection officers and local police waited outside. He made his excuses and left.

Back in Britain, his opportunities for meeting women were even more circumscribed. Friends, and the ever-attentive Mountbatten, tried to help out by organising group outings and parties with potential candidates for royal romance. One of these candidates – who prefers to remain anonymous – joined the Prince in the royal box at a theatre with several other young hopefuls. She and he exchanged only a few words, but the next day he called and haltingly asked her out. This was an era when a first date more usually involved a trip to the cinema or a visit to the pub. Charles issued an invitation to lunch at Windsor with the Queen and Prince Andrew followed by a polo match.

Subsequent dates followed a similar pattern, hemmed in by protocols and the Prince's worries about the press. 'He was very concerned about the effect the unwarranted attention would bring to me,' says his former flame. 'But there was no preparation, then or at any time, no advice from courtiers [regarding] travel plans and avoiding press, which was odd considering they were the enemy.' Finding time in the Prince's schedule, planned to the minute months in advance, added a further layer of difficulty. Nothing could be spontaneous. Dinner parties were staid affairs. 'People would be having fun, relaxing, smoking out of the windows, but then before he arrived they'd stub out cigarettes and stand to attention.' Guests, including this girlfriend – by now accorded that label by Prince and press – addressed him as 'sir', bowing or curtseying as he entered the room. She once thwacked her forehead on the princely chin, bending the knee as he leaned forward to kiss her. She doubts he was aiming for her mouth. Throughout her not-inconsiderable time as his official squeeze, they rarely kissed on the lips, much less spent a night together.

The distorting culture of Planet Windsor magnified the proprieties of the time. The sort of gels deemed suitable to be royal girlfriends must also fit the bill as suitable future wives. The Prince should leave them untouched and intact. Mountbatten advised his great-nephew that a man of his standing should 'choose a suitable, attractive and sweet-charactered girl before she met anyone else she might fall for. After all, [your] Mummy never seriously thought of anyone else after the Dartmouth encounter [with Prince Philip] when she was thirteen!' He added this helpful insight: 'I think it is disturbing for women to have experiences if they have to remain on a pedestal after marriage.'[7] Royal girlfriends who failed to meet these criteria quickly learned how icy the Queen and her courtiers could be.

Sexual experience was to be gained with experienced women, preferably married. Lady Tryon, an Australian married to an English peer, was widely reported to be just such a paramour based on the testimony of her friends and the journalists she contacted while promoting her fashion business, Kanga. This was her nickname – devised, she let slip, by Charles. The logistics of affairs, usually more complicated for the parties involved than pre-marital dating, were for the Prince a little easier to manage than his official love life. The landed gentry regularly hosted house parties and would welcome the wandering heir as an overnight guest. He was holidaying with Kanga and her husband at their lodge in Iceland when he heard the news of Mountbatten's murder.

Such relationships introduced the Prince to warmth and intimacy, but only in small portions. He never had to negotiate with his lovers, beyond working out plans for assignations. (An illicit recording of a telephone conversation in 1989 between the Prince and Camilla, then Mrs Parker Bowles, contains a detailed discussion about which friends' house they might use for a meeting, the likelihood of encountering traffic on the possible route and even which route to take. 'What do you do? Go on the M25 then down the M4, is it?' Charles asks. 'Yes,' Camilla replies. 'You go, um, and sort of Royston or M11 at that time of night.'[8] The geography is almost as much of a puzzle as how the conversation came to be recorded.) Such liaisons came with ready-made boundaries: they started from the premise that they could never be acknowledged; the demands the women might make on him were limited.

Failure to observe these rules carried risks. By the time Kanga died in November 1997, not yet fifty, she no longer belonged to the Prince's inner circle. Crippled by an unexplained fall from the window of a rehabilitation clinic called Farm Place where she had gone to try to shake an addiction to painkillers, she had later been detained under the Mental Health Act. Four months before her death from septicaemia, she had spotted Charles at a polo match and attempted vainly to reach him in her wheelchair. Officials blocked her route. A source says he did not see her. He may never have done so clearly.

Only Camilla has ever been able to be fully herself around Charles because she has nothing to hide from him. Robust and cheerful, she entered the relationship free from neuroses and, ironically, from any expectation of being his Queen. Lucia Santa Cruz brought the couple together in 1971. 'My father was Ambassador in London for five years and then he came back to Chile,' says Santa Cruz. 'I stayed on and Camilla and I lived in the same building. She was on the ground floor, I was on the second floor. Although I'd known her before, we became very, very close because I was left on my own and she was amazingly kind and generous. We saw each other every day. I never did forget the first Christmas I was on my own: I spent it with her family. They made a pillow full of presents.'

When it occurred to Santa Cruz that her friend might be a good match for the Prince, she wasn't thinking like a courtier. Camilla Shand was sixteen months older than Charles and wouldn't have passed Mountbatten's pedestal test. The Prince wasn't her first boyfriend. She had been passionately involved with one of his friends, Andrew Parker Bowles. She once donned leathers and rode a motorbike in the US. She smoked and drank and enjoyed life rather too visibly for comfort. But Santa Cruz correctly anticipated that Camilla would appeal to the Prince. 'I always thought that he needed more emotional life,' she says. 'And I thought that Camilla was such a human, down-to-earth, warm person that she would be a very good addition to his life. I thought, she's someone who's going to appreciate him, in spite of his position, and that was his greatest need. To be appreciated for what he was in spite of what he represented. Anyway, he was coming for a drink or to pick me up and I said: "Can Camilla come up?"'

The rest is – mostly inaccurate – history. A media legend grew up that Camilla had approached the Prince on the polo field and introduced herself with brazen wit: 'My great-grandmother was your great-great-grandfather's mistress, so how about it?' A similar joke was made at the first meeting, but not by Camilla. Santa Cruz presented Camilla to the Prince, 'and I said: "Now you two watch your genes" because of Alice Keppel'.[9]

With Camilla, the Prince would eventually develop his first – and, arguably, only – truly adult relationship combining love and passion, respect and equality, plus a sense of humour that often leaves both of them guffawing and weeping. Camilla is 'rude and raunchy', says Emma Thompson, approvingly.[10]

Charles and Camilla enhance and complement each other. It seems obvious they should have stayed together and spared everyone, especially their spouses, considerable aggravation. But the Prince hadn't begun to learn to be a good partner to anyone. He had few measures against which to judge his feelings for Camilla, and was still lacking in confidence. Choosing her would have meant over-riding his family, the Buckingham Palace apparatus and his own belief that in doing so he risked damaging the monarchy he had been brought up to serve.

'It was out of the question for [the Prince] to marry Camilla because she was older, and there was this idea that you had to be a virgin and with no past that the press could do anything about,' says Santa Cruz. 'Lord Mountbatten had been very firm about that and he had a lot of influence over Prince Charles and so [the Prince] went away to the Navy and then Camilla started seeing Andrew again and married him. Emotions are complicated and she had this kind of obsession about Andrew. The other thing was out of the question, and she thought she shouldn't keep [the Prince] in this involvement because his duty was to marry and procreate.'[11]

The Prince convulsed in anguish when he heard the news, but he did nothing to intervene. Mountbatten responded to the Prince's distress by intensifying his campaign to promote his own grand-daughter Amanda Knatchbull, sister of Tim, as a prospective royal bride. Those closest to the Prince have not always easily distinguished their interests from his, and Mountbatten wished to bind his dynasty, already intertwined with the Windsors through Prince Philip, yet closer to the monarchy.

Amanda Knatchbull, more than eight years Prince Charles's junior, rejected his offer of marriage when eventually he made it. She had seen enough of his life to know what being Princess of Wales might entail. Mountbatten didn't live to see the Prince walk up the aisle with a woman who in every respect fulfilled the marital prospectus he had laid out, nor would he witness the toxic fruits of his advice.

To this day, the Prince apparently maintains the denial he issued in Jonathan Dimbleby's 1994 film about him: that he did not resume his relationship with Camilla until after the irretrievable breakdown of his relationship with Diana. This seems to him an important point – a point of honour. Despite everything that has happened, a source says he still doesn't realise that it is also semantic. Whether or not he and Camilla consummated their passion in the early years of his marriage to Diana, they never entirely relinquished it. There were, as Diana observed, three people in her marriage.

Lady Diana Spencer had accepted the Prince's proposal in the belief that she was in love with him and he with her, no matter that he publicly queried what 'in love' might mean. She had scant understanding of the process that had selected her or the life that awaited her. Yet only five months after getting engaged, she already suspected her fiancé's commitment. During a joint interview broadcast on the eve of their wedding she averred that Charles had been 'a tower of strength' as she learned to deal with the unfamiliar pressure of media attention. 'Gracious!' he interjected, instinctively rejecting such undeserved praise. 'I had to say that because you're sitting there,' she shot back, smiling but possibly not joking.

Her answers also betrayed a blankness about the future. She had plotted every second of her three-minute walk down the aisle of St Paul's Cathedral but not a single moment of her subsequent reality.

'After the marriage how do you see your role developing, Lady Diana, as Princess of Wales?' one of the interviewers asked. 'Well, I very much look forward to going to Wales and meeting everybody,' she replied, stumbling over her answer. 'But my life will be a great challenge.'[12]

It already was. Behind the scenes, both bride and bridegroom grappled with swirling anxieties and separately persuaded themselves that to bolt would prove more damaging than to continue the pageant. Curled venomously amongst a pile of wedding presents and cards, Diana had discovered a bracelet bearing the initials 'GF', intended for Camilla. (A piece of jewellery for Kanga escaped her notice.) Diana already recognised in Camilla not a potential friend but a rival. The Princess told Andrew Morton that the initials stood for 'Gladys' and 'Fred', supposedly Camilla and Charles's pet names for each other; Charles's biographer Jonathan Dimbleby reported that they stood for 'Girl Friday', the Prince's sobriquet for Camilla. Both versions are plausible, the first reflecting the Prince and Camilla's shared sense of humour, the second the Prince's reliance on her.

Since they first met there have been few areas of Fred's life not susceptible to advice from Gladys. She has been his sounding board even in matters that directly concerned her and therefore should have excluded her counsel. He consulted her as he havered over marriage to Diana and then got cold feet ahead of the ceremony. He shared with her the manifestations of Diana's distress, much of it caused by justified jealousy.

He courted Diana only briefly before the engagement, itself just five months long. He didn't understand her at all or recognise the baggage she carried from an upbringing as difficult in its way as his own. The more he sensed she was not the jolly country girl he had assumed, the more she revealed her vulnerabilities and began to succumb to the eating disorder that would dog her for much of the rest of her life, the more he struggled with the prospect of marriage. Family members and most friends encouraged him to get a move on, though there were dissenting voices, including that of Nicholas Soames. On the eve of the wedding, the Prince, says a member of his inner circle, 'was desperate. "I can't go through with it … I can't do it." I always told him afterwards that if it had been a Catholic marriage, it could have been declared null. Because he wasn't really [committed], because she started with the bulimia and everything before the wedding.'

The British royals and their advisers believe – and they're probably right – that their hereditary monarchy relies for its survival on the inertia of tradition. For as long as the show continues without obvious hiccups, low key but offering occasional excitements such as weddings and births, most subjects of the Crown seem content. Ruptures spark questions. Older courtiers – and the Queen herself – shudder at the memory of the national soul-searching that attended Edward VIII's abdication to marry the American double divorcee Wallis Simpson. His face had already been printed on coronation memorabilia when he signed away his birthright on 10 December 1936. Forty-four years later the prospect of redundant souvenirs proved sufficient to persuade a fearful Diana to go through with her looming marriage. After she found the bracelet for Camilla, she contemplated calling it off. 'I went upstairs, had lunch with my sisters who were there and said: "I can't marry him, I can't do this, this is absolutely unbelievable." They were wonderful and said: "Well, bad luck, Duch [her nickname, short for Duchess], your face is on the tea towels so you're too late to chicken out."'[13] She had no idea her bridegroom also had to be coaxed to the altar.

So Charles and Diana took their vows, had their sons, made a stab at building a marriage and a much better job of destroying it. Defined not only by this period, but so often defined against Diana, the Prince is most frequently mistaken for a person lacking in feelings. A man who did not already know what love means might have developed a deeper affection for his fragile partner. Guilt often pushes people into behaving worse, not better. Damaged by formative years of being told to deal with his feelings by burying them, criticised for his failure to do so, the Prince sometimes meted out similar treatment to his wife, like the syndrome of an abused child who grows up to abuse.

The question of whether he ever loved her is problematic, like everything about the relationship. At the beginning of the marriage he imagined he could love her. He loved the idea of enveloping domesticity and children. He always loved the boys. Yet he was at sea when it came to dealing with his wife. When trying his hardest to respond to her obvious turmoil, he turned to the wrong people for the support he could not provide: not only to Laurens van der Post, but most startlingly to Jimmy Savile. But better advice – the best – could never have reconciled the Waleses. Their brief period of amity was based on the sense of a joint project done well: they revelled in the experience of pleasing Queen and country. Greater forces pulled them apart. This wasn't just the clash of two ill-suited people, beauty versus beast, or of their courts and champions, though it became all of those things. It wasn't simply that Diana discovered that her star power had grown independent of the institution that granted it. It wasn't just about a lack of common ground. Camilla shares only some of Charles's interests. In many ways – in the intensity of their emotions, their febrile passions, their desire to make an impact – Diana and Charles more closely resembled each other. Both grew up starved of affection. Both sometimes channelled their neediness into acts of great kindness, at other times gave in to self-absorption. The unbridgeable conflict was generational.

'[Diana] was the expression of a huge change in our way of relating to each other, that has happened in the last forty years, where emotion has completely taken over reason,' says Lucia Santa Cruz. 'The previous generation were taught that emotions were a bad adviser, that they had to be subordinated because emotions include fear, hatred, resentment, anxiety and so forth and therefore they must be controlled. He was very much an expression of that old upbringing.'[14]

There is an irony here. Much of the philosophy the Prince now advocates, explained in later chapters of this book, revolves around the conviction that too rational an approach is reductive; the spirit – and the emotions – must be equally engaged for a holistic, harmonious relationship with the world and, presumably, your spouse. 'He's completely intuitive,' says Tim Knatchbull. 'I know very few people who are as emotionally intelligent as Prince Charles because that's all part and parcel of the spiritual intelligence of the man as well. It's not just about doing, it's about feeling. It's about intuition and it's about faith. It's about the metaphysical. It's about love. And therefore if you're in that territory it's second nature that it's about emotion as well. He's a very emotional man. And many of the most emotional people I know, if they don't choose to wear it on their sleeve all the time, they carry it around with them and it will come pouring out in other ways, in their appreciation of great art or music or ballet or whatever their outlet is.'[15]

Watching Charles now it is easy to see how close to the surface his emotions always are. He has a thin-skinned quality, veins that pulse when he's displeased, a childlike delight that sometimes breaks through. But as a young man raised in the post-war era by the most austere of parents, the Prince not only lacked the equipment to understand his young bride, he recoiled from the messiness of the emotions she so liberally splattered. She brought to their combustible pairing an upbringing at least as dysfunctional as his own, but with radically different results. His background endowed him with a homeopathic reflex, to treat like with like. If the burden of royal life is making you sick, the answer must be to take on more of the burden.

Archbishop Runcie remembered having tea with Sarah, Duchess of York, 'in a very lofty corner of Buckingham Palace' during her break-up with Prince Andrew. 'She'd just come back from some public engagement, and was trying to live in that echoing place, and I felt sympathy for her ... And she said, "I just can't take the stiff-upper-lip syndrome. And the you-are-never-ill syndrome. And that's what got Diana.'"[16]

If the Princess had swerved at the altar or if her fiancé's fevered eve-of-marriage misgivings had led him to break off the engagement, the monarchy would doubtless have faced an immediate backlash. Instead it would be the disintegration of the ill-matched, ill-considered union that posed the most serious threat to the monarchy since the abdication. In 1992, the *annus horribilis*, Princess Anne also divorced her first husband Captain Mark Phillips and Prince Andrew separated from the ebullient Sarah. The siblings' failed marriages, though far from demographically unusual as UK divorce rates spiralled, undermined one of the key symbolic functions of monarchy: to present to its subjects an idealised view of themselves, happy and glorious.

Diana understood that transaction as she understood the implications of destroying the illusion. She was many things, but she was never, ever dumb, though she at least once described herself as 'thick as a plank'.[17] She could read people including her husband as he could not read her, and she could seduce almost anyone if she set her mind to it, male or female. Charles never entirely succumbed. The legacy of that rare failure and the ensuing battle for public sympathy endures in a global fan base that stoutly leaps to Diana's defence and a global media that still sometimes fights her corner, even if an increasing proportion of her army barely remembers her.

During the last decade of the twentieth century, the Waleses' conflict polarised Fleet Street and spilled across television screens and bookshelves. That there was public appetite for royal gossip had been clear since the publication in 1950 of *The Little Princesses*, an account by a former governess to the Queen and her sister Margaret of their childhood. It became a best-seller, earning its author, Marion

'Crawfie' Crawford, a fair whack of money and a painful estrangement from her erstwhile charges. Her revelations, by today's standards, were a tame brew. The thirteen-year-old Princess Elizabeth seems much taken on a visit to the Royal Naval College in Dartmouth by an eighteen-year-old cadet, Prince Philip of Greece, a 'fair-haired boy, rather like a Viking, with a sharp face and piercing blue eyes ... good-looking though rather offhand in his manner'. At the tennis courts, the boy 'showed off a good deal, but the little girls were much impressed', recounted Crawfie. 'Lilibet said, "How good he is, Crawfie. How high he can jump."'[18]

This sort of stuff was grist for satirists who continued chipping away at the edges of monarchical reverence and never succumbed to the self-censorship that gripped newsrooms for the first half of Elizabeth II's reign. In 1963 the comedy series *That Was The Week That Was* ran a sketch sending up the commentaries of Richard Dimbleby, father of Jonathan. He was the BBC's first war correspondent and went on to front coverage of the Queen's coronation and other big moments in royal life. In the sketch, the royal barge sinks, pitching the Queen into the water. 'The Queen, smiling radiantly, is swimming for dear life,' says a Dimbleby soundalike. 'Her Majesty is wearing a silk ensemble in canary yellow.'

The latex Windsors created by the television show *Spitting Image* in 1984 depicted the royals as both stupid and venal, abusing commoners, each other and every vowel. In one memorable episode they resort to crime after being forced by unpaid taxes into a council 'hyse'. 'Charles' is distinguished by hydraulically controlled ears and a compulsion to cavil about 'monstrous carbuncles', the term his real-life original used to torpedo a planned extension to the National Gallery. *Spitting Image* also conceived its own version of the Changing of the Guard ceremony, 'that most glorious of royal traditions, steeped in history, the Changing of the Wives'. 'Of course it looks so easy but to make it all possible, there's actually been a lot of hard work and precision-planning,' the announcer intones. 'By Camilla.' Diana might well have chortled at that scene. According to the actor Stephen Fry, who knew her and remains close to Charles, the Princess confided that she was a regular viewer of *Spitting Image*. Her in-laws hated it, she told Fry. 'I absolutely adore it.'[19]

Before Morton, newspapers assumed, probably correctly, that their readers would not thank them for this sort of lese-majesty. Columnists might sometimes question the cost of the monarchy and turn a sceptical eye on the Prince's advocacy for the environment or against carbuncles, but many editors chose to downplay the gathering omens of the Waleses' marital implosion. So potent was faith in the integrity of palace briefings and, more generally, in the decorum of royalty, that a cadre of loyalists simply couldn't bring themselves to believe that Morton's *Diana: Her True Story* could, as billed, be true. Here is Max Hastings, at the time Editor of the *Daily Telegraph*: 'Some of my executives, who were much more savvy and sensible than I was, formed up to me not once but repeatedly and they said to me: "Max, you've got to get real. The Morton story is true." That all this is for real. That Princess Diana had confided in this guy, she's unbelievably unhappy, this marriage is cracking up. "You have got to start reporting this story." And I hung on and hung on, going on digging my hole ever deeper, insisting that this couldn't be true, that Diana couldn't have done this, and of course I was absolutely wrong ... I want the Great British institutions to survive and prosper. I don't want to be involved in bringing them down. That's the end of town I come from. But that sometimes means, and it did in this case, that one sometimes failed in one's job as a journalist.'[20]

Executives at Rupert Murdoch's News International group decided to mothball one of the biggest potential scoops they had ever received. A retired bank manager called Cyril Reenan, whose hobby involved using a scanner to listen in on radio communications, approached the *Sun* newspaper in 1990, with a tape of a telephone conversation he had tuned into the previous New Year's Eve. The woman on the tape sounded just like Diana, and *Sun* reporters would identify the man who crooned: 'I love you, love you, love you' and called her 'Squidgy' as an upper-crust businessman named James Gilbey. After discussions at News International, the tape – which would later become known as 'Squidgygate' – was locked in a safe.

'It just didn't seem right or proper to carry it,' recalled Andrew Knight, at the time chairman of the company. 'The feeling of myself, and I'd always been a royalist and remain one, and also of Rupert Murdoch, was simply that these stories were too explosive to carry. The irony is that by the time these events started coming out, Mr Murdoch had come to the belief that the royal family, although it was the pinnacle of a system of snobbery that he didn't relish, nevertheless on balance was a good thing and he was reluctant to see it undermined … He knew that Middle Britain, the sort of stalwart core of Britain, is pro-royalist and it wasn't his job to undermine it.'[21]

It took another two years until Murdoch changed his mind and green-lit the Morton serialisation. In the meanwhile, Reenan's wasn't the only tape in circulation. Two or three more copies of the same conversation did the rounds while the *Daily Mirror* laid hands on a counterpart recording, inevitably dubbed 'Camillagate'. This was the late-night conversation in which Charles and Camilla planned their next assignation and chatted with an intimacy that was not only sexual but emotional.

The War of the Waleses blurred the definition of public-interest journalism. Nobody would doubt the prurient fascination of hearing the Princess comparing herself to a soap-opera character who gets pregnant by a man who is not her husband[22] or the Prince, combining his trademarks of humour and self-pity into one unfortunate, unforgettable image that sees him transformed into a tampon in his attempt to maintain sexual contact with his mistress. 'My luck to be chucked down the lavatory and go on and on, forever swirling round on the top, never going down,' he said.[23] This was certainly stuff that inter-ested the public, but didn't necessarily qualify as public-interest journalism. Public figures are entitled to private lives, however messy. After Morton's book destroyed the compact between the British press and the palace, editors would argue that publication of Squidgygate and Camillagate served the public interest in a more profound way, as defined by their recently established regulatory body, the Press Complaints Commission (PCC): 'Preventing the public from being misled by an action or statement of an individual or organisation.' The Establishment had tried to cover up the sham at its heart. The 1993 Calcutt Report, a review into the effectiveness of the PCC, unwittingly upheld a lie, 'that rumours linking the Princess and her friends with involvement in leaking information to the press were baseless'.[24]

The palace hadn't told journalists the truth about the Waleses and not just because the truth represented a danger to the monarchy. Officials didn't always know what the Waleses were up to and when they did, they sought to draw the line at commenting on matters that crossed the line into the private domain. They were used to being helped in this endeavour by their charges who had historically approached most interactions with the media with all the enthusiasm of vampires invited to dip carrot batons in aioli.

The Princess was a different proposition, an instinctive media player, who could 'sense a camera at a thousand yards', as Gilbey said admiringly.[25] About a year after the publication of Morton's book, Charles's biographer Anthony Holden received a mysterious phone call. It came, he says, from 'a mutual friend [who] told me to be at [the restaurant] San Lorenzo at Knightsbridge circa twelve-forty p.m.' Holden had written a cover story about Diana for *Vanity Fair*. She 'swept in' with her sons, pretended surprise at spying her friend and 'said: "Oh, what are you doing here? Wonderful to see you! Come and join us for lunch." It was all her pre-planned thing and she thanked me,' Holden remembers. 'I thought A) this is wonderful and it's fun; B) Prince Charles has never thanked me for anything and for ten, fifteen years I've been a better PR man for him than the ones he employed. And I thought: "I like this woman," and a friendship grew from there. Several more lunches in her favourite restaurants … and then finally six months before her death I had a one-on-one in Kensington Palace once the divorce and the [settlement of] £17 million was safely in the bank.'[26]

She played innocent when the Morton biography first appeared. Dickie Arbiter, Royal Press Secretary at the time, at first accepted Diana's assurances that she had had no involvement with the tell-all. 'I said to Diana: "I want you to look me straight in the eye. What do you know about Andrew Morton's book?" And she did look me straight in the eye and she said: "I don't know anything",' he remembered.[27] Patrick Jephson, the Princess's Private Secretary, resigned after she bypassed him in order secretly to film her *Panorama* interview. He later remarked: 'I always thought that Diana did her best talking when she kept her mouth shut.'[28] Many in the royal households, including the Queen herself, harbour similar sentiments about the Prince and despaired as he let himself be drawn into fighting the Princess on her terms.

Two years before the Morton bombshell, the Prince invited Jonathan Dimbleby to Highgrove. Dimbleby had established a reputation for hard-hitting foreign-affairs journalism. He found the Prince 'just outside in the garden on the patio. He was wearing a white suit and looking fresh and crisp and he was alone and we shook hands in the slightly limp way that royals shake hands and he said: "I hope you don't mind being out here," and I was looking at this beautiful environment and I said: "Well, I think I can bear it." He laughed and that broke the ice and of course I'd taken an interest in what he'd done already and I was attuned and sympathetic to quite a lot of it so we sat down,' says Dimbleby. 'He said: "What's this idea to make a film?" He affected that it was something that was going to come from me as opposed to coming, obviously ... [from the Prince's aides]. In reality they had said to themselves: "We need to do something," I presume.'[29]

The ostensible peg for the film would be the twenty-fifth anniversary in 1994 of Charles's investiture as Prince of Wales; the real spur was the Prince's PR problem. He could certainly draw attention to issues, but not, as his wife did, primarily by letting images speak. Charles's loud forays into issues such as architecture and the environment galvanised debate but also drew scathing commentary and fed ready-made material to stand-ups. The Prince hoped Dimbleby would set out his stall as a serious public figure, counter some of the negative publicity he had been reaping and perhaps wrest some of the limelight back from his wife. As the conversation with Dimbleby continued, the Prince said: 'I suppose you'll want to write a book as well, will you?'[30]

The Prince granted access to his private correspondence and diaries, facilitated meetings with his friends and family, and eventually read and annotated Dimbleby's manuscript. He provided lengthy interviews and allowed Dimbleby to observe him at close quarters.

The twin-track studies provided the clearest picture yet of Dimbleby's conflicted protagonist. Yet appearing after Morton's *Diana: Her True Story* had painted the Prince as a cold fish, whose cheating drove the Princess to an eating disorder and suicide attempts, Dimbleby's project inevitably became the vehicle for the Prince's riposte. As the cameras rolled for the documentary, Charles admitted that he had been unfaithful to Diana, uttering the line he still maintains, that he renewed his relationship with Camilla only after his marriage was irretrievable. He too was a casualty of the broken relationship and of the system that pushed two such ill-prepared, ill-suited people together. Dimbleby had begun to wonder if Diana might suffer from an underlying psychological condition because of problems she had acknowledged and the testimony of people who

Uneasy lies the head: Charles glimpses the future at the Queen's coronation, 1953.

The Beatles era, Windsor-style, 1968. *Left to right*: Philip, Andrew, Charles, Elizabeth, Edward, Anne and a corgi.

The student Prince: In 1968, on the steps of Trinity College, Cambridge.

A different kind of coming of age: Charles is invested as Prince of Wales by his mother in 1969.

In command but not master of his fate: Charles on the bridge of the minesweeper HMS *Bronington* in 1976.

His Royal Heart-throb: Prince Andrew serving Mother and Country in 1983.

No longer in play: Charles talks to Camilla at a 1975 polo match. She had married Andrew Parker Bowles two years earlier.

A fairy tale unfolds: Charles and Diana kiss for a rapt public on their wedding day, 29 July 1981. Both suspected their relationship might not endure.

Unhappy family: The couple doted on their children, but by 1986 the union was failing.

Not single spies but battalions: The Waleses in March 1992 after news that Diana's father had died. The *annus horribilis* would end with the announcement of their separation.

Happier family: The Queen follows newly married Charles and Camilla after their blessing at St George's Chapel, Windsor Castle, in 2005. The logistics of the wedding proved tricky.

Father figure: His great-uncle Louis Mountbatten, here with Charles in 1970, gave copious advice, good and bad.

Enduring influence: Prince Charles with the Queen Mother at the Royal Lodge, Windsor, in 1954.

Peace and reconciliation: An unofficial theme of Charles and Camilla's life together; this was also the official theme of their 2014 visit to Colombia.

'Better than sex': Emma Thompson's joke to *TIME* magazine about the pleasure of dancing with her long-time friend Charles made global headlines in 2013.

Men of God: Charles with his university friend, Richard Chartres, Bishop of London, during a 2010 visit to St Mellitus theological training college.

'Guru' as godfather: Laurens van der Post, *top right*, gains a new role at the 1982 baptism of Prince William.

Close friend, not girlfriend: Lucia Santa Cruz leaves a London theatre with Charles in 1970.

Altar ego: Nicholas Soames, friend of Charles since boyhood, serves as his equerry in Bermuda in 1970. Soames later raised concerns about the marriage to Diana.

His not-so-humble servant: Michael Fawcett, then Charles's valet, keeps the dogs on the lead during a 1990 shoot on the Sandringham estate.

Keeping her distance: Elizabeth Buchanan, *far right*, during a 2008 engagement with Charles and Camilla.

knew her (but not, he insists, of Charles himself), but in the end the biographer chose not to speculate. 'I was curious enough to test the proposition that she might have been suffering from one or another form of personality disorder,' he explains. 'However, I came to the conclusion that it would be wrong to publish such a sensational conclusion: too speculative and certain to cause distress to all closely involved, not least my subject.'[31]

Another author, Penny Junor, was one of the first journalists to go into print with the speculative diagnosis that Diana suffered from Borderline Personality Disorder. Junor also published the first detailed response to the Morton revelations, in *Today* newspaper, entitled 'CHARLES: HIS TRUE STORY'.

The newspaper attributed the rebuttal to friends of the Prince. 'All sorts of people, self-appointed members of his party, attempted to hit back,' recalls Richard Chartres. 'But I don't think he inspired all that.'[32] Other members of Charles's inner circle say that he explicitly asked them not to get embroiled in a briefing war. Hostilities ensued on both sides anyway. Nicholas Soames, by this stage Minister for the Armed Forces, gave an interview on the BBC after the broadcaster had screened Diana's *Panorama* confessional, suggesting that the Princess was in the 'advanced stages of paranoia'. She had certainly been right about the Prince's undimmed love for Camilla. 'Well, there were three of us in this marriage, so it was a bit crowded,' she told Bashir.[33]

These days the irrepressible Soames proves circumspect about the Princess and her state of mind. He says only that the failure of the marriage was 'one of nature's great tragedies', adding: 'Of course the press loved the fairy tale going wrong, the wicked man and another woman.'[34]

In April 2014 *King Charles III* premiered at the Almeida theatre in Islington, north London. Written by Mike Bartlett, the play tells the story of the Queen's death and the accession of the Prince as

Shakespearean tragi-comedy, or more accurately comi-tragedy. The characters – the fresh-baked King, Camilla, William and Kate, Harry, the Archbishop of Canterbury, politicians and others, real and imaginary – speak in iambic pentameter that incorporates modern idiom. 'Shall I be mother?' Charles asks his Prime Minister, offering to pour the tea at their first audience.

Charles is a sympathetic character, Hamlet crossed with Macbeth, desperate to do the right thing, at the mercy of his indecision and of the strong women around him. Adding to the confusion, a ghost stalks across the stage. Charles doesn't recognise her at first but in a later encounter she speaks. 'You think I didn't love you, that's not true / I always cared, I always wanted best / But you rejected me and so away / I went ...' Diana predicts that Charles will 'be the greatest King we ever have'.[35]

There is, of course, a catch. Charles fulfils the prophecy by abdicating in favour of William, a move which Diana, in life, suggested might benefit the Crown. She understood the potency of the idea and its power to hurt the errant husband who had caused her so much pain. The idea survived her and regularly sends knotweed-like tendrils into the foundations of the monarchy. Yet the Princess knew as surely as the news editors who regularly recycle the idea that the palace and its key players would never contemplate skipping Charles and handing the crown straight to William any more than the Queen would ever consider following the example of her cousin Beatrix who in 2013 retired as Queen of the Netherlands.

As the marriage disintegrated, palace aides and the Prince himself began to realise the dangers of Diana unleashed, to the monarchy but especially to the Prince's brand and the charitable empire he had painstakingly built. Diana did the traditional royal thing – the wordless symbolism – better than her husband ever could, and with a dimension the otherwise spotless Queen certainly never brought to the job. The Princess radiated empathy, or at least appeared to, and the sense that she was herself a victim deepened this aura. The Prince, for all that he has endured hardships, is least attractive when he lets his own victimhood show, nor is he a type that photographs well sitting at a hospital bedside or stroking a hand.

The Princess also won every test of strength. When the Prince sent Mother Teresa flowers for her birthday, Diana caught a flight to Rome to visit Mother Teresa in person. Diana responded to rumours of her instability with displays of defiance. 'Ladies and gentlemen, you are very lucky to have your patron here today,' she told an audience at an event for the charity Wellbeing of Women. 'I am supposed to have my head down the loo for most of the day. I am supposed to be dragged off the minute I leave here by men in white coats. If it is all right with you, I thought I would postpone my nervous breakdown to a more appropriate moment.'[36] She warned the royals via *Panorama* that they shouldn't underestimate her. 'She won't go quietly, that's the problem.'[37]

As she grew stronger, Charles declined. Those close to the Prince were alarmed. His emotions cycled rapidly; his mistrust and isolation increased, 'the slough of despond somehow mixed up with the "people are out to get me" bug,' as an insider said. 'I've seen him kicking paving stones in the belief that they jumped up and hit him.' The Prince felt under pressure from all directions: Diana, his parents, the press. Some in his retinue, far from helping him to regain perspective, played politics for their own advantage, said the source.

His friends did his best to buoy him. Emma Thompson wasn't yet a household name when she got to know the Prince – they met through her then husband Kenneth Branagh when the Prince became a patron of Branagh's Renaissance Theatre Company. She would send Charles entertaining bulletins about the 'theatrical adventures [of the Renaissance Theatre Company]. I thought, he's patron of so many things, I wonder what kind of feedback he gets,' says Thompson. She became aware of his misery and isolation as the marriage disintegrated. 'The Diana business was so difficult for both of them, so much expected and sort of arranged, so tremendously difficult,' she says. The Prince would be so downcast that 'I would get periodic messages from the boys that look after him at Highgrove saying: "You couldn't drop him a note because he's a bit low in the water," so I'd pick up my pen and write as funny a letter as I could think of.'[38]

Charles came away from the marriage with his reputation disfigured, his girlfriend vilified, his relationship with his sons bruised, his claim to the throne apparently weakened. Diana emerged a global icon in her glowing prime. To those who didn't know the realities of her difficult existence – the constant press attention, the anguish at frequent separations from her sons, the obstacles to finding a new partner and her own unresolved turbulences – her future looked bright. Financially she was sitting pretty too, entitled to the use of Kensington Palace, and given a reported settlement of £17 million.

The divorce provided a tantalising peek into the Prince's finances. Geoffrey Bignell, an adviser to the Prince, claimed that Diana's lump sum required the liquidation of 'everything, all his investments, so that [the Prince] could give her the cash. He was very unhappy about that … She took him to the cleaners.'[39] Palace sources dispute the idea that the settlement left the Prince strapped and he would anyway never have been in danger of real penury, thanks to his mother's considerable wealth and his income from the Duchy of Cornwall.

The balance of public opinion at the time of the divorce, and most likely now, was that Diana deserved every penny she got. If the Prince hoped the split represented the possibility of a fresh start – and an end to the war of the Waleses – he was quickly disappointed. Editorials attacked him and his mother for their supposedly mean-spirited decision to 'strip' Diana of the style 'Her Royal Highness', though the proposal emanated from Diana herself. As a plain Princess, the newly single Diana immediately cut back her charitable patronages from over a hundred to six, and adopted a new cause, lobbying on behalf of the Red Cross for a global landmine treaty. In so doing, she strayed beyond the skull-and-crossbones signs demarcating territory which the Prince believed he had claimed for himself. Suddenly she appeared to be repositioning herself as an activist, and one at least as effective as the Prince, possibly more so.

Her January 1997 trip to Angola attracted the sort of criticism that until then had also been his sole privilege. A Junior Defence Minister, Earl Howe, described her trip as 'ill advised ... not helpful or realistic'. 'We do not need a loose cannon like her,' he said.[40] She had landed in Luanda accompanied by a disoriented pack of royal reporters used to the sort of trips the Windsors usually took, pre-planned to the finest detail, recce'd to the max. Instead they found themselves trailing the Princess to the desolation of Huambo, a town ripped apart by conflict, and thence to the yet riskier Cuito Cuanavale, where, in body armour and a visor – photogenic, but little protection against a blast – she twice picked her way through a minefield, in an area that had been at the centre of a six-month battle during the country's civil war. At the battle's conclusion, both sides claimed victory. In the ongoing war of the Waleses, she seemed to have gained the upper hand.

In December of the same year, the United Nations General Assembly adopted the Ottawa Treaty, banning the use, production, stockpiling and transfer of anti-personnel mines. Diana did not live to witness a triumph that she had helped to secure. Her death in the Paris car crash, and the Queen's muted reaction, deepened the crisis around the throne. Some conspiracy theorists blamed landmine manu-facturers or the Windsors – or an unholy alliance of the two. Others preferred to blame secret cults or giant lizards. The Prince, seized not only by grief but guilt about his failure as a husband, blamed himself. He focused on his sons' obvious needs, worrying about their loss and never acknowledging his own.

That the accident freed the Prince from daily competition and conflict and removed the most obvious obstacle to his eventual marriage to Camilla intensified his discomfort. He appears to be sensitive to accusations that he benefited from Diana's death, perhaps not least because on some level he may fear that is true. After the convulsive sorrow of her funeral and the scrappy years that followed, the royal scandals and inquests, the Prince has arrived on what Nicholas Soames calls 'the broad sunlit uplands ... He's a happy man now, Prince Charles. He's got a rhythm to his life. He's content.'[41]

Would the Prince have reached this equilibrium if Diana still lived? The question is unanswerable but there's one factor that would certainly have played into any alternative outcome. The media rarely treats older women kindly and would likely have shredded a Princess past her tabloid prime. Instead Diana remains a presence, a threat too diffuse and gauzy to combat easily. She has come to represent the limitations of an old, crusty institution that seemingly couldn't cope with her modernity, an unlikely champion for the republican cause. She has mutated into a symbol of female empowerment, the docile child bride transformed into a broad-shouldered Amazon eternally striding through minefields. Another incarnation conflates her with Mother Teresa, who died just five days after the Princess on 5 September 1997 and was beatified in 2003.

Dealing with his ex-wife would never have been easy for the Prince; combating an immaculate wraith is impossible. This Diana will never fade, never go quietly.

Chapter 5

'Wolf Hall'

The court of the heir to the throne crackles with tension. His strengths and fallibilities result in creative but combustible constellations. Avid for knowledge and always insecure about how much he already knows, the Prince is strangely unguarded as he hoovers up ideas, from books and articles and radio programmes, and most often from the people he meets. In a room heaving with guests, he'll suddenly freeze like a truffle hound scenting a delicious possibility. He co-opts new advisers on slight acquaintance because they talk a good talk or come recommended by one of his established sages. (Others might term members of his kitchen cabinet 'gurus' but this word has uncomfortable resonances for someone so often mocked as a hippy.)

Charles hasn't always chosen his sages wisely. Fame, and especially his brand of relentless, lifelong fame, muddies signals. It's hard to know whom to trust; soft soap is always in greater abundance than gritty truth-telling. That factor, combined with his native insecurity, means he doesn't always believe he's earned the praise that comes his way, while criticism has the power to cast him into despair. Like many in the public eye, he is shaped by celebrity, resentful of press intrusion yet also dependent on the external validation it provides. Diana suffered from this syndrome more acutely than he; Camilla appears unusually resistant to it.

Some advisers arrive at his court already household names or prominent in their fields. Elites gravitate towards each other because they imagine they have less to fear from each other. Ad-hoc consultants cohabit uneasily with Charles's paid employees. Turf battles between these classes and especially within the ranks of those who call him 'the Boss' are common and bloody. Life at court and its offshoots can be every bit as brutal as in the days when a twitching arras might signal a hidden assassin. One former householder refers to Clarence House as 'Wolf Hall', in reference to the treacherous and opportunistic world depicted by Hilary Mantel in her fictionalised account of the rise of Thomas Cromwell under Henry VIII.

Such impulses are intensified by the Prince's habit of expanding his aides' jurisdictions. Apart from his time in the Navy, he has never held a paying job and doesn't understand the anxiety such moves can create; no student of management theory, he believes rivalries promote better performance, rather than recognising the glitches and strains which territorial disputes can cause.

His mother's courtiers tried to rein Charles in during his youth as he struggled to build the Prince's Trust. He won't let that happen now. 'What he really doesn't like people doing is fobbing him off. He'll just ask five other people,' says Andrew Wright. He adds: 'The Prince likes getting three or four opinions on a subject so you know he isn't just going to come to you and say: "What about this?" so that's reality and you may as well enjoy it. Which most people do. It's an extraordinary but stimulating environment.'[1]

Wright appears to relish his job in its infinite variety. Appointed as Treasurer to the Prince and director of his charitable foundation, the chartered accountant and former senior banker unexpectedly found himself also immersed in the Prince's Romanian interests. But some others within Charles's court feel oppressed by their changing job descriptions or threatened as colleagues are instructed to undertake work on turf they consider their own. Moreover, efforts to rationalise and restructure the Prince's charities, to future-proof them against a time when Charles can no longer do as much to sustain them because he has ascended to the throne or some other place, have been triggering bouts of infighting for years. One casualty was a plan to bring all the charities and initiatives under one roof in London's King's Cross redevelopment area, creating cost efficiencies and also higher awareness and better branding. Sources say internal conflicts scuppered the scheme after it was already significantly advanced, wasting more than £100,000 instead of saving money.

Changes to the charities and Clarence House reporting lines have been running in tandem – and not infrequently at cross purposes – with Buckingham Palace's drive to accommodate the Queen's slowing pace and the eventual transition to a new head of state. When the 'big house', as Clarence House insiders call Buckingham Palace, embarked on reintegrating the devolved royal press operations under Sally Osman, originally hired in April 2013 to head up the Prince's communications team, their efforts encountered unexpected – and fierce – resistance. Charles is increasingly looking for ways to build his activities into the head-of-state role rather than tapering them off as the big house envisages. His independence, asserted over many years, is also not something he will readily cede, a sentiment echoed at Kensington Palace, where the young Princes are unfurling their wings.

The culture of each court reflects its principals: Buckingham Palace is measured and stately; Kensington Palace is more relaxed in outlook, a little hipper but also inclined to make beginner's errors. The Clarence House and St James's Palace complex is passionate, stocked with aides who, like the Boss, are more likely to attract censure for caring too much than caring too little. 'New people would come into the office and I would say to them: "Number one, you're going to work harder than you've ever worked in your life." They'll say: "I've always worked hard," and I'd say: "No, you haven't. You absolutely haven't." Three weeks later they turn up: "I'm so exhausted," and I'll say: "I did tell you,'" says Elizabeth Buchanan, the Prince's former Private Secretary. 'In the ten years I worked for him, I would probably count ten weekends when I didn't have conversations with him on the weekend … He's trying to save the world, dammit! If you can't stand the heat, get out of the kitchen.'[2]

Organisational weaknesses in that kitchen sometimes impel Charles's charities and initiatives either to retrench or to embark on more thoroughgoing reinventions including name changes and mergers. So prolific is his brand of philanthropy that nobody at Clarence House can say how many charities he has founded over the years, though the count certainly stands at well over twenty-five. After a recent period of rationalisation that saw some of these folded into others or closed altogether, he still heads fifteen organisations in the UK and more abroad, grouped into four loose categories: 'responsible business and enterprise', 'education and young people', 'the built environment' and 'global sustainability'. He spearheads nine awareness-raising initiatives, including Accounting for Sustainability, which urges business and the public sector to factor environmental impacts into every decision. On top of that there's the Prince of Wales Charitable Foundation, which serves a dual function as a grant-making body and incubator for fledgling initiatives with counterpart organisations in Australia, China, Canada and the US.

Seeing is Believing, a programme devised by the Prince and run by his charity Business in the Community, organises a regular series of excursions that extract business leaders from limousines and executive suites to confront them with the realities of life in some of the poorest corners of Britain. 'What the Prince understood was that businesses needed to be involved in the community in a very direct way as opposed to a distant way,' says Dame Amelia Fawcett, the US-born Chair of the Hedge Fund Standards Board and of the Prince's Charitable Foundation and a non-executive director of the *Guardian*'s parent company. 'He created a movement here that ultimately transported itself to the United States. The concept of businesses feeling they have a direct responsibility for their communities and being actively involved in many ways beyond just donations, from employee mentoring and volunteering, working with young people, acting as school governors, was started here and took root here in a more fundamental way earlier than in the States.'[3]

Only with great reluctance has the Prince ever given up on a charity that he believed was still needed. The Prince's Foundation for Integrated Health closed in 2010 after its former Finance Director George Gray received a three-year custodial sentence for siphoning off £253,000 of its funds. Charles chose not to set up a successor organisation under the umbrella of his own charities but instead supports the work of an independent charity, the College of Medicine, in promoting complementary health care, a crusade covered later in the book.

Charles's ideas-first, feasibility-second approach has never been checked by the realities that impact ordinary start-ups. As soon as he is seized by a notion, he asks several different people to begin work on realising his vision. His position and resources mean that his brainchildren have a better chance of entering the world than if they were conceived by a common-or-garden commoner, and have sometimes been kept alive when other operations would falter and die.

Yet the glaring systemic weaknesses of the court also make the achievements of the Prince and his courtiers all the more astonishing. The court has become the headquarters of an umbrella organisation fostering established charities and start-ups, initiatives and events, and that's in addition to the daily grind of more traditional royal work. One reason it is able to do this is because its de-facto chief executive is passionate and driven and instils these impulses in his staff. Courtiers may not always wish the best for each other, but they are dedicated to the Prince.

He is largely unaware of the machinations of internal politics and when complaints are brought to his attention, he is sometimes apt to penalise the complainant. Suspicious of the world at large, he values individuals who seem to him to have proved their loyalty and takes criticism of those individuals not as a sign that he should reassess that faith but as a reason to redouble it.

Michael Fawcett (no relation of Dame Amelia) is a conspicuous beneficiary of this tendency. He ascended through the ranks from being a Buckingham Palace footman to serve as the Prince's valet. He resigned amid allegations of bullying only to be reinstated and named the Prince's Personal Consultant in recognition of his trusted position. In November 2002, Fawcett came under a different kind of pressure in the wake of an aborted trial. Diana's former butler Paul Burrell had been charged with stealing items of her property. Burrell pleaded not guilty, forcing the courts of Charles and his mother to divulge at least some of their secrets to a court of law, which they did, with great reluctance, until Regina v Burrell came to a skidding halt. Regina – the Queen – recalled that Burrell told her he had taken some of Diana's papers into safe-keeping. Less than five weeks later, the Crown abandoned a parallel trial against another former royal butler, Harold Brown, accused of selling official gifts. (Like official residences, such gifts belong to the state, not to the royals.) Brown, too, rejected the charges.

The police investigations had taken evidence from Diana's eldest sister Lady Sarah McCorquodale about a missing microtape, allegedy recorded by Diana and containing a rape claim by a valet called George Smith against another member of Charles's household. Smith – a Falklands veteran, who suffered from post-traumatic stress syndrome – had left the Prince's employ with a £30,000 settlement and assistance with medical bills including residential treatment for alcoholism. He would die, aged just forty-four, in 2005. Journalists looking for further signs of dysfunction in Charles's court focused on the disposal of his gifts, quickly discovering that the aide they dubbed 'Fawcett the Fence' oversaw much of the process.

At the request of the Prince, his then Principal Private Secretary Michael Peat and Queen's Counsel Edmund Lawson launched an internal inquiry into these reports. The inquiry did not weigh the rape claim. 'A serious allegation of this sort should not, in our opinion, have been treated so dismissively, even though there was universal disbelief as to its veracity, without (at minimum) full and documented consideration of the decision not to investigate,' concluded Peat and Lawson. They also found that Fawcett and other staff had sold official gifts in the absence of explicit guidance not to do so, and that Fawcett had 'infringed internal rules relating to gifts from suppliers', accepting 'as a mark of gratitude' from 'professional friends' both low- and high-value gifts, from champagne and chocolates to a Tiffany watch, a Cartier alarm clock and a Pasha pen.

But, they added, 'opprobrium cannot attach to this [the selling of items or accepting of gifts] because the rules were not enforced and he [Fawcett] made no secret of such gifts. Press suspicions were understandably aroused by his involvement in the sale of gifts (which, unknown to the media, were all authorised by the Prince of Wales) and by it being widely known that he received valuable benefits from third parties.' They went on to identify at least some of the reasons that resentment against Fawcett had bubbled. 'His robust approach to dealing with some people combined, perhaps, with his having been promoted from a relatively junior position within the household, undoubtedly caused jealousy and friction in some quarters.'[*]

Though cleared and backed by the Prince, Fawcett resigned again, only to reappear in a new guise, as an independent events organiser. His first client was Charles, who promptly hired his erstwhile aide to oversee Prince William's twenty-first birthday celebrations in June 2003. By that November, Fawcett featured at the centre of less festive coverage after the *Guardian* successfully appealed an injunction originally lodged to stop the *Mail on Sunday* from running a story naming him as the royal servant about whom another royal servant – presumed to be George Smith – had made unspecified allegations (unrelated to the rape allegations) concerning an anonymous senior royal.

The *Guardian* did not identify the senior royal as Charles; Peat did that, in an interview that raised more questions than it answered. 'I just want to make it entirely clear,' Peat said, 'even though I can't refer to the specifics of the allegation, that it is totally untrue and without a shred of substance ... Firstly, the Prince of Wales has told me it is untrue and I believe him implicitly. Secondly, anyone who knows the Prince of Wales at all would appreciate that the allegation is totally ludicrous and, indeed, risible. And thirdly, the person who has made the allegation unfortunately has suffered from health problems and has made other, unrelated allegations which have been investigated by the police and found to be unsubstantiated.'[5]

Someone of a different temperament from the Prince might have cut Fawcett adrift at this point. His refusal to do so did little to quash the fanciful speculation about the nature of the bond between the married Fawcett and the uxorious Prince. A front-page story in the *News of the World* claimed that Peat had asked Mark Bolland, the Prince's former Deputy Private Secretary, whether Charles might be bisexual. Bolland, by this stage writing a gossip column for the *News of the World*, reported that he told Peat 'emphatically that the Prince was not gay or bisexual'.[6] In such a context, any denials are as likely to stoke scepticism as to quell rumours, though Bolland, himself gay, later made clear that he had meant what he said. The Prince 'pays a lot of attention to his appearance, but a lot of straight men are like that', Bolland told the *British Journalism Review* in 2004. 'I always remember him leaving a Versace show and talking to his bodyguard about the models, and Naomi Campbell in particular. It was very much a boys' conversation. I said I felt excluded, and he said: "But Mark, there was plenty for you to look at as well." He's very liberal, and there isn't an ounce of homophobia in him, but there's no way he's got any tendencies in that direction.'[7]

There has long been smoke without fire billowing around the Prince's sexuality. There is also a thriving gay subculture at the Windsor courts that fuels gossip and trades in it. The Queen Mother is reputed to have reprimanded two retainers holding forth outside her door: 'When you two old queens have stopped nattering, this old Queen is dying for a gin.' The high camp of royal life holds an allure that attracts gay men to all the royal households and in the Prince has also found an employer who identifies with people who feel themselves to be outsiders. That's not much use to anyone who is made to feel an outsider once in his employ.

In 2004, Elaine Day, a former personal assistant to Mark Bolland, alleged sex discrimination and unfair dismissal from her St James's Palace job, producing the annotated memo to support the allegations which the tribunal later rejected. 'What is wrong with everyone nowadays?' the Prince had scrawled in the margin. 'Why do they all seem to think they are qualified to do things far beyond their technical capabilities? People think they can all be pop stars, high court judges, brilliant TV personalities or infinitely more competent heads of state without ever putting in the necessary work or having natural ability.' He questioned 'the learning culture in schools' and a 'child-centred system which admits no failure'.[8]

His rant drew wide coverage, not least because it mirrored charges frequently levelled at the Prince himself: that he imagines himself qualified to pronounce on issues that should properly be left to experts or elected government. His critics challenge his right to intervene and his abilities to do so meaningfully. The invective also seemed to confirm that Charles believed, as Day told the tribunal, that 'people can't rise above their station'. The reality is more complex. A closer examination of his book *Harmony* and Charles's philosophical underpinnings reveals a belief in a natural order that is inherently conservative, but as he pointed out in a blast against Day's charge at a private Lambeth Palace seminar, he created the Prince's Trust to promote social mobility. 'The idea that I think that people should not try to rise above their station is a travesty of the truth, nor indeed have I ever used any such words or anything like them,' he told an audience of bishops. 'For the last thirty years, I have done all I can to give young people who have limited opportunities, usually through no fault of their own, a chance to succeed.'[9]

Fawcett's rise stands in mute support of this point, but his history also demonstrates a weakness in the Clarence House human-resources framework that failed to smooth the edges off his management style or shield him from resentment.

More than a few people privately blame bruising experiences working for Charles – or unceremonious departures from his side – on Fawcett and others who gain the princely ear. A prominent businessman, coaxed by the Prince on the basis of a few meetings to help set up an event with his household, speaks with amazement about the glaring flaws in its organisational structure. 'No company would be expected to run along these lines,' he says. His impression was that aides obstructed planning in order to be able to tell the Boss of problems that they then would solve. 'There was a lot of back-stabbing,' says the businessman. 'There are certain people who because they're pretty cunning in the dark arts but loyal and able and they're good at their timing also involve themselves in the dark arts of undermining other people,' says an insider. 'I think [the Prince] hasn't always been best served by this.'

While Charles may not run a cohesive ship, many of the individuals aboard are properly talented. One of these, for all the criticisms lobbed against him, is Fawcett. The Prince, always liable to empathise with victims, may therefore have been more determined to protect his aide than to discipline him, but he also recognised in

Fawcett a rare skill set. In 2011 the Prince made Fawcett Chief Executive of a project close to his heart, Dumfries House, 'not the wisest deal that's ever been done' says an insider, who then admits, with surprise, that Fawcett seems to be doing a good job.

The former aide has a gimlet eye for detail that he brings to bear in planning functions and latterly also in overseeing the restoration of the house and grounds and working to put the estate's finances on a sustainable basis. He mixes easily with the Bond villains at fund-raising dinners but never imagines himself to be a guest. He is always watchful, always alert to potential disruptions in plans and schedules. He defers to Camilla and she tolerates him; she appreciates the people who help to keep her husband on an even keel. The Prince can relax around Fawcett because he trusts him to get things done. Slimmer and sleeker than in the days of his tabloid infamy, Fawcett has grown a beard that would sit nicely above a ruff and doublet. His power at court is undimmed.

Mark Bolland didn't fare quite so well. He had joined the Prince's staff in 1996 and the following year earned promotion to the rank of Deputy Private Secretary. His greatest achievement in the turbulent years that followed was to start easing public acceptance of Camilla's relationship with Charles. But complaints about Bolland flowed from Buckingham Palace and in particular from aides to Princes Andrew and Edward who accused Bolland of promoting his charges at the expense of members of their household. 'In the minutely plotted world of spin and manipulation, it seems that if the Prince's stock is to rise, another's must fall,' reported journalist Peter Foster in a long *Daily Telegraph* profile of Bolland that appeared to have been briefed by Bolland's enemies within the palaces. 'The Earl and Countess of Wessex are not alone in believing that they have been the victim of an aggressive campaign to blacken their names.'[10] The piece revealed Prince William's nickname for Bolland – Blackadder – the Machiavellian lord played by Rowan Atkinson in the eponymous television comedy and later the name Bolland adopted to write his column for the *News of the World*.

When Bolland left in 2002, he did so with a freelance contract to advise the Prince, though without the gong that routinely rewards former aides for their services. This looser relationship ended, said Bolland, after Charles found he could not get hold of him to discuss a story that had blown up. 'That went down very badly with him and made him think: "Well, is Mark really there for me any more?" One had a sense that he felt a great unhappiness. I did have a peculiarly clear understanding of him at a particular moment in his life, simply because I knew Camilla so well, and I had grown to understand him through her eyes. Sometimes you end up knowing too much about people and their characters, and you lose a sense of detachment. I was starting to be used by him directly, and by him through her, as a way of second-guessing other people who worked for him. While I was there, people coped with that. When I was merely a consultant, I think it irritated them. It wasn't fair on them, and it was proving very distracting for me.'[11] Insiders suggest that Bolland might well have eventually returned into the inner orbits if he had not backed the *Mail on Sunday* in its decision to publish the Prince's China diaries. The Prince had always liked him.

In 2005 Charles launched his first-ever private legal action after the newspaper published extracts of a diary he had written eight years earlier, recording his trip to Hong Kong for the handover of the islands from British to Chinese rule. In the document entitled *The Handover of Hong Kong or the Great Chinese Takeaway*, he describes the Chinese communist leadership as 'appalling old waxworks', recounts his struggles to deliver a speech in a downpour ('As it transpired, no one could hear anything I said because of the noise of the rain on the umbrellas. The things one thinks one is doing for England!!!') and summed up one difference between royalty and elected representatives. Politicians 'are all in such a hurry, so never really learn about everything', he observed. 'In this case [Tony Blair] had flown out to Hong Kong for 14 hours, stayed in HK for 14 hours and flown back to the UK for another 14 hours. They then take decisions based on marketing research or focus groups, or the papers produced by political advisers or civil servants, none of whom will have ever experienced what it is they are taking decisions about.'[12]

Bolland provided a witness statement supporting the *Mail*'s right to publish on the basis that the Prince might have expected his journals to reach public attention. The court went on to disagree. During Bolland's years working for Charles, such journals had been circulated to as many as 'fifty to seventy-five people ... politicians, media people, journalists and actors as well as friends of the Prince', said Bolland.[13] He also drew a picture of a politicised Prince, whose 'very definite aim ... as he explained to me, was to influence opinion. He saw that as part of the job of the heir apparent. He carried [it] out in a very considered, thoughtful and researched way. He often referred to himself as a "dissident" working against the prevailing political consensus.'[14]

Bolland burned bridges, but those who make it into Charles's circle of trust rarely find themselves fully exiled. More often, working for the Prince is like a stay at the Hotel California: you can check out any time you like, but you never quite leave. Elizabeth Buchanan resigned as the Prince's Private Secretary in 2008. The *Daily Mail* marked her departure with an article headlined 'CAMILLA AND THE BLONDE PRIVATE SECRETARY WHO'S PAID THE PRICE FOR BEING TOO CLOSE TO PRINCE CHARLES'. 'Those who observed the icy atmosphere between the tall and imperious "Miss Nannypenny" – as the unmarried Ms Buchanan was known around the Prince's office – and the Duchess, always believed the private secretary would go sooner, rather than later,' reported the *Mail*'s Richard Kay and Geoffrey Levy.[15] But Buchanan had not been banished. After the death of her father she faced either selling her family farm or running it herself. She chose the second option. The Prince had asked her to stay but accepted her decision and called her on the first day of her new life to check that she was in good spirits.

'I'm covered in cow dung normally,' she says, sitting in the lounge of a plush London hotel near the Clarence House and St James's Palace complex, her hair – blonde as advertised – well brushed and not a trace of the farmyard about her person, her manner far from imperious. She remains deeply engaged in the Prince's work, advising on his many schemes and initiatives aimed at rural communities.[16] Though Clarence House attracts its share of bone-dry mandarins such as former Principal Private Secretary William Nye, who left in 2015 to work as Secretary General for the Archbishops' Council and General Synod of the Church of England, and Simon Martin, Deputy Private Secretary on secondment from the Foreign Office (and its previous head of protocol), Charles likes to surround himself with warmer types such as Nye's replacement Clive Alderton too.

He has always opened up in the company of flamboyant women who refuse to recognise the cold boundaries of royal formality, even if they all dutifully call him 'sir'. Kristina Kyriacou, the Prince's combative communications secretary who in May 2015 pulled the cover off the microphone of a journalist asking about his black spider memos, built a career in music management and working for Comic Relief before joining the Prince's staff. He recruited Kyriacou personally, asking her then client Gary Barlow if he would mind sharing her time.

The effervescent Julia Cleverdon held key positions in the Prince's household across three decades. For seventeen years she built up Business in the Community as its Chief Executive, working to instil a commitment to corporate social responsibility in British companies and turning the Prince's ideas into workable programmes, including Seeing is Believing. Cleverdon was most recently employed as the Prince's chief adviser coordinating his charities in Clarence House. That post disappeared in the restructuring, and sources suggested she had fumbled the launch of a campaign called Step Up to Serve, but even then she retained a role at court, still billed as Vice President of BITC and Special Adviser to the Prince's Charities on responsible business practice. The Prince doesn't like to let anyone go if he can help it.

At the beginning of his married life, even as he began to perceive the obstacles to building any kind of stability with Diana, Charles tried not to let her go. He was hampered in his efforts by his inadequate understanding of her distress or her difficulties in adjusting to life at court. It is all he has ever known whereas immigrants to the planet are rarely prepared for the lack of privacy, or for the chill of its climate. The palaces are literally cold and then there's the bracing culture that expects inhabitants to grit their teeth and do their duty.

In the depths of misery, the Prince could tap reservoirs of Windsor spirit in his public work. 'From when he was little, he's always looked anguished, as if the weight of the world was on his shoulders,' observes Emma Thompson. 'He's the eldest son of the Queen. It's a heavy burden and there's no question about the fact that it's deeply isolating and can be very lonely … Like stardom of any kind, you are required – he is required on a daily basis and at all times – to be incredibly nice and open and warm to lots and lots of people who cannot feel themselves to be on a level with him, so he has to be even nicer so that they don't feel he's being superior. Compensating for the position is terrifically hard.'[17]

In private, as his marriage festered, he could be querulous or almost catatonic with gloom. Equipped with only two entwined responses to problems – the Windsor way and the Gordonstoun way – and realising neither of these worked for Diana, he let himself be persuaded to seek sustenance in equally unpromising places. His mentor Laurens van der Post recommended the services of his own wife Ingaret, 'a gifted interpreter of dreams', though not a trained analyst.[18] Charles consulted her. For Diana van der Post recommended the services of Dr Alan McGlashan, an aged Jungian psychiatrist. After several sessions with the Princess, McGlashan concluded she was unhappy but not unstable.

After a journalist spotted the Prince emerging from McGlashan's consulting rooms in 1995, Charles was widely reported to be in analysis. In an interview after McGlashan's death, his widow Sasha denied that his relationship with the Prince was professional. It had been, she said 'a supportive friendship'.[19] Whatever its basis, the relationship mattered enough to Charles that he visited McGlashan regularly, and later added a bronze bust of the psychiatrist to a kind of informal shrine he has erected in the gardens at Highgrove to people he admires. (His friend Patrick Holden is also represented in the line-up; so is environmental activist Vandana Shiva.)

The Princess had long stopped seeing McGlashan but continued with therapy, formal and informal, seeking out mainstream practitioners and a fringe of alternative and complementary options, from clairvoyants to colonic irrigation. Unconvincing as some of these choices appear, none now seems so jaw-dropping as the guidance provided by Jimmy Savile, DJ, broadcaster and now known sex offender.

Charles and Diana were by no means the only people Savile duped. Most of the British Establishment saw Savile not for the criminal he was, but as a pillar of the community and beloved broadcaster. His catchphrase 'Now then, now then' entered the national lexicon. Margaret Thatcher took him for the kind of self-made man she most admired. He befuddled the upper echelons of broadcasting, the police service, the judiciary and medicine. He met royalty through charity work for the Royal Marines which brought him into contact with Mountbatten. Mountbatten introduced Savile to Prince Philip and other royals. 'Whenever it came to doing anything, [Mountbatten] would say: "I'll cut the ribbon but get Savile down. He can do the speeches. He does it better than me,"'

Savile told Dan Davies, a journalist whose childhood treat – his mother took him to the filming of an episode of Savile's most famous television series, *Jim'll Fix It* – left him with an abiding, and canny, mistrust of Savile's public persona.[20]

Davies originally planned to write an autobiographical account of his search for the real Savile, to be called *Apocalypse Now Then*. He instead used the phrase as a chapter heading for *In Plain Sight*, the darker biography he completed after Savile's death and the post-mortem investigations that have thus far turned up more than 500 alleged counts of sexual assault.

Savile described himself to Davies as a kind of 'court jester'. 'Royalty are surrounded by people who don't know how to deal with it … I have a freshness of approach which they obviously find to their liking.'[21] In mistaking Savile's act for rough-hewn authenticity, the Waleses were at least in good company. He was the most unreliable of witnesses, but an auction of effects from his estate in July 2012 corroborated the evidence of the favour he had found in many parts of society and more than one palace. In his book Davies lists highlights from thirty-five lots including 'gifts and cards from Prince Charles, Princess Diana, Prince Andrew and Sarah Ferguson'.[22] Davies emails that Savile's 'relationship was arguably closer with Diana than Charles', but adds that names from Savile's contacts book included 'staff at Balmoral, Highgrove, Buckingham Palace, etc'.[23]

The biographer also saw material that has never come into the public domain and interviewed Janet Cope, Savile's personal assistant for three decades, who told him of a thick file of correspondence between Diana and Savile. Cope described her memory of this correspondence as 'along the lines of: "It was so lovely to talk to you, I feel so much better now. Thank you for your advice, I know where you are when I need you."'[24] That accords with Diana's casual mention of a conversation with Savile in the Squidgygate tape. 'Jimmy Savile rang me up yesterday, and he said: "I'm just ringing up, my girl, to tell you that His Nibs [Charles] has asked me to come and help out the redhead [the Duchess of York], and I'm just letting you know, so that you don't find out through her or him; and I hope it's all right by you.'"[25]

It speaks to the congested communications of the Prince's court that he would encourage Savile to 'help out' his sister-in-law. Savile's behaviour during his visits to St James's Palace had rung alarms but nobody seems to have told Charles. In her account of palace life, Sarah Goodall, a former Lady Clerk to the Prince, describes seeing a 'middle-aged man with white hair, dressed in a white boiler suit and covered in gold jewellery' roaming the offices. She watches him lift the hand of a female colleague 'as though to kiss it, and then he does the most extraordinary thing. He appears to be licking her hand. Now he is coming over to my desk. He takes my hand and does the same thing. He is looking at me and grinning. "Oh, oooh, oooh! Whoarr! Lovely girl."' A colleague tells Goodall that Savile is helping to arrange a rapprochement between Charles and Diana. 'I stand there stunned at the thought of Jimmy Savile, the television personality who utters curious warbling noises and dresses in weird clothing, helping His Royal Highness and the Princess of Wales to fix their relationship! This cannot be true ... He hardly seems the best qualified or most appropriate person to give marital advice.'[26] Goodall's book, written in the form of a diary, bears signs of embroidery but she is not being wise after the fact about Savile. Her book came out in 2006 and it was not until his death in 2011 that his history of sexual assaults against children began to be confirmed.

Clarence House did not dignify Goodall's recollections with a public response but issued a statement to *Panorama*, the series that gave Diana a platform for her bombshell interview, ahead of its 2014 investigation *Jimmy Savile: the Power to Abuse*. The programme reiterated Goodall's claim that Savile had provided marriage-guidance counselling to the Waleses. 'It is ridiculous to suggest that His Royal

Highness sought marital advice from Jimmy Savile. On the few occasions Jimmy Savile visited St James's Palace, it was as a guest of a member of the household and as such he would have been accompanied,' said the Clarence House statement, broadcast as part of the *Panorama* film.

The statement also responded to a claim in the film that health officials were 'gobsmacked' to find Savile at a Highgrove meeting convened by the Prince to protest the threatened closure of emergency services at a nearby hospital. After the meeting finished and the Prince departed, Savile allegedly warned one of the officials present that making the Prince unhappy could cost the official a knighthood. 'It is possible that such a meeting took place,' the Clarence House statement continued. 'However, we cannot comment on any alleged threats after the Prince left the room. It is certainly not the case that he knew, sanctioned or encouraged this form of behaviour by anyone.'[27]

That sounds all too likely. Courtiers and advisers not infrequently do things in Charles's name that he would be unlikely to sanction or encourage. Yet the detail of the meeting also rings true. People working for the Prince are used to finding their projects disrupted by unwanted input from unlikely quarters. The Prince 'is basically as distrustful as ministers are of advice from one source', says an insider. 'So you have a tendency to get some pretty surprising people reading things, checking things, coming up with an alternative view, some of whom are really quite difficult.'

Savile had persuaded top politicians and National Health authorities to give him the run of Leeds General Infirmary, Stoke Mandeville – a hospital that is home to a famous spinal injuries unit – Broadmoor high-security psychiatric hospital and other institutions, trusting him to make policy and personnel decisions and move unchaperoned among patients. To the Prince this made Savile an obvious person to tap for advice on navigating Britain's health authorities.

But Charles also consulted Savile on other matters. One source tells of an occasion when the Prince asked his famous occasional adviser to read over a speech he was due to give on a topic unrelated to health care or any field in which Savile had expertise. Savile made no amendments on that occasion.

Nobody – and certainly not Savile – would have been able to fix the Waleses' relationship. As the two camps washed dirty linen in public, the House of Windsor faced its toughest test since the abdication. Only the occasional beam of daylight had caught the sovereign and her children behind the scenes. The documentary *Royal Family*, based on footage of its titular subjects shot over an entire year as Charles prepared for his investiture as Prince of Wales, enjoyed just one outing only, in 1969, attracting audiences of 23 million in Britain and a further 350 million worldwide, before the Queen demanded the film be withdrawn. The royals are seen struggling to barbecue sausages; in another scene the Queen makes awkward small talk with President Richard Nixon, who would resign in 1974, a move precipitated by revelations of conversations he assumed would stay private. Anne, the Princess Royal, summed up the family's distaste for their telly adventure: 'I always thought it was a rotten idea. The attention that had been brought on one ever since one was a child, you just didn't want any more. The last thing you needed was greater access.'[28]

She was right, but only up to a point. The reason that the monarchy continues to flourish while other pillars of the Establishment totter is because it is rarely seen to chase popularity by yielding to popular opinion. Its unique selling point is consistency. Yet its success is also based on managing change, rather than standing against change. The institution develops in parallel with the people it claims to represent. As televisions took pride of place in British living rooms, the Windsors had to let cameras into their living rooms. The family learned from the mistake of the first documentary, quickly working out how to hide in plain sight, carefully controlling subsequent access and output. But the nature of that output had to change too. The greatest stumble of the Queen's reign came after Diana's death when the sovereign didn't realise her subjects had come to believe only in emotions they could see. Old-school Windsor restraint sits uneasily with the touchier-feelier, therapised, confessional spirit that found its zenith in Diana.

Charles himself remains caught uneasily between those two impulses, schooled to royal *omertà* and the product of a culture that tells him that to express emotion is to cheapen it, yet also brimming with emotions. To Nicholas Soames, this struggle appears heroic. 'The other day someone was on a television show and apparently they didn't show enough emotion so there was a terrible row in the *Daily Mail*, they haven't shown enough empathy, whatever the bloody hell it is, they haven't cried when they've won a competition,' he says. 'Well, there is no point looking to the Prince of Wales to do that. He will not play that game, because he is in my view morally honest and intellectually honest.'[29]

The problem for the Prince is that he did, for a while, play the game, just not enthusiastically or well. The Waleses' conflict damaged the control mechanisms and opened Walter Bagehot's dictum about preserving the mystery of monarchy to ridicule. 'How on earth this sentiment is relevant ... is beyond me, because it suggests two things that are completely false; the first is that when it comes to the monarchy we should be kept in the dark and, secondly, that there is any magic left ... What has been cast on the Royals recently is not a little ray of sunshine but a bloody great battery of floodlights,' wrote columnist Suzanne Moore in March 2003 in the *Mail on Sunday*.[30] Diana had been dead for five years, but the revelations continued to flow thanks to a tidal wave of official reports, inquiries, acrimonious court cases and a roaring trade in gossip and harder-edged information.

The paradox of palaces is that they are at once thoroughfares, their carpets worn thin by visitors and retinues, and nests of secrecy and intrigue. They are the least private of homes and the most resistant to oversight. They breed plots and foment mysteries.

Neither journalistic investigations nor legal inquiries have ever finally pinpointed the source of the Squidgygate and Camillagate recordings. The tabloids' initial reticence to publish the transcripts could seem to exonerate them from involvement. The quality of the recordings, and the odds against one or more radio ham staying locked onto the signals for the duration of the calls, raised doubts that such amateurs could have picked up the transmissions unaided. Audio analysts commissioned by the *Sunday Times* found anomalies suggesting the conversations might have been recorded and rebroadcast for Cyril Reenan and other radio enthusiasts to discover.

Meaningful motives are just as difficult to establish. Both sides in the War of the Waleses sustained damage from the release of the tapes. As for potential perpetrators, GCHQ had the capacity to tap into conversations but joined with the other intelligence services in a statement in 1993 giving 'categorical assurances denying any involvement in intercepting, recording or disclosing telephone calls involving members of the Royal Family'. GCHQ's former chief, Sir John Ayde, and Sir Richard Dearlove, head of MI6 until 2004, repeated these denials in person at the inquest into the deaths of Diana, her boyfriend Dodi Fayed and their driver Henri Paul. Lord Fellowes, Diana's brother-in-law through marriage to her sister Jane and, at the time the recordings emerged, the Queen's Private Secretary, also testified that the involvement of spies seemed 'unlikely ... they have better things to do'.[31]

But Fellowes told the inquest – which ran from October 2007 to April 2008 at London's Royal Courts of Justice, at a cost to the taxpayer of £2.8 million – that the Queen routinely ordered Buckingham Palace to be swept for bugs and revealed that the tapes had triggered 'discussions' with the security services. The aim, he said, was 'obviously if there had been anything nefarious done, that it should be discovered and punished. But the main strand of thinking in Buckingham Palace, if I can put it broadly, was that this had happened and what action should be taken to ensure that it did not happen again.'[32]

Fellowes's dry confirmation of palace fears of bugging, sensational in another context, sank in a welter of wilder claims and intimate details as 268 witnesses gave statements or took the stand. They ranged from people who happened to be on the scene of Diana's death to key figures from her life. Paul Burrell told the court on the first day of his three-day testimony that he knew his employer's 'every waking thought'. By day three, he rowed back. 'I'm not sure I knew her better than most, but I knew her very well.' Hasnat Khan, Diana's lover from 1995 until she met Dodi, provided a statement full of pathos. The Princess, like her ex-husband, observed normal life from enforced distance. 'Diana was also not used to doing everyday things that the rest of us take for granted,' Khan's statement revealed. 'For example, we once went to the pub together and Diana asked if she could order the drinks because she had never done so before. She really enjoyed the experience and chatted away happily to the barman.'

Some familiar faces stayed absent from this parade. Neither Charles nor any blood members of his family were called to give evidence, sparing short-term embarrassment but reinforcing the sense of royal exceptionalism and an Establishment quick to close the shutters. To conspiracy theorists, this appeared more significant, a sign of guilt. When Dodi Fayed died alongside the Princess, his father Mohamed Fayed, the owner of the department store Harrods, expected to be embraced by the Windsors in shared grief. The embrace never came. The royals recoiled from Fayed, believing he had flaunted his links with Diana in life and now would turn her death into a promotional opportunity. As she travelled to Paris with the Prince to retrieve the Princess's body, Diana's sister Sarah McCorquodale asked Charles about the arrangements for transporting the coffin on arrival back in the UK. 'One thing's for sure,' he replied. 'She's not going into London in a green carriage drawn by horses.'[33] The Harrods carriage, painted in the store's green and gold livery, was often deployed to ferry celebrities to the launch of its seasonal sales.

Fayed at first blamed the paparazzi pursuing Diana and Dodi for provoking the fatal collision in the Pont de l'Alma tunnel. He came instead to imagine 'that Dracula family', as he called the Windsors, had orchestrated the crash to prevent the Princess from marrying his Muslim son. At the inquest, he anatomised an elaborate plot, alleging the knowledge or active participation of the senior royals, Tony Blair, the security services, Fellowes, some of Diana's friends, former London police chiefs, the British Ambassador to France, French toxicologists and medics, three of his former employees and Henri Paul, who lost his own life in the crash.[34]

Conspiracy theories are hardy plants that flourish in the most arid of soils. The rich compost of this tragedy continues to nourish all sorts of exotic blooms. The inquest reached the same central conclusion as earlier investigations in France and Britain: that the car hit the wall of the tunnel not by design but by accident, caused by Paul driving at excessive speeds after drinking, with paparazzi in pursuit. Yet anyone entering 'Diana death' in online search engines falls down a rabbit hole into a universe in which Fayed's version of events seems positively tame. Scenarios involve different methods of forcing the crash: a bright light beamed into Paul's eyes or a sniper lurking in the Parisian underpass. In some versions the murderers hijack the Princess, forcing her into a vehicle concealed as an ambulance before doing the deed; another hypothesis sees the Mercedes, and its occupants, compacted in a crusher. The inquest jury heard detailed medical evidence about Diana's menstrual cycles in the weeks leading up to her death but in this parallel universe she and Dodi expected a baby, furnishing her royal ex-laws with additional reasons to wish her ill. A persistent meme depicts the Windsors as giant shape-shifting extraterrestrial lizards, who snuffed out the Princess and continue to pose an existential threat to all surviving humanity.

Such views remain on the fringes, but cloud wider opinions of Charles.

———

There is, of course, a world that most people don't get to see. It doesn't have the swagger of its fictional portrayals or operate to clear-cut distinctions between good and evil, though many people working in intelligence certainly aim to be on the side of the angels. The Prince has seen their dedication to public service up close. As heir to the throne and in his duties representing the Queen, he receives regular briefings from intelligence officials and has made private visits to the headquarters of MI5, MI6 and GCHQ. ('You can usually ensure a moment when large numbers of staff gather round a central atrium,' says an aide.) Charles has also met teams in Northern Ireland and further-flung locations. A statement provided for this book by the three agencies emphasises that such visits are appreciated. A former field operative remembers Charles's appearance in the operations base in slightly more colourful terms: it was 'slightly unreal but [it] cheered everybody up'.

In 2012 the Prince took on a formal role with the services at their request, becoming their first royal patron. He and Camilla also attended the premiere of the James Bond movie *Skyfall*, asking that monies raised should benefit charities helping former and serving members of the intelligence services. He had held the first annual Prince of Wales Intelligence Community Awards a year earlier. It had been his idea to find a way to celebrate achievements by members of the intelligence services; the three agencies then got together to agree the criteria. The lunchtime ceremony is held every year in the St James's Palace State Apartments. 'His Royal Highness has often commented that due to the secret nature of the three agencies' work, their successes often remain unrecognised and unreported,' says the statement from the intelligence services. 'The awards complement the public honours and recognise staff for their outstanding efforts to keep the country safe.'

Many royal engagements are announced in advance. These awards are only reported a day after the event, to maintain confidentiality. The attendees, numbering around 200, include friends and family, the services heads and the Ministers with oversight of the services. Citations are given to whole teams, and are directed not just to field agents but also for excellence in administration, management and what in a corporate setting might be termed information technology. Charles conducts the ceremony with the same high formality with which he doles out public honours. 'The Prince's appreciation of the work of the intelligence agencies came across very strongly and it was great to hear how much he values what we do ... We were really proud to receive the award,' says one 2014 recipient. 'It was fantastic to see the Prince appreciate the work that goes into joint operations,' says another. 'His questions showed just how interested he is in our work.'

Most people employed in intelligence are unable to tell any but those closest to them how they spend their days and then only in circumscribed form. To outsiders, spies often describe themselves as 'consultants' or 'civil servants', deflecting curiosity by pretending to specialise in areas so boring or abstruse as to discourage further enquiries. The awards offer a rare chance to operate in daylight. 'I was delighted my parents could glimpse into my world.' 'Our work being recognised by the Prince of Wales in front of our colleagues and family made me very proud, and my mum more so.' 'There are not many occasions where you can speak so openly about our work – this is one.' 'Being in the shadows, it was extraordinary to be at St James's Palace talking to the Prince about our work.'

That positive reinforcement is all the more welcome in the changed and rugged landscape which spies refer to as 'Snowdonia'. In 2013, a former CIA systems administrator Edward Snowden leaked thousands of classified documents obtained during his work as an outside contractor to the US National Security Agency (NSA), a conjoined sibling of GCHQ. The documents revealed that the US and UK in concert with other countries were scooping up huge amounts of data from electronic communications of all kinds, snooping on allies in their efforts to contain terrorism and circumventing restrictions against spying on their own citizens by sharing data between them. A core group of five countries – Five Eyes – jointly operating many of the surveillance programmes originally came together during the Second World War when Britain reunited with its former anglophone colonies, the US, Australia, Canada and New Zealand, to plan for the post-war world and continued their cooperation into the Cold War era and beyond. Snowden's leaks didn't just disrupt relations with friendly countries that found they had been targeted and damage the reputations of the intelligence agencies involved – and, according to those agencies, compromise active operations and operatives as well as future capacities – but raised questions almost as bottomless as the NSA archives, about privacy versus security and accountability versus secrecy.

The backwash is engulfing public and corporate life, urging new safeguards for individual privacy and greater institutional transparency. The arguments don't hinge simply on ethics but also on the practical difficulties of blocking the spread of information in a porous world. That part of the debate isn't new but has aquired more urgency in 'Snowdonia', a region short on trust.

The monarchy, for now, retains the faith of the public in a way that few other institutions do, yet the institution as always must keep pace with the times. In many ways it appears to be doing so. The press operations at Buckingham Palace and Clarence House have expanded and professionalised, and stocked their ranks with talented people who have worked in mainstream news organisations, wrangled celebrity clients or survived the white heat of government media management. There are dedicated teams assigned to the main royal brands; the Queen personally approved a slick royal website and separate feeds on social media such as Facebook, Twitter and Flickr that seem to dovetail nicely with her mantra of being seen to be believed. Her children and their children may appear more open than she is, but apart from her eldest, they rarely talk about anything of substance. Their private lives, for the most part, remain private. Camilla, styled HRH Duchess of Cornwall on her marriage to Charles, has made a smooth transition from public enemy to royal asset. Everything appears calm. Yet the royals are no closer to solving the old dilemma of how much daylight to let in or confronting the new reality: that they may not have a choice in the matter.

It's not just that confidentiality agreements have failed to deter serial former employees from 'doing a Crawfie', publishing memoirs of royal service that tend to be far less gentle than Marion Crawford's sunshine-infused original. During the War of the Waleses, media organisations that played by the existing book floundered in a brash new free-for-all, read-all-about-it scrum in which not only Murdoch's *Sunday Times* but its red-top stablemates the *Sun* and the *News of the World* turned out to be the newspapers of record. Now all mainstream news organisations are trying to navigate still bigger changes. Their representatives know the rules, even if they sometimes transgress them. New media and citizen journalists – and that's everyone on Twitter – may not know there are any rules and are as likely to take cues from Snowden and Julian Assange as from dusty jurisdictions mumbling about privileged communications and the right to privacy.

Outside the palace gates, the pressure for transparency is growing. Within palace walls sits a future king whose irrepressible desire to communicate should logically herald fresh moves towards greater openness. That isn't happening. His court has grown more clenched. Yet Charles has many things to be proud of, not least his first and biggest charity.

Chapter 6

A Matter of Trust

In June 2014, in a classroom in the south London suburb of Merton, ten kids struggle to compile a shopping list. Rajan Patel, nineteen, stands by an easel, noting items on a large pad. Behind him a poster warns against bullying, under the slogan: 'NOT ALL JOKES ARE FUNNY'. His teammates ranged around a U-shaped table periodically forget that message, directing snide remarks at Patel or each other and shouting down suggestions. 'You need to listen to each other. It's respect,' says David Tovey, their team leader. A girl raises her head from the table and stares at him with kohl-rimmed eyes. 'I wasn't talking,' she says. 'I was sleeping. You lot are waking me up.'

That's the central purpose of the twelve-week Team Programme, the seventy-fourth run at this location, and of every programme and project run by the Prince's Trust: to wake people up, then to provide them with the tools to realise their potential. Seventeen-year-old Tanya Djemal knows that, even as she puts on her small show of defiance. She is beginning to think she might harbour ambitions in the longer term to go to college, she says in a voice so small that the whirr of an overheated computer threatens to drown her out. Her acting up in front of the group masks a crippling timidity that complicates one of the tasks the Trust has set participants: to secure a three-week work placement. The Team Programme is aimed at sixteen- to twenty-five-year-old NEETs – the reductive acronym denotes young people Not in Education, Employment or Training; by the end of the course, they will hopefully be moving towards college, apprenticeship or a job. Djemal recoils from the idea of interaction with children. Her work experience must involve 'food or animals', she says.

For her and the thousands of others who pass through the Prince's Trust programmes every year – 56,077 in the financial year 2014–15 – the placement will provide a glimpse into a world that seemed beyond reach, in which life isn't just about survival but holds the possibility of love and friendship and personal development and professional achievement. 'I came to the Prince's Trust to get a brighter future and to change my past,' says twenty-year-old Matt Jelinek, who spent the first half of his life in Poland and the second being bounced around the English education system and excluded from three schools. Everyone has different stories about how he or she arrived at the Prince's Trust but all the narratives describe alienation and exclusion.

Patel and Jelinek and Djemal and their fellow participants, encouraged by Tovey to function not as competing individuals but as a cooperative unit, are beginning to taste the unfamiliar sweetness of belonging. Tovey has already helped them to bond during a week at an adventure centre in the Peak District. They hiked, went caving, learned the rudiments of rock climbing. For several of their number, it was the first time they had ever ventured beyond city limits. Tovey, a former advertising executive who retrained as a teacher and Prince's Trust Team Leader, laughs when remembering the fascination sheep held for these children of grubby suburbia, then grows serious as he talks about a hike up Kinder Scout and a tranquil moment with Jelinek as they stopped to admire the view. 'Matt was telling me how amazing it was to get away from everything to centre himself. If he gets nothing else from these twelve weeks, he's got that.'

The shopping expedition the group is planning will salve the sting of deprivation, not by furnishing team members with the things consumer culture has taught them to equate with happiness, but by enabling them to give to other people. They have a budget of £500, partly generated by their own fund-raising efforts and the rest provided by the Prince's Trust, to create a remembrance garden in a Wimbledon churchyard. Only a few of them have ever tried their hand at gardening, so making the list is heavy weather. 'What's a rake?' 'Like a fork.' 'A fork you eat with?' 'We need a trowel.' 'Trowel? Like trousers?' asks Patel, trying to keep up with the rapid-fire proposals. When someone suggests a 'hoe', the boys snigger and the girls ignore them. 'Anybody got seeds?' 'Yeah, all the boys.' 'What about an extension lead?' 'Polish person here,' Jelinek sings out. 'I got an extension lead.'

The vicar has promised to dedicate a church service to the team in thanks for the garden. 'What's a church service?' asks Kieron Tayler, seventeen, who has come to the Trust 'to get myself back on track'. His neighbour attempts to explain. Mention of the Prince of Wales – to clarify the presence of his biographer in the classroom – produces universal blankness. Not one among this recent intake to the Prince's Trust has linked the organisation to a real live Prince. Some charities with charismatic founders resemble reverent cults, in which the founder serves as a demigod and personification of values. The Prince's Trust, by contrast, aims to imbue its alumni with a sense of their own potency – *plus est en vous*.

If clients do encounter the Prince when he visits Trust projects or holds fund-raisers or events to honour the achievements of Trust participants, they see an older man in a double-breasted suit, surprisingly easy to talk to, ready with a joke, but apparently light years away from their own experience. They are right, of course. Yet Charles too was young once, isolated, vulnerable and directionless. In learning to give to others, he found his direction.

Like most organisations set up by the Prince, his largest and most successful charity sprang into life without a detailed plan or defined target, but from a single idea that gripped its creator. In 1972, George Pratt, the Deputy Chief Probation Officer for Inner London, defended a pilot scheme he had helped to devise under which some offenders guilty of minor crimes undertook community work instead of serving custodial sentences. The scheme proved so effective that within three years it had become a nationwide standard, but its debut attracted hostile headlines about soft options and pampered criminals. 'These are sentences without shame, in that offenders are not ashamed to do the tasks and get something out of it too in the way of satisfaction. The scheme is telling us a lot about offenders: if you break the cycle of court appearances followed by prison, and gel them into another, socially acceptable cycle you have some hope of making them change,' Pratt explained.[1]

After Charles heard Pratt's radio interview on the BBC Home Service, he invited the probation officer to Buckingham Palace to discuss whether young people might be coaxed away from potential criminality by getting them involved in Gordonstoun-style volunteering. The Prince proposed setting up a network of community fire brigades on inner-city estates. Pratt warned him that putting firefighting equipment in the hands of vandals might not produce the anticipated effect. Undeterred, Charles convened a series of meetings with Pratt – who would become the Trust's first Chairman – and with social workers and a range of experts he thought might be able to refine his idea into something practicable and constructive. The Director of Social Services for a London borough recalled the Prince 'pacing up and down this room in the Palace like a caged tiger, frustrated, by what? By what he wanted to do, by what he couldn't do, what he wasn't allowed to do ...'[2]

Jon Snow, now Channel 4's news anchor but at the time working in a homeless day centre with teenage kids, received 'this extraordinary call from Squadron Leader David Checketts who was [Charles's] Private Secretary. He says: "Um, hello, you won't know me but I'm ringing on behalf of His Royal Highness Prince Charles." I said: "Really? Have you got the right number?" and he said: "Yes, we'd very much like you to come and see him. It's about a project we want to look at.'" Snow laughs. 'So I turned up at Buckingham Palace on my bike and it turned out there were two of us who had been invited, just two, me and a guy from Save the Children, and we were shown to what's called the White Drawing Room, where there were, I'd say, two more flunkies and Charles. He was wearing double-breasted, and he opened up almost immediately. He said: "You know I've brought you here because I want to do something with my life. I want to start something which will make a difference." And we had a really good discussion. Both of us really said much the same thing to him which was that if you use your kudos and your name to set up a kind of foundation that would help to resource the kind of people we're working with, you could make a really fantastic difference because the cachet of using your name would make life very much easier for us and indeed for them. Because at the moment it's very difficult to get anything done at all.'[3]

Social workers and charities were confronted by spiralling problems as the post-war boom and 1960s euphoria curdled. Inflation in the cost of consumer goods peaked at more than 25 per cent as national debt also increased and the queues of unemployed lengthened. Those Britons lucky enough to afford television sets – still mostly black and white, though the BBC and ITV began transmitting in colour at the turn of the decade – were succumbing to Hahn's feared spectatoritis, spending twenty-two hours a week in front of their tellies by the end of the decade.[4] They watched Eric Morecambe joyously rework the same joke again and again. 'What do you think of it so far?' he would ask during one of Ernie Wise's playlets, holding up a bust or a set of false teeth or some other prop and ventriloquising a single word: 'Rubbish!' And this was the age of rubbish, mouldering piles that festered in the streets as industrial action stopped domestic collections, blockaded refuse dumps and closed down sewage works. The number of days lost to strikes multiplied faster than British television-viewing hours, not least because of power cuts forced by miners' stoppages that regularly blacked out homes, interrupting *The Morecambe & Wise Show* and *Doctor Who*. The trades unions fought to preserve settlements that the moribund economy could no longer support; the political classes failed to present clear-eyed alternatives. The competition for dwindling jobs and resources sharpened resentments that had already been building.

Charles had still been at Cambridge University when the then Conservative Shadow Defence Secretary Enoch Powell delivered an inflammatory speech warning of 'immigrant communities [that] can organise to consolidate their members, to agitate and campaign against their fellow citizens, and to overawe and dominate the rest with the legal weapons which the ignorant and the ill-informed have provided. As I look ahead, I am filled with foreboding; like the Roman, I seem to see "the River Tiber foaming with much blood".'[5] The Prince wrote to Mountbatten at the time, concerned by the way Powell's words had infected public sentiment and concluding: 'I fear the whole problem is going to get far worse in the near future.'[6] This proved prescient, not least as 28,000 Ugandan Asians arrived in Britain, expelled by the dictator Idi Amin in his efforts to 'africanise' Uganda. It was in this difficult context and against the upward sweep of youth crime and joblessness that Charles surveyed opinions about how he could help his inner-city counterparts, whether British born or from immigrant communities. 'I just felt what we need at that young age is somebody to take an interest and to show concern but also to give you that self-confidence and self-esteem which I do believe is absolutely critical if you're going to be able to achieve anything later,' he says.[7]

That mission and the notion of empowering the disempowered by placing faith in them, for example by giving out small grants without requiring guarantees or demanding the completion of laborious paperwork, remain central to the Prince's Trust. 'I tried to put myself in other people's positions, which is not easy, of course,' Charles admitted. Yet he had no difficulty imagining 'having to endure constant red tape and constant delays and procrastination' as Palace aides and government bureaucrats did their best to impede his plans. 'If you're operating in very deprived circumstances, and you are confronted with all of that, you just say: "Well, to hell with this,"' he concluded.⁸

Despite his more privileged circumstances, he too came close to giving up, but instead learned to push back. He sometimes did so with the combustive anger of a person unused to asserting himself, and sometimes still does, or more often slides into bleak moods that those close to him learn to negotiate. 'He always reminds me of a day in April,' says an insider. 'It can be bright sunshine and then the clouds suddenly appear from nowhere and then they clear and it's bright sunshine. He's got a million things on his mind all of the time, but when the sun comes out he can have you crying laughing with him within seconds.'

There were longer depressions and more frequent squalls after Charles left active service in the Navy in 1976 – the same year the Prince's Trust came into formal existence – and in trying to work out how to spend his life found himself blocked and hemmed in. He had commanded a ship but back in the palace, he was expected not only to bow to the Queen – whom he has always revered – but accept directions from courtiers who treated him with condescension.

In his twenties, the Prince entered his years of teenaged rebellion. While his contemporaries demonstrated their independence of spirit by growing their hair, dabbling – in life experiences, rather than affairs of state – and heading to rock festivals, Charles stuck to his guns about the direction of the Prince's Trust. When officials cited security risks and cancelled his excursions to see inner-city hardships at first hand, he insisted that alternative visits be organised. When Buckingham Palace tried to put the brakes on his activities, the Prince forged on regardless, overriding the voice he found hardest to ignore. His father had tackled Checketts about potential overlap between the Prince's new Trust, a fund planned to mark the Queen's Silver Jubilee and the existing King George's Jubilee Trust. In fact, the biggest concern in the palace was not that the heir's evolving charity duplicated efforts but that it might be controversial, directed to the undeserving poor – troublemakers and offenders – rather than the traditional virtuous recipients of royal beneficence.

Scepticism about the Trust wasn't entirely unfounded. Its first programmes – including a Gordonstounian notion of training young offenders as lifeguards – were small-scale and experimental. The charity had scant resources and the Prince had not yet learned, in the words of Sir William Castell, Chairman of the Wellcome Trust since 2006 and from 1998 to 2003 of the Prince's Trust, to 'pick pockets'.[9] The organisation's start-up funds were far from princely: its founder's Navy severance pay of £7,400, his fee of £4,000 for an interview about George III given to a US television company (the first time but not the last the Prince would argue that Mad King George was cruelly underrated), and a £2,000 donation from Harry Secombe. With Peter Sellers and Spike Milligan, Secombe had gained an ardent fan and frequent imitator in the Prince of their radio comedy, *The Goon Show*. If the Prince sings in the bath – and an overnight guest claims to have heard him doing so – the Goons' 'Ying Tong Song' features on the set list: 'Ying tong ying tong / Ying tong ying tong / Ying tong iddle I po!' The Prince's Goon impressions are legendary – albeit in the restricted circle of his friends and family, many of whom are too young to have heard the original.

His musical tastes have always been eclectic, from the Goons to classical music. 'He's immensely knowledgeable about opera,' says

Nicholas Soames. Rock, however, has always been something of a blind spot. 'The Three Degrees were our heroes. We loved the Three Degrees,' Soames declares. 'Prince Charles met one of them somewhere. I think he saw them at the Royal Variety Performance, and they adored him. I think they came and sang for him at one of his parties. It's so bloody long ago, Jesus Christ. I'm reluctant to say rock music passed us by, because it didn't. We never went to a rock concert or anything. Diana Ross, he loved Diana Ross. And the Supremes, that was who he loved. Do I mean the Supremes? They were three bloody pretty black girls anyway. They were absolutely adorable.'[10]

In 1978, the Prince performed 'the Bump' with the Three Degrees during a small concert for the Prince's Trust at the King's Country Club in Eastbourne and the same year danced with the group's Sheila Ferguson at his birthday party. She reminisced: 'It was funny, we started off the dance, he and I, and I was holding my handbag. And he said to me: "Sheila, you don't have to hold your handbag," and I said: "What are you talking about?" and he replied:"You're at Buckingham Palace!" So I told him: "You can take the girl out of the ghetto, but you can't take the ghetto out of the girl!"'[11]

When forced to listen to less euphonious music, the Prince sometimes wears earplugs, and from the early 1980s he has donned earplugs for the Trust on a regular basis. Status Quo headlined the Trust's first big rock fund-raiser, in May 1982, more than three years before Live Aid. Such events became a moneymaking staple, in the early 2000s generating more than £1 million from each of a series of multi-artist gigs. Big names used to be easy to snare – they got to do good at the same time as boosting their music and merchandise sales – but that model broke when consumers discovered they could download music for next to nothing or nothing, forcing musicians to earn their keep from live performances. The Trust, now a slick professional operation, headed by a shrewd Chief Executive Martina Milburn and headquartered in the City of London, among the best locations for 'pickpockets', has become nimble and entrepreneurial, finding alternative ways to harness the music industry to raise money and awareness, for example partnering with Beyoncé on her 2014 UK tour. The initiative promoted the Trust on the singer's website and during the concerts, an ideal matching of brands with no risk and only upside for the charity.

These days the Trust needs to raise about £1 million per week just to break even. About a third of its income comes from private donations, mostly at corporate level or from wealthy individual donors, many of them personally persuaded to their generosity by the Prince. As he takes on additional head-of-state duties, the pressure on his time is increasing and the Trust is adjusting accordingly. 'It's about using his time much more effectively and more cleverly,' says Martina Milburn. 'He's going to have less time, he's going to have more demands on what he does, so we have to be cleverer.'[12]

It's still not as easy to raise money for the benefit of the Trust's spiky clientele as for children or, in the UK, animals. Nevertheless, potential donors have become more alert to the problems of social exclusion and youth unemployment, not least since these blights manifested themselves in noisy movements such as Occupy, pitching tents at the steps of St Paul's Cathedral or Zuccotti Park on Wall Street, and in less choate protests such as the riots that ignited in Tottenham, north London, in 2011. Thirty years earlier, similar alarm calls sounded among the comfortable classes as violence spread from one English inner city to another. Then, as with the more recent riots, politicians disagreed over the causes of the unrest but nobody could assume the problem would go away of its own accord or keep to itself in the rougher parts of town, visiting misery only on those who already had little to lose.

For the nascent Trust, the trouble carried a silver lining: easier access to funds, not only from private donors but the state sector, which now accounts for about a third of the Prince's Trust income.

Sir Angus Ogilvy, husband of the Queen's first cousin Princess Alexandra, knew his way around government. Brought on board by Charles as a trustee, he persuaded Margaret Thatcher's Secretary of State for Employment, Lord Young, to match any funding the Trust raised for its newest programme, providing seed-corn funding to young entrepreneurs. In 1988 Young's pledge delivered a delicious windfall to the Trust, when a fund-raising drive to mark the Prince's fortieth birthday succeeded in hitting its £40 million target and the government had to match that figure.

Ogilvy continued to wheedle subventions from successive administrations. 'Angus did a brilliant job for the Trust and he was rigorous on the fund-raising,' says Castell. 'We'd go to functions, the two of us, and Angus would say: "This is Bill Castell of the Prince's Trust," and I'd say: "Actually, we're the Prince's pickpockets," and so given that we needed to raise substantial amounts of money we used to encourage people to think compassionately about those who were lost to society. Angus said: "We'll get a match out of Tony Blair and so we did. We got the Prime Minister to agree that he would match us one for one, up to fifty million quid. And it was much easier to go after major donors to say if you give us a pound we get a pound out of Her Majesty's Government.'[13]

Tom Shebbeare, an amiable former Eurocrat, who joined the Trust as Chief Executive in 1987, diversified the Trust's programmes and scaled them up significantly. On his watch the Trust made the leap from niche player to the leading interventionist charity of its kind, not only complementing state-run initiatives, but clearly influencing them. The Blair government's welfare-to-work programme, the New Deal, outsourced its volunteering strand to the Prince's Trust; at the Trust's urging, the New Deal also included a business start-up option, rather than putting all efforts into getting the unemployed into existing jobs. The after-school clubs the government introduced during the same period took their inspiration from the Trust's initiative to provide a haven for pupils whose turbulent home environment might disrupt studying.

As the Trust grew, the Prince dedicated ballooning hours to helping the charity grow further still and to building additional charities and initiatives, some conceptually related, such as the Prince's Youth Business Trust (later folded back into the Prince's Trust) and Business in the Community (BITC); others, such as the Prince of Wales' Institute of Architecture, representing different strands of interest. His Gordonstounian impulses also kept trying to find expression in programmes designed to reintroduce to Britain a form of national service that would inculcate in British youth the sense that by helping their communities they could also help themselves. The Prince of Wales Community Venture, tested in Sunderland, Llanelli and Birmingham from 1986 to 1989, was its first incarnation. The Prince's Trust Volunteers was launched in 1990 as an initiative with the Speaker's Commission on Citizenship, with all-party support and government funding, and eventually developed into the Team Programme. Another version of this vision emerged in 2013 with the launch of the Prince's Step Up to Serve campaign to bolster youth volunteering, backed by all three main political parties.

Always on the move, a habit he has never since broken, he shuttled from one meeting to another, schmoozing donations, discussing strategies, ever more focused in his desire to make a difference. His increased activity reflected a growing sense of purpose and his own power to make things happen, but also coincided with the final disintegration of a home life that had never been homely. This was no coincidence, says Julia Cleverdon. 'As the marriage became more separate, like many in that situation he became more and more of an entrepreneurial workaholic and the charitable initiatives began to multiply.'[14]

Money enables, but without conviction and credibility the Trust would not have survived. The best advertisements for the Trust are its alumni. Idris Elba, who at sixteen joined the National Youth Music

Theatre with a grant from the Trust, went on to star in television shows such as *The Wire* and *Luther* and in the film *Mandela: Long Walk to Freedom.* Steven Frayne, better known as the magician Dynamo, got money for the laptop and video equipment that he needed to make a DVD of his stunts, *Underground Magic*, which launched his career. He has his own television series and, as he revealed to an interviewer: 'I've peed in the same toilet as the Queen.' A regular at the Prince's receptions at St James's Palace on behalf of the Trust, he baffles fellow guests with sleight-of-hand illusions. 'P. Diddy ain't got nothing on Prince Charles when it comes to putting on a party,' he once enthused. 'Charles throws the best parties.'[15]

James Sommerville, since 2013 Vice President, Global Design at Coca-Cola, is another Trust success story. He co-founded the design company Attik in 1986 with a £2,000 loan, eventually selling the business to advertising giant Dentsu. 'If [the Prince] was in industry he would be a [Richard] Branson or the late Steve Jobs, he'd be one of those entrepreneurs of the world who've got that great vision,' says Sommerville. 'He's got the ability to see things others don't and the mind to speak to many different levels of people and different subjects and remember his conversations.'[16] Sir Charles Dunstone, co-founder of the Carphone Warehouse, Chairman of the Talk Talk Group and since 2009 of the Prince's Trust, makes a similar point. 'I always think of [the Prince] as the Richard Branson of charities. If he comes across something he thinks needs to happen or is a really good idea, he'll start it and try and do it and see what can be achieved,' says Dunstone. 'If it doesn't work – and not everything's going to work – that shouldn't in any way be seen as a failure. It represents his enthusiasm and his passion and his kind of optimistic nature.'[17]

The comparisons are apt. Jobs accumulated a track record as a brilliant innovator but sometimes teetered on the edge of failure when his ambitions outstripped his abilities to deliver. A similar pattern defines Branson's long career of serial entrepreneurship.

Quite a few of the people working for the Prince 'can't add up', says one insider. The Prince's Trust for a long time lacked rigour. The statistics produced didn't always stand up to scrutiny; the effectiveness of programmes wasn't always closely enough monitored. John Pervin joined the Prince's Trust on secondment from Unilever in 1985. He found an amateurish organisation: 'I said to them: "Money has to be tracked." They said: "We've got advisers for that," and I said to them: "What you want is business people."'[18] Tom Shebbeare was the Trust's first full-time employee. Until then, the organisation had been stocked by people on secondment and enthusiastic co-optees and volunteers. 'He's a fantastic bloke, the Prince, absolutely fantastic bloke in a most impossible position and for me – not a mad monarchist – I found him absolutely fantastic to work for,' says Shebbeare, who now works for Richard Branson, as the Chairman of Virgin Money Giving and Virgin StartUp, the Virgin Group's two non-profit arms. 'He's sometimes tremendously inspiring and lateral thinking and says yes to things most people would say no to. He was a great boss, great company. But,' says Shebbeare, 'possibly too nice.'[19]

Every year, the two wellsprings of the Trust's success share a London stage. The Prince, whose commitment has never wavered, presides over the annual Celebrate Success Awards, summoning Trust alumni to the podium in the Odeon Leicester Square to honour projects completed, businesses started, lives turned around – living proof that the Trust is effective.

Groups of kids, forged into teams by Trust programmes, troop up to applause for impressive community services excellently rendered. At the 2014 ceremony pupils at a Scottish school earned praise for a stark film about cyber-bullying; nine jobless young people had laboured to preserve Newhaven Fort, a significant military installation during both world wars; thirteen NEETs came together for an initiative similar to the Merton team's memorial garden: they removed a stretch of concrete to create vegetable and flower beds in front of a residential home for adults with learning disabilities.

The awards to individuals highlighted the severity of the challenges the Trust's clients often face and often in combination: abuse and neglect, drugs and alcohol dependencies, mental and physical illness, the stigma of criminal records, inadequate education and grinding hopelessness. The people who came to the stage to shake the Prince's hand may never entirely escape their demons but like the Prince himself, they have already slain dragons. 'I may as well have been a f*cking pigeon back in the day,' said Karine Harris in a video shown to explain her Flying Start Award, pointing at birds milling aimlessly on a disused games court where as a homeless teenager she used to wish her hours away. 'I was nothing to no one back in the day. I was just stuck here.' The Team Programme followed by one-on-one support helped Harris to find work in the building industry, managing construction teams for Kier Group.

Shaun McPherson collected a prize as the Trust's Young Ambassador of the Year, for turning his own experience at the Trust – and the trauma of his earlier years – to use in mentoring newer Trust clients and spreading the word about its programmes to people who might benefit. Tall and mild-mannered, McPherson arrived in Britain from South Africa with a container-load of hurt and unresolved issues; parents and step-parents themselves too scarred to look after him (though his parents are now doing better he says), a brother who died, grandparents who tried to intervene but could not curb their grandson's wildness. He stole compulsively. 'I went off the rails, drugs and weed. I was expelled from school three times before fifteen,' he reveals. It's a history he finds viscerally painful to revisit yet he has shared it with hundreds of young people in his efforts to help them avoid or escape similar pain.[20]

At college he studied economics, catering and harder drugs. By the time he followed a girlfriend to the UK, he had little confidence in his abilities to do anything apart from welding, a skill his grandfather had taught him. That skill helped him to hold down a job but his experiences marked him out as an outsider to co-workers who, from McPherson's account, enjoyed getting a rise out of their sensitive colleague. 'If you try and do something different and you think with initiative, you get a lot of backlash and I found myself getting verbally attacked on a regular basis and even physically attacked,' he says.

When orders to his company slackened as the economy declined, he whiled away dead hours at work by fashioning figurines out of nuts and bolts, metal rods and steel from the scrap bin. He devised the first of his pond covers after his father-in-law lost one of his koi carp to a heron. 'My signature is a spider web,' says McPherson. 'The original product was a decorative web that stops children from falling into ornamental water. I couldn't find a net online and I liked natural engineering so this fits over a pond beautifully, very delicate strands of steel.' After an altercation with a colleague – the 'last straw', he says – he resigned from his job, and a few months later, in April 2011, enrolled in the Prince's Trust Enterprise Programme. 'After those four days, I was blown away because it was a free course. They even paid for my travel. I can't believe this, how is this even possible? The tutelage was absolutely brilliant,' he says. 'Everybody was there to learn, it was serious, there was nobody messing around. By that time I was serious, I was giving them everything I could, because I didn't want to go back to working for somebody because of all these bad experiences.'

Assigned a mentor at the end of the course, he continued developing a business plan and his product. Banks had rejected his application for a loan to cover start-up costs, so the Trust stepped in with £2,500 as a deposit on a workshop and to equip him with basic tools and materials for fulfilling his first orders. He could rely on advice as he set up a website and navigated his fledgling business through teething problems. His one-man company, Elite Pond Covers, now makes enough to support him and his wife and son. Life is not plain sailing. He gets so many orders he's had to work round the clock to meet target delivery dates, and the pressures of combining his work with his ambassadorial role for the Trust – regularly confronting the shadows of his own past – risk plunging him into depression. But he says: "The pros [of representing the Trust] outweighed the cons and I just thought it was my calling; I'd wanted to give back. I'd wanted to do something with a charity for ages and then all of a sudden it just fell in my lap. So I wasn't going to turn away from it."[21]

McPherson 'didn't know the Prince from a bar of soap' when he first got involved in the Trust, he says, but by the time he collected his award he had heard both good and bad. 'It's hard because so many people talk about the royals in a negative way and you hear all this horrible stuff. I know as far as history goes back, the royals have been quite harsh to South Africa and America, and all over the world the English and Europeans went about stamping their feet and taking over the world. But everything I've been told about the Prince, he's an eco-activist and he's all into wind farms and natural, sustainable agriculture and then he's got so many of these awesome charities, so I can't personally see how he's bad. You know what I mean?' He pauses. 'I really wanted to meet the Prince and shake his hand and just say thank you for setting up this charity. It absolutely changed my life and my family's life.' [22]

The model and methods that proved so effective for McPherson and thousands of other Trust alumni are being exported to other countries and cultures. As youth unemployment has risen since the global financial crisis, twenty governments or government-affiliated organisations outside the UK have contacted the Trust for advice and with a view to launching Trust programmes or their own schemes. Despite the burgeoning calls on his time, the Prince insists on retaining his role in the overarching strategy of the Trust as well as its fund-raising side. Martina Milburn – approachable, unforced and un-posh, like many of the Prince's preferred people – has run the charity since 2004, merging several of its offshoots into one entity, more closely defining the targets of its help and establishing improved systems to track Trust alumni, both to monitor the longer-term impact of programmes and to be able to intervene where necessary. She says she's used to the Prince 'holding my feet to the fire. He will regularly say he doesn't mind how many people we help as long as the help we give those young people is the best it can be.'[23]

She has noticed – it is impossible not to – that the Prince is most at ease where he should be least at home, far from Planet Windsor and surrounded not by courtiers or sycophants but young people, finding a welcome and a sense of kinship that eluded him in his own youth. 'He has an amazing ability to talk to teenagers,' says Milburn. 'I've sat with him in colleges, in classrooms, in prisons, sink estates, youth clubs, you name it, he just has a connection … He is genuinely interested in their lives and somehow they sense that, with that human connection. I've seen other people do it, notably politicians, and get it badly wrong because they're not really that interested, and they come to tell young people their view or the latest government policy change. The Prince does it completely the opposite way round. The Prince always asks them first. Somehow they sense he's genuine.'[24]

It is more than that. The Prince sees himself in every Prince's Trust client. 'My great problem in life is that I do not really know what my role in life is,' he told an audience at Cambridge University when he was twenty-nine. 'At the moment I do not have one, but somehow I must find one.'[25] The Prince's Trust came to his rescue, as it has continued to assist many others, to find a purpose in life.

Back in Merton in August 2014, the Team Programme comes to an end. Participants who have completed the course – and that's all but one of the original intake – take part in a final ceremony, witnessed by friends and family. One by one they describe to the audience what they've got out of their experiences – the residential segment in Derbyshire, building the garden, taking up work placements, undergoing mock interviews, fund-raising, feeling part of a group and of the wider community – and what they plan to do in the future. That may not sound like a big deal, but two months earlier not one of them had much of a life plan beyond getting through another day. Kieron Tayler hopes to train as an electrician. Rajan Patel wants to do something in IT or finance. He tells an anecdote about his mock interview, when the interviewer asked him 'a random question. If I was a cereal what would I be? I said Fruit Loops because they're colourful and taste good.'

Matt Jelinek, who put on a boisterous front from the early days, now seems more quietly assured, less the class clown. 'Something you learn on the course is you get back what you give,' he says. 'The entire programme was amazing.'

Everybody looks different, calmer, confident, more upright, more open. Tanya Djemal has undergone what may be the greatest transformation. She has found her voice. As her mother and grandmother watch with pride and astonishment, she stands up in front of a room full of people and begins to speak, fluently and clearly. She found a work placement in a hair salon, and has thrived. She's heading back to college to retake her English and maths exams and she thinks she knows what she might want to do further down the road. She's fascinated by bats and would like to join an organisation dedicated to protecting creatures that are often misrepresented and misunderstood. It's an ambition the founder of the Prince's Trust would surely applaud.

Chapter 7

Long to Rain Over Us

He sits on a garden bench. He's wearing a well-worn shooting jacket, a pair of Hunter Argylls – a wellington boot favoured by farmers – and an expression familiar to his friends. Charles is trying to compose his face into an appropriate mask, sufficiently serious for a serious occasion, but bubbles of laughter are rising inside the royal chest. This isn't one of his regular garden perches. It's on the back of a muddy trailer. The incongruity is heightened by sweet little bunches of flowers and ribbons affixed to the arms of this improvised throne and a garland festooned across its backrest. The whole thing shakes and shudders as a tractor tows the trailer through an inland sea of mud.

The rain started over the United Kingdom in December 2013 and for two months rarely let up. By this drear beginning of February, roads have turned into rivers, fields are lakes. Island villages, ringed by citadels of sandbags, wonder when outside help might come. On dry land, their compatriots speculate about the causes of the flooding. 'I wrote to David Cameron … to warn him that disasters would accompany the passage of his Same Sex Marriage Bill, but he went ahead,' complained UKIP councillor David Silvester in a letter to his local newspaper.[1] Meteorologists perceived a different set of connections behind the biblical torrents, between jet streams and an intense polar vortex.

Residents of the low-lying Somerset Levels, afflicted earlier and worse than other regions, blamed not only God or Nature for their predicament. Too little had been done to protect against flooding by dredging existing waterways and constructing new defences. Relief efforts were patchy. Politicians, safe and warm in Westminster, appeared not to notice or care. Lord Smith of Finsbury, better known as Tony Blair-era Minister Chris Smith, at this juncture Chairman of the Environment Agency responsible for water management, stayed at home, penning a piece for the *Sunday Telegraph* that seemed to suggest Somerset might be less of a priority than metropolitan areas. 'Yes, agricultural land matters and we do whatever we can with what we have to make sure it is protected,' he wrote. 'Rules from successive governments give the highest priority to lives and homes; and I think most people would agree that this is the right approach. But this involves tricky issues of policy and priority: town or country, front rooms or farmland?'[2]

Owen Paterson, then Secretary of State for the Environment and a rare countryman in Cabinet, became the first senior politician to make the journey to south-western England, but his 27 January visit intensified anger after claims he used polished city shoes to sidestep local people waiting to meet him at a pumping station. 'Where has he been at the end of the day? Who's he actually spoken to? He's spoken to no one, has he?' lamented Becky Reilly, a Somerset farmer and police community support officer. 'We've got the farmers here, we've got members of the public here, we've got people who live here, and he's not here. He's not here listening to the actual people who are having to go through what they're going through, the flooding with the water. No, it's not on. It's not right.'

More than 500 miles to the north, at Birkhall, Charles watched the news reports, as he often does, and worried, as he always does, about how he might help. That same evening he wrote letters to key parties and spoke to aides. On 4 February, clad like the countryman he is, the 'Prince of Wellies' (© the *Sun*) arrived in Somerset and waded into the muddy waters of political controversy.

He looked regal on his bench once he had controlled his impulse to laugh. His behaviour was princely. Unlike Paterson, the Prince gave generously of his time to hear the stories of people directly impacted by the flooding. 'One of the most important things is listening,' he says. 'You don't just have to bang on at people.'[3] He brought comfort, not only of a pastoral nature but a chunk of aid, £50,000 from the Prince's Countryside Fund matched by a donation from the Duke of Westminster, one of Britain's largest landowners. So far, so stately: but then a microphone picked up a comment to a local farmer during the sort of conversation that by palace convention is deemed private. 'There's nothing like a jolly good disaster to get people to start doing something,' said the Prince. 'The tragedy is that nothing happened for so long.'

A Downing Street spokesman responded swiftly: 'The Prime Minister has repeatedly said that the situation that a number of communities in the Somerset area find themselves in is unacceptable.' By 7 February, Cameron had pulled on his own wellingtons to survey the 'heartbreaking' damage, promising the government would 'do everything that can be done' and attributing the disaster to cuts made during Blair's adminstration. 'The pause in dredging that took place in the late nineties – that was wrong,' he suggested. Smith fetched up in Somerset the same day, drawing renewed criticism by avoiding hard-hit areas and keeping his wellingtons clean. By 11 February, so many politicians had togged up in waterproofs to tour scenes of devastation that the appropriately named Jim Waterson of website BuzzFeedUK was able to compile a photo feature entitled *21 Pictures of Politicians in Wellies Staring at Floods*.[4] Along with the deluge of fresh publicity, benefits to flood victims flowed, not only an extra £140 million for flood defences allocated in the government's March budget, but immediate help from major banks in the form of repayment holidays, extensions to loans and reductions or waivers of fees, a commitment that totted up to £750 million.

Jonathan Jones, who more usually writes about art for the *Guardian*, assisted readers to square this apparent triumph of Princely intervention with their concerns about Charles and his position. His piece likened the heir to the throne to King Cnut – the spelling is a valid alternative to 'Canute' – and acknowledged widespread approval for the Prince's actions. 'In an age that hates professional politicians, there may be real popular enthusiasm for a king who tells the government where to get off. Republicans who have dreamed for decades of a clumsy Charles becoming an unpopular monarch may be sorely disappointed. His canny stand in Somerset could mark the beginning of a powerful mystic repudiation of the bureaucrats and metropolitan elite. Speak for Olde England, Charles!'

Jones concludes with a punchline, or rather a flurry of sharp jabs. 'There's just one problem, for a democracy. Those Cnuts in Westminster are elected. The Prince of the Marsh is not. Somewhere in that mud there's a *Monty Python* peasant saying: "Well, I didn't vote for you."'[5]

The day after his Somerset trip, suited and de-booted, the Prince returned to the ground zero of another political debate. He originally came to Tottenham in north London in August 2011 as glass still crunched underfoot and buildings still smouldered. Five people died over six nights in the riots that enveloped the borough spread across the capital and to other English cities; businesses, homes and cars were torched. In the aftermath, policymakers tussled over possible reasons for the unrest with all the determination of looters competing for a crate of designer trainers. 'The riots weren't about protest, unemployment or cuts. They weren't about the future, about tomorrow and a person's place in the world. They were about today, about now,' averred Conservative Home Secretary Theresa May. 'They were about instant gratification.' She quoted a rioter. '"It wasn't political, it was shopping."'[6]

Local Tottenham MP, Labour's David Lammy, standing in the debris, spoke passionately about the suffering caused to ordinary people by the riots, questioning not only the policing that sparked the unrest (police shot and killed a Tottenham resident called Mark Duggan), but also the motivations of the rioters. 'A community that was already hurting has now had the heart ripped out of it. The post office, fitness shop, newsagents, mobile phone shops, council buildings that deal with customer complaints, smashed to pieces by mindless, mindless people.' The Prince offered an interpretation that contrasted with both these schools of thought, seeing not a mob on the rampage but a group of individuals expressing the anguish that he knows from personal experience a lack of direction and identity can cause. 'I still think half the problem is that people join gangs because it is a cry for help, the fact that they're looking for a framework, a sense of belonging, and a meaning,' he said.[7]

Though their off-the-cuff analyses differed, Lammy doesn't resent the Prince's intercession – indeed, he facilitated it. Just days after the riots, Charles and Camilla cut short their summer break at Birkhall to make their initial visit to Tottenham, overriding the warnings of personal protection officers to mingle with crowds. Lammy had invited them after a phone call from the Prince. 'We had quite a bit to do with each other when I was Minister for Culture – he's got this passion for heritage and he discovered that so had I, for different reasons – so he rang and he said: "What can I do?" and I said: "You can come but the key thing is please keep coming back."'[8]

Lammy speaks as he waits in the 639 Enterprise Centre on Tottenham High Road to welcome the Prince on what will be his fourth visit to the borough since the riots. In the intervening period, the Prince's charities have been collaborating with each other and other bodies and agencies to speed Tottenham's recovery and alleviate some of the root causes of the original conflagration. The Blooming Scent café at the centre is run by Gina Moffatt, who set up a floristry business while serving time for drugs smuggling. 'I thought he was my knight in shining armour,' Moffatt told the *Mirror* of the drug dealer who persuaded her to be a mule. 'But he was grooming me for what he wanted.'[9] She found a more reliable knight in the Prince. On her release, with the support of the Prince's Trust she has diversified into cafés and founded further outlets in Tottenham. Another of Charles's charities, Business in the Community, has deployed senior company executives on lengthy secondments from Sainsbury's and Argos to help local businesses get back on their feet; it is one of six of his charities delivering a programme of activities in local schools. Others include the Prince's Foundation for Children and the Arts, his Drawing School, his School for Traditional Arts and his Teaching Institute. His architecture foundation led a community consultation to canvass local views on how to regenerate Tottenham Green, the potential heart of the community, and is working with other agencies to realise the plans that evolved. The Prince's Initiative for Mature Enterprise (PRIME) is running a programme out of Tottenham's Enterprise Centre to mentor over-fifties who want to set up their own business. 'He has come back,' says Lammy. 'No other major national figure has been back as often as he has, and bringing all of his charities. That is commitment and it's an unsung commitment because it's not done with fanfare.'

As the Prince emerges from his car and greets waiting local officials and charity workers like old friends, Lammy says something out of the corner of his mouth. 'That's why we don't want presidents [of Britain]. They'd come once and never again.'[10] The assessment seems to be true of party leaders too. At the time Lammy makes the comment, Cameron and Labour's then leader Ed Miliband have put in a single post-riots appearance in Tottenham apiece. Only the Mayor of London, Boris Johnson, equals the Prince's total.

Lammy describes himself as a 'big, big fan' of the Prince but among Westminster politicians, opinions of Charles, like attitudes to the monarchy, are divided and often deliberately obscure. A noble stud of republican warhorses continues to raise important questions in both Houses. There are almost certainly more republican MPs than the fifteen of the Commons' 650 members who are openly signed up to the campaign group Republic especially since the Scottish National Party won 56 seats in the May 2015 elections. Jeremy Corbyn, who took over as Labour leader four months later drew flack for refusing to sing the national anthem during a memorial service, then quickly gave an interview promising not to abolish the monarchy. Even before approval ratings rose for the Windsors and plummeted for the political classes, republicanism looked a potential vote-loser. In January 2002, Labour MPs secretly convened a meeting to form a republican all-party parliamentary group. Republic's then spokesman Jon Temple told the *Guardian*: 'We had to be covert about the meeting. Republicanism is still one of those iffy areas.'[11] The group lapsed. An initiative to set up a republican group inside the Labour party coinciding with the celebration of the Queen's Diamond Jubilee in 2012 drew criticism from two prominent republicans on Labour benches. There was 'no point stirring it up this year', said Paul Flynn, MP for Newport since 1987. 'You can hold republican views but you respect the current monarch, particularly in this year of all years,' reproved Stephen Pound, since 1997 the MP for Ealing North.[12]

The assumption among Westminster republicans echoes the wider view: the Queen is inviolable; her son and heir is not. 'Some of [the Prince's] ideas are fine, some foolish, and some eccentric. But he cannot keep a lid on them. He suffers from a compulsive urge to influence government,' Flynn complained.[13] John Major demurs. 'He [the Prince] never in my experience overstepped the marks of propriety at all. He would bring to the attention of my Ministers things he thought were worthy of being brought to our attention, and fine. Any citizen in the country can do that but of course you're more likely to see it if it's from the Prince of Wales but I think that's entirely proper.'[14]

Ministers and former Ministers from various eras, the recipients of the Prince's famous black spider memos, paint a more complicated picture. Charles has supporters and critics on the Right and the Left. In their descriptions he often emerges as political, but rarely party political. The Prince 'avoids a simplistic Left-or-Right characterisation. He doesn't go venturing views about tax rates,' says a former Cabinet minister. 'The issues he's chosen – environment, conservation, inner-city renewal, youth – they're not Left or Right issues.'

Serving and former Ministers say conversations with Charles have aided their thinking or given them a new slant on issues. Another former Cabinet Minister found him harmless but faintly comical. A meeting requested by the Prince at Clarence House started badly – Charles wrongly assumed the politician shared his aversion for the juxtaposition of modern and historic buildings; not so said the politician, citing the vibrancy of New York – and slid downhill from there. As they passed a Canaletto depicting a view of St Paul's Cathedral, the politician joked that it would look better with the Gherkin added to the skyline. Charles, usually swift to laugh at jokes as well as crack them, remained stony.

Nicholas Soames issues a stout defence of his friend's dealings with the body politic. 'When I became a Minister, Prince Charles did get in touch with me on official matters. He came back through Hong Kong when we still had a big military presence there and he said: "I think you ought to know ..." and told me something and I was very, very, very grateful to be told. It was something we had not been told and I needed to know,' says Soames. 'There were endless occasions when he wrote to us, never officiously, and said: "I do think that this is causing very considerable difficulty." It was always "difficulty"; it wasn't that he was criticising the government. He was just explaining the consequences of a lot of things that we did that we buggered up.'

Soames leans back in his chair and the skulls on his braces grin a little more widely. 'It's easier to see from his point of view almost than anyone else's. Because people have absolute trust and confidence in him and they talk to him. And from time to time he thinks Ministers ought to know about it. Well, good for him, I say. I don't know a single Minister who minded.'[15] Another former Defence Minister gives a similar account. He says the Prince takes his role as Royal Colonel or Colonel-in-Chief of twenty regiments in Britain and the Realms extremely seriously and that includes speaking up for them. In anonymous interviews for this book, both Labour and Tory grandees spoke up for the Prince.

Charles's intersecting circles of contacts create a Venn diagram that links unlikely bedfellows, from Hollywood to hill-farming communities, poets (Ted Hughes and Kathleen Raine numbered among his close friends) and polo players, the Dalai Lama and Augusto Pinochet. In 1998 the Chilean general was arrested in London where he was recuperating from back surgery; the indictment, issued in Spain, cited multiple human-rights violations under the military dictatorship he imposed on Chile after the overthrow of its elected government in 1973. Lucia Santa Cruz campaigned against Pinochet's detention.

The Prince, says Emma Thompson drily, 'has friends from all political persuasions'. She recalls an evening spent with the Prince and Duchess during Pinochet's involuntarily extended London sojourn. 'We were sitting at dinner, just [Charles] and Camilla and [Thompson's actor husband] Greg [Wise] and me, and she was saying: "I do think you ought to lend Pinochet your plane," and there was a loud snort from HRH who looked over at me and said: "I don't think Em would approve," knowing me to be a raving lefty.'[16]

'There are two very different issues,' says the first former Cabinet Minister, mulling the question of Princely interventions. 'One is a constitutional propriety issue and another is the content of his views. What I think is happening is that those who don't like the contents of his views are alleging constitutional impropriety as a way of undermining the views he holds. Secondly, those who don't like his views present them as wacky. Both the charge of impropriety and the charge of wackiness seem to me to be completely unfounded. I took him seriously and he took me seriously.' The speaker rejects an idea that is central to concerns about the Prince: that he wields disproportionate behind-the-scenes influence because of his royal status. 'There's the issue: does his passion overreach the boundaries of his constitutionally limited role? Well, not if you're a serious Minister because if you're a serious Minister you decide whether you agree with him or not. There's no injunction to agree with him.'

Tony Blair frequently disagreed with Charles. Over two volumes of edited diary extracts, Blair's former communications chief Alastair Campbell detailed the tensions that flared between Prime Minister and Prince over a range of issues. The Prince opposed Labour's proposed ban on fox hunting and gave Blair 'a long paper on hunting and why it was good for the environment'. The Prince's fears that the creation of a European defence force, backed by Blair, would undermine NATO and Britain's special relationship with the United States were leaked to the *Daily Mail*. The Prince expressed reservations to Blair about Britain's rapprochment with China, saying he felt 'very strongly' about China's actions in Tibet; he failed to attend a state banquet for Jiang Zemin. The Prince's aides publicly denied an intended snub towards the Chinese leader but Campbell claims they surreptitiously briefed the opposite and one of the aides – Mark Bolland – backed up that allegation in the court case about the *Mail*'s publication of the Prince's Hong Kong travel journal. The Prince took issue with Labour's handling of the 2001 epidemic of foot-and-mouth disease and sent Blair what Campbell describes as 'about a six-page letter from Prince Charles full of *Daily Telegraph*-speak suggesting it was all down to closed abattoirs, lack of understanding of the countryside, etc'. 'Charles can't resist jumping on the bandwagon,' Blair sighed, in Campbell's account.[17]

The Prince and Blair also tangled, repeatedly, over Blair's promotion of genetically modified crops as a potential solution to global food shortages. Here's Campbell's diary entry for 31 May 1999: 'Prince Charles's office sent through the article he was doing for the *Mail* tomorrow on GM food, which would be a huge hit. He was basically saying we didn't need this stuff at all, and would no doubt have all the pressure groups out saying how marvellous he was. I tried to contact TB but he was playing tennis. I formulated a line that they had sent us the article, we have been calling for a sensible, rational debate and it should be seen in that context. When I finally got round to reading the article in full, it was dreadful. It could easily have been written by the *Mail*. It was clearly going to lead the news tomorrow and I would have to pretend that we were totally unbothered by it. Re-reading it, I felt that it was over the top and it might backfire on Charles. There was a sense of it being gratuitously anti-science from someone whose locus in the debate wasn't clear.'[18]

'It is very hard for people to know who is right,' the Prince had written. 'Few of us are able to interpret all the scientific information which is available – and even the experts don't always agree. But what I believe the public's reaction shows is that instinctively we are nervous about tampering with Nature when we can't be sure that we know enough about all the consequences.'[19]

Each of these examples reflects core characteristics of the Prince's interactions with politics and politicians. His palette of tools includes speeches, signed articles, co-authored books, occasional television documentaries, private conversations and private letters. Additional support for his views comes from his charities and initiatives, with representatives from these organisations arranging meetings and briefings with key figures in government and opposition. On GM as with quite a few other topics, the Prince stands at odds with the Establishment – and in particular the scientific Establishment – but he is closely aligned with public sentiment and environmental pressure groups in his impulse to protect Nature-with-a-capital-N. His contributions to the debate on GM foods almost certainly helped to slow the process of political sign-up to the technology, which is still banned for commercial growing in the UK and must be licensed in other European countries. In Blair's government, at least, he found a quiet ally too. Michael Meacher, Minister of State for the Environment from 1997 to 2003, said: 'There were always tensions in government and I knew that he largely agreed with me and he knew that I largely agreed with him ... We were together in trying to persuade Tony Blair to change course [on GM].'[20]

But on none of the points of conflict with Blair did the Prince prove decisive. There is increasing pressure within government to review the British stance on GM; the uptake elsewhere in the world is considerable, in cultivation by 17 million farmers in twenty-eight countries. The notion of a European defence force foundered amid straitened budgets and rising euroscepsis. The Prince's continued backing for the Dalai Lama occasionally ripples diplomatic waters but has no deep impact on Britain's relations with China, according to Foreign Office assessments. Indeed there is despair among the Dalai Lama's supporters as China's economic muscle trumps human-rights issues in its relations with most world governments. In August 2014, William opened the Dickson Poon University of Oxford China Centre, a facility dedicated to the study of China. (Kate, due to attend as well, cried off at the last minute, precipitating an announcement by Kensington Palace that she was expecting a second child.) William also travelled to China in February 2015 to promote UK–China relations helping, said the *Mail on Sunday*, to 'repair the damage caused by Prince Charles's diary description of Chinese officials as "appalling old waxworks".'[21] He charmed his hosts into giving him a slot on Chinese TV to highlight his concerns over illegal wildlife trade.

On foot-and-mouth Charles failed in his advocacy for vaccinating herds rather than slaughtering them. It turns out he had been a comparatively recent convert to the idea. 'He used to say to me: "I can't understand why you waste your life on vaccines," and I said: "Well, I don't regard it as a waste, sir. I used to make a lot of vaccines,"' says William Castell. 'And then we had the foot-and-mouth disease outbreak and eventually I got him briefed. I used to run seven foot-and-mouth disease vaccine factories around the world and I got my experts over and I sent them into Number Ten and I sent them to see the Prince and he eventually became supportive of a different approach to leaving the cattle on the land just lying there as carcasses.'[22] The Prince continues to try to help the farmers still recovering from the crisis. His Campaign for Wool is one manifestation of that concern.

'I think people generally feel that we're not getting leadership from politicians because we all feel they're doing deals and saying what we want them to say because then they'll get into power,' says one of the Prince's informal advisers. 'With [the Prince], whether you agree with him or not, this is a person who's got views, who's full of conviction – I don't want to compare him to [UKIP leader] Nigel Farage, but I think people felt "at least this person is saying what he believes" and with Prince Charles you know where you stand with him. Probably because we all know him so well now, we all know how he would react to something almost before it's happened. We know which causes, the unpopular, the unfashionable, you know those things he's always going to try and champion.'

'I want to make it clear that I always found my discussions and correspondence with Prince Charles immensely helpful,' protested Blair in a letter to the *Guardian* after the newspaper serialised Campbell's diaries. 'I thought he had a perfect right to raise questions and did so in a way that was both informative and insightful.'[23]

Clarence House's website asserts that 'when issues become a matter for party political debate or the subject of Government policy, the Prince stops raising them publicly'.[24] In practice Charles has snagged his foot in that fox trap more than once. Charles's views, like the brimming emotions Nicholas Soames admires him for restraining, threaten to come spilling out at any moment. People familiar with his letters insist that few would rouse controversy if published, and more because of an urgency of tone rather than their content. It's tough to judge. Over the years only small numbers of spidery memos have crawled into the public domain, a fraction of his voluminous output.

In a documentary profile of the Prince that was aired in 2008, Julia Cleverdon produced six of the memos he had sent to her the previous week. She rifled through a folder, describing each of the missives in turn: 'One about digging up the roads, what was [energy company] EDF doing about it; one about cause-related marketing for hill farmers; one about small abattoirs; one about Islam and the environment; one about a marvellous project going on in Middlesbrough where they're growing vegetables in public spaces; one about de-radicalising extremist prisoners.' She reads from a memo: '"Forgive me mentioning this, but do you think we could find a way of tackling the supermarkets again over the whole issue of plastic bags and plastic wrapping. I know that M&S under Stuart Rose is doing its best, but [it's] still not enough. However the others: are they doing anything more? Can you send me a note about who's doing what best?"' Cleverdon laughs. 'Pages and pages and pages.'[25]

The disparate subject range is typical of Charles and explains his reputation for dilettantism among people who have not read his manifesto, *Harmony* – and that's most people, not least thanks to the determination in some corners of Clarence House to keep the book as far below the radar as possible. *Harmony* makes clear that for the Prince there is a thread – a 'golden thread of ancient understanding' – that connects apparently unrelated areas of activity, winding through his concerns about Islam, slaughterhouses, carrots, fundamentalism and shopping bags. His philosophy, its roots and surprising conclusions are dissected in later chapters.

When the Freedom of Information Act (FOIA) came into effect in 2005, the *Guardian*'s then editor Alan Rusbridger asked the journalist Rob Evans to see if he could use the legislation to get sight of the heir to the throne's correspondence with Ministers. 'Either the monarchy doesn't matter in the sense that it doesn't have an active role in influencing things in policy or politics, in which case you can make an argument for it in one set of terms – a tourist attraction, stability, continuity, a sort of head of state that is above politics. I can see the value of all of that but that does rather depend on [the royals] just being ceremonial. If you then have somebody who is number two who is deeply interested in having an influence on politics then that seems to me to change the deal,' says Rusbridger. 'Or if you want to have a monarchy that is entitled to interfere because they're such brilliant people and they have a unique perspective on the world then we have to have that debate too.'[26]

As a young reporter, Rusbridger had reluctantly filed stories about Charles and Diana's Australian trip to the *Guardian*. As editor of the *Guardian*, he expanded the newspaper's royal coverage. 'There came a moment when we were discussing what we thought of the royals in general and there was a feeling that we understood the attraction of the current monarch but felt that the *Guardian* couldn't really support a monarchical system,' he says. 'So we came out as a republican paper. But I thought it was a bit dull just to say we were a republican paper so I wanted to try and find a way that would tackle what was wrong about it, and try and dramatise a bit.'

His first wheeze was to challenge the 1848 Treason Felony Act, still theoretically in force, which made advocating republicanism a criminal offence, punishable by life sentence. Lawyers for the *Guardian* argued that the law was incompatible with the 1998 Human Rights Act, but the House of Lords dismissed the case on the basis that the *Guardian*'s own campaign for a republic hadn't attracted prosecution. The newspaper also looked into mounting an assault on the Act of Settlement on grounds of religious and gender discrimination. The act, passed in 1701 and amended to include Scotland after Union in 1707, not only specifies that the sovereign must be in communion with the Churches of England and Scotland, but that he or she may not be Catholic or married to a Catholic. Until the Commonwealth Realms agreed a change in 2011, the law also favoured male heirs, queue-jumping them ahead of females. 'I got a reporter to go through the list of succession – there's a list of about three hundred and they're all Hapsburgs or Saxe-Coburgs or whatever and half of them are now running car dealerships in Ohio. I was just trying to find someone who would say: "I was denied that job [as monarch] because of my religion or because I'm the wrong sex,"' says Rusbridger.[27] He abandoned that scheme after he couldn't find any far-flung royal progeny to join the *Guardian*'s legal action.

Undaunted, Rusbridger alighted on the Freedom of Information Act as the surest means yet to force open palace blinds and let daylight do for the monarchy what it generally does for Transylvanian blood-suckers. Tony Blair had arrived in Downing Street in 1997 promising 'a new relationship between government and people', founded on transparency and enabled by legislation. The FOIA gave anyone living in the UK the right to apply to public authorities for informa-tion held by those authorities. (Environmental information held by authorities is covered by a similar protocol, the EIR.) The authorities in question must comply where possible but can refuse if to do so would cost too much, if the request is 'vexatious' or repeated, or is covered by exemptions – for example, if releasing the information might prejudice a criminal trial, damage commercial interests or compromise the privacy of individuals.

Blair came to regret the FOIA. 'It's not practical for government,' he told an interviewer. 'If you are trying to take a difficult decision and you're weighing up the pros and cons, you have frank conversa-tions. Everybody knows this in their walk of life. Whether you are in business – or running a newspaper – there are conversations you want to have preliminary to taking a decision that are frank. And if those conversations then are put out in a published form that afterwards are liable to be highlighted in particular ways, you are going to be very cautious.'[28] In his autobiography, he complained the most avid users of the legislation were not 'the people' but only one slice of people, journalists. 'For political leaders, it's like saying to someone who is hitting you over the head with a stick: "Hey, try this instead," and handing them a mallet. The information is neither sought because the journalist is curious to know, nor given to bestow knowledge on "the people". It's used as a weapon.'[29]

The political classes felt the mallet early and hard after journalists lodged requests for details of parliamentarians' expenses claims. The authorities tried to block access but a series of appeals – and a whole-sale leak of data to the Telegraph group – revealed eye-popping examples of the non-essential goods and services some politicians had sought to charge to the taxpayer (a 'floating duck island' for a garden pond! A glittery toilet seat! Soft-core porn movies!) Five MPs and two members of the House of Lords served jail terms as a result of such revelations; many more stood accused not of any criminality but of showing themselves to be penny wise, politically foolish.

Meanwhile Rob Evans lodged a request to view correspondence between Charles and seven government departments covering an eight-month period in 2004–05. In its original form, the act excluded communications with the royals from general access, but did make provision for a public-interest test. An amendment in 2010 granted an absolute exemption to communications with the Queen, Charles and William and any correspondence about conferring knighthoods and other honours. The exemption is valid for twenty years from the creation of any letter or document or five years from the death of its author. It does not apply in Scotland.

The change came too late to stop the *Guardian*'s legal team from making progress, winning a 2012 appeal to the Upper Tribunal.

Later the same year, then Attorney General Dominic Grieve vetoed that ruling. In his judgement, Grieve argued that the Prince's 'advocacy letters' were part of his preparation for kingship. But Grieve added a startling paragraph: 'It is highly important that [the Prince] is not considered by the public to favour one political party or another. This risk will arise if, through these letters, the Prince of Wales was viewed by others as disagreeing with government policy. Any such perception would be seriously damaging to his role as future monarch, because if he forfeits his position of political neutrality as heir to the throne, he cannot easily recover it when he is king.'[30]

The ruling achieved a rare first, uniting the *Guardian* and Clarence House, albeit in outrage. The *Guardian* appealed. The Prince's aides privately seethed at Grieve's wording, which far from protecting the Prince implied he is not only political (as undoubtedly he is), but partisan. Grieve 'appeared to suggest a greater degree of sex appeal in the correspondence than actually existed, to put it mildly', says one Clarence House insider: 'The Prince of Wales's style is faultlessly courteous and much of what he writes makes generous use of conditionals.' That point was proved when the Supreme Court in March 2015 decided in favour of the *Guardian*, triggering the release of 44 partially redacted black spider memos, with the Scottish government releasing extracts from a further six. 'I particularly hope that the illegal fishing of the Patagonian Toothfish will be high on your list of priorities because until that trade is stopped, there is little hope for the poor old albatross, for which I shall continue to campaign,' Charles had written to the Secretary of State for the Environment in 2004.

Greater transparency is clearly in the public interest if it results in exposing the abuse of a lax expenses regimen or clarifies how a constitutional monarchy should interact with the legislature. But the greater transparency that is the logical response to a draining of trust does not reliably restore trust. When President Obama published his birth certificate to disprove reports that he had been born outside the US – a circumstance that would have invalidated his election to the White House – conspiracy theorists collectively known as 'birthers' retorted that the certificate had been faked; a strain of twenty-first-century America is as wilfully gullible as the seventeenth-century Britons who fell for the propaganda yarn that a baby had been smuggled into the palace in a warming pan to replace the dead infant Prince of Wales.

These days such a story would have spread irresistibly and globally on social media. There would be few trusted voices to puncture it because there are fewer trusted institutions than ever. Voters watch the national and local governments they elect floundering in the face of international forces and trying to spin their way back to popularity. Scandals have eroded faith in the political classes to act for the public good. Watergate marked the end of American innocence and most countries have experienced their own Watergates. In Britain during the 1990s some parliamentarians turned out to have accepted fees for asking questions. Disclosures during Blair's government that 'intelligence' ahead of the 2003 invasion of Iraq had been souped up proved more damaging still. Then came the expenses scandal. A majority of UK voters say that politicians never tell the truth. People don't have much faith in the media to do so either. The 2013 British Social Attitudes survey revealed a slump in approval for the way journalism is carried out, from 53 per cent in 1983 to 27 per cent, a trend the researchers presumed to be exacerbated by the phone-hacking scandal that in 2011 killed off the *News of the World* and spawned a series of investigations and criminal prosecutions.[31]

The practice came to light with the arrest in 2006 of Clive Goodman, the royal editor of the *News of the World*, and a private investigator, Glenn Mulcaire, on retainer to the tabloid. Goodman had published a series of scoops about the young royals in the Blackadder column (proud motto: 'Your snake in the grass of the rich and powerful'). His predecessor as Blackadder was Mark Bolland, whose time working for Charles and Camilla furnished him with deep and wide contacts. Goodman's links weren't quite so lofty. He gained a second pseudonym among colleagues, 'the eternal flame', because he never seemed to go out, instead turning up items for the column from his desk.

The titbits seemed innocuous enough, but contained information only a small number of people could have known. 'Royal action man Prince William has had to postpone a mountain rescue course – after being crocked by a 10-year-old during football training,' Goodman reported in November 2005, attributing the story to an anonymous 'pal', who had apparently divulged the circumstances of William's injury and details of his treatment, observing: 'The really important thing is that his leg heals before he starts Sandhurst in January. He doesn't want to inherit Prince Harry's nickname, Sicknote.'[32]Another item later the same month revealed that William planned to borrow a portable editing suite from Tom Bradby, then ITV's royal editor and later the correspondent invited to interview William and Kate on their engagement. The royals and their aides conferred with Bradby to try to work out who was leaking. They quickly suspected that Goodman must have access to messages left on their mobiles. Police asked the presumed targets not to do anything that might alert Goodman that he had been rumbled, but to collate evidence against him. It wasn't hard to do. One hacking victim shakes his head with residual disbelief, remembering that Goodman frequently quoted wholesale from messages, without any efforts to disguise the wording.

'Shame-faced Prince Harry has been given a furious dressing-down by [then girlfriend] Chelsy Davy over his late-night antics in a lapdancing bar ... Yesterday the repentant prince took an ear-bashing call as news broke,' read a story, jointly bylined with the *News of the World*'s chief reporter Neville Thurlbeck. "'It's Chelsy. How could you? I see you had a lovely time without me. But I miss you so much, you big ginger, and I want you to know I love you," said a hysterical voice. Luckily the caller was joker brother, Prince William.'[33]

At the beginning of 2007, Goodman and Mulcaire received custodial sentences and *News of the World* editor, Andy Coulson, stepped down. A Rubicon in royal reporting had been crossed, but this didn't look to be a breach on the scale of any of the 'gates – certainly no Watergate, but not a Squidgygate or Camillagate either. The hacking victims emerged with reputations intact, the monarchy appeared unscathed and the culprits had been identified and dealt with. Mobile hacking required little technical expertise; messages could be accessed remotely by dialling the number when the mobile was in use or switched off and inputting a pin code. Many users failed to change their default pin codes and if they did, a clever blagger could persuade the phone company to return the codes to factory settings.

But the initial police investigation had actually uncovered evidence pointing to a much wider pattern of hacking. The authorities chose not to pursue these leads. The decision left a much larger malignancy that may have gone undetected but for the arrival in Downing Street in May 2010 of Conservative Prime Minister, David Cameron, bringing as his Director of Communications Andy Coulson. Coulson's appointment stoked the determination of the *Guardian* and other news organisations to investigate what else may have gone on during his tenure as *News of the World* editor. In January of 2011 amid a flurry of fresh allegations, Coulson quit, saying: 'When the spokesman needs a spokesman it's time to move on.'

If the sense that the Establishment colludes to cover up uncomfortable truths is pervasive, that is because the Establishment, in its different incarnations, so often appears to do just that. The excavations continued, laying bare the infrastructure of interlocking institutions and natural class allegiances. The Metropolitan Police press office employed former News International staffers; the News International titles, including the *News of the World*, employed serving or former police officers as columnists. Rebekah Brooks, who worked her way up through the News International ranks to the editorships of the *News of the World* and the *Sun* before taking the throne as the company's Chief Executive, had even enjoyed the use of a retired police horse, called Raisa. Brooks returned the nag 'in a poor but not serious condition' after two years, according to Scotland Yard. 'The horse was subsequently re-housed with a police officer in 2010, and later died of natural causes.'[34]

Raisa rested in peace. The story did not. The Prime Minister would eventually end mounting speculation with an admission: he had ridden the horse as a guest of Brooks and her husband, his close friends and country-home neighbours. 'I am very sorry to hear that Raisa is no longer with us and I think I should probably conclude by saying I don't think I will be getting back into the saddle any time soon,' said Cameron.

Such details provoked mirth. Others roused concern, even revulsion. The *News of the World* had hacked phone messages left for a murdered thirteen-year-old schoolgirl called Milly Dowler. Until that moment, hacking to most people seemed a victimless crime, impacting only inhabitants of the human zoo already dehumanised by fame: them, not us. Mass-market newspapers position themselves as the voices of ordinary Britons. In targeting Milly Dowler, the *News of the World* shredded that illusion and severed its bond with its readers. The backlash gained extra force from a rare mistake in the *Guardian*'s sharp reporting, alleging that the hackers deleted some of the messages, giving Dowler's parents false hope that she was still alive.

Rupert Murdoch shuttered the newspaper (later replacing it with the *Sun on Sunday*) and embarked on damage limitation. His guillotine fell too late to protect his British operations (renamed News UK since 2013) and other media organisations from the kinds of scrutiny they more regularly dole out. Three separate police investigations into phone hacking, computer hacking and bribery of public officials played out in the courts. On the 138th day of the trial, Coulson was found guilty of conspiracy to hack phones. Brooks and the other defendants were cleared of all charges. She returned to her role as Chief Executive of News UK in September 2015.

The judge-led Leveson Inquiry separately devoted seventy-two days to examining the context of the hacking and the wider culture and practices of the press, to the outrage of some witnesses brought before its inquisitors. 'Let's keep all this in proportion,' said Paul Dacre, Editor of the *Daily Mail* and Editor-in-Chief of publisher Associated Newspapers about the scandal that precipitated his grudging attendance. 'Britain's cities weren't looted as a result. No one died. The banks didn't collapse because of the *News of the World*. Elected politicians continued to steal from the people they were paid to represent. The nation didn't go to war. Yet the response has been a judicial inquiry with greater powers than those possessed by the public inquiries into the Iraq war.' Dacre continued, his complexion growing as florid as his prose. 'Indeed, am I alone in detecting the rank smells of hypocrisy and revenge in the political class's current moral indignation over a British press that dared to expose their greed and corruption – the same political class, incidentally, that, until a few weeks ago, had spent years indulging in sickening genuflection to the Murdoch press?'[35]

Dacre's diatribe illuminated in a few sentences the dysfunction the inquiry so laboriously sought to understand. He also undermined his own argument. The relationships at the core of the British Establishment have corroded into abusive co-dependencies, weakening each element. The nation didn't go to war but it is at war with itself. Every successive scandal – whether about parliamentary expenses or hacking or the failure of the BBC and the police to pursue complaints against Jimmy Savile – confirms public cynicism.

The press, no longer trusted to regulate itself, is trading blows over the legitimacy of IPSO, the successor to the PCC. There's agreement on one point: that politicians can't be counted on to protect valuable freedoms. If doubts remained about the duplicity of the state, the combined efforts of Wikileaks and Chelsea née Bradley Manning and Edward Snowden in making public reams of classified material that often showed governments doing one thing and saying another have blown them away.

Since nobody can be trusted, nobody can be trusted. Or as Piers Morgan, former Editor of the *News of the World* and the *Mirror*, says in a documentary about Diana's inquest: 'When you have the head of the British security services calmly announcing: "We have never killed anybody in the last fifty years," I laughed out loud. What's the point of them then? We've all been to James Bond movies, thanks. We know the British security services do a lot of dark stuff so the idea that we're supposed to believe that in fifty years British agents haven't killed anyone, I don't believe it. So if you don't believe that, where does that leave the rest of the Establishment evidence?'[36] This is a world in which James Bond commands more faith than his real-life counterparts.

In this same world just a handful of institutions retains any significant credibility: in Britain they are the National Health Service, trades unions and the monarchy, a strange, anachronistic construct of pomp and flummery.[37] The government spent more than £400,000 in legal fees trying to stop the public from getting to know more about the man who is set to lead the last and oldest of these.[38] What made the battle over the black spiders even odder is that Charles has been spreading his views for years, vigorously.

Chapter 8

Architecture of Controversy

The Prince often prompts debate. Sometimes he simply overpowers.

Peter Ahrends lives in a lovely Georgian town house in London, and at first that seems funny, because in conversation at Birkhall, Charles has said that he imagines modernist architects live in nice eighteenth-century houses.[1] Yet Ahrends is hardly the heartless ideologue the Prince's supposition entails, surrounded by beauty and comfort while foisting soulless rat runs of plate glass and concrete on the masses. The architect and the cat that shares his home both conduct themselves with the caution of the elderly to whom life has not always been kind. When Ahrends arrived in Britain as an eighteen-year-old, he had already experienced Nazi Germany as the son of a Jewish father and, after emigrating to South Africa, the first dismal clench of apartheid. Yet it would be a run-in with the Establishment of his adopted homeland – and especially with the heir to its throne – that left the most obvious bruises.

After qualifying as an architect, Ahrends founded the practice ABK with two friends, Richard Burton and Paul Koralek, tapping into the optimism of the post-war period that had seen the creation of new British institutions such as the National Health Service, and on the southern bank of the Thames the Royal Festival Hall and other modernist structures commissioned for the 1951 Festival of Britain 'to celebrate and to build hope for the building of a new Britain in a changed world'.[2] To idealistic architects, modernism's break from the past represented the possibility of a better future. The Prince saw only ugliness in the transformation of British landscapes in the name of progress. 'I couldn't bear the physical aspect of destroying town centres and historical places, digging up all the hedgerows, cutting down trees, making terrifying prairies covered in chemicals. All that stuff. I thought this was insanity,' he says.[3]

Ahrends suggests another underpinning to the Prince's reaction. The royal family, he muses, 'must be conserving of their position of that fundamental structure of monarchy in relation to the political scene that Parliament enacts and to that extent it's almost impossible to envisage that Charles could have a view other than the one he occupies' which Ahrends characterises as 'wanting the past to go on being represented through the idioms that history tells you were prevalent in earlier times'. There is more than an element of truth to that, but the sadness of the conflict that pitted Ahrends against the Prince is that both men always had the best of intentions.

To a Prince immersed in the aesthetic of palaces and accustomed to finding solace from his own unhappiness in wide open spaces, tower blocks looked like penal colonies in which the clients of the Prince's Trust had been condemned to serve life sentences. His involvement with inner-city charities took him to sink estates; he saw few examples of good modern architecture and he anyway carries ideological baggage alongside his cushion and other homely comforts. A later section of the book explores the Prince's religious and spiritual beliefs and his philosophy of harmony, which, ironically, has created the greatest disharmonies in his life, seeming to pit him against entire professions. It explains his unyielding opposition to modernism, which rejects tenets that he holds not only dear but sacred. 'It is a sad fact that our modern outlook does not recognise geometry as a language by which we may understand Divine order

... It is humanity that has always embedded this geometry in the world's greatest works of art and architecture, simply because we resonate with these hidden patterns,' he observes in the foreword to a book by Keith Critchlow, Professor Emeritus at the Prince's School of Traditional Arts and co-founder of Temenos, an association promulgating the teaching of 'perennial wisdom' and a key source of the Prince's thinking.[4] Charles is often misunderstood as someone wedded to classicism, but for him this question goes far deeper than questions of style. Modernist buildings, to someone who believes in perennialism and sacred geometry, are not just unlovely but profane.

In the 1970s, Charles's ideas were only just beginning to find shape as Britain's economic decline slowed its building boom, restricting the funds that had flowed into the construction of state institutions and social housing. When Margaret Thatcher came to power at the end of the decade, promoting free-market economics and privatising large segments of the public sector, architects had to become entrepreneurs, forging commercial relationships with developers to get things built. Even without the Prince's influence, that would have meant fewer radical designs and more crowd pleasers and dull post-modernist frontages, offensive only in their desire to offend nobody. Thatcher's deregulation of the City of London provided some opportunities for landmark new buildings such as Richard Rogers's Lloyds of London headquarters, but large-scale public-sector building projects dried up. Even the planned extension to the National Gallery, a grand nineteenth-century building with a soaring portico entrance on the north side of London's Trafalgar Square, had to rely on commercial funding. To make the scheme work, architects – jousting for the contract in a public competition and eventually whittled down to a shortlist of six firms – had to squeeze enough office space into their plans to make the scheme profitable as well as allocating sufficient room for the substantial Renaissance collection, all on the limited footprint left when a Second World War German bomb demolished a furniture store next to the gallery.

Rogers submitted a futuristic design that was voted both most popular and least popular by the public and drew a compliment from Owen Luder, then President of the Royal Institute of British Architects (RIBA). It was, said Luder, 'the work of a man who has said "this is what I think the answer is and sod you!"'[5] Both the comment and the design reinforced a sense among the public – and in palaces – of a profession primed to bang on and never to listen.

The concept delivered by Ahrends and his partners proved less controversial, securing nearly as many votes in favour as Rogers's but with fewer against, and convincing the judges – who included representatives of the National Gallery and of the government's Property Services Agency – to award ABK and the developer Trafalgar House the contract, subject to alterations and final approvals. The design went through several iterations as the architects took on board the wishes of the client, adding to the gallery space at the expense of some of the elegance of the original concept. A circular courtyard, echoing the circular space next to Admiralty Arch at the other end of Trafalgar Square, became too constricted; the exterior looked heavier. Eventually, despite reservations which Ahrends had detected on the part of some trustees, the gallery approved the plans, submitted a planning proposal and opened the scheme to public enquiry, both routine procedures in such circumstances.

The lead architect of the extension didn't go to Hampton Court for RIBA's 150th anniversary dinner on 17 May 1984 nor did he expect a speech made at the dinner to be the first item on *News at Ten*. Ahrends switched on his television to discover that the Prince had used his keynote address to launch an aerial bombardment on ABK's work. The speech had started conventionally enough, with compliments to Charles Correa, recipient that evening of the Royal Gold Medal for Architecture, and, of course, with a joke, not one of the Prince's better efforts. 'It would seem that sesquicentenaries are coming thick and fast nowadays. Last year I was invited to become President of the British Medical

Association for its one hundred and fiftieth anniversary and greatly enjoyed holding that particular office,' said the Prince. 'I am enormously relieved, I must say, that you have not asked me to be President of the RIBA this year because while it is comparatively easy to be a practising hypochondriac it is probably much more difficult to become the architectural equivalent.'[6] For many architects, the speech proved him to be a more dangerous phenomenon than a malingerer or bed-blocker; like an untrained fantasist scrubbing up and preparing to operate on a patient, the Prince had come to excise the malignancies he perceived in their profession.

He took a turn into territory now familiar but startling to his audience and horrifying to Ahrends as the television news recapped its loudest passages. Charles tore into architects and planners who failed to consult sufficiently before imposing buildings on communities or neglected to pay sufficient heed to disabled access; he bemoaned the tendency to tear down old buildings rather than rehabilitating them; he complained that architects too often preferred modern styles over traditional; all, but for the last complaint, fair points well made. From there, it was but a short hop to the key note of his keynote: the damage inflicted on London in his view by modern – and in particular modernist – buildings pitched next to old ones.

'It is hard to imagine that London before the last war must have had one of the most beautiful skylines of any great city, if those who recall it are to be believed. Those who do, say that the affinity between buildings and the earth, in spite of the city's immense size, was so close and organic that the houses looked almost as though they had grown out of the earth and had not been imposed upon it – grown, moreover, in such a way that as few trees as possible were thrust out of the way,' he said. 'Those who knew it then and loved it, as so many British love Venice without concrete stumps and glass towers, and those who can imagine what it was like, must associate with the sentiments in one of Aldous Huxley's earliest and most successful novels, *Antic Hay*, where the main character, an unsuccessful architect, reveals a model of London as Christopher Wren wanted to rebuild it after the Great Fire, and describes how Wren was so obsessed with the opportunity the fire gave the city to rebuild itself into a greater and more glorious vision.'

The Prince was working himself up to a pitch. 'What, then, are we doing to our capital city now? What have we done to it since the bombing during the war? What are we shortly to do to one of its most famous areas – Trafalgar Square? Instead of designing an extension to the elegant facade of the National Gallery which complements it and continues the concept of columns and domes, it looks as if we may be presented with a kind of municipal fire station, complete with the sort of tower that contains the siren. I would understand better this type of high-tech approach if you demolished the whole of Trafalgar Square and started again with a single architect responsible for the entire layout, but what is proposed is like a monstrous carbuncle on the face of a much-loved and elegant friend.'

With another flourish of rhetorical questions and a few more sideswipes, the Prince reached his ungracious conclusion. 'Goethe once said: "There is nothing more dreadful than imagination without taste." In this one hundred and fiftieth anniversary year, which provides an opportunity for a fresh look at the path ahead and in which by now you are probably regretting having asked me to take part, may I express the earnest hope that the next hundred and fifty years will see a new harmony between imagination and taste and in the relationship between the architects and the people of this country.'[7] With one speech, he roiled that relationship and in trying to lay the foundations of a pantheon of useful ideas about British architecture planted the cornerstone of a coliseum of miscommunication.

When Ahrends attended a scheduled breakfast the next morning with Trafalgar House, he believed the extension could be saved.

He was still too much of a foreigner, he says, to understand the power of monarchy. The developers put him right. They knew the scheme was effectively dead, even though the planning application continued to grind on until then Secretary of State for the Environment, Patrick Jenkin, delivered a final *coup de grâce* some months later.

Ahrends met Charles around the same time, first as his guest at a dinner held by the Prince to discuss architecture and then when his royal nemesis accepted ABK's invitation to 'a perfectly nice lunch, well-cooked salmon and salad' at the firm's office. 'We had a mews office surrounded by early- to mid-Victorian houses and journalists had found their way into these houses with suitable lenses,' Ahrends recalls. 'On the way out of the lunch, which was a bit extended – we talked a while about his position and our position – and on the way out he turned to us and he said: "I'm sorry it had to be you." Well, I thought to myself afterwards, why did it have to be us?' ABK was struggling. 'The practice suffered enormously,' Ahrends says quietly. 'It was a battle to survive.'[8]

Other practices felt the chill too. The Prince had helped to speed a climate change that meant planners could be expected to favour safe options over statement buildings. When the National Gallery finally got its extension – the Sainsbury Wing opened in 1991 – it was an undistinguished postmodern lump by architects Venturi, Scott Brown, selected over more interesting contenders during a second competition. Peter Davey, editor of the *Architectural Review*, called it 'picturesque, mediocre slime'. 'I am rather pleased, I must say, with the result,' said Charles, by this stage a trustee of the Gallery (he served as trustee from 1986 to 1993). 'It hasn't produced a rather raucous young person standing beside [the old] saying, "Look how old and wrinkled you are", so to speak.'[9]

He had not only stimulated discussion around important issues, but polarised the debate so sharply that some of these issues were submerged in rancour, especially as he continued to make inflammatory speeches. 'You have, ladies and gentlemen, to give this much to the Luftwaffe,' he told a Mansion House dinner in 1987. 'When it knocked down our buildings, it didn't replace them with anything more offensive than rubble. We did that.'[10] The specific target of that speech, a scheme by Richard Rogers for the redevelopment of Paternoster Square, next to St Paul's, bit the dust. The architect John Simpson came up with an alternative classicist masterplan, a lively pastiche with multiple shop frontages to leaven the dead weight of office buildings, supported by the Prince and the public but without developer backing. After the site changed hands, the new owners opted for a third design, influenced by Simpson but without the positives of Simpson's vision, the humdrum product of too many compromises.

Another planned development by Rogers – Lord Rogers since 1996 – for Chelsea Barracks caught the Prince's attention and, as Charles wrote in a letter to Sheikh Hamad bin Jassim bin Jabr Al-Thani, the head of the Qatar Investment Authority and its property arm Qatari Diar, made his heart sink. The letter emerged in 2010 during a bust-up between developers Christian and Nick Candy and the management of Qatari Diar, in partnership to build high-density accommodation on former Ministry of Defence land along the Thames Embankment in Chelsea. After the Qataris withdrew the planning application for the Rogers scheme, the Candy brothers sued for breach of contract, blaming the Prince's intervention for the Qataris' change of heart.

Lawyers revealed the full content of the Prince's letter in court. It began with an apology: 'I hope you will forgive me for writing but I only do so because of a particular concern for the future of the capital city of this country. For the entire duration of my life we have had to witness the destruction of so many parts of London, with one more "Brutalist" development after another. This gigantic experiment with the very soul of our capital city – and with many others in the UK and elsewhere – has reached the point where it is no longer sustainable in our day and age particularly in view of the immense challenges the world faces.' He urged the Sheikh to consider alternative plans drawn up by one of his favourite classicist architects, Quinlan Terry, and urged a collaboration with his own architecture foundation to achieve a 'timeless approach' that 'enhances all those qualities of neighbourliness, community, human-scale, proportion, and, dare I say it, "old-fashioned" beauty'.[11]

The author of these rococo phrases remains unrepentant. 'It just seemed to me that you have to start drawing lines in the sand about how much London is going to be mucked about with,' he said. 'I'd seen some of the plans and I thought, this seems insane. I just wrote a letter – a confidential letter to somebody I happen to know. I didn't do anything in public. It only came into play when they, for some reason or other, leaked my letter. Frequently, I've written letters to people that they pay no attention to at all.'[12]

The Prince's communications channels with Middle Eastern royals, so keenly appreciated by the Foreign Office, had again proved their efficacy. Dominic Richards, former Executive Director of the Prince's Foundation for Building Community, reckons his boss was more catalyst than sledgehammer: 'I think it was a confluence of the Prince saying what most people thought and the Qataris not wanting to do something so brutal in the heart of London that would have been a ghetto for rich people.' Richards, engaging and floppy-haired, is sitting with Hank Dittmar, a dapper American, former White House adviser on transport and sustainability and director of organisations promoting public transit and walkable cities, and at the time of the conversation joint head with Richards of the Foundation. 'Lord Rogers was [Labour Deputy Prime Minister] John Prescott's adviser on the built environment, he was [Labour Mayor of London] Ken Livingstone's adviser on the built environment, he vetted most commissions in London for fifteen to twenty years,' says Dittmar. 'So who's the Establishment here?' chimes Richards.[13] Lord Rogers continues to seethe. 'The prince always goes round the back to wield his influence, using phone calls or in the case of the Chelsea barracks, a private letter. It is an abuse of power because he is not willing to debate,' he said.[14]

That's not quite accurate – Charles often convenes architects for discussions and dares to beard lions in their dens, as he showed by accepting ABK's invitation to lunch. What he doesn't do is debate publicly, maintaining traditions of palace media management that make better sense for some models of royalty than others. The result has been a form of asymmetrical warfare between some strands of architecture and the royal knight errant. As for the wider impact on British cities, that has been mixed: on the debit side, less daring and more mediocrity of new build, but some positives too.

Good ideas promoted by the Prince have gone on to become mainstream: sustainability in design, better attention to the public-health impacts of town planning. Planning authorities give preference to schemes that mingle income groups, 'pepper-potting' social tenants and others on lower incomes with the wealthy, a practice Charles has long championed. He has also argued for more interactive planning processes. In 2011, the government signed off on the Localism Act and new planning guidelines both incorporating key ideas and practice promoted by his Foundation, especially through the concept of neighbourhood planning under which planning authorities must support neighbourhoods that wish to pursue their own development plans. More than 800 such plans are in process around the country. 'My experience is if you sit down with people, local people who don't normally get sat down with, you get a remarkable consensus outlook, which frequently revolves around reintroducing local identity and tradition and human scale,' says the Prince.[15]

Architects accuse the Prince of being overbearing. He throws the accusation back at them. Architect Ewen Miller is willing to agree that his profession can be too arrogant. 'There's little or no listening; you will have my building, and the fact you're going to live in it, you should be grateful,' he says.[16] But he is no fan of Charles and expected to be infuriated by the Prince's second RIBA speech, in 2009, this one marking the institution's 175th anniversary. 'I sat down with a glass of wine ready to throw it at the telly and start shouting,' says Miller. 'I was quite upset that he really started to make a lot of sense … What engaged me was that he was encouraging architects to engage with people and communities and listen to what they need and to guide them. I thought, oh crikey, I've judged him too harshly.'[17]

The problem for many architects – and for them the fatal flaw in the Prince's approach to architecture – is that his philosophy of harmony makes him conflate really important ideas about what makes buildings and towns liveable with narrow definitions of beauty. His highest term of praise is 'timeless', yet many of the buildings he lauds would have looked aggressively modern in their own eras. 'It's when [the Prince] starts to engage in stylistic argument, that's when I struggle,' says Miller. 'Good architecture should be good architecture whether it's an Arts and Crafts revival building, a Classical revival building or a glass box on the side of a cliff. Good architecture should transcend the style debate.'[18]

If anyone should have a beef with the Prince, it's Miller, whose only project linked with him – Poundbury's fire station – won a place on the shortlist for the least coveted of architectural awards, *Building Design* magazine's Carbuncle Cup, 'architecture's only prize for sheer downright ugliness'.[19]

Poundbury is what happened when the Prince decided that his speeches and articles and books and documentaries and letters and conversations were not enough. In his 1988 documentary and 1989 book – both entitled *A Vision of Britain* – Charles had fleshed out his thoughts about what makes for good and bad buildings and towns, and inserted more than a few jibes against anticipated criticism. 'For those readers who may happen to be professional architects, I dare say my expressed views have merely confirmed the opinion of those critics who say that since I have no professional training in archi-tecture I should not be voicing my views so publicly,' he correctly surmised, following up with a sentence that showed a lack of under-standing for the concept of the democratic mandate. 'The trouble with that particular criticism is that if you develop it logically, you will find it precludes most politicians fr om expressing their views on most subjects.'[20] But, he asserts, in the planning and commissioning of new buildings and larger developments, 'we *can* do better. Our fellow citizens are demanding we do better. It is up to developers, the architects, the planners and the politicians to respond.'[21] And, he might have added, 'princes'. By creating on Duchy of Cornwall land an urban extension to Dorchester, he built a real community and a test bed for principles of community architecture.

The best-looking buildings in Poundbury are pretty cottages and a row of four white Arts and Crafts-inspired houses. 'We're not striving for iconic architecture; we're striving for ordinary buildings and most buildings in a neighbourhood are background buildings,' says Dittmar. 'Most architects are trained to do iconic buildings that say look at me.'[22]

Poundbury's fire station might be accused of a certain look-at-me-ism. It is hard to miss because its form and its function are so bizarrely ill-matched. *Building Design*, explaining the building's Carbuncle Cup nomination, derided 'a collection of pasty sand-coloured brick and inelegant glazing'.[23] The writer and critic Justin McGuirk went further, launching a demolition in the *Guardian* of the 'dumpy neoclassical Georgian palace with three garage doors attached to it. It's the Parthenon meets *Brookside* [a TV soap set in an architecturally monotonous urban close].'[24] The relish with which McGuirk attacks the fire station may not be unconnected to his misplaced belief that the Prince – the very person who had criticised ABK's National Gallery extension for resembling a 'municipal fire station' – had designed Poundbury's pompous pump house. The *Daily*

Mail also ran an article mocking the Prince as the architect of the fire station. As Miller explains, that was not the case.

Nevertheless, everything in Poundbury does bear the Prince's stamp. He selected as master planner Leon Krier, a flamboyant Luxembourgeois, and has worked closely with him on the evolving settlement, though not always in perfect harmony. Jonathan Dimbleby's biography of Charles charts disagreements over Krier's original master plan, not only because accountants at the Duchy of Cornwall judged his 6,000-square-foot family houses too 'heroic in scale' but because the Prince found Krier's neoclassical designs jarring and preferred to aim for a Dorset vernacular.[25] Prince and master planner found a modus vivendi and since then the Prince's distinctive black ink commentaries have often adorned artists' impressions of buildings sent to him by Krier for his input. Their joint vision can be praised or blamed for streetscapes that stray far from Dorset, jumping from Georgian to Gothic, rustic to urban, an eclectic mix that *Building Design* called a 'fruity melee of architectural costumes' – anything, in other words, but modern.[26]

That wide range in theory gave Miller a lot of options to play with as he mulled over a design for Poundbury's fire station that would be in sympathy with existing buildings. In 2006, his practice Calderpeel had taken over another architectural firm that had already won the contract to build the fire station. Miller decided the best solution would be an open-sided barn structure. 'Fire engines are pretty large brutes and therefore require big garage-door openings and it's difficult to make a building look historically accurate when you're making an opening in spans or structures that are physically larger than would have been possible in days gone by with the advent now of concrete and steel structures,' says Miller. Krier accepted the internal design, but not the exterior, which he proceeded to re-imagine as a neoclassical mansion. The result, admits Miller, 'looks a little bit ridiculous. If Leon Krier had his way we'd have taken the appliances out and put in horse-drawn carriages with buckets of water. It's a modern fire station in a modern building that's trying to be an old building. It's always going to struggle with identity.'[27]

Poundbury is the physical manifestation of a struggle with identity and of the tension between the old and the new. 'I've always wanted to bring the baby back – that went out with the bathwater. Out went all sorts of really valuable things,' says the Prince.[28]

In Poundbury, he is attempting to rediscover a lost England of his imagination. The emissary from Planet Windsor arrived on earth with romantic notions about villages and towns that were not just conurbations but communities, self-regulating ecosystems in which residents of different income levels and interests could flourish. Walt Disney had a similar idea. He planned EPCOT in Florida – the acronym stands for Experimental Prototype Community of Tomorrow – as a new town, announcing the scheme at a 1966 press conference. 'It will be a planned, controlled community; a showcase for American industry and research, schools, cultural and educational opportunities,' Disney pledged. 'In EPCOT there will be no slum areas because we won't let them develop. There will be no landowners and therefore no voting control. People will rent houses instead of buying them, and at modest rentals. There will be no retirees because everyone will be employed according to their ability. One of our requirements is that the people who live in EPCOT must help keep it alive.'[29] In the end, EPCOT became a theme park, an annexe to Disneyworld. When Disney Corporation did develop a new town, Celebration in Florida, critics carped about its lack of authenticity. It felt unreal, they said. That's a charge often levelled at the Prince's English experimental prototype community of tomorrow.

That misses the point about Poundbury: it is remarkably pleasant; its residents, who number over 2,000, enjoy living there; in many of its ambitions, Poundbury is successful. Children do play on the village green. People of diverse ages and income levels live and work alongside each other, congregate in its public spaces, take tea in its cafés and walk along peaceful lanes to the shops. 'This is the joy of it,' says John Ivall, a pensioner who moved to Poundbury in 2011. 'You've got everything from people in their late seventies like us to young-sters starting out on life with their first kids and first flat or house, and you've got affordable housing mixed in and honestly you wouldn't know where they were. They've blended in so well.' He and his wife slotted in just as seamlessly. 'We got ourselves into the community very quickly,' Ivall says. 'We got into the events club, we arrange events every month. Another couple that we're very friendly with, they do potlucks there. Potluck suppers every few months. I belong to the Pathfinders and we do long walks every week and I coordinate that so you know we really got ourselves involved.'[30] Are there any downsides? Yes, says Ivall. The idea of mixing business with resi-dential units functions less well in some areas of Poundbury than others. And the gravel used in place of paving stones gets everywhere it shouldn't be. (Poundbury's unseen directors, like the *Truman Show* producers, keep closely in touch with developing narratives and have been quietly retiring the gravel for some time.)

Some of Poundbury's design solutions are innovative rather than old-fashioned. There are no *Brookside*-style closes, the cul-de-sacs popular among the builders of new housing estates that studies suggest foster higher car use. Thoroughfares – all Poundbury roads are through roads – counterintuitively encourage people to walk or cycle because routes are more direct and therefore shorter. Traffic-calming measures in Poundbury are often subliminal and rarely rely on signage.

'First thing I did was shout: "Stop, stop the car. What is that?"' says Tim Knatchbull, describing his initial reaction to one of these measures. 'There was this massive tree in the middle of the road and all the traffic was driving around the tree.' The friend who brought him to Poundbury explained: '"What they found is the tree slows traffic down, it makes people make eye contact with each other, they've cut the accident rate and it's a great success." And we went round the next corner into a square and there was a pub and people making eye contact and there was a factory just beside this pretty row of houses and although there were some things that just seemed wrong to me at first sight, that may have been because they were unusual. In any case I thought: "Wow, I would love to live somewhere like this,"' says Knatchbull.[31]

Though he is a close friend and supporter of the Prince, it was 2005, twelve years after construction started, before Knatchbull finally toured Poundbury. On the death of his grandfather Lord Mountbatten, he had inherited part of the Broadlands estate abutting Romsey in Hampshire and for decades came under pressure from volume house-builders to let them develop housing on the land. He says he felt 'fiercely protective of Romsey when developers started circling', but his sense of civic duty and a request by the local authority to enable an urban extension to the town sent him on a lengthy and depressing search for a sympathetic developer. He rejected one scheme after another, feeling, as the Prince did, that social problems correlated to poor housing and planning might be alleviated by better design, but he scoffed when a friend suggested a fact-finding mission to Poundbury. 'I said: "You've got to be kidding, right? You didn't make that comment seriously, did you?" Because anybody who reads the newspapers knows it's a little nonsensical, neoclassical pastiche that only somebody as influential as the Prince of Wales could possibly bring about.'[32]

Seeing is believing. Knatchbull's Poundbury tour inspired him to begin developing plans at Romsey with regular input from the Prince and in collaboration with Hank Dittmar and the Prince's Foundation for Building Community, which has been changing like an urban skyline. (Dittmar stepped down from the Foundation in 2014, Richards in 2015.) The Prince's vision of the potential of architecture for social good is finding expression across the world. One of the best examples sits close to the heart of metropolitan London.

Highbury Gardens, a housing development north of Highbury Corner in Islington, turns an expressionless face to the traffic and fumes of Holloway Road. Only after you pass through an archway into a courtyard does it begin to impress. The architectural practice Porphyrios Associates has created a bubble of calm in a noisy location, setting two wings of accommodation in a shared green space with the tranquillity of a Japanese garden. Apartments are, of course, pepper-potted, mixing private ownership with part-owned, part-rented flats reserved for key workers such as teachers and with social housing, all finished to the same high standards irrespective of the type of occupancy.

Angela Stephenson loves her flat so much, she says, that: 'When I first saw it, I cried.' A social tenant, born with the bone disorder fibrodysplasia, she was rehoused in Highbury Gardens with her son and daughter in 2011. Shehnaz O'Mallie, teaching media studies at an inner-city comprehensive, says: 'Pretty much everyone I work with lives somewhere that is too small or too expensive.' She and her partner bought 25 per cent of the flat and at the time of the interview in September 2013 had a combined mortgage repayment, rental bill and service charge of around £1,200 per month, reasonable by London's inflated standards, and especially for a spacious flat with views across the city and access to the shared garden. O'Mallie mentions she feels defensive when she sees negative coverage of Charles. 'We've lost quite a lot of faith in public figures,' she says. 'It's nice to have faith in someone.'[33]

The Prince's Foundation for Building Community is enthroned with the Prince's School of Traditional Arts and the Prince's Drawing School in an attractive converted warehouse in Shoreditch, next to a media studio and café and opposite a barber's shop that has styled many a Hoxton fin and trimmed many a hipster beard. Like this part of London, the Foundation has known more than one incarnation, once at the edge of things, but these days at the pulsing heart of discourse. The Prince's Institute of Architecture – the first iteration – opened in 1992, merging with his Urban Villages Forum and Regeneration Through Heritage in 1998 to form the Prince's Foundation for Architecture and the Building Arts and subsequently splitting again to form the drawing and traditional arts schools and the Prince's Foundation for the Built Environment, which was rebranded in 2012 to become the Prince's Foundation for Building Community.

Maps on its website show the extent of its current reach, if not the significant breadth and depth of the Foundation's influence, listing projects on the Galapagos Islands, Rosetown in Jamaica, and locations in China, Haiti and elsewhere. In Britain, the Foundation claims involvement in more than thirty developments; it also operates an educational strand, running courses in planning, sustainable design and traditional crafts that otherwise threaten to become extinct, and it promotes community engagement, convening planners, designers, builders, local authorities, community groups and local and national government officials.

On a drenching day in March 2014 – the polar vortex is still intense – the Foundation brings representatives of all those groups to join the Prince for a symposium and launch of a report, 'Housing London: a mid-rise solution'. 'In London we find ourselves in a situation where the average house price is 10 times the annual salary of a primary school teacher – a huge rise in comparison to just 20 years ago – when the average house price was 2.9 times a primary teacher's annual salary,' says Charles ahead of the event.[34] Price rises threaten to drive the young and those on low and medium incomes out of the capital. Before he moves to the podium, to bring the proceedings to a climax and a conclusion, Dominic Richards tries to explain his then Boss and the 'golden thread' that links his enterprises.

Everything the Prince does 'is about creating a harmonious society', he declares. 'I would like you to welcome His Royal Highness as a true leader.'

The true leader opens his speech with his usual studied diffidence. 'I am finding myself in the utterly unenviable position of the last to speak on the subject, particularly when there are such a distinguished range of experts here. I am afraid I'm not really sure what I can usefully add without being in constant danger of repetition,' says Charles, grimacing comically. 'Although I can promise a cup of tea at the end!'

The speech skitters across his usual preoccupations to focus on the findings of the report, a proposal for a greater provision of high-density, mid-rise blocks with an emphasis on 'walkable, sustainable urbanism'. The inevitable barb is directed not at modernism as such but at over-investment in luxury high-rises.

This is a political speech at a sensitive moment. The symposium comes two days before Mayor Boris Johnson will unveil his own housing strategy to try to tackle London's shortage of affordable housing. Some of the roots of that shortage date back to the creation of a green belt around the city, restricting room to sprawl; other drivers of the crisis can be traced to the era when Charles first jumped into the architecture debate – as social-housing construction continued to decline, the Thatcher government made it possible for council tenants to buy their properties, taking a chunk of public housing into the private sector. In 1990, less than a month before Thatcher's ousting, Michael Spicer, Minister of State at the Department of the Environment, attended a conference on homelessness chaired by Charles, noting in his diary: 'Prince getting more and more involved in what he thinks is a non-political subject. He's quite wrong about this. Homelessness could not be more political as shown by some of the presentations. They blame the government for not building enough houses. I say we had built considerably more per head of population. The problem is the break-up of families which is going on around Europe.'[35]

Spicer also recorded the presence of Diana. 'This is the first time for some weeks that the two HRHs have been seen together.' Two years later, the HRHs would follow the Europe-wide trend, but whatever the factors increasing pressure on housing, the government Spicer represented failed to ensure that supply kept pace with demand. Its successors would do no better.

However, in recent years a new bogeyman has emerged for Londoners struggling to afford the most basic accommodation in their city. The prime property market is booming, boosted by Thatcher's Big Bang and subsequent governments' relentless promotion of the financial sector and eagerness to attract as many Bond villains to Britain as possible in the belief that their wealth may trickle down. Popular wisdom blames the luxury market for fuelling surging prices lower down the ladder and sees the dark windows of super-luxe apartments that stand empty as their jet-set owners jet-set around the globe as both symbols and causes of the crisis. The most prominent totem of such divisive development is an ungainly quartet of glass-and-steel towers, One Hyde Park, designed by Richard Rogers, marketed by the Candy brothers, and reputed to be the most expensive address, per square foot, on the planet.

In levelling his lance at Gucci ghettos, Charles is continuing a quest in which he positions himself not as an avatar of privilege but as a Robin Hood, challenging vested power rather than wielding it. This self-image is entirely sincere, however awkwardly it fits into the continuum of British history and the nation's problematic colonial legacy.

Chapter 9

The Knight of the Realms

Camilla smiles on the podium. She's wearing a blue that's more cobalt than royal, designed to tone with her Nova Scotia tartan collar and scarf, and beginning to accessorise with her fingers on this unseasonably frigid morning. The Duchess of Cornwall has adjusted smoothly to many of the oddities of being a royal, but she wasn't born with the Windsor metabolism. She feels the cold, unlike her poikilothermic husband and in-laws, and finds foreign trips gruelling. It doesn't help that the Prince demands jam-packed schedules that allocate no slots to lunches or quiet lie-downs, irrespective of the time zones overflown. Then there are the endless ceremonials. She's often required to spend more time being welcomed and waved off than actually looking at a place, and everything she sees has been pre-rehearsed and sanitised.

On 19 May 2014, that's probably a good thing. She has been spared the freezing run-through of Nova Scotia's welcoming ceremony on Halifax's Grand Parade. By 9 a.m., the event had already attracted a small but patriotic crush. A choir of schoolchildren shivered in harmony as their adult overlords wrapped up against the cold. No matter: everyone was excited. The authorities had deployed a guard of honour and a platform of movers and shakers including then Justice Minister Peter MacKay, sent to Canada's federal parliament by the voters of a Nova Scotian constituency. A military band, perplexingly, played 'What Shall We Do With the Drunken Sailor?' until MacKay moved to the microphone to check sound levels, announcing his pleasure in welcoming 'the Prince and Princess of Wales' to his country. By the time he delivers his speech to the Prince and the Duchess, MacKay has corrected his mistake, though he will mangle another set of titles, referring to the absent William and Kate as 'the Prince and Princess of Cambridge'. It's a foretaste of a four-day trip during which avidity for the spectacle of royalty masks a deeper confusion about who the visitors are and what they're doing in Canada.

Some of that confusion is stirred by the ghost of Diana, who already hovered above the proceedings before MacKay inadvertently named her. Mell Kirkland and Kim Burke have been pressed up against a barrier from early morning to secure a good view. Kirkland proclaims herself content that her city is pulling out the stops for Charles. She doesn't even begrudge Camilla her moment in the elusive sun. She has come to get close to Canada's royalty. 'We all feel the connection, but sometimes you need to be in the presence,' she says. Yet Kirkland feels no natural affinity for Charles, who seems to her 'of another generation'. The Diana brand maintains its potency. 'She is still a huge part of people's lives,' says Kirkland. For Kirkland and Burke, as for many across the Realms and beyond, the Princess remains the world's premier symbol of compassionate humanity. 'We all need role models,' says Burke.

The Prince's brand, by contrast – and as a result – lacks definition and appeal, an errant husband, buttoned up and closed down, his love for Camilla an aberration, his failure to love Diana proving him a dry stick. The women are surprised to learn that Charles does much of anything to try to help other people, though they have heard of the Prince's Trust. They assume Charles has come to Canada purely to help himself and the institution he represents.

That is certainly part of the plan. In his speech to the people of Halifax – struggling through a chest cold that will worsen as he tours the country – the Prince quotes his grandmother, who in 1939 accompanied her husband George VI on a month-long tour of Canada. 'Seeing this country, with all its varied beauty and interest, has been a real delight to me,' said (that) Queen Elizabeth. 'But what has warmed my heart in a way I cannot express in words is the proof you have given us everywhere that you were glad to see us.' The couple routinely drew crowds in the tens of thousands. So did Charles and Diana on their first trip to Canada in 1983. The Halifax authorities estimated that as many as 15,000 to 20,000 people planted themselves at Garrison Grounds to glimpse the Prince and, in particular, the Princess. 'At times Diana, breathtakingly lovely and surprisingly thin, simply disappeared in the throng. Only the bright red silk ribbons of her hat peeked above the crowd,' reported the *Toronto Star*. 'Undeniably, Diana was the drawing card ... "It's really the royal visit of the Princess of Wales," Jeff Williams, Nova Scotia's director of information, said. "The Prince is playing second fiddle."'[1]

Charles and Camilla's whistle-stop tour to Halifax, Pictou County, Charlottetown and Winnipeg never commands such big attendances – the weather refuses to improve; and the trip coincides with a national holiday which means some people use their leisure not to rubberneck at royals but to travel out of town – but everywhere they go, the couple is greeted by respectable numbers of well-wishers propelled onto the streets by the impulse that brought Kirkland to the Grand Parade, the desire to breathe the same air as royalty. It's not a cheap shot of nitrogen, oxygen and argon for those who wave flags or the far larger numbers subsidising the experience at a distance. The trip costs Canadian taxpayers around £390,000 plus £500,000 for security, according to press estimates. The first figure includes £45,000 for a snowbound recce by the Prince's officials to plan the trip, a total released under Canadian Access to Information laws.

'I'm the minister so I have to be able to defend the costs,' said Shelly Glover who at the time had temporarily dismounted from a lofty career in the Canadian Royal Mounted Police to render a different form of public service as Federal Minister for Canadian Heritage. 'We're always concerned about value for dollars.' How did she assess that value? Glover might reasonably have pointed out that the cost to Canada of each visit by the monarch or her family members, though steep in total, averages out at less than a cent per taxpayer excluding security, or maximum a few cents all-inclusive. The expense of maintaining the Governor-General and ten provincial Lieutenant-Governors would not disappear if they were no longer the Queen's representatives and might even rise. A 2012 study of monarchies and republics by Herman Matthijs at the University of Ghent suggested that royals generally get higher 'salaries' than republican heads of state, but republicans get better pensions. France's powerful President is substantially more costly than any monarchy. Germany's ceremonial presidency is a little cheaper than the Dutch monarchy or the House of Windsor.[2]

Instead Glover cited a more diaphanous argument for the Crown: the feel-good factor. She was standing in an aircraft hangar on the last full day of Charles and Camilla's tour, ahead of their joint event with Canada's then Prime Minister Stephen Harper. 'Look at the crowds of Canadians who take an interest in this wonderful relationship [with the Crown],' Glover urged. 'Just look at the smiles. They just love the Prince and the Duchess ... The media here and in the UK are very different in outlook. I see media here covering the royal visit with smiles. The Canadian media are just as excited as the rest of us.'[3]

That wasn't much of an exaggeration. As busloads of children, their faces painted with the Canadian maple leaf, tipped up at the hangar, a local broadcast journalist snarled: 'Kids with flags. He's such a robot. You have to import the emotion.' The reporter's ire was directed at Harper, not the Prince, whom he pronounced 'warm and human', and that's before the cameras, and his descriptive powers, started rolling.

Some Canadian media outlets raised questions about the use of taxpayer dollars, but most Canadian coverage was indeed infused with a spirit unfamiliar to the small press pack that had travelled with the royal party from Britain: unfettered enthusiasm. The state broadcaster CBC streamed every event live. Other channels confected royal specials and dusted down archival footage from the Prince's previous sixteen trips to his future kingdom. Local newspapers splashed the visit on their front pages and showered the royals with praise. When Charles fed sandwiches to a polar bear called Hudson at a Manitoba zoo, Canadian journalists clapped like seals offered particularly tasty mackerel.

Britain's fourth estate couldn't have cared less. At the height of Dianamania hundreds of British journalists followed the Prince's overseas tours. Just seven members of the UK press were accredited for his 2014 Canada trip. There were two writers – a reporter from the Press Association and the *Daily Mail*'s royal correspondent Rebecca English – and five lens-men including the *Sun*'s veteran royal photographer Arthur Edwards. They all fly on the Canadian Air Force jet that transports the royal party from the military base of Brize Norton in Oxfordshire to Halifax, then ride around in the royal convoys from one destination to the next, muttering throughout about the lack of stories or pictures to excite editors back home. Charles and Camilla are no William and Kate – or Charles and Diana.

At first only one story from Canada makes it into the British newspapers and then barely scraping onto two or three inside pages. After the welcome ceremony in Halifax, Charles and Camilla visit a local resource centre for military families to highlight its work supporting the spouses and children of troops and to draw attention to one of the Prince's initiatives. His Operation Entrepreneur provides Canadian military personnel with grants, training and mentoring as they prepare for transition out of the services. At the centre he and Camilla chat to a trio of volunteers costumed as a carrot, a bunch of grapes and a banana as part of a drive to promote healthy eating.

Linda Dunn, the grapes, works with disabled children as an educational programme assistant. She's impressed by Charles. 'I think he represents his family very well. He does a lot of great volunteer work,' she says. In the UK, the image inspires a gag as inevitable as some of the Prince's own punchlines: that he has moved on from talking to plants to holding conversations with fruit.

An encounter later the same day will create a volume of coverage back in Britain that surpasses even Diana's high-water mark or the Cambridges' overseas missions. Rebecca English secures a front-page splash in the *Daily Mail* with a report about a tea party for Second World War veterans and war brides at the Canadian Museum of Immigration at Pier 21. Charles and Camilla chatted to guests as a band played Glenn Miller's 'Moonlight Serenade' while press, penned at the edge of the floor, strained to eavesdrop. After cookies had been dunked and tea drunk, the royals headed towards the exit, accompanied by eighty-seven-year-old Marianne Ferguson. A volunteer at the museum, Ferguson née Echt first arrived at Pier 21 aboard a ship called the *Andania* in February 1939, three months before King George and Queen Elizabeth landed on Canadian shores. She was a Jewish refugee from Danzig, who had witnessed the brutality of Nazism. 'These men came at night, broke the doors and windows of some of the people's houses, and brought the head of the family to a place which was unknown to all other people,' Echt recalled in a memoir which she wrote, aged sixteen, after her family settled in Nova Scotia. 'The next day, the family of such persons would get a little gift. This gift consisted of a dainty, little parcel, mostly a box, wrapped in tissue paper and tied with a brightly colored ribbon. When it was opened, one found in the box the remains or ashes of the person of the family which had disappeared the night before. Also a little card was enclosed, a card of sympathy.'[*]

How much of her story she revealed to Charles in the few minutes they spent in each other's company – or what, exactly, he said in response – remains unclear. Neither the Prince nor his aides would comment on the 'private conversation' after English reported that the Prince compared Vladimir Putin to Hitler. The remark, according to English's article, was 'heard by several witnesses. Mother-of-three Mrs Ferguson said: "I had finished showing him the exhibit and talked with him about my own family background and how I came to Canada. The Prince then said: "And now Putin is doing just about the same as Hitler." I must say that I agree with him and am sure a lot of people do. I was very surprised that he made the comment as I know [members of the royal family] aren't meant to say these things but it was very heartfelt and honest.'[5]

English had been told of the exchange by a photographer, and Ferguson herself later cast some doubt on the exact wording, but the Prince had almost certainly drawn a parallel between Nazi aggression and Russia's incursions in Ukraine. Two separate sources in his household doubt he used the 'H-word' but agree the sentiment in other respects sounded characteristic of the Boss. The story broke as the royal party flew from Prince Edward Island to Manitoba, for the last full day of the trip. British politicians tripped over themselves in the rush to slap down the Prince or to defend him. 'If Prince Charles wants to make controversial statements on national or international issues he should abdicate and stand for election,' tweeted Labour MP Mike Gapes. His party leader, Ed Miliband, read the public temperature with unusual accuracy. 'I think lots of people across the country will share Prince Charles's concern about President Putin and his actions in the Ukraine,' he said. One commenter on the BBC website summed up the bulk of responses: 'Charles is only saying what the rest of us have been thinking – if you behave like a bully don't be surprised if people think you are a bully.'

Russia hit back. State-funded broadcaster Russia Today reminded viewers of the Windsors' German antecedents and historic susceptibility to Nazism: the infamous 1937 visit paid by the Duke of Windsor

– as Edward VIII became on abdication – to Hitler, Prince Philip's SS brother-in-law and, rather more tenuously, the swastika armband Prince Harry once wore, not as a political statement but to attend a fancy-dress party. Putin weighed in too, riposting that Prince Charles's alleged comment did not live up to standards of 'royal behaviour' – a criticism that provoked snickering in the Foreign Office given the fate of the Romanovs – but the Russian President downplayed the seriousness of the diplomatic spat. 'I think that if our partners in Great Britain, just as I am, are guided by national interests rather than some other considerations, then all this will pass quite quickly and we'll continue to co-operate as we have done before,' he pronounced magisterially.[6]

The world hadn't shifted on its axis. The fracas confirmed the Prince's critics in their analysis that he is dangerously outspoken but endeared him to another constituency that is tired of political plati-tudes. Despite the churning coverage, it wasn't really a big deal. But Charles, for all he assumed a brave face for his last duties in Canada, flew back to Brize Norton sicker than he left. 'I'm quietly expiring from a particularly frightful lurgy I picked up on the other side of the Atlantic,' he told a group of Canadian business people at one of the last events in his schedule, to publicise the Seeing is Believing initiative and the launch of pilot projects in Halifax, Toronto and Winnipeg. 'I look forward to seeing you again. If I'm still alive.' His cold had worsened but more than anything else, he felt demoralised. Once again controversy had proved his only reliable route to British headlines and muddied waters that were already far from crystal clear. He had travelled with an agenda and a higher purpose, as a representative of Canada's head of state and as the nation's presumed next head of state, not only to shore up support for the monarchy, but also to showcase its potential future form. His programme of activities made little distinction between head-of-state functions and the Prince's promotion of various causes. In this blurring of lines, he had the support of his hosts. 'The Canadian government sees his charities as being an important element in the relationship with the Crown and part of its value,' said a well-placed source.

The Prince may be Britain's most prolific philanthropist by many measures but that's not how Britons see him. His image further afield, clouded though it is by memories of Diana, more often acknowledges the scale of his charitable work. 'Coming from somewhere other than here, I saw the Prince as a leader,' says Hank Dittmar.[7] 'I didn't come with a lot of other baggage British people have about the system.' Another of Charles's American-born advisers, Dame Amelia Fawcett, lauds the Prince as an unsung hero. 'In the United States he would be lionised,' she says. 'The sniping, the envy, the "how-dare-he", "he's-too-privileged". No one would think like that. They'd think: "Wow, look at what he's doing – here's a man who has got everything, who is wealthy and privileged, who doesn't need to do anything but he's doing so much for so many."'[8]

America might well share Britain's conflicted attitudes to wealth, privilege and the Crown had the nation not shaken off the colonial yoke – and the British Crown – in 1776. Australia, Canada, Jamaica, New Zealand and the other far-flung Commonwealth Realms never made a full break and retain some of the symptoms of adolescence as a result. Australia, in particular, is often truculent towards the royals, then screams like a kid at a pop concert when they pay a visit. As Charles contemplates the relationship between the House of Windsor and the Realms, wondering how to get it onto a more mature footing, or mulls his possible future role as head of the wider Commonwealth, the lessons of history carry both comfort and warning. The monarchy may appear sturdy and adaptable, but empires, countries, solid-looking world and social orders have all proved friable.

The growth of the British Empire reflected the nation's military strength, entrepreneurial spirit and sense of destiny. It crumbled together with those defining characteristics and as the ideological, commercial and strategic logic of the British brand of colonialism failed. The brutality deployed to retain dependencies tore away the fig leaf of the Empire's moral purpose and jarred with the very notion of Britishness. The costs of fighting global wars eventually far exceeded the revenues from distant territories. In 1947, Charles's great-uncle Mountbatten, as the last Governor General of India, declared the partition of India and Pakistan. Both nations became independent republics. Two years later, UK Prime Minister Clement Attlee agreed that India could remain a member of the Commonwealth of Nations, up to that point an association of countries ruled directly or indirectly by Britain. Over the years more countries joined, former colonies and others without historical ties, all hoping for diplomatic advantage from the association.

The Commonwealth, in turn, has attempted to promote democracy, human rights and the rule of law. Its inability to bring to heel members in flagrant breach of these values raises questions about how long the association will endure. Then there's the small matter of what happens when the Queen dies. There is no automatic guarantee that her son will be welcomed to the role. In his memoir, Don McKinnon, Commonwealth Secretary General from 2000 to 2008, records a conversation with Olusegun Obasanjo, at the time President of Nigeria. 'After the death of the Queen, you, Secretary General, must talk to all heads of government to establish a consensus around the new King and announce it. We don't want to be put in a position of scrutiny by the public or the media, and certainly we don't want to be confronted with anything resembling a vote on the issue.'[9] Whatever the process, John Major thinks the Prince will be a shoo-in. 'The Queen has a special bond with the Commonwealth but Prince Charles has quite a bond ... I have no doubt from what I know of Commonwealth leaders over the years that Prince Charles will become head of the Commonwealth in precisely the same way the Queen has,' he told the BBC.[10] Geoffrey Robertson, a leading barrister, gave an opposing view to the same programme. 'I act for a number of Commonwealth countries,' he said. 'I've been privy to conversations about this for some time. And I don't think he would be acceptable. I don't think it's a personal thing. I think they believe it's time for the Commonwealth to move beyond the mother country ... A British hereditary monarch will not be the first choice.'

The palace is leaving as little as possible to chance. In a piece of theatre so significant that the Queen rose from her sickbed to attend, McKinnon's successor used the signing of a new Commonwealth charter in March 2013 to firm up Charles's candidacy. 'You have carried forward with untiring dedication and conviction the task laid upon you of following your father as Head of the Commonwealth,' Kamalesh Sharma told the Queen. 'Throughout the Commonwealth's existence, the Crown has symbolised the free association of our nations and our peoples, promoting the right and proper purpose of assembly and dialogue. The ties forged between the people and communities of the Commonwealth have been reinforced by the care which you have taken to visit and meet so many of them over more than sixty years. The support given to you in this endeavour by the Prince of Wales and other members of the royal family deepens the Commonwealth's links to the Crown.'[11]

That support often takes the form of visits designed to project the deathless continuity of those links. Yet many of the destinations on such trips spark intimations of their mortality too. On Charles and Camilla's 2013 trip to India, they visited a military academy at Dehradun established in the latter stages of the country's struggle for independence against British imperial rule. Many destinations on their 2014 Canadian itinerary carried similar resonances. The history of how Canada came to have – and retain – a British monarch is a history of turbulence and change. Europeans made landfall in the seventeenth century, first the French, then the British, and fought across the continent, battling for territory and in proxy for their wider imperial conflict, deploying soldiers and corporate entities such as the Hudson's Bay Company to secure their claims. France ceded its Canadian lands to Britain in the 1763 Treaty of Paris but then weighed in against its old foe in the American War of Independence, helping the United States to cast off its British rulers.

Canada itself is only a century and a half old, formed by the melding of British colonies into a dominion with a significant degree of autonomy. Its population reflects a narrative of forced migrations: arrivals like Ferguson's at Pier 21 and the 187 Scots sent in search of a new home by the Highland Clearances who in 1773 disembarked in Pictou from the ship *Hector*, but also ragged exoduses: of indigenous peoples and of Acadians, the descendants of French colonialists, who were persecuted and expelled when Britain suspected them of aiding the French. In 1931 Canada finally gained formal independence from the UK, though for another fifty years Westminster would retain residual powers to amend the Canadian constitution. From some perspectives, the apparatus of monarchy looks like a similar piece of historical detritus, as picturesque as the replica of *Hector* that the Prince and Duchess stop to admire during their visit to Pictou – and about as seaworthy.

Supporters of the Canadian monarchy rehearse the standard arguments for the institution, starting with its unifying function in a sprawling federation of provinces and three territories that encompasses First Nation peoples, Inuit and Métis and a variety of anglophone and francophone populations distributed across a land mass that stretches from temperate British Columbia to the tundra of Nunavut. Then there are the constitutional functions anchored by royalty plus, of course, the overarching guarantee that a monarch provides – but which republicans argue an elected head of state would more appropriately enact – in safeguarding democracy. The Monarchist League of Canada quotes on its website a statement issued in 1978, during a flaring of Quebec nationalism, by the nation's then provincial leaders: 'Provinces agree that the system of democratic parliamentary government requires an ultimate authority to ensure its responsible nature and to safeguard against abuses of power. That ultimate power must not be an instrument of the federal Cabinet.' The Supreme Court is another such check.

The League trots out an additional argument too, a peculiarly Canadian spin on the interplay between the monarchy and national identity – the Windsors represent a bulwark against US cultural imperialism. 'A central reality of Canadian life is the inevitably overwhelming influence of our friendly neighbour, the United States of America,' the website declares. 'Free Trade. Continental defence and secure borders in a post-9/11 environment. A porous frontier ranging from television and the Internet to popular music and culture. These and other factors often tend to overwhelm Canada's national identity. Every nation needs to understand and foster the existence of distinct images and institutions; thus for Canada, constitutional monarchy is of particular importance.' The republican counterblast is predictable: the Queen isn't even Canadian; the head-of-state role must be 'canadianised'.

Opinion polls in Canada broadly mirror trends in the other Realms: a falling-off in support for the monarchy during the 1990s and the first decade of the twenty-first century, followed recently by a revival in interest in the younger generations and especially William and Kate and baby George. A 2013 Forum Poll for the *National Post* rated William almost three times more popular than his father and produced some confusing data on the appeal of the monarchy in general, with a majority of respondents in favour of keeping the Crown but 63 per cent also saying the head of state should be Canadian and reside in Canada.[12]

The blizzards of polls and flurries of disputes between committed monarchists and ardent republicans that accompany royal visits succeed like a good Canadian dump of snow in disguising the significant features of the landscape. There's a broad, flat plain of apathy out there – Canadians who really don't care very much either way – and the electric fence that encircles the institution of the monarchy means they're right not to waste too much energy on the issue. The patriation of Canada's constitution in 1982, though symbolic of its independent nationhood, entrenched the overseas monarchy more firmly at its heart, requiring any constitutional amendment affecting the Crown to secure the unanimous support of the federal and provincial governments, about as likely as catching a tan in the Nunavut winter.

The solidity of the constitutional arrangements might be assumed to place Canada low on the priorities of the Windsors when other Realms and voting populations could far more easily mobilise the tumbrels. That would be to misunderstand the sense of duty – and destiny – shared by the Queen and her son that compels them to render the service they believe themselves born to fulfil. Both, in their own distinctive ways, believe in adding value to their roles. In return – and though the Queen disguises this impulse far better than her thin-skinned son – they want to be wanted.

The 2009 autobiography of a New Zealand-born, Australia-based show-business impresario called Harry M. Miller claimed that Charles wondered 'why Australia bothered with us – we really are yesterday's news'. The Prince supposedly made this impolitic observation during a private conversation over dinner. Miller's memoir, covering a royal trip to Australia some thirty-two years earlier, included a number of other details which, if true, the Prince might have hoped to keep under wraps – not least his alleged use of Miller's house 'to entertain a handful of young women, including his friend Lady Dale "Kanga" Tryon and the very pretty daughter of a well-known [New South Wales] politician'.[13] Government House, the usual digs for visiting royals, lacked privacy according to Miller, whose revelations underscored the rarity with which the Prince enjoys that particular commodity.

At the time of this 1977 visit, the Prince had not entirely given up on a move that might have solved his problem of what to do with his life but would have created new headaches in its place: becoming Governor General of Australia. There were many flaws with this idea, not least the anger sown two years earlier when the then Governor General deployed the royal prerogative to dismiss Prime Minister Gough Whitlam whose Labor government had managed to reshape the country's image at home and abroad in three years – introducing equal pay for women and beginning to reassert Aboriginal land rights – before becoming mired in stalemate. 'I have seen students in Melbourne jostle [the Prince], brandish beer cans and call him a "parasite". I have seen polls concluding that only some 20% are actively in favour of his becoming Governor General,' reported Anthony Holden who accompanied the Prince to Australia. Holden also assumed that the Prince had been too sheltered from the realities of public hostilities to absorb the right message. 'Were I the Prince of Wales's private secretary – which I am not, nor am ever like to be – I could not advise HRH to pursue his undisguised hopes of one day governing Australia. As a Pom at the end of his first visit to this country, made in the company of the heir to its throne, I should come to a very different conclusion. The Prince should hope to mark Australia's bicentenary in 1988 by presiding over the independence celebrations of a new republic within the Commonwealth.'[14]

Miller's autobiography suggests that the Prince had indeed got the message, only for the idea of the Governor Generalship to resurface a decade later when the outgoing incumbent approached Charles to consider the role. The Prince took soundings, discovering that Australian republicanism had grown no less raucous, and in a downbeat letter to Nicholas Soames observed: 'I must say I'm in two minds nowadays about how to approach Australia – let alone

Canada or New Zealand.'[15] By 1994, Charles had decided that the best and only option must be to encourage debate and, if necessary, change, rather than standing in its way. 'Personally, I happen to think that it is the sign of a mature and self-confident nation to debate those issues and to use the democratic process to re-examine the way in which you want to face the future,' he told an audience at an Australia Day reception in Sydney.[16] Earlier the same day, a student had run at the Prince, firing a starter pistol. The Prince, in barely flinching, boosted his popularity in the former colony. As it happened, the protestor's cause was not republicanism but to draw attention to the fate of Cambodian refugees held in detention camps in Australia.

Nevertheless, the incident highlighted the unpredictability of the Prince's reception in the Realms. He accepts that support for his future reign is nowhere automatic, but that does not mean he intends to preside over a process of attrition that sees the Crown lose one foothold after another. Though his chief focus has been on turning his existing position to meaningful use, he has been thinking about the longer term too, for many years and now with increasing urgency. In Canada he is developing another test bed for his ideas, a virtual Duchy Home Farm or Poundbury. The strategy was reflected in every part of his 2014 Canadian itinerary and briefed to the Monarchist League. 'The frequent returns to Canada by the Prince of Wales and Duchess of Cornwall are not only the result of Ottawa's enthusiasm for the Canadian Crown,' read the editorial in a special charities-focused edition of its newsletter, *Canadian Monarchist News*, published ahead of the trip. 'They mark a refreshed, visible commitment on the part of Charles that he values the Maple Realm and fully intends one day to be its King. With wise counsellors both new and old having his ear here, he also realizes that there is no substitute for his regular, physical presence in the country. But more – and as significant – he has invested a great deal of thought and energy in bringing to Canada

the vehicle that in no small measure has been the engine of his rehabilitation – together with the faultless, sensitive public role of his
devoted wife – in the affections of Britons; namely, his passionate
involvement with and practical facilitation of numerous good works
which are assembled under the banner of the Prince's Trust.'

The editorial's concluding paragraph recalls the Prince's short-
lived incarnation as fearless, full-of-fun Charlie. Aged twenty-six, he
dived under the Arctic ice of Nunavut's Resolute Bay, emerging to
the delight of waiting photographers with a bowler hat and umbrella
and then inflating his dry suit in a display of the kind of slapstick
that has always made him laugh and sometimes his audiences too.
As the newsletter points out, the funny business cloaked another
piece of funny business: signalling Canadian sovereignty over the
country's northern sprawl, still a source of friction with Russia and
the United States. Canadians were charmed but their affection for
Charles soured in tandem with his first marriage.

The editorial suggests that redemption is at hand. 'As monarchists,
as Canadians, as admirers of Charles, we think [the] imaginative
energy and diverse outreach [of his Canadian charities] deserve to
be better known and to succeed – for [their] good works' sake, yes;
and as much for how [they] can assist in re-developing the bond
between Prince and Canadians which we felt so keenly in his youth
and early adulthood … It is not too late to rejuvenate an appreciation
of a remarkable man of restless energy and determined mien, who
merits, in the fullness of time, being welcomed and hailed – not
merely tolerated in expectation of better things – as our King and
head of the nation, as opposed to simply being head of state.'

In devising a new model of monarchy for the Realms, the Prince
hopes to defeat their new model armies of republicanism. Canada,
with small but committed forces on either side and larger phalanxes
of don't-knows and couldn't-cares, makes a good testing ground.

'The trip is a blinding success, talking to fruit, insulting one of the world's great nations,' jokes a member of the Prince's retinue. 'We should get the Boss to say he hates maple syrup and that Mounties are second rate.' Yet despite the gallows humour that grips the party and the malaise that envelops its principal, it has been a largely positive mission in the narrow terms of its objectives.

The Prince has converted at least a few don't-knows, convinced some waverers, and firmed up support for the monarchy in Canada, though the tartan army of Canadians of Scottish heritage that turns out in Pictou to meet him clearly needs no persuasion. 'This area is very, very pro-royal,' says Sue MacLachlan. Scottish nationalism Canadian-style, unlike the home-grown variety, is unambiguous in its devotion to the Windsors. 'Everyone is very excited. When William and Kate got married, most of us had wedding parties in the middle of the night. We had cucumber sandwiches.' MacLachlan is sitting spinning near an enclosure of rare-breed sheep. One of the Prince's aims in Pictou is to give a push to his Campaign for Wool, newly launched in Canada and running in eleven other countries to promote wool for its sustainability and to help traditional sheep farmers struggling to survive. The campaign claims responsibility for a threefold increase in the price of raw wool since 2010, though rising demand in China and low production of wool have also played a part. As the Prince makes a beeline for the sheep, he's mobbed by well-wishers and Camilla loses sight of him. 'Oh dear, I've mislaid my husband again,' she sighs.

So long have people waited to inhale royal molecules that a woman faints with exhaustion and the paramedics move in. As they work to make the casualty comfortable, the Prince and Duchess reunite to sit in biting winds and watch a series of performances. There are Highland reels and 'These Hands', a folk song written and performed by Dave Gunning, a local singer-songwriter with national profile. The chorus is apposite not only to the medical emergency but the

Prince's life: 'Some hands can stop a life from dying / So tell me what shall I do with these hands of mine?' An answer comes in the final stanza: 'The world could use a hero of the human kind.'

That chimes with Greg Baker's message for the Prince. The Senior Manager, Engineering, for the Halifax Port Authority talks to the royals as they stroll through Seaport Farmers' Market in the city, and tells Charles about Halifax's race with New York to see which can first install giant charging stations so cruise ships can connect to the local grid when docked. This will enable ships to shut down their auxiliary engines, reducing emissions. 'I see the Prince's real potential not in sporadic visits but in taking a leadership position for the people of Canada and providing a voice for programmes, issues etc. that politicians do not want to touch in this highly capitalistic society we live in,' emails Baker later. 'I would like to see him be less involved in scripted visits and more of a constant involvement … He has quite a unique position and status to be a leader in environmental issues and many others (we saw some of this from both him and his wife) where the current politicians, business people, celebrities fall short.' Baker has watched the Putin story unfolding and concludes: the Prince 'should not within reason be censored'.[17]

The Prince's charities in Canada get a boost from his presence too, even if Joelle Foster, Director of Manitoba, Saskatchewan, Nunavut and the Northwest Territories for Futurpreneur, an offshoot of the Prince's Youth Business International organisation, regrets that Hudson the polar bear hand-fed by Charles steals some of her thunder. 'The darned bear has gotten more coverage than Innovation Alley,' she laments.[18] The Prince has toured a stretch of Winnipeg's Exchange District that serves as tech hub and an incubator for start-up companies, many founded with the assistance of Futurpreneur and other organisations working to foster entrepreneurship. The Futurpreneur methodology is familiar to anyone who knows the work of the Prince's Trust: 'We look at character, not collateral, when providing youth aged 18–39 with pre-launch coaching, business resources, start-up financing and mentoring to help them launch and sustain successful businesses,' explains its website. Foster says 95 per cent of loans are repaid.

One problem for this model is recruiting mentors, senior business people with the knowledge to help and the willingness to do so. Charles's visit produced a new stream of potential mentors. 'My LinkedIn has gone nuts,' says Foster. 'I'm getting twenty-five-plus requests a day. The increase in mentors has been enormous.' Better yet, the Manitoba provincial government has taken an interest and may come on board with funding. Individual companies highlighted as the Prince toured Innovation Alley benefited too, despite Hudson's long shaggy shadow, especially VisualSpection, a tech business developing ways to make it easier for workers in the energy industry to locate and deal with problems. When the Prince stopped at the company's display and donned a pair of Google glasses, the resulting image proved sufficiently startling to induce editors across the world – even in Britain – to build pieces around it. The *Mail*'s article names VisualSpection and describes the nature of its business exactly as Charles's press handlers would wish, but the headline carries a sting. 'DOES ONE LOOK A GLASSHOLE IN THESE?' it wonders.[19]

Chapter 10

A Foreign Asset

The Prince is the butt of jokes as often as he cracks them. He long ago learned what the photographers wanted and frequently indulges them. 'No arty shit,' says royal photographer Arthur Edwards derisively. 'If you have to write a caption explaining the picture, it's no good.' So in Canada, apart from posing with fruit, the Prince wields a giant mallet and stares in mock perplexity at a carving of a woman's naked torso. Over the years he stepped into horse-drawn vehicles in which two other passengers already waited, braced against inevitable gags about 'three of us in this carriage'. He has let people of both sexes and all ages kiss him, tolerated babies tweaking his nose and tried on more headgear than Pope Francis.

On a visit to Saudi Arabia in February 2014 he donned a ghutra, the traditional cotton headdress folded over a keffiyeh, or skullcap, and the full-length shirt called a thawb, to participate in a sword dance. 'I'm a fake sheikh,' he told a wide-eyed child. The ostensible reason for this display was to celebrate the Janadriyah Festival, an annual cultural event. His footwork wasn't up to the standard that makes Emma Thompson go into a mock swoon or over the years has enlivened Balmoral balls, put a spring into tea dances, gingered up the Rio Carnival and impressed at least one Degree of the Three. Nor did it win him approval among critics of Saudi Arabia, a kingdom ruled over by an absolute monarchy that only introduced the country's Basic Law in 1992, after the first Gulf War, and retained its clutch throughout the Arab Spring. King Abdullah had been hailed as a moderniser and he was – but only by the arch-conservative standards of his predecessor and older brother, King Fahd. Abdullah, who died in January 2015, brooked no dissent. His successor, half-brother Salman, continues a regime that sees anyone organising protests or publicly criticising the government risk prosecution and swingeing penalties. 'Tarnishing the reputation of the state' is defined as an act of terrorism. So is atheism. Yet despite the country's sweeping anti-terror laws, the oil-rich nation (it straddles almost a fifth of the world's proven oil reserves) remains a crucible and source of funding for the kind of jihadism that produced Osama bin Laden and continues to inspire violent Sunni organisations such as al-Shabab, Boko Haram and the self-styled Islamic State – also known as ISIS, the Islamic State of Iraq and Syria, or ISIL, the Islamic State of Iraq and the Levant. Generations of Saudi rulers have promoted the ultra-orthodox Wahhabist sect as part of a ploy to maintain power, ironically creating their own most potent enemy.

Among the other primary targets of Sunni jihadists are Shia Muslims, now the majority population in Iran and Iraq as well as Azerbaijan and Bahrain, and with significant presences in Indonesia, Kuwait, Lebanon, Nigeria, Pakistan, Syria, Turkey, Yemen and other countries including Saudi Arabia, who after the death of the Prophet Muhammad in 632 made the fateful decision to follow the hereditary principle and support his descendants in the struggle to lead Islam. The Sunnis back then called for a democratically chosen Caliph but the people who kill in the name of Sunni Islam care little for democractic mandates, reserving a special animosity towards Western democracies and in particular the 'Great Satan', America. The term was originally coined by the Shia cleric Ayatollah Ruhollah Khomeini, who led the revolution that deposed Iran's royalty. Iran has helped to finance Shia militant groups including Lebanon-based Hezbollah and the Palestinian organisation Hamas that direct their fire against Sunni and Western targets. In the intricate history of the Sunni and Shia conflict and Islam's conflict with the West, enemies' enemies are rarely friends.

As Charles acknowledged in a 1993 speech, the hostilities owe some of their venom and a good deal of their complexity to Western interventions over fourteen centuries. 'Extremism is no more the monopoly of Islam than it is the monopoly of other religions, including Christianity,' he said and set to illustrating the point. 'To Western schoolchildren, the two hundred years of the Crusades are tradition-ally seen as a series of heroic, chivalrous exploits in which the kings, knights, princes – and children – of Europe tried to wrest Jerusalem from the wicked Muslim infidel. To Muslims, the Crusades were an episode of great cruelty and terrible plunder, of Western infidel soldiers of fortune and horrific atrocities, perhaps exemplified best by the massacres committed by the Crusaders when, in 1099, they took back Jerusalem, the third holiest city in Islam. For us in the West, 1492 speaks of human endeavour and new horizons, of Columbus and the discovery of the Americas. To Muslims, 1492 is a year of tragedy – the year Granada fell to Ferdinand and Isabella, signifying the end of eight centuries of Muslim civilisation in Europe.

'The point, I think, is not that one or other picture is more true, or has a monopoly of truth. It is that misunderstandings arise when we fail to appreciate how others look at the world, its history, and our respective roles in it. The corollary of how we in the West see our history has so often been to regard Islam as a threat – in medi-eval times as a military conqueror, and in more modern times as a source of intolerance, extremism and terrorism.'[1]

The speech stood at odds with much mainstream Western thinking. 'At that time, he was far ahead of others in coming up with the view that something needs to be done to bring about a better understanding between the Islamic world and the West,' says Farhan Nizami, the founding Director of the Oxford Centre for Islamic Studies and the Prince of Wales Fellow at Magdalen College. 'To be calling for the Islamic world and the West to work together, to say we were almost at the crossroads, I think was remarkably prescient.'[2]

It was also a highly political speech and carefully strategised, ahead of a trip to the Gulf that the Prince feared would be a rerun of previous trips – polite, content-free meetings in air-conditioned rooms. His speech changed that. The Prince used the platform to draw attention to 'the terrible sufferings' of Bosnian Muslims and to inveigh against Saddam Hussein's persecution of the Marsh Arabs of Southern Iraq. Charles also appeared to hold up Islam as an antidote to Western materialism, already betraying his concerns about post-Enlightenment Christianity and its acceptance of 'mechanistic science' that would find much more detailed expression in *Harmony* and are explored in the next chapters of this book. The future Defender of the (Anglican) Faith lauded Islam for its holistic thinking. 'At the heart of Islam is its preservation of an integral view of the universe,' the Prince told his audience at the Sheldonian Theatre in Oxford. 'Islam – like Buddhism and Hinduism – refuses to separate man and nature, religion and science, mind and matter, and has preserved a metaphysical and unified view of ourselves and the world around us.'[3]

In the Gulf nations, as in the wider Muslim world, Charles's speech drew warm applause. When the Prince arrived in Saudi Arabia, King Fahd set aside usual protocols to greet him at his guest house before dawn, rather than awaiting the Prince at his palace. In Britain, the heir to the throne's views on Islam, expounded in further speeches and enthusiastically demonstrated through many more visits and meetings, interfaith initiatives and his patronage of the institution run by Nizami – in receipt of funding from Saudi Arabia as well, says Nizami, as from donors 'across the Muslim world, from Turkey and the Gulf to South East Asia ... British and US foundations and indeed the FCO' – have aroused the mixture of amusement and rancour that often attends his efforts.[4] Columnists mock him: does he not know the penalties for adultery under sharia law? In Saudi Arabia cheating on your spouse carries a potential death sentence.

Conspiracists of all waters find in his connections with the Muslim world confirmation of his murky aims. 'Prince Charles has been placed by the Queen at the head of [the] British-Saudi Empire terror machine, utilising relationships he has developed over more than a quarter of a century,' declare Richard Freeman and William F. Wertz, Jr., the authors of an essay published by Lyndon LaRouche, an arch-conspiracist, failed US presidential candidate and convicted fraudster. 'Charles is [also] at the forefront of Queen Elizabeth's drive, through starvation, disease, war, and murder, to reduce the world's population from its present 7 billion persons to 1 billion. According to Charles' semi-official biography, *The Prince of Wales* by Jonathan Dimbleby, the Prince held a two-day international seminar, on board the royal yacht *Britannia*, which set the agenda for the 1992 Rio Earth Summit. The summit launched the Intergovernmental Panel on Climate Change (IPCC)'s campaign promoting the genocidal hoax of anthropomorphic global warming, as the vehicle to shut down industry and civilisation.'[5]

Dianaists posit that the Prince's interest in Islam stems from his need to compete with his former wife's Muslim boyfriends, Hasnat Khan and Dodi Fayed, ignoring not only a psychology that makes that interpretation implausible but a timeline that makes it impossible. Another persistent theme insists that the Prince is a Muslim revert. On the far Right website Stormfront a user calling himself 'Fight_ For_England' posted this question: 'After many arguments with the wog muslim in my dorm room about Islam and Prince Charles being a muslim i thought i would come to my brothers and sisters on here and see what you people think.' 'Aha!' replied 'Raffles'. 'Someone else shares my pet theory. This jug-eared Balloon likes nothing better than cavorting around in Wog hats.'[6]

To many liberals, the Prince's tendresse for Islam equates to support for repressive interpretations of the faith and for the regimes that rule in its name, especially Saudi Arabia and its dictatorial monarchy. After the Saudi government arrested Briton Sandy Mitchell in 2000 for his alleged involvement in two car bombings, despite Mitchell's impeccable alibi and strong evidence pointing to al Qaeda, the Prince interceded on his behalf with Abdullah, then Saudi Arabia's Crown Prince and de-facto ruler. 'Abdullah listened politely and nodded without commenting,' recounted investigative journalist Mark Hollingsworth in *Saudi Babylon*, a book written with Mitchell. The Prince's intervention and subsequent frequent pleadings bore no obvious fruit – Mitchell spent thirty-two months in detention, subjected to physical and mental torture including a death sentence that hung over him until his eventual release and in 2005 his formal exoneration by the Wiltshire coroner at the inquest for Christopher Rodway, the victim of one of the car bombings.

Mitchell and Hollingsworth accuse the Prince on the one hand of being ineffectual and naive in his dealings with the Saudi royals, on the other of blocking efforts by the British authorities to investigate allegations by relatives of the September 11 victims that the upper echelons of the Saudi regime had helped to fund al Qaeda. *Saudi Babylon* relates that Alan Gerson, a lawyer for the 9/11 families, asked in a 2003 meeting at New Scotland Yard if the UK authorities had 'uncovered anything to show the charities run by some members of the Saudi royal family were channelling money to the terrorists'. Stephen Ratcliffe, a Special Branch officer tasked with tracing terrorist money, is described as appearing 'hesitant and a little sheepish' in response. "'Our ability to investigate the Saudis is very limited,'" he said. He then paused, looked across at a photograph of Prince Charles on the wall, raised his eyebrows and smiled knowingly without saying a word. "He did not say anything but the message was crystal clear when he looked at the picture," said a police officer who was present. "It was Prince

Charles's special relationship with the Saudis which was a problem. [Ratcliffe] gave no other reason why they were restricted."'[7]

The Salman Rushdie affair saw Charles side with Islamic conservatives; Ayatollah Khomeini issued a fatwa against Rushdie in 1989 for his novel *The Satanic Verses*. The ostensible grounds for Khomeini's call to murder Rushdie was that his book had insulted Islam; the cleric's deeper aim was to position Shia Iran and not Sunni-led Saudi Arabia as the fulcrum of the Islamic revolution. This twisted view of events, in which Rushdie rather than his persecutors was the offender found some powerful allies in Margaret Thatcher's government – she appears in cameo in *The Satanic Verses* as 'Mrs Torture' – and in Lambeth Palace. Archbishop of Canterbury Robert Runcie let it be known he could 'well understand the devout Muslims' reaction, wounded by what they hold most dear and would themselves die for'. Nor did the literary world stand foursquare behind Rushdie. John le Carré and Rushdie exchanged furious letters, reconciling in 2012, though le Carré did not resile from his initial concerns about Rushdie's book. 'Should we be free to burn Korans, mock the passionately held religions of others?' he asked. 'Maybe we should: but should we also be surprised when the believers we have offended respond in fury? I couldn't answer that question at the time and, with all good will, I still can't. But I am a little proud, in retrospect, that I spoke against the easy trend, reckoning with the wrath of outraged Western intellectuals, and suffering it in all its righteous glory. And if I met Salman tomorrow? I would warmly shake the hand of a brilliant fellow writer.'[8]

Elsewhere, blows were traded in place of words, spilling over into riots in which forty-two people died and violent attacks on those involved in publishing the book. A would-be Rushdie assassin accidentally blew himself up. The book's Japanese translator was stabbed to death. Rushdie went into hiding. In this febrile atmosphere Rushdie's friend and fellow author, Martin Amis found himself at a dining table in royal company. 'I had an argument with Prince Charles at a small dinner party,' Amis recalled in an interview marking the twenty-fifth anniversary of the fatwa. 'He said – very typically, it seems to me – "I'm sorry, but if someone insults someone else's deepest convictions, well then," blah blah blah … And I said that a novel doesn't set out to insult anyone. "It sets out to give pleasure to its readers," I told him. "A novel is an essentially playful undertaking, and this is an exceedingly playful novel." The Prince took it on board, but I'd suppose the next night at a different party he would have said the same thing.'[9]

It's unlikely Charles had read *The Satanic Verses*. In their Cambridge days, Lucia Santa Cruz persuaded her friend to read *Anna Karenina*, she says, remarking that despite the false, fervid speculation that attended their platonic friendship the novel was the only new experience with which she provided him. 'He said he liked [the novel], but he never wanted to read another one, I don't think. He always wanted to stick to history or essays,' she adds.[10]

In Rushdie's most famous work the Prince may have been surprised to find a measure of what he says he wants to foster – a serious engagement with Islam that does not shrink from criticism. In 2006, Charles used a speech at the Imam Muhammad bin Saud University in Riyadh to issue a call for a more flexible reading of scripture that Brian Whitaker, the former Middle East editor of the *Guardian*, hailed as 'sensational and revolutionary stuff' within the context of the deeply conservative Islamic institution.[11] 'I think we need to recover the depth, the subtlety, the generosity of imagination, the respect for wisdom that so marked Islam in its great ages. Islam called Jews and Christians the peoples of the book, because they, like Muslims, are a part of a religion of sacred texts,' said the Prince. 'And what was so distinctive of the great ages of faith surely was that they understood that, as well as sacred texts, there is the art of interpretation of sacred texts – between the meaning of God's word for all time and its meaning for this time.'[12] Charles 'was seeking to defend Islam from anti-Muslim prejudice in the West and at the same time supporting Islamic reform against clerics whose mentality is frozen in backwardness,' wrote Whitaker. 'The big question ... is whether the Prince's words will fall on deaf ears.'[13]

More recently, Charles has begun to campaign for Christian communities that are being targeted by fundamentalists in Egypt, Iraq, Syria and other predominantly Muslim countries. In December 2013, he spent a day meeting Christians from the Middle East with his friend the Bishop of London and with Prince Ghazi of Jordan, another proponent of interfaith understanding who the following year would welcome Pope Francis to the Al-Aqsa mosque in East Jerusalem. Both men then joined him for an Advent reception at Clarence House that brought together the leaders of Coptic and Orthodox Churches in Britain with the Archbishop of Canterbury Justin Welby, Vincent Nichols, the head of the Catholic Church in the UK, and Britain's Chief Rabbi Ephraim Mirvis. The Prince also took his message of concern about Christian persecution direct to the Gulf, on the £228,426 trip to Saudi Arabia, Qatar, Abu Dhabi and Bahrain in February 2014 that produced the images of him participating in the sword dance.

His critics spotted blood on the dance floor. Amnesty UK called on the Prince to raise human-rights abuses with his Saudi hosts while its Twitter feed posted a link to the video. 'Prince Charles's sword dance,' read the accompanying tweet. 'Yes, they like swords in Saudi Arabia. Including for public executions.' George Galloway, at that time an MP representing the left-wing Respect party, used his regular slot on Press TV to tear into the Prince for his Saudi visit. 'Thirteen of the nineteen mass murderers on 9/11 were from the very same Saudi Arabia,' intoned Galloway. 'They used sharp blades to cut the throats of young women, air stewardesses on those aeroplanes, as they flew them to destruction and mass murder in the Twin Towers.

Why doesn't Prince Charles ask how that came to happen, out of which well this poison is coming. He knows ... where that well is located. That young man [Fusilier Drummer Lee Rigby] that was murdered, butchered, in broad daylight on the streets of south London in Woolwich, they cut his head off, these fanatics. Where do they get their money, where do they get their mindset, where do they get the political support? The very same Saudi Arabia where Prince Charles was dancing like an idiot, like a clown.'[14]

Press TV is funded by Iran, Saudi Arabia's geopolitical rival and Shia enemy. Galloway, expelled from the Labour party in 2003 after officials found he had breached an internal rule against 'bringing the Labour Party into disrepute by behaviour that is prejudicial or grossly detrimental to the party', was once recorded apparently telling Saddam Hussein: 'I salute your courage, your strength, your indefatigability.' Galloway successfully sued the *Daily Telegraph* for suggesting that he had been a paid apologist for Saddam, explaining to the court he had been addressing the Iraqi people in general rather than Saddam and adding, 'I was trying to stop a disastrous war.'[15] It seems unlikely he would grant the Prince a similar defence.

It did nothing to dispel dark interpretations of the Prince's 2014 mission that the British aerospace company BAE Systems announced the conclusion of a deal to sell Typhoon jets to the Saudi government the day after he left Riyadh for Doha. In the *Guardian*, defence and security writer Richard Norton-Taylor quoted Andrew Smith, spokesman for the Campaign Against the Arms Trade, CAAT: 'It is clear that Prince Charles has been used by the UK government and BAE Systems as an arms dealer.' The Prince's aides deny – with unusual ferocity – that the arms deal came up in any of his conversations. No matter. 'It did not have to,' wrote Norton-Taylor. 'The Saudis must have got the message. It was the heir to the British throne's tenth official visit to the feudal monarchy. He made his trip, we are told, at the request of the Foreign Office.'[16]

The Prince, so often criticised for cross-cutting with ministerial work, had indeed dutifully carried out the wishes of Her Majesty's government in travelling to Saudi Arabia, according to sources in HM government. He went at the FCO's request and with an agenda briefed to him in advance. His own objectives included raising his anxieties about Christian communities in the Gulf states and about the luxury-oriented, car-centred, energy-spendthrift cities in the Middle East that call into question his notion that Islam is naturally in sympathy with the environment. He met young entrepreneurs in Riyadh, ecologists in Doha, participated in an interfaith dialogue. Yet his government business took precedence.

Ever since the Prince's Oxford speech, he has had the confidence of key contacts in the region, not least the Gulf royals who regard him not only as an equal, but as a defender of Islam. 'I do not know of another major Western figure anywhere who would have as high a standing in the Muslim world as the Prince of Wales,' says Nizami.[17] 'The value he brings to this is the value of long-term relationships, not short-term transactional ones,' says an insider. 'That is immensely reassuring to his interlocutors.'

This has made the Prince an effective asset for the Foreign Office and the British intelligence community in certain key regions, able to transmit the British viewpoint to major players and to glean information that may not be so readily divulged to a Minister of State or diplomat. Sources say these missions always take account of the constitutional limits to his role: he would not be asked to nego-tiate or conclude deals, whether political or commercial, but to advise and warn, promote and listen. A source close to the Prince says he doesn't like being used to market weaponry and now sidesteps such activities where possible. That wasn't always the case. In Jonathan Dimbleby's 1994 documentary, Charles defends his appearance at the Dubai arms fair on the basis that he is boosting British trade, arguing without much conviction that the arms will likely be used as a deterrent and if the UK doesn't sell them, someone else will. If he has changed his mind, why doesn't the dissident Prince speak up? One answer, according to insiders, is that he has done so, in – thus far – private communications. If he is uncomfortable with his itineraries, he will say so, in terms, and in ink with underlinings.

Another answer is that any noisy protests on his part would diminish his usefulness in the Gulf. Some of the objectives of his recent trip to Saudi Arabia relied on that vanishing commodity: secrecy. All of them relied on his close skein of relationships in the region. 'It's soft, it's track five diplomacy, under über-Chatham House rules,' says a source. As the Prince put on his headdress, picked up his sword and set to dancing, London harboured deepening fears that Saudi support for the Syrian insurgency had not only failed in the objective of toppling President Assad, but continued to strengthen jihadi groups that draw many of their fighters from radicalised youth from outside Syria. The conflict has also displaced millions of people. At private meetings with King Abdullah and other Saudi royals, the Prince discussed how the Saudis could best target humanitarian aid and articulated the risk of blowback as battle-hardened militants returned home – whether to Saudi Arabia or the UK. The Prince also communicated British worries about wider regional stability and in particular the capture by ISIS of the Iraqi city of Fallujah.

There must be questions about any initiative that gives succour to the Saudi regime or attempts to appease the unappeasable. At the time, Britain aimed to do both. Less than two months after Charles's visit, Prince Bandar bin Sultan, Saudi Arabia's intelligence chief and driver of the misfired Syria policy, stood down. The choice of his successor, Interior Minister Mohamed bin Nayef, signalled closer strategic and intelligence cooperation between Saudi Arabia and its Western allies just as the crisis in the region sharpened, with ISIS forces sweeping into Iraq. Bin Nayef was subsequently appointed Salman's heir. The Saudis are deeply problematic allies, says a source.

British and US foreign policy is in disarray but for now there is no alternative to trying to work with the Saudis. The Prince's discussions, while not conclusive, 'may well have aided clear thinking in exalted [Saudi] circles', the source adds.

Charles does not always work with the Foreign Office. In May 2013 he became the first Windsor to visit Armenia, accepting an invitation from a foundation called Yerevan My Love, set up by the Armenian Ambassador to Britain and former Armenian Prime Minister, Armen Sarkissian. The Prince is its Patron and its aims and scope are straight from his playbook, 'a heritage-led regeneration project dedicated to preserving architecturally significant buildings in Yerevan and, by adaptive reuse, to improve the life experience of disabled children, young people and disadvantaged families'.[18] The Prince also met Catholicos Karekin II, the leader of the Armenian Orthodox Church, and was accompanied throughout by Bishop Vahan Hovhanessian, the Primate of the Armenian Church in the UK.

'There was one thing that was very clear, that the visit was to the Church not to the state,' says the Bishop. 'He didn't do the routine kind of politically correct things that others may have to do … I've been with some dignitaries, you can tell after the five, ten minutes they have seen what they came to see and now they want to leave. Not with His Royal Highness. Had we had other old buildings to show, he would have spent another two, three hours with us and everybody felt that.' Hovhanessian had met Charles at charitable fund-raising events, but had never before spent more than a few minutes in his company. 'He impressed me by his humility. He was joking with me as we were talking. He made everybody around him feel comfortable and relaxed and enjoy what we were doing because we felt that he was genuinely interested. He was genuinely concerned about the Church and the future of the Church and Christianity and the importance of preserving these roots, the earliest roots of eastern Christianity.'[19]

Hovhanessian is speaking in Armenia's London embassy, under photographs of Yerevan so old that daylight has bleached them to sepia. The building is in fancy Kensington, an area populated by members of the Armenian community rich enough to help fund Yerevan's regeneration and, indeed, to contribute to the Prince's charities – the Manoukian family supports Yerevan My Love and has endowed an outdoor activity centre at Dumfries House – but Armenia's threadbare diplomacy reflects its marginalised status. Its neighbours Azerbaijan and Turkey maintain closed borders against it. Baku harbours an enduring grudge over Nagorno-Karabakh, a predominantly ethnic Armenian region of Azerbaijan that sparked war between Armenia and Azerbaijan after the dissolution of the Soviet Union and is now formally recognised by the United Nations as occupied Azerbaijani territory. Ankara reacts with neuralgia to Armenian insistence that the massacres of Armenians in Turkey before and after the First World War amount to a holocaust. Although the devolved parliaments of Northern Ireland, Scotland and Wales have joined with eighteen other countries in condemning the Turkish 'genocide', the UK Parliament prefers to fudge the issue, talking about 'massacres' but stopping short of the stronger term, which carries legal as well as diplomatic implications. In visiting not only the fourth-century Etchmiadzin Cathedral but the twentieth-century Memorial to the Armenian Genocide, Charles risked diplomatic friction. FCO officials say they weren't worried by any aspect of the Prince's Armenian travels. 'We don't have a file for him marked "Handle with Care", you know,' says one.

By contrast Charles's support for the Dalai Lama – and criticisms of the Chinese leadership in the travel journal he wrote to amuse himself and friends that in 2005 wound up as a *Mail on Sunday* splash – did trigger a few migraines in the Foreign Office's ornate premises. Speaking in defence of the *Mail*'s right to publish, the Prince's former aide Mark Bolland claimed that contrary to public assurances, Charles had indeed made a point of missing a 1999 state banquet in London with China's President Jiang Zemin 'as a deliberate snub to the Chinese because he did not approve of the Chinese regime and is a great supporter of the Dalai Lama whom he views as being oppressed by the Chinese'. Bolland's statement continued: 'The Prince was aware of the political and economic importance of the state visit. Nevertheless, he wanted to make a public stand against the Chinese – hence his decision to boycott the banquet. We tried to persuade him to attend, but to no avail.'[20]

The Prince's lawyer disputed this version of events, but many Tibetans believe it. 'Some say [a boycott] wasn't in the plan but the fact that it became a big story also sent a message to the Chinese people and the Chinese government that something wasn't right,' says Thubten Samdup, the representative of the Dalai Lama in Europe. 'That got a huge coverage that Tibetans remember. So little acts like that matter. Also today everybody in the world seems to be very afraid of being seen with the Dalai Lama – you know, they always find a quiet place where they can meet somewhere so they can tell the press and public: "Oh yes, we've met with the Dalai Lama." But [Charles] is very open about it. Tibetans are going through a very difficult period and you know having somebody like him means a lot.'[21]

In December 2014, the Vatican cited the 'delicate situation' with China in declining a meeting between the Dalai Lama and Pope Francis. The Prince has rarely let such concerns stand in the way. He first met the Dalai Lama at a conference in 1991 and has entertained him once at Highgrove in 1999 and three times at his London residences. (The Dalai Lama, an inveterate giggler, has always entertained the Prince.) In 2004 Charles held a reception at St James's Palace for the Dalai Lama. Tony Blair, Prime Minister and future head of an eponymous Faith Foundation, cited diary pressures in declining a meeting with the Dalai Lama during that London sojourn. In 2008, the Prince again hosted the Dalai Lama. Gordon Brown, by now installed as Prime

Minister in Blair's place, also swerved a Downing Street meeting with the Dalai Lama, opting for a chat at an interfaith conference. In 2009, Charles held a private meeting with Chinese premier Hu Jintao, raising the Tibetan cause. In June 2012, Tibet's spiritual leader returned to St James's Palace, chucked the Prince under his chin, held his hand and declared him 'very close, best of friends. Right from the beginning, I felt "very nice person, good human". He [has] proved a very wonderful, sensible, good human being.'[22] The Dalai Lama's 2015 UK perambulations didn't include a similar encounter. The Prince navigated a Chinese state visit later in the year by meeting President Xi Jinping behind closed doors and again sidestepping the banquet.

When Charles made his first foray into foreign policy in 1989, mandarins had been aware of his concerns about President Ceaușescu's targeted destruction of traditional villages in Romania for some months. Black spiders had been insinuating themselves into FCO inboxes, including a letter to the then Foreign Secretary Geoffrey Howe: 'I do believe the situation in Romania should be an <u>urgent</u> priority for the European nations to address. After all, for <u>what</u> did so many of our courageous countrymen die during the last war? Was it merely to see one system of tyranny and misery exchanged for another?'[23]

Frustrated by Howe's apparent reluctance to act, the Prince deployed the same weapon that had proved effective, if indiscriminate, in his battle against modernism. In his speech at the opening of the Build a Better Britain exhibition, he suddenly pivoted from the blight of the UK's 'know-all planners' to a frontal assault on Ceaușescu and his 'wholesale destruction of his country's cultural and human heritage'. Pausing to explain 'for the benefit of those who specialise in making headlines from the most unlikely sources' that he was not drawing an equivalence between Britain's travails and the excesses of the Romanian despot, the Prince sketched out for his audience the impact of Ceaușescu's policy of 'systemisation'. 'It is difficult, I find, to remain silent as the peasant traditions and ancient buildings of a fellow European society are bulldozed to make way for a uniform and deathly mock-modernity,' he said.

He had not yet honed his routine about having a stake in Romania and the context was anyway too serious for vampire jokes, but he did explain his familial connection with Transylvania. 'Believe it or not, I have a small personal share in this unfolding tragedy because the tomb of my great-great-great-grandmother – Claudina, Countess Rhedey, who was my great-grandmother Queen Mary's grandmother, and Hungarian – is in the village of Singiorge de Padure and threatened with demolition.'[24]

The public response of the Foreign Office to the Prince's intervention – a spokesman claimed advance knowledge of the speech – belied behind-the-scenes debates about its wisdom and constitutional propriety. Still, in calling for action on an issue that had hitherto scarcely been debated, the Prince gained an unlikely ally. He had been lobbying the government to strip Ceaușescu of his Knight Grand Cross, the order awarded by the Queen during the Romanian President's 1978 state visit. Paul Flynn, less than two years into his role as Labour backbench MP and scourge of the monarchy, in a single documented instance of agreement with Charles took up the cudgels too. The government eventually agreed, removing Ceaușescu's gong later the same year, but by then small gestures had become irrelevant. The Romanian people, enraged by the regime's manifold human-rights abuses and brought onto the streets by the shooting of anti-government demonstrators, ousted Ceaușescu. The dictator and his wife were executed by firing squad on Christmas Day.

That might have signalled a new lease of life for Romania's rural heritage had Ceaușescu's fall not coincided with wider geopolitical convulsions. He had once said that Romania's most valuable exports were 'oil, Jews and Germans'; his regime sold exit visas for Jewish Romanians and ethnic Germans – members of Romania's German-speaking Saxon population – to Israel and West Germany.[25] Until his demise, the number of Saxons allowed to leave had been capped at 12,000 per annum. As the Eastern bloc crumbled, West German leaders talking up the logic of German reunification emphasised that all ethnic Germans were entitled to exercise their 'right of return' to a country most of them had never seen. In 1990 there were around 90,000 Saxons left in Transylvania. By 1996 their numbers had dwindled to below 20,000, not only because of the lure of German prosperity but also because of discord at home as tensions spiked between the ethnic Hungarian population and Romanian nationalists. The buildings Charles had campaigned to preserve stood empty; the farming culture he admired from a distance fell into disuse. Roma Gypsies moved into the area bringing different priorities and traditions.

A young Briton called William Blacker witnessed the consequences as he travelled through the Carpathians soon after the Romanian revolution, and eventually distilled his fears into a 1997 pamphlet, 'The Plight of the Saxons of Transylvania and Their Fortified Churches', published with the assistance of [a charity called] the Mihai Eminescu Trust and, says Blacker, 'a very nice man at Kall Kwik on the King's Road. It was all photocopied except the cover which was printed, and then we stapled it together. So it was really the most basic thing you can imagine.'[26] One of the 500 copies produced in this way made it into the Prince's hands. 'He wants to go to Romania. You know you've really given us an enormous amount more work,' sighed one of Charles's Private Secretaries when he bumped into Blacker at a London theatre. He was 'regretting that he'd ever shown this pamphlet to Prince Charles in the first place. But I was thinking secretly: "Oh good!"' says Blacker. 'The chap was joking, of course.'[27]

It's a joke that sometimes wears a little thin among aides, as yet another cause catches the Prince's attention, based on a fleeting conversation or an item on BBC Radio 4's *Today* programme. 'Have you heard about his idea for geothermals?' sighs one staffer to another.

Or: 'Now he's interested in WEEE' – presumably the European Union's Waste Electrical and Electronic Equipment Directive. Their Boss has been known to change tack just as suddenly, but more often he's tenacious, demanding progress reports and swift action.

Stroll around the Transylvanian villages of Viscri or Zalanpatak and you'll see what can happen if you give a Prince a pamphlet. Local residents enthuse about Charles's (partial) mastery of the Romanian language and dedication to promoting the country. In Britain, the Prince issues royal warrants as a mark of recognition to favoured suppliers of goods or services to his household. In Romania, the tables are turned, with his name garnishing all sorts of enterprises to which he has no connection. It's a mark of appreciation and a sign too that the Prince's efforts to promote the area to tourists are making an impact, if not always in ways he would wish.

He first visited in 1998 – at a low ebb in his personal life – and has returned with increasing frequency, now spending at least a few days in the country every year, usually centred on private expeditions to his house in the remote village of Zalanpatak, itself remote from the village, down a long track that in warm months is fringed with wild flowers and in winter blanketed in snow. Camilla has never accompanied him on these trips. He does snatch quality time with friends there but this is also his personal Mount Athos, a place of retreat. He doesn't go anywhere without some degree of security – and there are, as always, staff on hand, and usually gaggles of people involved in his Romanian strategies – but he gets to brew his own tea, sit and paint in silence or stride off on lengthy hikes admiring the unspoiled landscapes.

A high point of the Queen's childhood experience was to ride the London Underground incognito. For her son, the freedoms he grasps in Romania are the rarest of luxuries. Dominic Richards, the former director of the Prince's architecture foundation, remembers the first time he decided, on a whim, to hire one of London's on-street rental bikes, to cycle to Clarence House. As Richards passed through security checks at the gate, he felt 'a sudden overwhelming sense of sadness. [The Prince] can't have this thing. He can't. People don't understand that he works so hard, his diary is so controlled, he doesn't have that kind of personal freedom that to me is worth a billion dollars.'[28]

Throughout his adult life, Charles has tried to find escape routes from his overplanned existence to the riotous natural world in which he perceives a different kind of order. Laurens van der Post in 1977 tantalised Charles with the prospect of a seven-week trek in the Kalahari. Van der Post's BBC series, *The Lost World of the Kalahari*, and later book of the same name had been huge hits during the Prince's childhood. The Foreign Office stymied van der Post's plan because of the deepening conflict around Rhodesia so the lengthy trek became a short hop to Kenya. The journey to the Kalahari eventually took place a decade later, truncated to just four days.

That has been the lifelong pattern of princely travels: tasters, days here, days there, trailed by retainers and royal protection officers and others. If a Prince slips into the wilderness and someone is there to observe him, is it still wilderness? When Charles flew to the so-called Empty Quarter, the desert in Abu Dhabi, in 1993, Jonathan Dimbleby and a film crew followed his every footprint in the sand dunes. 'The whole sort of problem on these trips, these exercises, is that you're suddenly flown and bumped out to somewhere like this for literally half an hour, then you turn around and go back again,' he told his shadows ruefully.[29] In November 2013, during his official visit to India en route for the Commonwealth Heads of Government Meeting in Sri Lanka, the Prince's exasperation boiled over. He had driven two and a half hours into the Keralan jungle near Kochi with his brother-in-law Mark Shand, founder and chairman of Elephant Family, a conservation organisation, hoping to see elephant in the wild. At the watering hole, thickets of police and military determined to ensure royal safety ensured that no terrorist penetrated the shield – but neither did any pachyderms.

Charles arrived at his next destination under torrential rains, walking through the mud in his white linen suit and white shoes and gamely abandoning his umbrella so that Arthur Edwards and other photographers in attendance could get the images they needed. But although he smiled, he spoke through gritted teeth. 'On every other occasion in my life that I've gone to these things it's the same – it's the security that ruins everything … It's Murphy's Law. Everybody always says, "the day before people saw God knows what".'[30]

Only on the Balmoral estate and in Transylvania has the Prince regularly and reliably escaped the madding crowds and in Romania that is becoming increasingly difficult. The first houses he bought in Transylvania – or more precisely, that a subsidiary of the Prince of Wales Charitable Foundation purchased – are in Viscri and Malancrav. He offloaded the Malancrav house in 2002 and no longer stays at the Viscri property because he has in some ways been too successful in promoting tourism to Viscri, becoming an attraction in his own right.

Both the Zalanpatak and Viscri properties are available for rental. The logistics are handled by Count Tibor Kalnoky, scion of Hungarian Transylvanian nobility who successfully reclaimed his family's ancestral home and has joined with the Prince in trying to conserve heritage buildings and the natural environment by attracting upscale ecotourism to the area. Kalnoky's website describes the 'rich biodiversity' of the Prince's Zalanpatak lodge, where guests will be looked after by 'discreet staff and the resident ecologist'. Tour companies operating without Charles's imprimatur take a different approach. For example, the 'Live Like a King' package offered by the agency Touring Romania starts with a night at Zalanpatak. 'After a good-night sleep in Prince Charles' bed, we will enjoy the beauty of site. After lunch, we leave for Miclosoara, another dear place of Prince Charles. When he comes to Miclosoara, the Prince goes to his good friend, Count Kalnoky. For one night we will accommodate here. We will have plenty of time to enjoy the beauty of the area [and] the wonderful dishes of the traditional Romanian Cuisine, so appreciated by Prince Charles. After breakfast, we are heading to another dear place of His Highness – Viscri village, where the Prince of Wales bought a house. Viscri was a rusty village until Prince Charles put his foot down there. The village was reborn, and the villagers developed a taste for tourism.'[31]

It's another example of Murphy's Law: tourism, as a tool of development, is hard to control and sometimes threatens to destroy the very things it seeks to promote, plonking eyesore hotels in sites of natural beauty and in Transylvania felling tracts of virgin forest to create ski runs. This couldn't be further from the Prince's aspirations for the region, which he sees as one of the world's last remaining models of traditional sustainability, the old ways of agriculture enhancing nature rather than destroying it. 'The key thing I think in Romania, Transylvania in particular, is that there's so much we can learn from the last corner of Europe where you can see true sustainability and complete resilience and the maintenance of entire ecosystems to the benefit of mankind and also for nature and there's so much we should learn from that before it's too late,' he says in a documentary called *Wild Carpathia*.

The interviewer pushes, gently. 'Presumably this is why it's so important to preserve it for the future?' The Prince, in characteristic fashion, anticipates the criticism his words may attract. 'And people will say: "Ah well, you know you're just trying to preserve things in aspic and trying to prevent progress and so on," but don't you think by now we might have learned a few lessons from the things that have gone wrong with an agro-industrial approach to everything?'[32]

Just as Canada has become the proving ground for the Prince's ideas of how his reign might play out, so Romania allows him to grapple with big issues that obsess him, about how to combine tradition and innovation, conserve without constricting, achieve, in that other favourite word of his, *harmony*. In Romania, in contrast to Britain and the Realms, he runs into little opposition and enjoys a great deal of appreciation for what he does. 'I've never seen anybody that has got a bad word to say about him frankly; everybody loves him. Everybody wants to give him time, everyone wants to interview him, and everyone thinks he's wonderful,' says Craig Turp, an Englishman resident in the Romanian capital Bucharest, the Editor-in-Chief of the *In Your Pocket* city guides.[33] Turp, an exception to the rule, frequently uses his blog to mock the Prince. 'It is all very well visiting a Romanian village for a day or two and saying how jolly marvellous it is (especially when you stay in some rather agreeable accommodation), quite another to have to live in one your entire life,' wrote Turp during the Prince's 2011 excursion to Transylvania. 'But then what would one of the most privileged men in the world know about hardship?'[34]

In conversation, Turp turns out to be better disposed towards the Prince than his blog suggests. 'There are some things about him that I actually quite like,' he says. Turp is closely acquainted with the Romanian countryside and its grinding poverty – his parents-in-law are subsistence farmers in northern Transylvania. It transpires that his greatest objection to the Prince is not that he meddles in Romania, but that he meddles too narrowly, seeming to focus only on the former Saxon enclaves. Turp wishes Charles would use his influence to highlight rural poverty in areas that aren't graced with Saxon architecture; he also questions whether high-end tourism is a sustainable industry in the places that are.

Justin Mundy, the Director of the Prince's International Sustainability Unit, says Charles is keenly aware that tourism on its own is not a solution. 'His concern has been, as it has been in other parts of the UK and the world, to try and find what are the key drivers of issues of rural poverty, what are the key drivers to try and enhance the build-up of skills and resilience within these rural communities in order not only to safeguard and to ensure that the architecture in the villages maintains economic integrity and therefore can participate properly but also to find a way in which the very complex mosaic of agricultural activities can be maintained.'[35]

Mundy is one of the Prince's most influential advisers. Soft-spoken, he once operated in the back rooms of Blair's government and now maintains a deliberately low profile while steering some of the Prince's most ambitious projects. He was instrumental in finding practical mechanisms to realise the Prince's conviction that the way to preserve rainforests is to make them more valuable alive than dead. Under his auspices the ISU has undertaken valuable research into creating sustainable and secure food systems, offering concrete proposals to help industries, such as fishing, transition to models that will benefit both the workforce and the wider environment. He is sitting in his Clarence House office with Jeremy Staniforth, an ISU adviser who also advises the Romanian government and is based for about one week every month in Bucharest. 'We managed to get the Ministry of the Environment and the Ministry of Tourism to talk together and to start putting in programmes to use sensitive systems ... They've designated certain villages that they want to focus on in the Carpathians so they'll have a sort of agro-ecotourism. They've put in some bicycle trails, walking trails. There's masses and masses of sheep and there we're trying to introduce improved cheeses so that they don't just keep them at home and eat them [but] actually produce a cheese that can then be marketed outside of Romania and marketed into the hotels. If you go to the hotels there you'll see the packs of butter, they're all brought in from Germany and other places in Europe,' says Staniforth.[36]

In his advisory capacity for the Romanian government, Staniforth has come to understand not only the physical terrain but also the political landscape that complicates efforts to help the country thrive. Ceaușescu uprooted all the administrative levels that came between government and villages, and these have never been fully restored. That means a lot of top-down decision-making, not only from Bucharest but more distant Brussels since Romania joined the European Union in 2007. Non-governmental organisations try to fill the void, but sometimes clash or overlap and can't always summon the concerted voice necessary to achieve their objectives. Charles, on his visits to Romania, often travels via Bucharest to talk to the Prime Minister or the President. 'I really can't but emphasise what a huge help it is to have Prince Charles involved in the way that he has been involved. His interest in the country has made a crucial difference in helping ordinary Romanians understand the importance of their historic old buildings and traditions,' says William Blacker, who now runs the Anglo-Romanian Trust for Traditional Architecture which he set up in 2009.[37] 'Because [the Prince] is totally apolitical, it works,' says Staniforth. 'It's a pure, simple desire to try and preserve, but not in aspic. He's not unrealistic. He realises that people have got to move on and it's got to be sustainable in an economic, financial way.'[38]

For all that, one of Turp's accusations resonates: that Charles romanticises peasant life in Romania. In finding practical ways to support people living these lives, the Prince is irrefutably helping to keep them where they are. The question is why he is impelled to do so.

'For me the biggest problem is that the Romania [the Prince] loves, these serf villages, they confirm his world view,' says Turp. He has read the Prince's book *Harmony* 'in a kind of ironic way' and detects 'this idea that there is a natural order of things, everybody knows their place. In Romania, in rural Romania especially, he finds that. It's a world which in Western Europe probably hasn't existed for hundreds of years. The peasant is still very much a peasant, the lord of the manor is still very much the lord of the manor. The peasant doesn't really have any ambition to climb socially.'[39]

This echoes Elaine Day's charge, that Charles thinks 'that people should not rise above their station'.[40] The many individuals for whom he helps to create opportunities to acquire education or skills, get jobs, start businesses would say otherwise. The Prince's Trust and many of his other charitable enterprises and initiatives are designed to alleviate the inequalities that place him in palaces and the poor man at his gate.

Yet perceptions of Charles as someone dedicated to maintaining the old order are not without foundation. The apparent contradictions in his aims can be traced to the intertwined histories of Empire and of the ecological movement. The philosopher Prince draws his ideas from some surprising sources.

Chapter 11

Harmonies and Disharmonies

Charles appears to be dancing. He's wearing a double-breasted suit the glaucous grey of a seagull's wing with a jaunty little purple flower tucked into the lapel. His brogues of ancient leather are planted on the lawn at St James's Palace in an effortless ballet 4th position as he sways his upper body. His right arm describes a large and graceful circle. Three men and four women stand in a wide arc facing him. Beyond them in the flickering shade of 140-year-old London plane trees, further groups of guests arranged in the same formations await completion by their royal host.

The Prince perceives naturally occurring patterns in everything, a hidden geometry in flowers that finds echoes in the glorious architecture of Chartres cathedral and in the five-pointed orbit of Venus, and perhaps that's not so surprising. Throughout his life, aides have coaxed the people he meets into neat configurations before he arrives. The semicircle is a kinder shape than a straight line, allowing people to chat with each other until he reaches them, and affording him a swift exit should Charles avail of the opportunity, which he almost never does. The tight timetable of this event, slotted into an afternoon in June 2014 during a week of keynote speeches and the publication of his annual review and before he heads to Scotland to welcome his parents to Dumfries House, means he ought already to have moved on from this first group. He has been engrossed in conversation with members of the Swarovski family whose business has been turning cut glass to commercial gold since the nineteenth century. Then, just as he turned to leave, Nadja Swarovski, the first female member of the company's executive board, asked him a question and he paused, mid-stride.

His answer involves the subject everyone has notionally gathered to discuss – the science of biomimetics – but quickly expands to encompass a philosophy that for Charles explains everything about the world, and to a befuddled world might handily explain pretty much everything about Charles. This belief system, like its exponent, is one-third complaint to two-thirds transfiguring faith. Its kernel is this: modern thinking – or more precisely Modernist thinking – has disconnected us from Nature-with-a-capital-N and from the trinity of celestial essences or objective Platonic values which she embodies, the True, the Beautiful and the Good. The result is alienation and destruction. Yet there is still time – just – to reconnect by creating 'virtuous circles'. It is one of these circles which the Prince is so enthusiastically pantomiming for Nadja Swarovski.

Biomimeticists have recognised what 'mechanistic science' overlooks, that Nature has been running her own research-and-development experiments from the dawn of time, rejecting poor designs and preserving only the best, he tells Swarovski. In co-opting those designs, it is possible to create things that are in sympathy with Nature and are therefore more energy-efficient to manufacture or deploy, biodegradable just as fur, scales, feathers, bones and vegetal life are, better, cleverer, more true, beautiful and good. Building a market for biomimetics will foster a deepening appreciation of Nature and her creations along with a recognition that the extinction of any life form means the loss of a natural solution engineered over millennia and often more technologically advanced than anything humans might come up with on their own. Products and services based on the invisible grammar of harmony will be in demand, and so businesses providing those biomimetics-based products and services will flourish, to the mutual, sustainable benefit of all in the circle, from micro-organisms and potentially endangered species to commercial organisations and consumers, maybe even Swarovski's customers.

In this instance he is preaching, if not to the converted then to people who are at least open enough to the potential of biomimetics to be exploring it. Swarovski designers have worked with Professor Andrew Parker, Research Leader in the Life Sciences department at the Natural History Museum and Senior Visiting Research Fellow at Green Templeton College in Oxford specialising in photonic structures and eyes, evolution, development and biomimetics, to imbue their famous crystals with the vivid hues of a hummingbird. This is done using structural colours made from transparent materials that refract and reflect, inspired by the micro-structures in hummingbird feathers. There's no need for environmentally damaging pigments and the optical effects are stunning.

Before arriving at St James's Palace, guests congregated at Prince Philip House just off the Mall for a presentation by Professor Parker and his business advisor Alastair Lukies, a former rugby player who founded the mobile banking company Monitise. They unveiled a new biomimetics company Lifescaped. Parker explained the science, and then Lukies evangelised, not for Christianity, though he mentioned his faith more than once, but for the commercial potential of biomimetics and its potential to transform the world for the better. 'It's about profitability and philanthropy,' he said. 'It's not about competition; it's about *cooperatition*.' Charles is a supporter of Lifescaped; neither Parker nor Lukies ruled out his formal involvement in the company.

It was with another virtuous circle in mind that the Prince founded Duchy Originals, aiming to create a market for sustainably produced goods to provide a boost to small farmers, benefit their free-ranging herds and flocks, protect the wildlife that flourishes in fields and hedgerows which have been allowed to grow without blankets of pesticide and herbicide, and provide assurance to the consumer, who can enjoy an organic Original Oaten Biscuit, organic British Beef Meatball or a slug of organic Old Ruby Ale safe in the knowledge that these and other Duchy Originals products are not tainted with chemicals or manufactured from the products of industrialised farming.

The Prince's Trust is based on the idea of turning vicious cycles into virtuous circles, re-routing the destructive path through child-hood deprivation, behavioural problems, poor prospects, crime, drugs and alcohol dependencies into a new circuit in which the possibility of a better life provides the motivation to do the things necessary to attain that goal. In Transylvania Charles is hoping to trigger a virtuous circle by using his celebrity to raise awareness of the natural environment, Saxon architecture and disappearing traditions, and stimulating the eco-tourism that nourishes all three – to the benefit of the local populations – while galvanising the government and non-govern-mental organisations into facilitating these positive developments.

Each virtuous circle operates inside an expanding ring of concentric virtuous circles, just as vicious cycles intersect and gain in force. In holding a reception for biomimetics, Charles is attempting to signal the promise of the science – and the dangers of ignoring Nature – and to encourage what he calls 'joined-up thinking', to create what he explains to Swarovski is 'an integrated picture in terms of water security, energy security, food security'. He frequently worries aloud about the dangers of unsustainable population growth coupled with climate change.

Most of the mechanisms that his International Sustainability Unit proposes for the mitigation of climate change are based on principles of enlightened self-interest in the form of tight virtuous circles that make it more profitable to conserve than destroy. Left unchecked, industries and countries interfere with ecosystems, which the Prince sees as the most fundamental virtuous circles of all, perpetuating themselves until malign or careless development upsets their natural balance.

'At the moment we are disrupting the teeming diversity of life and the "ecosystems" that sustain it – the forests and prairies, the woodland, moorland and fens, the oceans, rivers and streams,' Charles writes in *Harmony*. 'And this all adds up to the degree of "dis-ease" we are causing to the intricate balance that regulates the planet's climate, on which we so intimately depend.' He explains that his reason for writing the book – which happens to be his reason for just about everything he's done during four decades as a philanthropist and charitable entrepreneur – 'is that I feel I would be failing in my duty to future generations and to the Earth itself if I did not attempt to point this out and indicate possible ways we can heal the world'.[1]

He wrote the book with the BBC's Ian Skelly and Tony Juniper, a prominent environmentalist working for the ISU and other bodies and a former Director of Friends of the Earth. 'Tony and I would write a draft or a section,' says Skelly. 'Certain parts of the book were Tony's bag and certain parts of the book were my bag and then we would send what we'd written and it would come back with great reams of writing all over it and suggestions here, suggestions there. [The Prince] scribbles in red on texts and so it's full of red writing and then I'd take that and incorporate it and do this bit of research and go off and talk to this particular person and get a thought from here or there and then it would go back and forwards and sometimes it would come back on the same morning. There was one occasion when we were right up against a deadline and he was literally scribbling, looking at two or three pages of this between engagements. Scribbling away in a corridor, often in the car. So, over time it would be very difficult to say: "I did that, or Tony wrote that," or "The Prince wrote that." It really was a combined effort and he was definitely one of the three writers.'[2]

More than that, the 2010 book is phrased in the Prince's distinctive cadences, in the first person, and clearly intended as his statement of belief. He insisted, despite the reservations of the publisher, on the title *Harmony*, and made a documentary of the same name with US film-makers Julie Bergman Sender and Stuart Sender. The film premiered in 2012. 'The word is derived from the Ancient Greek *harmonia* which essentially means to join things up, so that was what he wanted to stress,' says Skelly. 'That Nature is joined up, it's a harmonic system. That doesn't mean to say it's completely at ease, it's not perfectly balanced, but there is this curious seeking of balance, and of course it's incredibly interconnected. It's our attempt at explaining something that is so complex in its interconnection that we can't conceive of it being so but you can draw this patterning from it and see that there is this astonishing association between things.'[3]

A list of acknowledgements at the back of the book reveals associations some people might find astonishing: Charles's unofficial circle of advisers. They include not only Andrew Parker but two exponents of alternative and complementary medicine, Mosaraf Ali and Michael Dixon, and Keith Critchlow who teaches at the Prince's School of Traditional Arts. His biography on the school's website reads: 'Professor Critchlow has published many books and papers on cosmology, architecture, and geometry, which he sees as a karma yoga. These include *Order in Space*, *Time Stands Still* and *Islamic Patterns: An Analytical and Cosmological Approach*. As he says, "All authentic academic research is based on the simultaneous pursuit of the True, the Beautiful, and the Good – if any is pursued separately, imbalance ensues." He continues his research into five-fold and ten-fold symmetries, an area that has held his interest for many years.'[4] Charles provided a foreword for another of Critchlow's books, *The Hidden Geometry of Flowers*. 'It is a sad fact,' the Prince observes, 'that our modern outlook does not recognise geometry as a language by which we may understand Divine order … The patterning hidden in a flower also enables all life to achieve an active state of balance that we call "harmony", which is the prerequisite of the health of each of the Earth's vital support systems.'[5]

Charles's overarching quest – the motivation behind everything he does – is to restore harmony. It is a particularly cruel irony that his mission frequently plunges him into conflicts and disharmony. He feels hurt by the controversies he creates and often not a little bewildered. A fan of the BBC comedy series *Blackadder*, he identifies, says someone who knows him well, not with the scheming anti-hero of the title or its dumb Prince but with the hapless Baldrick, a member of the lower orders whose 'cunning plans' are ridiculed but often turn out to be right. Like Baldrick, Charles sometimes reaches his right conclusions via some questionable pathways. Like Baldrick, sometimes he just gets things wrong.

In November 1948, General Jan Smuts sent a cable to King George: 'We pray that the Prince will be a blessing to our Commonwealth and to the world.'[6]

Smuts had resigned as premier of South Africa a few months before Charles's birth and would live just two more years, but his influence has permeated the Prince's life just as it continues to flow through significant streams of the conservation and environmental movement. Smuts was not only a politician and military strategist; he was also a keen amateur botanist, ecologist and the founder of holism – or 'whole-ism', as Charles prefers to spell it. Smuts set out his philosophy in his 1926 book *Holism and Evolution.* Nature tended to form wholes, he wrote. 'The whole is not a mere mechanical system . . . It is more than the sum of its parts.' This idea neatly served the fraying idea of Empire and provided a retrospective justifying principle for the 1910 union of the Orange Free State, Transvaal, Natal and Cape Province under the British Crown to create South Africa. It also underpinned some of Smuts's ideas about race. Although he opposed apartheid, he thought black populations should only gradually be entrusted with social and political rights and assumed a natural hierarchy 'with human races ranging from the very lowest to the highest', the white man. The quotation, from one of Smuts's private letters, is cited by Peder Anker in his book, *Imperial Ecology*.

The South African leader was reworking an older notion, about 'the harmony of nature and the simple people and the simple life in the countryside as opposed to the industrial world', says Anker, speaking from his office at Harvard University where he is Associate Professor of the History of Science and Environmental Studies. 'Essentially it's an old romantic idea dating back to [Jean-Jacques] Rousseau. You know the life of the noble savage and we can never lead the lives of savages again. But we can aspire to be the new noble savage.'[7]

The phrase first crops up in John Dryden's 1670s play *The Conquest of Granada*, when the hero Almanzor squares up to his love rival Mahomet Boabdelin, whom he has helped to restore to the kingship of Granada. 'Obeyed as sovereign by thy subjects be / But know that I alone am king of me / I am as free as nature first made man / Ere the base laws of servitude began / When wild in woods the noble savage ran.'[8]

Almanzor's identity is far from fixed. Kidnapped as a child by African natives, and fighting for the Moors against the Spanish, he only discovers late in the play that he is in fact a Spanish aristocrat. The idea of the noble savage has gone through at least as many plot twists and identity shifts. The sixteenth-century essayist Michel de Montaigne found him in the most unlikely place, in a colony of cannibals: 'They are savages at the same rate that we say fruit are wild, which nature produces of herself and by her own ordinary progress; whereas in truth, we ought rather to call those wild, whose natures we have changed by our artifice, and diverted from the common order.'[9] Rousseau popularised the notion of 'man in a state of Nature'. 'God makes all things good; man meddles with them and they become evil,' he wrote.[10]

That might appear to sum up a central idea of *Harmony* but Charles takes issue with Rousseau for insisting that 'there is a conflict between the "natural" human state and the "social" one'.[11] The Prince is convinced that man in his natural state, Adam before the apple, is essentially good. It is the post-Enlightenment world – a world corrupted by thinkers like Rousseau – that has interposed itself between man and his better nature.

You can see why the Prince might regard Rousseau with suspicion. The philosopher provided some of the inspiration for the French Revolution. His legacy is also visible in the founding principles of a phenomenon that induces at least as much horror in Charles as the fate of the Bourbons: modernist architecture. Its godfather, Le Corbusier, was born like Rousseau in Switzerland and, muses Anker, 'was a keen reader of Rousseau and lived in a small, simple little hut in the summer just to reach back to that savage life'. Modernists and anti-modernists share great chunks of ideology that instead of bringing them together make their antipathies more visceral. 'You can find in so many other modernist architects the same idea of the simple life and the simple structure without ornaments as being liberated from the burden of civilisation,' says Anker.[12]

In 2008 the Prince delivered the keynote address at the annual media awards held by the Foreign Press Association in London. His audience expected the usual fare for such an occasion – a homily about the importance of investigative journalism and conflict reporting or perhaps, if the Prince felt sufficiently daring, a rueful look back at his relationship with the British press. Instead 400 journalists and assorted actors, business leaders and politicians got what amounted to a preview of *Harmony* and the unifying philosophy behind all the Prince's charities and initiatives. The heir to the throne cantered through examples of the damage wrought by modernism: dependence on technology, rampant consumerism, 'noxious' high-rises, 'dis-ease', and he spoke, dangerously, of 'a fundamental disconnection from

Nature – from the organic order of things that Nature discloses; from the structure and cyclical process of Nature and from its laws [that] impose those natural limits'.[13]

To at least some members of his audience, the 'organic order' sounded indistinguishable from the idea of the hereditary order that placed him above any nationals from the Realms who might be present. 'He was making the case that monarchy was part of the natural order of things,' says Will Hutton, an economist, author and former Editor of the *Observer*. Craig Turps maintains a similar theme in his blog *Bucharest Life*. 'People: Prince Charles does not love Romania per se,' Turps admonished in a 2010 post. 'It is a certain way of life in a certain part of a country that just happens to be Romania he loves: a way of life that reminds him of the pre-industrial age, when there was a natural order of society. Everyone knew their place, there was zero social mobility and the lower orders didn't answer their betters back.'[14]

Charles is alert to such interpretations and in his speech to the Foreign Press Association tried to deflect criticism by inserting one of his typically defensive lines: 'You may believe that I have some curious and reactionary obsession with returning to a kind of mock-medieval, forelock-tugging past. In fact all I am saying is that we simply cannot contend with the global environmental crises we face by relying on clever technological "fixes" on their own.'[15] That was disingenuous. The Prince's philosophy is far more intricate than that. 'We thought … when we started to work we were making a kind of environmental movie but it's really a kind of bigger thing,' said Stuart Sender, director and co-producer of the *Harmony* movie, clearly still startled – and impressed – by the scope and ambition of the princely philosophy.[16]

The belief system set out in the film and more fully realised in the book starts from the premise that every human is intrinsically good and sets out a holistic view of the world that sees a gold thread linking everything. The Prince is also convinced that we are born imbued with perennial wisdoms and is deeply anxious that these risk being lost in the maelstrom of modern life. In *Harmony*, he describes the devastation wrought by the tsunami that raced across the Indian Ocean in December 2004 and that he witnessed at a year's distance on a visit to Sri Lanka. He mentions that an early-warning system has subsequently been developed. But is this technological solution the best one? The Prince claims there was already 'an early-warning system that was acted upon by those who could read it'. The Sentinelese, indigenous forest-dwelling hunter-gatherers living on one of the Southern Andaman Islands without electricity or any modern method to alert them to the coming wave, retreated to higher ground, 'told of the danger', Charles concludes, 'by Nature herself'.[17]

To the Prince, civilisation often appears as a serpent that comes between man and primal harmony. He would never use the term 'noble savage' but the iconography is recognisable. That gets him into trouble, because the concept has historically been pressed into service to justify keeping mankind in the grinding poverty of subsistence. In Smuts's holism, the savage takes on the guise of 'the bushman being happy living in the bushes', says Peder Anker. 'That's where they should live and that's where they will be in harmony. And that's why you need a Bantustan, a closed-off area for them, so they can live in their harmony. Which seen from the bushman's point of view is incredibly oppressive.'[18]

Laurens van der Post, a key architect of the Prince's thinking, had absorbed Smuts's holism at source in his native South Africa and blended it with other strains of thought, in particular the teachings of Swiss psychiatrist Carl Jung. Van der Post advocated Jung's concept of a collective unconscious that binds human beings whether they are Kalahari bushmen or princes in palaces. The trove of shared memory and experience is sometimes accessed through dreams. In *Venture to the Interior*, van der Post's richly embroidered memoir of his 1949 expedition to the Nyike and Mlange plateaus, the author meets a Briton, 'Michael Dowler' (a pseudonym), living with four African servants. 'The more I got to know Michael, the clearer became my impression that he gave these children of African nature the consideration and affection he would have liked to give his own dark, unfulfilled self, only centuries of so-called European civilised values prevented him from doing this,' writes van der Post.[19]

Van der Post was a charlatan; his biographer J. D. F. Jones produced evidence that he consistently exaggerated his achievements and lied compulsively; he also used his powers of seduction widely. In 1952, van der Post had sex with a fourteen-year-old South African girl he was supposed to be chaperoning during a sea voyage to the UK and continued to maintain her as his mistress in London until she became pregnant, a secret that came out only after his death. He duped many people, not least because he was mesmeric as well as famous. His brilliant storytelling in books and television programmes secured him a wide fan base. To a Prince condemned to the forced innocence of that chilly Eden, Planet Windsor, van der Post's vitality was also immensely attractive. Moreover in reworking the idea of the collective unconscious, van der Post provided Charles with the thing he most lacked, assurance of an automatic connection to people – and not only to the ermine ranks but simple, good, unspoiled people. Van der Post's anecdote about the character he calls Michael Dowler concludes: 'We all have a dark figure within ourselves, a Negro, a gipsy, an aboriginal with averted back. And, alas! The nearest many of us can get to making terms with him is to strike up these precarious friendships with him through the black people of Africa.'

This wouldn't have seemed so gratuitously offensive within the context of an age that institutionalised racial discrimination and routinely deployed pseudo-sciences to claim white superiority. Charles has moved on as culture has moved on. He may romanticise the idea of unspoiled humanity but he's no more racist (or indeed sexist) than many educated, affluent white British men, which is to say, of course, that he is by no means fully exempt from either charge. However, unlike many educated, affluent white British men, he has regular contact with people from different backgrounds and ethnic and cultural heritages. Moreover, his belief system fortifies his determination to create employment opportunities for former offenders and help disadvantaged young people reach their full potential. He understands, and tries to change, some of the drivers of twenty-first-century segregation that mean joblessness among black British men remains stubbornly double that of their white male counterparts.

The dubious origin of a good idea doesn't negate it, any more than its misappropriation invalidates it. But Charles's philosophy will always carry difficult resonances, not only from the past but the present. At times it can sound like a posh version of creationism, Intelligent Design but with better spelling and a wider vocabulary. That's because it is shot through with the mystical ontology of Smuts–Jung that he imbibed not only from the plausible van der Post and the people he brought into the Prince's life, especially the poet and Temenos Academy founder Kathleen Raine, but also from Charles's beloved grandmother, the Queen Mother, who knew Smuts well, and from Prince Philip, the father Charles could never wholly please. Though Prince Philip's environmentalism is well known, his brusque, brook-no-nonsense public persona has largely diverted attention from his fascination with the immaterial. He founded the Alliance of Religions and Conservation to encourage different faiths to preach the gospel of conservation and has spoken of a spiritual dimension to the natural world.[20]

'I've always been interested in Jung, his work, his ideas. And Philip is interested in Jung,' Sacha, Duchess of Abercorn, a friend of the Duke's, told Gyles Brandreth in 2004. 'Prince Philip is always questing, exploring, searching for meaning, testing ideas. We had riveting conversations about Jung.'

Riveting conversations were not a hallmark of Charles's first honeymoon. As the royal yacht carried him and his new bride to Italy and Greece, he left Diana to her own devices.[21] He sunbathed on deck, lost in van der Post's *Jung and the Study of Time.* Van der Post had already trained the Prince to note down his dreams. Charles's self-appointed guru did not believe in the Freudian analysis that dreams represent the disguised fulfilment of repressed wishes but the Jungian concept that they carry nuggets of the ancient wisdom which civilisation so wantonly destroys.

A leading British botanist named Arthur Tansley entered analysis with Sigmund Freud in 1922 and quickly developed a second strand to his career, writing and lecturing on psychology. Much of the rest of Tansley's time was spent locked in competition with different schools of botany in Britain and in South Africa. In 1924 British botanists and South Africans – richly funded, thanks to Smuts's patronage – faced off at the 1924 Imperial Botanical Conference in London, chaired by Tansley. Peder Anker's book *Imperial Ecology* examines the ways in which these rivalries helped to fuse botany and wider disciplines into a science that could secure the needs of Empire.

In contrast to Smuts – and in opposition to Smuts's ideas – Tansley defined himself as a 'mechanist'. 'All living organisms may be regarded as machines transforming energy from one form or another,' he stated. In 1935, in a tract criticising holism, which he despised, Tansley coined an expression and an idea: 'ecosystem': 'Ecosystems are of the most various kinds and sizes. They form one category of the multitudinous physical systems of the universe, which range from the universe as a whole down to the atom,' Tansley declared.[22]

Ecosystems may have become a matter of faith across ecology but their definition and the way they function remains a subject of fierce debate. Though most widely understood to represent a virtuous circle of self-regulation – a balancing mechanism – this paradigm too has been challenged. 'The metaphor of the balance of nature is not an appropriate metaphor for the technical understanding that had emerged from the science of ecology over the decades,' says Dr Steward T.A. Pickett, a plant ecologist at the University of Illinois, Urbana. 'The balance of nature is one of our big governing myths ... These ideas of harmony and balance of nature are classical Greek ideas. But that's really not at all useful as a way to couch or to communicate the richness of dynamism and contingency that we find in the natural world.'[23]

'Mechanists', with their adherence to evidence-based, physical science, repudiate holists who, like the original holist Smuts, reject the mechanistic approach as reductive and try to make room for the spiritual. 'Our object in studying and interpreting Nature is to be faithful to our experience of her,' wrote Smuts. 'We do not want to recreate Nature in our own image, and as far as possible we wish to eliminate errors of observation or construction which are due to us as observers. We do not wish to spread Nature on a sort of Procrustes bed of our concepts and cut off here and there what appears surplus or unnecessary or even nonexistent to our subjective standards ... A good deal of what we have hitherto felt certain may once more become uncertain; the solid and recognised landmarks may once more become blurred or shifting; the stable results of 19th century science may once more become unstable and uncertain.'[24]

These are ideas Charles has internalised, and just as the sight of brutalist tower blocks crystallised his distaste for modernist architecture so some of the uglier outcrops of technology and medicine have for him become totemic of the failure of mechanists to admit the spiritual dimension. In confronting 'mechanistic thinking' he hopes that the stable results of twentieth-century science may once more become unstable and uncertain, to make room in twenty-first-century science not so much for the God particle as for God.

That immediately cuts off some of his potential support. A significant tranche of the Prince's most strident critics – not least the constituency of concerned citizenry frequently described by the British media as 'Guardian readers' – shares his concerns about the industrialised world. Technology once promised space-age dreams in which everyone lived in cities, in sleek skyscrapers fitted out with all manner of clever white goods, their talkative Frigidaires fully stocked with mysterious foods. These happy future folk would commute to work in flying machines, if, in these utopias, they worked at all.

A significant portion of that vision has come horribly true. In nations including Argentina, Australia, Belgium, Brazil, Canada, Denmark, Finland, France, Norway, Sweden, the UK and the US, 80 per cent or more of the populations are concentrated in urban areas. In China, Russia and even in Romania more than half of the populations live in cities.[25] Yet many conurbations serve only their richest inhabitants well. São Paulo is the largest city in the southern hemisphere, also one of the most traffic-choked. Its wealthy residents have taken to the skies, pushing helicopter ownership to the highest per capita anywhere. There are helipads on the roofs of towering apartment blocks and office complexes, enabling the elite minority never to descend to street level but to overfly gridlock and some of the largest and nastiest favelas in Brazil where joblessness is more common than employment.

Similar sharp divisions have opened across the globe as wealthier populations soar above the problems associated with lower-income groups. A transnational apartheid has seen the affluent living longer and healthier lives than their poorer counterparts. That gap is now narrowing again but only because affluence is wreaking its own toll, with the longer lifespans gifted by clean water supplies and improved medical technologies eroding as a result of what Kurt Hahn called 'spectatoritis', unhealthily sedentary lifestyles, combined with smoking, excessive drinking and calorie-rich, content-poor diets. Obesity, until recently a signifier of urban poverty, is swelling among the better-off. Big Food and Big Pharma are flourishing. In July 2014, the US Centers for Disease Control and Prevention revealed that half of all Americans have at least one chronic disease, representing the main causes of poor health, disability and death, and accounting for most health-care expenditures.

The Prince has been trying to address these problems from a number of different angles over many years. His charities run programmes designed to reconnect urban children with the natural environment, to encourage physical activity and also to raise awareness of food sources. In promoting sustainable farming, he is simultaneously seeking to encourage better diets and to attack the vicious cycles of industrialised agriculture – an example he cites in *Harmony* is the US beef industry, forced to spend money on ammonia to cleanse meat of *E. coli* that continues to infect cattle reared not on grass but on corn in feed lots. When he first entered the debate on health-care provision more than three decades ago, he hoped to break another malign cycle, by encouraging policymakers to do more towards tackling the causes of chronic diseases before these diseases take hold and need to be treated, incurring costs that no system – including Britain's NHS – can sustain as more technologies and treatments become available. He has continued to warn of the folly of medicalising every complaint and throwing pills at patients when patients and taxpayers would benefit if these problems were averted upstream.

The Prince keeps making these important points and in confronting the sway of global corporations has been doing what few governments risk and few individuals have the access or influence to do meaningfully. Yet the manner in which he intervenes means some people find it hard to hear him. They may agree with him on numerous issues – as this author does – but, like this author, they may also struggle with the routes he takes to reach some of his views, in particular with the more mystical aspects of holism. For some people close to the Prince, his advocacy for complementary and alternative

The constant gardener: Charles at Highgrove in 1986.

The official London residence: Clarence House.

A favourite retreat: Birkhall in Scotland.

The heart is wherever the home is: Charles and Camilla at Llwynywermod in 2009.

Rescued: Dumfries House in East Ayrshire.

A stake in Romania: The guest house at Zalanpatak, Transylvania.

Soundings: In 1985 Charles speaks with Michael Elliott, *left*, and Mark Malloch Brown, both from less rarefied backgrounds than some of their colleagues at the *Economist*.

Three in the marriage: In 2012 Charles and
Camilla play host to the Dalai Lama.

A different kind of estate: Touring an
inner-London housing complex in 2001.

Diplomatic and offensive: Charles attends the 1997 Hong Kong handover ceremony
with, *left*, China's President Jiang Zemin and Tony Blair. His journal describing the trip
referred to Chinese officials as 'appalling old waxworks'.

Prey: Harry and William attracted press criticism by going hunting on the eve of a conference to protect wildlife. Here they are at the event with their father and, *in the background*, Kristina Kyriacou and Justin Mundy.

Rare breeds: William and Charles at Duchy Home Farm, 2004.

Fleet of foot: Charles showcases British talent during his 2014 trip to Mexico.

Blood on the dance floor: Charles's participation in a sword dance in Saudi Arabia in 2014 provoked cutting criticism.

Wading into controversy: Visiting the flood-hit Somerset Levels in 2014.

The heir: William at the controls of a Sea King helicopter, 2011.

The spare: Harry serving in Afghanistan in 2008.

Two families, four generations: Kate holds George at his 2013 christening, surrounded, *clockwise*, by the Queen, Philip, Charles, Camilla, Harry, Pippa Middleton, James Middleton, Carole and Michael Middleton, and William.

In his element: Charles wields a scythe during a 2005 hedge-laying competition at Duchy Home Farm.

therapies marks a Rubicon they cannot cross. 'I'd do anything for him except alternative medicine,' says William Castell.[26]

Supporters of the Prince's wider vision may also regret that his methods of delivery have a tendency to undercut his messages, whether about architecture or health. The Prince has spoken up so loudly in favour of integrated medicine – the blending of conventional and alternative approaches – that a section of his audience is permanently deafened.

Chapter 12

Are There Alternatives?

The lightest of breezes plays along the Suffolk coast and teases tiny cumulus clouds that never quite mask the sun or diminish its unseasonal warmth. It seems a crime against Nature to remain indoors on this March morning, but Edzard Ernst has serious matters to discuss. He believes the Prince is 'smuggling quackery into the NHS'.[1] His disagreements with the Prince led to Ernst's premature retirement from his role as Britain's first Professor of Complementary Medicine, at the University of Exeter. He also alleges that some therapies supported by the Prince are not only ineffective but potentially harmful to patients.

Ernst, like Peter Ahrends, was born into a Germany disfigured by Nazism, but Ernst is younger than the architect, born in the same year as Charles. Ernst and his royal adversary have more in common than numeric age and their German blood; they were both brought up to believe in complementary and alternative medicine. Homeopathy was the brainchild of a German physician, Samuel Hahnemann, who postulated that 'every effective drug provokes in the human body a sort of disease of its own, and the stronger the drug, the more characteristic, and the more marked and more violent the disease. We should imitate Nature, which sometimes cures a chronic affliction with another supervening disease, and prescribe for the illness we wish to cure, especially if chronic, a drug with power to provoke another, artificial disease, as similar as possible, and the former disease will be cured: fight like with like.'[2]

Britain's royals have been attempting to fight like with like ever since Queen Adelaide, German consort of King William IV, sought the services of a homeopath, a German practitioner called Johann Ernst Stapf, in the 1830s. The Queen Mother encouraged her grandson to take homeopathy seriously. The Queen still consults a homeopath.

The Prince favours not only homeopathy but also a wider range of therapies. 'He's always telling us to consult Dr Ali,' says a member of his inner circle. That's Mosaraf Ali, a doctor thanked for his contribution to *Harmony*, who according to his website is an 'expert in ayurvedic medicine and naturopathy with a holistic vision'. Mosaraf's website also carries a testimonial from Charles ('Dr Ali has done us a great favour in pointing out the way forward during the coming centuries') and includes the Prince on a list of 'endorsements from famous people' that also names Morgan Freeman, Sylvester Stallone, Samuel L. Jackson, Andrew Lloyd Webber and Kate Moss, while a second list of those Ali has treated adds Michael Douglas, Ernie Els, Colin Montgomery, Claudia Schiffer, Richard Branson, Michael Caine and Boris Becker to the starry line-up.[3]

The general practitioners who serve the royal court and accompany members of the family on their travels are not only qualified in conventional medicine but have taken time to learn about alternative therapies and to offer an integrated approach to treatment that in Germany would be seen as mainstream. In Edzard Ernst's – and the royals' – country of origin at least 75 per cent of the population uses at least one form of alternative therapy, the highest uptake in the Western world. 'Alternative medicine, particularly homeopathy, just fits into this Teutonic back-to-nature type of image and has an unbroken history of promotion,' says Ernst.[4]

Ernst trained as a conventional doctor, but took up his first post at a homeopathic hospital in Germany. He came to Exeter University in 1993 excited by the prospect of applying rigour to an area of medicine that he supported and felt would be enhanced by strong research to back its claims. His specialism up to that point had been blood rheology – the flow properties of blood – but he had also written some thirty papers on alternative therapies. He was startled, he says, to encounter hostility to his Exeter appointment among complementary and alternative practitioners in the UK. In Germany, qualified doctors such as himself promoted an integrated approach to health that excluded neither conventional nor alternative approaches and paid heed to diet and exercise. In Britain, battle lines were drawn between the mainstream and the largely unregulated fringes. Many in the second camp appeared 'anti-science', he says. It's an accusation he levels at Charles.

To illustrate this point, he indicates a passage in *Harmony*, one of the sections dealing with the Fibonacci sequence, the observation of a thirteenth-century Italian mathematician Leonardo Pisano Fibonacci of an apparent repeating pattern in the natural world, a sequence in which each number from three upwards is the sum of the two preceding it, so 1, 2, 3, 5, 8, 13 and so forth. 'If each of the numbers is measured either in inches or centimetres and plotted out on a piece of paper it produces a pattern of boxes,' explains the Prince. 'Joining the corners of those boxes produces a very familiar shape indeed' – a spiral.[5]

Charles claims that the spiral, found in so many guises and places, is evidence of 'sacred geometry'. Ernst – remember his specialism is blood flow – pours ridicule on a paragraph from *Harmony* which asserts that the spiral shape is present in all rivers and in the blood stream. 'I was fascinated when I first came across the work of the Austrian forester Viktor Schauberger who demonstrated in the 1920s that rivers do not flow as a block of water but via spiralling vortices,' the Prince (and co-authors) write. 'Our blood supply does the same.

In this way the friction that the blood would cause at it moves through our bodies is reduced and, indeed, the immense pressure on the veins and arteries. If the blood didn't do so, our veins would burst and our fingertips would burn to a frazzle.'[6]

Ernst says: 'Prince Charles displays bizarrely romantic concepts about human physiology: blood does certainly not flow in spirals and there is everything but "immense pressure" in veins.' A small-scale survey of mainstream scientific opinion – conducted by emailing the paragraph from *Harmony*, without identifying its authors, to experts in haemodynamics and vascular biology at top universities – offers only limited support for the book's version of how circulation works. 'Certainly there will be vortices present at various locations within the arterial system at various times within the cardiac cycle,' replies Dr Malachy O'Rourke, Lecturer in the School of Mechanical and Materials Engineering at University College Dublin, with particular expertise in fluid mechanics. But he adds: 'Friction is regulated somewhat by the fact that our arteries expand and contract as blood flows through them. Vortical structures have been linked with early stage atherosclerosis and other diseases of the cardiovascular system such as aneurysm and stenosis.'[7] 'In some arteries/veins (but not all) blood exhibits a spiral flow (as opposed to laminar flow whereby it flows in "layers" parallel to the vessel wall), and this spiral flow does tend to reduce the sheer stress on the vessel walls. However, the statement "If the blood didn't do so, our veins would burst and our fingertips would burn to a frazzle" seems exaggerated,' emails Georgios Mitsis, who specialises in cerebral haemodynamics and blood flow auto-regulation at McGill University in Montreal.[8]

Other correspondents point out that the Austrian forester-turned-biomimeticist whom Charles praises is lauded on many websites as an 'undiscovered genius', a frequent hallmark of cod science – though in this case, trout science might be the more apposite expression. Various biographies of Schauberger claim he used biomimetics to develop a 'trout turbine' based on his observations of how fish leap; this allegedly became the central propulsion device in his work for the Nazis developing flying saucers.

Schauberger's work has been widely pressed into service to peddle nonsensical devices to consumers looking for health remedies. The Internet is full of such vicious circles: bogus science gets debunked only to be picked up and promoted as a discovery too revolutionary or advanced to receive the recognition it deserves; mainstream scepticism finds itself misappropriated as a badge of honour used to market expensive forms of snake oil. Attempts to debunk the snake oil reinforce the narrative of suppression by an Establishment too rigid to recognise the truth.

Charles's susceptibility to such argumentation may have been increased by a feeling that he himself is trapped in a vicious cycle. In December 1982, seventeen months before his incendiary speech to the Royal Institute of British Architects, he delivered an address to the British Medical Association that packed almost as much gunpowder, chiding mainstream medicine for an 'objective, statistical, computerised approach to the healing of the sick. If disease is regarded as an objective problem isolated from all personal factors, then surgery plus more and more powerful drugs must be the answer.' He highlighted very real dilemmas involved in mass health-care provision and raised very important questions about the growing muscle of the pharmaceuticals industry in determining health-care policies, prescribing a more encompassing – holistic – approach to the assembled doctors: 'Wonderful as many of them are it should still be more widely stressed by doctors that the health of human beings is so often determined by their behaviour, their food and the nature of their environment.'[9]

This was not only sensible stuff; it needed – and still needs – to be said. But Charles framed his speech in polarising terms, opening with a complaint: 'I have often thought that one of the least attractive traits of various professional bodies and institutions is the deeply ingrained suspicion and outright hostility which they can exhibit towards anything unorthodox or unconventional,' he said. 'I suppose it is inevitable that something which is different should arouse strong feelings on the part of the majority whose conventional wisdom is being challenged or, in a more social sense, whose way of life and customs are being insulted by something rather alien. I suppose, too, that human nature is such that we are frequently prevented from seeing that what is taken for today's unorthodoxy is probably going to be tomorrow's convention. Perhaps we just have to accept it is God's will that the unorthodox individual is doomed to years of frustration, ridicule and failure in order to act out his role in the scheme of things, until his day arrives and mankind is ready to receive his message; a message which he probably finds hard to explain himself, but which he knows comes from a far deeper source than conscious thought.'[10]

Although the Prince went on to identify the 'unorthodox individual' of his speech as the sixteenth-century healer, Paracelsus, he clearly reflected – and anticipated – his own experience. He has endured years of frustration, ridicule and failure, as his interventions far from sowing harmony open him to attack, redoubling both his conviction that something needs to be done and his impulse to use his position to override criticism, encouraging him to do things that strengthen his critics. This is Charles's personal vicious cycle, and Edzard Ernst, for a while, became snared in its vortex.

The Professor filled time after his departure from Exeter University in May 2011 by writing a memoir, *A Scientist in Wonderland*, which was published in February 2015; the book recounts in detail his version of the events that led to his public clashes with the formal and informal courts of Charles. Sitting in his Suffolk home, Ernst appears a character straight from central casting with his light German accent, neat moustache and air of intellectual abstraction. When he comes to parts of the story that upset him – there are many such moments – he stirs his tea into Schaubergerian vortices.

His department was integrated into the newly formed Peninsula Medical School in 2000, run jointly by Exeter and Plymouth universities. This, he says, is where the problems started. As early as 2003, Ernst spotted an announcement in a newsletter published by the Prince's Foundation for Integrated Health: 'The Peninsula Medical School aims to become the UK's first medical school to include integrated medicine at postgraduate level.' Ernst says the university authorities told him the course had been suggested by Dr Michael Dixon, whom he knew to be a supporter of complementary medicine, and that funding had been facilitated by the Prince. Money for a fellowship came from the Barcapel Foundation, a charitable body that supports alternative and complementary therapies and by Nelsons, the family-owned business behind Bach™ Original Flower Remedies and Nelsons® Homeopathy.

Ernst's spoon speeds up as he describes his 2005 tangle with the Prince's Foundation over *Complementary Health Care*, a patient guide published by the Foundation, which Ernst dismissed to British journalists as 'over-optimistically misleading'. Later the same year Ernst incensed supporters of the Smallwood Report conducted under Charles's aegis 'to investigate the contribution which certain complementary therapies could potentially make to the delivery of healthcare in the UK'.[11] Ernst had provided information to the researchers of the report, and says he offered them his own findings on twenty-seven economic evaluations of popular forms of alternative therapy that proved inconclusive. His own primary research into alternative therapies, the basis for the 2008 book he co-wrote with Simon Singh, *Trick or Treatment*, dismissed most such therapies as having, at best, a placebo effect. The draft of the Smallwood Report did not reflect Ernst's input and he felt it included potentially dangerous recommendations – such as the use of homeopathy to treat asthma – so he asked for his name to be removed.

Ernst maintains that shortly before publication of the final report, he received a call from Mark Henderson, then Science Editor for *The Times*. 'I knew Mark from many encounters and we had a position of trust and he said: "Why aren't you on that document?" I said: "Well, I was on it. I asked them to take my name off it but unfortunately, Mark, I cannot tell you anything about the document because I promised to keep it confidential," and he said: "You don't need to – it's in front of me." It had been leaked to him and he read me passages out of it so I knew he had it in front of him. And he said: "I don't want you to disclose any contents of the report, but tell me a bit about it, about the methodology, why you pulled out." And then I didn't mince my words and the next day it was on the title page of *The Times*.'[12] The piece quoted Ernst not only tearing into the report but suggesting the Prince had overstepped his constitutional role.

Ernst says he received an email the following day from Christopher Smallwood, the report's author, accusing him of breach of confidentiality. That charge was repeated in a letter to *The Times* by Richard Horton, the Editor of the medical journal, the *Lancet*, and in a missive on Clarence House-headed paper, sent by Michael Peat to the Vice Chancellor of Exeter University, and reproduced in Ernst's memoir. 'I am writing both as the Prince of Wales's Private Secretary and as Acting Chairman of His Royal Highness's Foundation for Integrated Health,' it reads. 'There has been a breach of confidence by Professor Edzard Ernst in respect of a draft report on the efficacy of certain complementary therapies sent to him by Mr Christopher Smallwood. The report was commissioned by the Prince of Wales. Mr Smallwood sent Professor Ernst an early and, at that stage, incomplete draft of the report for comment. The accompanying email requested and stressed the need for confidentiality. Professor Ernst implicitly agreed to comment on the report on this basis but then, as you probably saw, gave his views about the report to the national press. I attach a copy of a letter from the editor of the *Lancet* published by *The Times* which summarises the issues well. I also attach a copy of the email sent to Professor Ernst by Mr Smallwood. I apologise for troubling you, but I felt that you should have this matter drawn to your attention.'[13]

Clarence House aides are adamant that Peat sent his letter not at the behest of the Prince but at the request of the trustees of the Foundation for Integrated Health, concerned about the 'breach of confidence' that Ernst denies. (Aides add that Peat should have used Foundation letterhead.) The university launched a thirteen-month investigation, eventually deciding not to issue Ernst with a formal disciplinary notice but warning him, Ernst says, that he risked sanctions if he did anything similar in future.

This did not deter him from participating in a television documentary, *Charles: the Meddling Prince*, that was aired in 2007, eliciting a seventeen-page rebuttal from Clarence House. Two years later, Ernst attacked Duchy Originals – and its founder – for selling a so-called Detox Tincture. 'Prince Charles contributes to the ill-health of the nation by pretending we can all over-indulge, then take his tincture and be fine again. Under the banner of holistic and integrative healthcare he thus promotes a quick fix and outright quackery,' Ernst told the *Guardian*.[14] Meanwhile, funds for Ernst's research unit at Exeter dried up. He claims he offered to retire to save the unit, but that the university instead shut it down in 2011.

The previous year the jailing for fraud of George Gray, Finance Director of the Prince's Foundation for Integrated Medicine, had signed that organisation's death warrant; the Foundation was wound up in 2012. No blame attached to Gray's colleagues. The Foundation's Medical Director Michael Dixon went on to chair the College of Medicine, which has no formal link to the Prince and functions outside the umbrella of the Prince's charities but pursues many of the same aims. Charles remains determined to facilitate research into alternative and complementary therapies, says Dixon. 'The Prince well understands the need for good evidence on effectiveness and safety and has spoken frequently of the need for good evidence, particularly, on cost effectiveness, but it has proved endlessly difficult to get proper research funding for this,' Dixon emails.[15] On this last point, Ernst might well agree.

The National Liberal Club, established in 1882 by Britain's four-time Prime Minister William Gladstone, occupies a substantial neo-Gothic building with a terrace that overlooks a lush garden and beyond its shrubbery two flows: London traffic along the Embankment and further still the mottled sweep of the Thames. Michael Dixon is a non-political club member and likes to show his guests the establishment's prize exhibit, kept under glass: the original Gladstone bag, created to honour the politician but a model for the cases many conventional – and less conventional – doctors carry. Dixon deposits his own bag next to a terrace table and prepares to discuss Charles. 'It's quite extraordinary,' he says. 'I've run some national organisations and deal an awful lot with the press who have almost invariably been straight with me. But as soon as they talk to me about my work with the Prince, it's always about trying to find some new answer that can be misinterpreted. Everyone wants to get a story that can be somehow a new angle but a negative angle.'[16]

Despite this, Dixon is relaxed and affable, emphasising key points not by raising his voice but by spreading his arms, as if crucified. This may be a familiar posture for the GP, who has become a lightning conductor not only for anger in the medical profession directed towards the Prince but also for Dixon's work as Chairman of the NHS Alliance, an independent association of medical practitioners that promotes its own vision of good patient care and the best way to structure the NHS. Dixon has argued for slimming down the central NHS administration and devolving more competences to clinical commissioning groups, regional bodies of GPs. He is also a passionate supporter of integrated medicine, offering a wide range of alternative therapies at his surgery in Devon under the motto: 'We treat the person, not just the symptoms.'[17]

'I was an extremely orthodox practitioner for ten years and then got slightly burnt out, because there were so many things from back pain to chronic tiredness to people with infections to irritable bowel disease which modern medicine simply has no real answers for,' says Dixon. 'The yawning gaps in what I could offer patients in terms of their expectations got greater and greater.' He found intimations of the way he might close those gaps and add to what he calls his 'armamentarium' when he attended a training afternoon showcasing alternative therapies. Soon afterwards, the wife of a local judge, a Christian healer, asked to offer her services from his surgery. 'I said: "Certainly not. I don't want to go into witchcraft in our nice clean NHS practice," but she was a determined woman, insisted on doing it and she did a lot of good for our patients,' Dixon recalls. 'Eventually I thought we had better do a scientific trial.'[18]

The study compared outcomes for patients who had been ill for six months and had tried conventional treatments before referral to the healer with patients who had also been ill for six months but had not consulted the healer. The first group did better, but the study attracted criticism on the basis that it didn't exclude the placebo effect: in other words, the patients may have done better because they believed they were being helped. The criticism 'always struck me as quite amusing really, because if placebo is the effect of one human being on another, well, that's what it is', says Dixon. 'Being able to do something as a GP was fantastically rewarding; to talk to someone with acute pain or make it better or get rid of it altogether. So I confirmed my journey through acupuncture, herbal medicine and the rest – aided and abetted by him.'[19]

'Him' – Charles – encouraged Dixon to go to India to learn about ayurvedic medicine and is for Dixon an inspirational figure. 'Whatever [the Prince] says is actually what he means and thinks. Most of the rest of the world says what they want other people to see them doing or saying ... I think we're incredibly lucky because he deeply cares. Almost to the point of pain, he suffers with his people and he gets tremendously fired up and upset when he thinks injustices are being done or opportunities are being missed.' Dixon extends his arms again. 'A lot of the calls I get are times when everyone else is celebrating New Year's Eve or Christmas Eve or bank holidays and he's still working. He's incredibly hard-working and serious and when it comes to health that is almost his natural territory. If he hadn't been a Prince I'm sure he'd be a doctor. I very much see him as the Healing Prince.'[20]

Dixon summons up a story from the reign of an earlier Charles as an analogy for the wisdom he sees in his Charles challenging the medical Establishment. 'During the Great Plague in 1665 the physicians and the surgeons fled from London and left only the apothecaries who then came out and saw the patients and looked after them as best they could. I'm sure their evidence base wasn't as good as the physicians' or surgeons' but quite frankly there wasn't much evidence base for the physicians and surgeons in those days. Anyway the physicians and surgeons come back after the Plague to London and say: "Clear off, you lot, you don't know what you're doing."'[21]

Like much of the debate around alternative medicine, this anecdote is open to various interpretations. Some historians suggest apothecaries were inclined to stay in London not for noble reasons but because they could potentially turn a profit selling their nostrums. The antipathy between apothecaries and physicians burned as bright as the fire that would eventually help to bring the epidemic under control and mirrors the polarities of the current debate between conventional and alternative practitioners. 'Nathaniel Hodges, a physician, took some satisfaction from the fact that these "blowers of the pestilential flame" [apothecaries] were themselves victims of the epidemic … He was severe in his condemnation of those "chymists and quacks" who were "equal strangers to all learning as well as physic" and yet "thrust into every hand some trash or other under the disguise of a pompous title",' writes Stephen Porter in *The Great Plague*.[22]

To Dixon, the apothecaries are avatars of the more caring and holistic approach which he and the Prince hope to inspire in the medical profession, one that is open to the possibility that conventional medicine doesn't hold all the answers. 'In a way what Charles the potential Third is doing is saying, to some extent, what biomedicine leaves behind is its patients,' says Dixon. 'Because frankly, if you have chronic tiredness and you're not anaemic and you haven't got an underactive thyroid [a conventional GP] will just have to say: "Well, I haven't found anything serious, good luck."'[23]

Elizabeth Buchanan, the Prince's former Private Secretary, tells a story about the Boss. During a walkabout in Wales, Charles met a woman who had recently been diagnosed with cancer. He immediately summoned Buchanan to get her details and make sure the woman got a referral to the Bristol Cancer Help Centre. The charity, later renamed Penny Brohn Cancer Care in memory of one of its founders, practises the 'whole person approach', described on its website as a 'unique combination of courses, tools and techniques which includes lifestyle measures such as healthy eating, physical activity, ways of managing stress and emotions, and a range of complementary approaches. It is designed to work alongside standard medical cancer treatments.'[24] Charles is its patron.

Buchanan unearths this anecdote to illustrate the Prince's caring side. The Boss apparently didn't just ask that the woman be introduced to the charity; he continued to ask for bulletins about her welfare. 'He empathises,' says Buchanan. 'He has the ability to empathise. And his kindness. He has the ability to be as concerned at the macro-level as at the micro-level. This is another thing that marks him out, I think, from other people.'[25]

There is another relevant aspect to this story and it lies in the history of the cancer charity. Its reputation suffered a heavy blow in 1990 with the publication of interim findings of research that appeared to show that patients attending the Bristol Cancer Help Centre with breast cancer were three times as likely to relapse and twice as likely to die from their malignancy as their counterparts receiving conventional treatment only. The clear implication was that the Bristol regime worsened cancer or undermined the patients' resistance.

In fact, the research had been badly structured, failing to take into account the fact that the women attending the Bristol Cancer Help Centre tended to suffer from more advanced or intractable forms of cancer and had sought out the charity after exhausting conventional routes. The therapies they received at the centre couldn't cure them but might have helped to improve the quality of the life they had left. Some patients involved in the research felt so strongly that the charity had been misrepresented – and suffered so much stress in the eye of the medical storm – that they founded the Bristol Survey Support Group. A book, *Fighting Spirit*, collected some of their testimonies. The actor Sheila Hancock, herself a patient of the Bristol Cancer Help Centre, supplied the foreword. 'They say that everyone remembers where they were when they heard Kennedy had died. I am ashamed to say I don't,' she wrote. 'But I do remember where I was when I heard I had doubled my chances of dying of my breast cancer by going to the Bristol Cancer Help Centre. I was in hospital recovering from a gall-bladder operation. I watched, listened and read in disbelief as members of the medical profession leapt, with obvious relish, to condemn complementary/alternative medicine (they seldom knew the difference) and all its evil ways. It seemed as if this was the weapon to lance the pent-up boil of resentment festering against women who had strayed from the path of orthodoxy. For me, feeling particularly vulnerable in my hospital bed, their pronouncements were profoundly disturbing.'[26]

The polarised ecosystem of the health-care debate maintains a balance of extremes, pitting the conventional against the alternative, the power of pharmaceutical giants against the profiteers of the snake-oil industry, rationalists against advocates for a spiritual dimension. One result was the Bristol Cancer Health Care debacle, an episode that not only demonised a legitimate approach but deepened confusion around the benefits, or otherwise, of complementary therapies, leaving cancer sufferers potentially more vulnerable to the blandishments of quacks promoting regimes that really are dangerous. Another is that alternative therapies which Ernst concedes do have benefits, such as yoga and Pilates, remain poorly regulated, with no single body ensuring that practitioners are qualified to independently set standards. Patients are most often the losers.

The Prince, as he usually does, has used back channels to try to promote his ideas. In Peter Hain, who served in the Cabinets of Tony Blair and Gordon Brown, he found a rare ally in wanting to encourage an integrated approach to medicine. Charles 'had been constantly frustrated at his inability to persuade any Health Ministers anywhere that that was a good idea, and so he, as he once described it to me, found me unique from this point of view, in being somebody that actually agreed with him on this, and might want to deliver it,' Hain told a BBC Radio 4 documentary. 'When I was Secretary of State for Northern Ireland in 2005 to '07, [the Prince] was delighted when I told him that since I was running the place I could more or less do what I wanted to do. I was able to introduce a trial for complementary medicine on the NHS, and it had spectacularly good results, that people's wellbeing and health was vastly improved. And when he learnt about this he was really enthusiastic and tried to persuade the Welsh government to do the same thing and the government in Whitehall to do the same thing for England, but not successfully.'[27]

Ernst responded to Hain's interview with a splenetic blog post questioning the legitimacy of the trial. 'So, is the whole "trial" story an utterly irrelevant old hat?' Ernst asks. 'Certainly not! Its true significance does not lie in the fact that a few amateurs are trying to push bogus treatments into the NHS via the flimsiest pseudo-research of the century. The true significance, I think, is that it shows how Prince Charles, once again, oversteps the boundaries of his constitutional role.'[28]

Such criticisms are unlikely to deflect Charles and not only because the concept of his constitutional role is as dynamic as the natural world and its ecosystems. The Prince is implacable because he is a believer, not just in alternative and complementary medicines and the potential of biomimetics, but in a larger picture that includes the unseen and the unknown. He is Prince Hamlet proclaiming more things in heaven and earth than we might dream. 'We live in a culture which doesn't really believe in the soul,' says Ian Skelly. 'You are seen as a bit of a crank if you talk in that way, yet actually if you talk to people individually they speak in a very spiritual way about love and about feelings for things. Culturally we've put that in a corner, and it has no part to play in the mainstream economic approach to life.'[29] This, too, is something Charles is determined to change.

Chapter 13

King Save the God

Despite alien bloodlines and planetary culture, the Queen's Englishness is as concentrated as the original Ribena cordial. The English of the so-called Silent Generation are defined as much by the things they don't say or do as by their words and deeds, and the monarch's mute actions speak volumes. She consigned the upbringing of her children to nannies and treats her dogs like princes. She is awfully fond of horses and has never done anything to frighten them. She dresses as if life were a perpetual church fete. In 2003, when Ryan Parry, a trainee reporter for the *Daily Mirror*, skivvied for two months as a footman at Buckingham Palace, he uncovered no vices, no unsuspected passions, no dynamic hidden side to the royal existence. The Queen's breakfast with her husband is a staid affair of oatmeal from Tupperware boxes, with an old Roberts radio on the table to supply the conversation. Princess Anne turned out to harbour a solitary weakness, for ripe-to-the-point-of-rotten bananas. Prince Andrew amused himself by finding new and more incongruous places around the palace to leave a toy monkey.

The extravagance Parry documented appeared neither compulsive nor joyful. Palace overstaffing and tedious ceremonial seemed to be vestiges of dusty history rather than symptoms of venality. It takes a team of ten servants — two footmen, two kitchen porters, two chefs, two silver pantry under-butlers, a page and a coffee-room maid – to prepare, deliver and remove the Queen's coffee tray. 'The maid waited two-and-a-half hours to pick up a pot of coffee from a hot plate and pour it into a silver jug. She then handed it to me. My role was to take the tray 20 metres to the page's vestibule and hand it to the page, who then carried it another eight metres to the Queen in her dining room,' Parry reported, his use of metric measures jarring.[1] Elizabeth II has always ruled, imperially, in yards, feet and inches.

As Supreme Governor she has served the Church of England well, reflecting and reinforcing attributes celebrated since the Reformation. Her faith, though devout, is quiet and undemonstrative. Her church-going is regular, but not so frequent as to seem showy. C of E may be Anglicanism's mother church, but it is often as honoured in the breach as the observance. British Prime Ministers, in the words of Tony Blair's spin doctor Alastair Campbell, 'don't do God', or, if forced, will occasionally tackle the subject with all the articulacy of a Richard Curtis hero confronted with his own repressed feelings.[2] Before David Cameron took up residence in 10 Downing Street, he described his faith as 'a bit like the reception for Magic FM in the Chilterns: it sort of comes and goes. That sums up a lot of people in the Church of England. We are racked with doubts, but sort of fundamentally believe, but don't sort of wear it on our sleeves or make too much of it.'[3] Once in office and after alienating different wings of the Church by introducing gay marriage and presiding over an economy that witnessed a burgeoning dependence on food banks, Cameron tried to strike a pious note. 'People who ... advocate some sort of secular neutrality fail to grasp the consequences of that neutrality, or the role that faith can play in helping people to have a moral code,' he wrote in an article for *Church Times*, then immediately recoiled from the implications of the sentence. 'Of course, faith is neither necessary nor sufficient for morality. Many atheists and agnostics live by a moral code – and there are Christians who don't.'[4]

Anglicanism is most likely to get itself in a tizzy when it cares too visibly, in an un-English sort of way. Some of the deepest schisms of recent times emerged in the gulf between the emotional supporters of Gene Robinson, a proudly gay man ordained in 2003 as Bishop of New Hampshire by the liberal, North American Episcopal Church, and the emotional opponents of gay clergy, noisily represented in the congregations of Africa and Asia. The General Synod is the Church of England's parliament; the ten-yearly Lambeth Conference sets wider Anglican policy. The Archbishop of Canterbury attempts, and often fails, to steer the debate rather than handing down doctrine like the Pope.

Such differences to Roman Catholicism are literally defining. The Church of England was formed in opposition to the Vatican after Henry VIII broke with Pope Clement VII over the latter's inclement refusal to annul the King's marriage to Catherine of Aragon. Laws passed once the Glorious Revolution had deposed Britain's last Catholic ruler, James II, simultaneously enshrined and interlocked the dominions of the Church of England and Britain's – exclusively and explicitly Anglican – sovereigns to come, while British colonialism expanded the sway of Anglicanism and the monarchy. C of E is the Established – state – Church; its Bishops help to make the country's laws. The Coronation Oath requires the monarch to 'maintain and preserve inviolably the settlement of the Church of England, and the doctrine, worship, discipline, and government thereof, as by law established in England' and to 'preserve unto the Bishops and Clergy of England, and to the Churches there committed to their charge, all such rights and privileges, as by law do or shall appertain to them or any of them'. The Queen serves as Defender of the Faith that defends her against interlopers and incense-wavers. This mantle was never likely to fall comfortably on her son.

The biggest revelation of Jonathan Dimbleby's 1994 documentary portrait of Charles almost got lost in the pandemonium surrounding another disclosure. Dimbleby's film and book had been swept into the tail stream of Andrew Morton's biography of Diana, focusing attention on any potential ripostes by the Prince to his wife's accusations of his infidelity with Camilla. 'I was very anxious for it not to be a sort of arms race, because the other book was actually such a real frustration to me ... I knew there were issues about "Was he faithful, wasn't he unfaithful?" and I had to deal with that,' says Dimbleby. He felt he must probe the marriage or see 'the whole rest of the film overwhelmed by the fact that I hadn't', but he started gently.[5] 'Were you – did you try to be faithful and honourable to your wife when you took on the vow of marriage?'

'Yes, absolutely,' said the Prince. 'And were you?' Dimbleby persisted. 'Yes,' the Prince repeated, 'until it became irretrievably broken down, us both having tried.'[6] The exchange confirmed that there had indeed been three people in the Waleses' marriage and raised questions that still rumble in conservative corners about the Prince's fitness to be a figurehead for the Church of England. But the more startling declaration came earlier in Dimbleby's film, during a discussion about the Prince's exploration of world religions and his assertion that there are 'common threads that link us all in one great and important tapestry'. 'Does that mean that spiritually and intellectually you feel at home walking between and within all those religions and don't feel tied to the Church of England, the Protestant Church?' Dimbleby wonders. 'Yes,' the Prince replies. 'I feel there is an enormous amount, once you begin to understand where we are linked, in common that can be immensely helpful. I'm one of those people who searches. I'm interested in pursuing a path, if I can find it, through the thickets.' So saying, Charles apparently swerves straight into a clump of thorn bushes.

'I personally would rather see [the role of the monarch] as Defender of Faith, not *the* Faith, because [the Faith] means just one particular interpretation of the Faith, which I think is sometimes something that causes a deal of a problem,' he declares. 'It has done for hundreds of years. People have fought each other to the death over these things, which seems to me a peculiar waste of people's energy, when we're all actually aiming for the same ultimate goal, I think. So I mean I would much rather it was seen as defending faith itself, which is so often under threat in our day where, you know, the whole concept of faith itself or belief in anything beyond this existence, beyond life itself, is considered almost old-fashioned and irrelevant.' The future co-author of *Harmony* begins to sketch out his nascent philosophy, mooting the idea that a monarch might be 'Defender of the Divine in existence, the pattern of the divine which is, I think, in all of us, but which because we are human beings can be expressed in so many different ways'. Lest there be any doubt about his message, he name-checks some of the other religions he envisages that he, as King, would be inclined to defend. 'I've always felt the Catholic subjects of the sovereign are equally as important as the Anglican ones or the Protestant ones. Likewise I think that the Islamic subjects or the Hindu subjects or the Zoroastrian subjects are of equal and vital importance.' In Charles's theology, all believers are equal to each other, if not to the sovereign.

These musings may not have roused as much tabloid excitement as his confession of adultery but they created consternation in Lambeth Palace. 'As heir, [the Prince] has to be concerned with every citizen, regardless of creed or colour,' the Archbishop of Canterbury George Carey told a BBC interviewer. 'I believe that is what he intended to say.'[7]

Carey suggested that tweaks to the coronation service – but not to the coronation oath – would fulfil the Prince's desire to see all faiths given the same prominence. In his biography of the Prince, published later the same year, Dimbleby rejected Carey's 'minimalist interpretation' and produced the transcript of a segment of the interview with the Prince that had been cut from the broadcast. In it, the Prince returns to his theme of the shared ground among religions. 'The great Middle Eastern religions – Judaism, Islam, Christianity, all stemming from the same geographical area – all have a great deal in common … There are aspects of Hinduism and Buddhism … which are attached by very profound threads to Islam, Christianity and Judaism.' The Prince also bemoans the schisms in Christianity between the Orthodox, Roman Catholic and Protestant Churches. 'I think [different branches of] Christianity had a great deal more in common a long time ago than [they do] now – sadly, in my opinion.'[8] Carey's attempt at firefighting had fanned the flames. Charles hadn't stumbled into the briars. He had made his points deliberately and with his usual determination to kindle debate. He was backed in this endeavour by his biographer. 'I was really furious,' says Dimbleby. 'I knew what [the Prince] meant; we'd talked about it a lot. A great deal.'[9]

Carey's predecessor will also have known what the Prince meant, though never could grasp quite what the Prince *meant*. Robert Runcie served as Archbishop of Canterbury from 1980 to 1991. He conducted Charles's marriage to Diana and a few years later was asked by the Prince to lunch with him and his unhappy wife 'on the basis of :"It's been rather a lot for Diana, because religion hasn't stuck much with her. And we feel we ought to mention it to you, because you married us,"' as Runcie told his biographer, Humphrey Carpenter.

In conversations with Carpenter recorded in 1993, before the Dimbleby revelations but after Morton's devastating book and the Waleses' separation, Runcie let slip deep unease about the Prince's religious moorings. He recounted to Carpenter a discussion at a party he had attended about whether Charles's now public private life might rule out his succession to the throne and as the Church's Supreme Governor. Runcie told his interlocutors: 'It depends whether the Prince wins his way with the British people over the next five to ten years. Also, it would quite help if he loved the Church of England a bit more.' He enlarged on this theme to Carpenter. 'That's one of the things that I found disappointing – that he was so disenchanted with it ... I think he'd given up on the Church of England before I arrived.'[10]

To Runcie, the Prince's views lacked consistency. The cleric couldn't reconcile Charles's apparent liberalism on issues such as urban poverty with his impulse to align himself with the sorts of conservatives who opposed moves to broaden the appeal of the Church by modernising its language. (Charles continues to fight that battle, remarking in 2012 that 'it is hard to escape the suspicion that so many changes have been made to the cadence of the language used just to lower the tone, in the mistaken belief that the rest of us wouldn't get the point if the word of God was a bit over our heads. But the word of God is supposed to be a bit over our heads.'[11]) Nor could Runcie understand how the Prince's mystic bent fitted into the picture. 'I think he was deeply into the Laurens van der Post spirituality,' said Runcie, concluding: 'I don't think he took the Church of England very seriously.'[12]

The Bishop of London, Richard Chartres, understands his old university friend far better. 'If people can't extract from [the Prince] what they want, they invent it and with immense confidence people are saying: "Well, of course he's not going to want a Christian coronation because he is Defender of Faith." Now he's an intelligent guy. And he is totally aware of the philosophical and spiritual incoherence of being a Defender of Faith as if you didn't have one for yourself but were looking down from some other more elevated level on the whole scene. Of course, like sensible people he recognises that faith communities have a role in social cohesion and spreading the practice of virtue and in their local manifestation they're often very central to most volunteering in local society. He's been trying to make absolutely clear that he has immense sympathy with the world of religion, the world of faith, because he sees very clearly how it relates to a view of the world in which human beings do not play the role of oppressive dominance but understand their connectedness with the health of the whole planet and the whole human race. But the idea that he doesn't really have a faith of his own is untrue. He is a convinced Christian.'[13]

The Bishop of London's own views are not always immediately easy to reconcile. When he enrolled at Cuddesdon theological college, he appeared to the college's then principal – Runcie – to be 'very right-wing ... Richard had a tremendous capacity to relate to the upper classes. An original Young Fogey. And behind it all was a shrewd, observant, discerning mind, a very good turn of phrase, and a very considerable presence and fluency.' Chartres 'believed in old-fashioned terrifying religion', Runcie told Carpenter.[14] Yet this is the same Chartres who as Runcie's Chaplain wrote a speech for the Archbishop to deliver at a memorial for the dead of the Falklands War that drew the ire of Margaret Thatcher and her government in commemorating the fallen on both sides and including a sharp line about 'those who stay at home, most violent in their attitudes and untouched in themselves'.[15] Bishop of London since 1995, Chartres has appeared a pillar of the Establishment, officiating at Prince William's confirmation and his wedding, at the memorial for Princess Diana on the tenth anniversary of her death and at the funeral of Baroness Thatcher. He also delivered a box of chocolates to the Occupy protesters encamped next to the steps of St Paul's Cathedral and has expressed concerns about the impact of unbridled capitalism. 'For about 15 years I said repeatedly that the prospect of growth without limit, with no end in view beyond the process itself, was unsustainable and a frail foundation for any civilisation. But for a long time that caused no resonances, nobody was listening,' he said in 2013.[16]

An environmentalist, Chartres drives a hybrid car when he drives at all. To a journalist who asked him if he had any frivolous pursuits, he replied: 'I have to admit, and this is rather embarrassing, but I'm very interested in the history of farming.' During the same interview he talked about the loneliness of leadership and said: 'Faith isn't about having good ideas in your head, it's about the ability to listen, which can be very difficult for a bishop.'[17] The phrase sounds familiar. 'One of the most important things is listening,' the Prince says. 'You don't just have to bang on at people.'[18]

The similarities between Chartres and Charles go beyond shared phrases, fears of unsustainable growth, a fascination with farming and adherence to the rich language of the Book of Common Prayer; beyond their age (the Bishop is the elder by only sixteen months) and university education. For one thing, both men know what it is to hover on the edge of the top job at an age at which their contemporaries might consider retirement. In 2012, Chartres ruled himself out of the race to become Archbishop of Canterbury, reportedly worried that at sixty-four he was too old to take on such a huge responsibility. The strength – and the apparent polarities – of his views might also have rendered support for his candidacy less sturdy than it appeared.

Like his friend, he is often misunderstood. Far from being inconsistent or contradictory, the Bishop and the Prince are true to complex belief systems. 'You can be a loyal member of the Church of England and you can appreciate the extraordinary quality of the spiritual life that other people have in their traditions,' says Chartres, adding that the Prince's book *Harmony* 'is a very important contribution at the present moment when we are looking for a global conversation among the wisdom traditions. And anybody who's involved in a religious body, as I am, ought to feel very humble indeed as we look at the comparative success of economists and scientists in developing the kind of global conversations that we need in order to confront series of promises and perils which are not to be confined to one continent or one nation'.[19]

There are philosophical points of disagreement – Chartres does not elaborate – but in a broad sense he and the heir to the throne are in concert, traditionalists and radicals of the Establishment and just as liable to challenge the Establishment view as to uphold it. They mirror each other because, long-time friends that they are, they have influenced each other's thinking over many years and collaborated on interfaith initiatives and recently on the Prince's campaign to protect Orthodox Christians in the Middle East. The Bishop praises the Prince's 'energy, the hard work – we're not talking about going around occasional discourses of an anodyne kind, we're talking about the shaping of institutions to make a long-term difference in areas which when he started on them were not very obvious to the majority of opinion'. Chartres cites Business in the Community and the Prince's Trust as examples. 'These are institutional responses to a series of problems very profoundly understood and sustained over the long term by his commitment to them and his determination to make sure they have the funds and the wherewithal to make a difference ... He doesn't flit. There is a coherence about all of his interests that runs through the Temenos Academy and *Harmony* and the Prince's Trust. There is a coherent view and it is fundamentally spiritual.'[20]

For much of its early history, Shrewsbury, an English market town on the Welsh border, came under siege from the Welsh. These days it's the headquarters of a small campaign against the Prince of Wales. 'I've had a good life apart from having to live in the same timescale as Charles Windsor,' says Frederick Phipps, a former prison officer, retired and suffering from prostate cancer.[21] Since hearing of the decision to allow Charles to marry Camilla, Phipps has collected signatures on a petition (twelve: his fellow residents in sheltered accommodation) and written a series of protest letters to the Archbishop of Canterbury – Rowan Williams and latterly Justin Welby – as well as to his MP and more recently this missive to the Queen: 'I wrote to the Archbishop challenging the right of the Prince of Wales to become Monarch on your demise. I based my challenge on the grounds that, just as your uncle, Edward VIII, was denied the throne because of his determination to marry a divorcee, Mrs Simpson, so the would-be Charles III should be disqualified on the grounds of his adulterous relationship with the now Duchess of Cornwall … If your son becomes King, the Church of England will become a mockery.'[22]

Phipps sent his letter to the Queen as a last-ditch attempt to draw attention to his cause after receiving a rebuff from Lambeth Palace: 'It needs to be understood that we live in a hereditary monarchy,' wrote Andrew Nunn, the Archbishop's Correspondence Secretary. 'It follows then that the Prince of Wales will inherit the throne when Her Majesty dies – an event that we hope is some while off yet. The alternative to that arrangement would be a republic with an elected Head of State. No serious proposals to that effect are being put forward at this time. Should you and the other anti-monarchists at [Phipps's sheltered accommodation address] wish to promote Republicanism, then you should do so through your MP, not through the Archbishop.' Nunn signs off: 'In bringing your long correspondence with Lambeth Palace to a close, I can promise you the Archbishop's prayers.'[23]

Phipps says his fellow residents, far from being anti-monarchists, are supporters of the monarchy. He has come to be a republican 'simply because I cannot tolerate the idea of [the Prince]'. A convert from Roman Catholicism to the Church of England, Phipps says he may now leave the Church 'that would allow [the remarriage] to happen … I believe in the New Testament, I pray to Jesus Christ and where does that leave me in the Church of England? I'm intrigued by Pope Francis. I might go back there.'[24] In response to a query about the correspondence, Nunn emailed that Phipps's correspondence with the Archbishop and his predecessor had lasted a very long time: 'Mr Phipps has been writing to this Archbishop and his predecessor for [many] years now, often in shockingly abusive terms about the Prince of Wales, the Duchess of Cornwall, and others. My

May 2013 letter was intended to close the correspondence between him and the Archbishop's office for good. (The digression into Republicanism was a cheap dig, but I was riled.)' He signs off this email with a phrase in inverted commas: '"Publish and be damned."'

The engagement of the Prince to Camilla Parker Bowles, announced in February 2005, brought to a head questions that had hung over the couple since the relationship became public: how might the wedding be organised, given the Church of England's interdict on marrying divorcees with living spouses if the marriage might be 'tantamount to consecrating an old infidelity'? And what would the marriage mean for the Prince's position as a representative and future Supreme Governor of the Church?

The first question received a swift answer – too swift, according to critics. The wedding would be a civil ceremony, followed by a Church dedication. 'These arrangements have my strong support and are consistent with Church of England guidelines concerning remarriage which the Prince of Wales fully accepts as a committed Anglican and as prospective Supreme Governor of the Church of England,' said then Archbishop of Canterbury, Rowan Williams, in a statement.[25]

Sidestepping an immediate problem created a fresh controversy. Two statutes – the Marriage Act of 1836 and the 1949 Marriage Act – appeared to bar members of the royal family from registry-office weddings, the first law explicitly, the second via a clause, 79(5), that reads 'nothing in this act shall affect any law or custom relating to the marriage of members of the Royal Family'. This had been widely understood to mean the ban was still in force. In 1992, the Queen's *annus horribilis*, Princess Anne avoided this possible bear trap by taking advantage of the Church of Scotland's more relaxed approach and plighting her troth to second husband Timothy Laurence in Crathie church near Balmoral. Charles and Camilla accepted the advice that the Prince's future Church of England role ruled out a similar solution.

Two successive Labour governments rode to the rescue. Blair's Lord Chancellor Lord Falconer issued a statement based on legal advice he had taken. 'In our view, section 79(5) of the 1949 Act preserves ancient procedures applying to Royal marriages, for example the availability of customary forms of marriage and registration. It also preserves the effect of the Royal Marriages Act 1772, which requires the sovereign's consent for certain marriages. But it does not have the effect of excluding Royal marriages from the scope of Part III, which provides for civil ceremonies. As the heading to section 79 indicates [Repeals and Savings] it is a saving, not an exclusion. We are aware that different views have been taken in the past, but we consider that these were over-cautious.' He added that the Human Rights Act required legislation to be 'interpreted wherever possible in a way that is compatible with the right to marry'.[26]

In 2008, long after the confetti had drifted down over the happy pair and with Gordon Brown now installed in Downing Street, his Secretary of State for Justice Jack Straw turned down a Freedom of Information request to view the advice on which Falconer had based his decision. In his appeal to the Information Commissioner, Michael Jones, the journalist who had lodged the request, set out evidence challenging Falconer's interpretation of the Marriage Act and laying out his fears 'that Lord Falconer's reinterpretation of the 1949 Act and his dubious invoking of the Human Rights Act opens the way to the changing of laws of this country by Ministerial decree without Parliament's authority or the sanction of the courts or the even-handed disclosure of the advice Ministers receive'.[27] The Information Commissioner rejected Jones's appeal because of the 'sensitivity and significance of [Falconer's] advice' and because 'the issue relates to the rights of specific individuals'.[28]

The decision made further probes into the circumstances of the wedding unlikely. The marriage has transformed Charles's life. He is as contented as someone of his temperament is ever likely to be.

People who know him well – and especially those who weathered the tempests of earlier decades – wonder how differently, and better, things might have turned out if he and Camilla had never parted.

The ceremony – both ceremonies – were joyous affairs. The couple got officially hitched in Windsor Guildhall in April 2005, exchanging wedding rings of Welsh gold, in front of their children and other family members before heading to St George's Chapel at Windsor Castle for a service of prayer and dedication led by Rowan Williams. There they were joined by the Queen and Prince Philip, who did not attend the civil ceremony, and by friends such as Nicholas Soames, dignitaries and foreign royalty including a clutch of Saudis and Romania's exiled Crown Princess Margarita and Prince Radu. There was one notable absentee. Richard Chartres, who had been present for the Prince's marriage to Diana, stayed away, happy for his old friend, charmed by Camilla, but perhaps uncomfortable about the potential impact on the Church of England and worried about the erosion of tradition. It was a response that in any other circumstances the Prince might well have shared.

Chapter 14

Sacred Spaces

Frequently accused of arrogance by the professions he riles, Charles has always wrestled with insecurity. His diffidence is not assumed. He sounds most vehement when masking his fears – and that of course means when making interventions that are likely to be controversial, sometimes in self-fulfilling prophecy. He confesses to getting knots in his stomach before speeches. 'I've had conversations with him – and he probably won't remember me saying so – but "You're an elder now," "You're no longer the student, you're the one who knows this stuff",'" says Ian Skelly. 'I think he's always seen himself as a student at the feet of the great and wise and rather like the ugly duckling and the swan, he doesn't realise how fully fledged he is.'[1]

Charles was far from fledged in the late 1970s when he met Laurens van der Post at the Suffolk house of a mutual friend, Captain Robin Sheepshanks. It seems to have been a union of mutual needs, between a Prince longing to find meaning in his existence and a storyteller who could weave apparent answers out of thin air, the one insecure but with the glossiest of social pedigrees, the other self-invented to a stupefying degree. 'There were many phone calls (and a code: a phone bell broken off and then repeated, to which Laurens would respond with a reverential "Sir! …"),' recounts van der Post's biographer J. D. F. Jones. 'There were small dinner parties in London, and Laurens would visit Highgrove, the Prince's estate in Gloucestershire, or Sandringham, the royal residence in East Anglia. There were annual visits to Balmoral in Scotland.'[2] Van der Post liked to believe his association with Charles served a higher purpose; he confided in a note to Arianna Huffington: 'I am sometimes almost inclined to think that perhaps I am serving in a kind of Holy Grail and a Round Table summons with people like Prince Charles to rally in defence of the spirit of man.'[3]

Throughout the 1980s and into the 1990s, van der Post plugged his protégé into a wider network of ideas and people. In the poet Kathleen Raine, the Prince discovered both a safe friendship with a substantially older woman and a repository of the ideas that fascinated and sustained him. Raine had founded a journal 'devoted to the arts of the imagination', *Temenos* (the word means 'sacred space'), with Keith Critchlow and two other men: Brian Keeble, an author and publisher, and Philip Sherrard, who translated the *Philokalia*, the fourth- and fifth-century texts from Mount Athos which Charles likes to read in his Highgrove sanctuary. Van der Post introduced the Prince to the journal, and eventually to Raine, over dinner in Kensington Palace. 'I thought, that poor young man – anything I can do for him, I will do, because he is very lonely,' she said later.[4]

Van der Post died in 1996, three months after Charles's divorce came through, leaving his younger friend in a wilderness more impervious than any they had visited together. During the years of bleakness, anyone the Prince felt he could trust took on more importance to him than ever; his instinct to search for wider and higher meanings became more urgent. He made frequent visits to Raine's house in Chelsea for tea and cake and long discussions about 'flowers and gardens ... the encroaching technology and materialism of the modern world ... art and architecture, music and poetry'.[5] Always they talked about their joint project, to return the world to an awareness of ancient wisdoms.

At their first dinner, she had quoted one of the exponents of Perennialism, the art historian Ananda Kentish Coomaraswamy: 'It takes four years to get the best university education, but it takes 40 to get over it.'[6] That this message found a receptive audience in the first Prince of Wales with a university degree says something about how unrewarding his experience of Cambridge and Aberystwyth had been. In 1990, with Charles's encouragement, Raine set up the Temenos Academy, and for a period from 1992 ran the organisation from a perch within the Prince's newly established Institute of Architecture. The founding aim of the Academy, and its journal, relaunched as the *Temenos Academy Review*, was to spread the philosophy of Perennialism – the notion of a universal truth that underpins all the major religions and is not the sole preserve of the Church of England or any Christian communion. 'The arts of the imagination flourish … in the Temenos – the precinct of that sacred centre, be that centre temple, synagogue, church, mosque, or the invisible sanctuary within the heart,' explained Raine in a statement that still garnishes the Temenos website. 'Since knowledge is universal, we seek to learn from all traditions.'[7]

In 2003, aged ninety-five and still vigorous, Raine was killed by a car reversing outside her house. A letter from the grieving Prince mailed out to subscribers of the *Temenos Academy Review* promised he would 'ensure that the great, enduring message of perennial wisdom is guarded and nurtured in an increasingly uncertain and forgetful world' and he has kept that pledge, as the Academy's patron and champion, speaking at its events, writing for the review and holding fund-raisers.[8] Charles attended Raine's small private funeral and spoke at a remembrance service held later the same year at St James's Palace. He revealed that Raine had sympathised with him, seeing his role as heir to the throne as 'the most difficult task in England'. He quoted her advice: 'Dear, dear Prince, don't give that riff-raff an inch of ground, not a hair's breadth; stand firm on the holy ground of the heart. The only way to deal with the evil forces of their world is from a higher level, not to meet them on their own.' In closing his eulogy, he adapted a line from *Hamlet*: 'May God rest her dear departed soul and may flights of angels sing her to her rest.'[9]

Once as anguished as the Prince of Denmark, the Prince of Britain and the Realms through his associations with Raine and van der Post acquired a vision of the world in which everything made some kind of sense. He has continued to elaborate that vision and his confidence is growing in step with his personal happiness. 'He has assumed a certainty in the time I've known him,' says Skelly, these days Chairman of the Temenos Academy. 'He's much more sure of himself, philosophically. He has a wisdom about him.'[10] Charles remembers his mentors with fondness and gratitude. Some in the British Establishment, indeed in Buckingham Palace, regard their legacy with deep mistrust.

The Temenos Academy offers a £1,400 two-year, part-time diploma course in the Perennial philosophy, covering subject areas such as Hinduism, Islamic mysticism, metaphysics, Taoism and the visionary imagination. Temenos lectures are open to members and the public and 'may range over an astonishing range of subjects,' says the Prince. 'But so often they expose this crisis in our collective perception. They demonstrate that before the advent of the modern era, a far more integrated view of the world prevailed.' In a video message, recorded for a Temenos conference in 2013, he speaks of the need to recognise the 'beingness of things', the limitations of rational thought and the 'wisdom born not of reductionist analysis but of contemplation and ultimately of revelation'. He ends with a message to rally the troops. Temenos keeps alive 'an important flame. It is a form of prayer in action.'[11]

The Prince isn't exaggerating Temenos's subject range. The Academy's 2014 programme featured talks about *Hamlet*, Bob Dylan's album *Blood on the Tracks* and an audience with Vandana Shiva, whose bronze head sits in the Highgrove gardens. Listed as one of the Prince's advisers on sustainability, she has decried genetically modified organisms in terms that fit with Temenos's concerns – 'GMO stands for "God, move over"' – and she delivered a blast against globalisation.[12] A July 2014 lecture by the composer Patrick Hawes, who created the *Highgrove Suite* for the Prince, communicated an idiosyncratic view of music history, in which the Enlightenment should be understood as the 'Endarkenment', the point when humans began relying too much on thinking and too little on the soul, and when Western music began moving away, to its detriment, from its roots in Christian plainsong. At one point Hawes challenged the audience with a series of three questions: 'Is it wrong to commit murder?', 'Should a murderer be subject to the death penalty?' and then the third question: 'Is Jesus the son of God?'

This was not a typical Temenos talk, according to Ian Skelly. Many Temenos speakers are billed to address religious matters, but they more rarely evangelise. The organisation is devoted to finding common ground and shared understanding rather than to preaching. Nevertheless, meetings can feel churchy. On one of the long, rain-swept evenings in March 2014, Dr Margaret Barker, a biblical scholar and Lambeth Doctor of Divinity – a title awarded by the Archbishop of Canterbury – delivered a disquisition entitled 'Jesus in the Gospel of St John', setting out her signature approach to biblical studies, Temple theology. Her theory marks a startling departure from the usual narrative of Christian history. Barker says that the Old Testament is not the text known to the first Christians and that Christianity itself was heir to a so-called Temple tradition that saw the temple as a microcosm of creation, the original Eden, Adam as the original high priest and Jesus as the keeper of the ways in the first temple in Jerusalem. Before Barker spoke, a candle was lit and dedicated to the 'light of the world'.

Barker's sonorous intonations have been honed at the pulpit as a

Methodist preacher; her audience, ranging in age from perhaps late forties into the seventies, clad in corduroys or long skirts, looked like any C of E congregation on a wet Sunday, until closer inspection revealed not only a smattering of bracelets made of copper, an alternative therapy to ward off rheumatoid arthritis, but also red string wristlets, thought by followers of the Kabbalah to ward off the evil eye. A lively question-and-answer session focused on the links which Temple theology sees between Christianity and the other Abrahamic traditions.

This is a characteristic preoccupation for disciples of Temenos and its core philosophy. Perennialism traces its roots back to Marsilio Ficino, a fifteenth-century Italian priest, lauded by the Prince in *Harmony* for persuading 'many painters, writers and musicians throughout Europe to make a fresh connection with Nature and the eternal principles that she displays'.[13] Ficino articulated an idea that to some religions (and philosophers) might still sound blasphemous and in an era in which theologians held that knowledge was imparted by divine revelation was pretty daring: 'lawful religion is no different from true philosophy'.[14] He translated Plato and other ancient philosophers, and cited from their works in his efforts to reconcile Christianity with philosophic traditions.

In *Harmony*, the Prince traces a 'golden thread' of wisdom 'from Pythagoras and Plato to Shakespeare and Ficino, from [Italian Renaissance painter] Giorgione, Bach and Handel to Wordsworth, Poussin and Blake – all of these great artists were very clear that there is a harmony to the world that must be maintained'.[15] Oddly, the Prince does not follow the thread to a significant twentieth-century destination, French-Egyptian philosopher René Guénon, or onwards to German-French-Swiss-US resident Frithjof Schuon. Both men interwove strands of Islamic esoterism, in particular Sufism, into Traditionalism, a philosophical branch closely allied to Perennialism.

Schuon founded a Sufi order, the Alawiyya, later the Maryamiyya.

One of the order's members, Martin Lings, a convert also known as Abu Bakr Siraj Ad-Din, became a fellow of Temenos and gave lectures about Guénon and Schuon. He died in 2005 aged ninety-six, and in 2009, Temenos commemorated what would have been Lings' centenary by inviting Temenos fellow Seyyed Hossein Nasr to deliver a keynote. The Iranian-American Nasr, Professor of Islamic Studies at George Washington University, had long taken up the thread of Islamic Traditionalism, stitching it not only into Western thinking but feeding it back into parts of the Islamic world.

Lings and Nasr aren't just linked to the Prince through Temenos; both gave guest lectures at the Visual Islamic and Traditional Arts programme set up by Keith Critchlow and incorporated since 1993 into the various incarnations of the Prince's School of Traditional Arts. The Prince has contributed to *Sacred Web*, a biannual journal focused on Traditionalism, and provided recorded messages for its conferences. 'Although, very sadly, I cannot be with you, I do want to say that I am always delighted to receive the latest issue of *Sacred Web* because, so often, I come across such deeply revealing and enlightening articles, rich in content and diverse in subject matter,' he told delegates in 2006. 'In addition, through the work of the Temenos Academy, of which I am Patron, I have been fortunate to enjoy the writings of some of your colleagues – people such as Professor Seyyed Hossein Nasr and, of course, the late Dr Martin Lings, whose presence amongst us is so profoundly missed.' In 2014 Charles again sent his regrets and a video message to a *Sacred Web* conference. The main speaker and guest of honour was Nasr, who opened with an anecdote which might have been spun by van der Post. An indigenous man is challenged to define what is sacred. He answers: 'If you ask the fish: "What is water?", he will ask: "How can I tell you what water is?" Everything is sacred.'[16]

The speakers who followed wielded their maces against secularism, which they saw as a threat to human happiness and the natural world.

The themes are familiar to anyone who spends time around Charles; so too is the close identification between Islamic Traditionalism and environmentalism. 'Prince Charles is more of an anti-modernist than a Traditionalist,' writes academic and historian Dr Mark Sedgwick in his book *Against the Modern World*, which tracks the skein of Traditionalist influences in the twentieth century. But Sedgwick adds that 'Traditionalism may also lie behind an approach to Islam [by the Prince] that is significantly more sympathetic than is normal in British public life'.[17]

The Prince may not name-check all of his influences in *Harmony* but he does summon up a Sufi aphorism: 'Although there are many lamps, it is all the same light.'[18] This is the view of religion that strikes fear into some of the functionaries of Lambeth and Buckingham Palaces, gets mistaken for pick-and-mix New Ageism and also feeds conspiracy theories about the Prince's secret conversion to Islam or to Orthodoxy. It is the fundament of the Prince's determination to be a Defender of Faith, rather than *the* Faith. Yet it is also the fundament of the Prince's faith, and that faith is Anglican, albeit Higher Church and more mystically inclined than that of many of his co-confessionals. Prayer is as much a part of the Prince's late-night routine as his red boxes. In Charles the Church of England stands to gain a Supreme Governor who takes his duties, and his religion, exceptionally seriously.

Prominent among those duties, as he interprets them, is interfaith work, helping Crown and country – and its Established Church – to come to terms with an increasingly diverse population and in turn help that population to live harmoniously. The 2011 Census of England and Wales produced stark figures: 59.3 per cent of the population identified themselves as Christian, down from 71.1 per cent at the census a decade earlier. The Muslim population, though still small by comparison, has grown from 3 per cent of the total in 2001 to 4.8 per cent, and in some inner-city areas is a far more significant presence

— 34.5 per cent in the London borough of Tower Hamlets. More than 22 per cent of Londoners practise a religion other than Christianity.[19] A similar proportion, slightly lower in London, slightly higher across England and Wales, has no faith affiliation.

These changes represent challenges to what politicians have taken to calling 'community cohesion', most often when that spirit is lacking. At the sharp end, in areas of high unemployment and deprivation, the competition for scarce resources easily takes on sectarian and racial tones that populist movements encourage and exploit. Islamophobia is increasing; so too is the appeal to some younger Muslims and British converts of forms of Islam that are irredeemably at odds with notions of happy multiculturalism. The toll of hate crimes against religions continues to rise; the proportion carried out in the name of religion is less frequently documented, but the murder of Lee Rigby in May 2013 by two Britons of Nigerian descent who had converted to Islam became the pretext for a spate of attacks not only against Muslim targets but other faith groups. Sectarian enmities from distant conflicts also play out on British streets.

The answer, Charles believes, must be 'to remind people of what we share in common', and he uses speeches, meetings and more formalised initiatives to try to do that, as well as visiting, again and again, churches of different denominations, synagogues, mosques and temples, in Britain and elsewhere.[20] 'I can't tell you what a joy it is to worship with you today,' he told the congregation at Jesus House Church in North London. He was attending a 2007 service that happened to fall on his birthday, with the aim of celebrating the work of black-majority churches. A survey two years earlier had revealed that although people of African and Caribbean origin constituted just 2 per cent of the British population, they represented 7 per cent of churchgoing nationwide and in London accounted for more than two-thirds of worshippers.[21] 'Britain is such a welcoming country to so many people of different backgrounds but I always think that, at the end of the day, you can't be hospitable without a home and, in our case, a Christian home to which to welcome people,' he said. 'And you welcome people in your own wonderful way. You are all a marvellous example of how so many people whose families originate from the Commonwealth, have yourselves brought new life into the Christian Church in the United Kingdom thereby completing the cycle started by missionaries from Britain so many years ago. So we have that to thank you for.'[22]

Many initiatives involve bringing different faith groups together. In 2006 the Prince opened St Ethelburga's Centre for Peace and Reconciliation, established by the Bishop of London in a London church rebuilt after an IRA bombing. 'You don't just sit back and say you know [all faiths] are marvellous; you engage, you create friendships, you devise methodology like scriptural reasoning where you sit down with Sikhs, with Jews, with Muslims,' says Chartres. 'We take as a horizon a pressing contemporary problem and we actually draw resources out of our own scriptures not arguing with one another but listening acutely and accountably speaking to one another and you always emerge from that more deeply convinced about your own Christian identity and more deeply respectful at the same time.'[23]

'The royals in general and HRH in particular do interfaith better than anyone,' says Lord Sacks.[24] At the time of the conversation in August 2013, Jonathan Sacks is entering his last fortnight as Chief Rabbi of the United Hebrew Congregations of the Commonwealth. He first met Charles seventeen years earlier aboard a private jet to London, after the funeral of Israel's murdered Prime Minister Yitzhak Rabin. The then leaders of Britain's two main opposition parties, Labour's Tony Blair and the Liberal Democrats' Paddy Ashdown, also hitched a ride. As the Prince sat, nose in a book, Blair leaned over and asked him what he was reading. It turned out to be the Hebrew Bible, and soon everyone present had been drawn into a wide-ranging discussion. Sacks remembers being impressed not only by Charles's theological knowledge but his broader take on issues. 'He had so carefully thought through positions,' Sacks recalls. 'You cannot be with HRH for very long without realising that he has thought immensely about really big vision-type issues. He thinks on a very broad canvas and he has an integrated world view.'

The Rabbi also recalls the Prince's vulnerability. 'It was really self-evident that he was really under siege; this was the most difficult moment.'[25] The embattled Knight of the Realms had drawn up the drawbridge, and like Kathleen Raine, Sacks's impulse was to try to penetrate Charles's defences in order to alleviate this isolation. Sacks still seems a little startled by how well he succeeded, quite quickly forging a relationship with the Prince that remains important to both men. In June 2013, at a dinner for Sacks, Charles gave a funny, affectionate speech in tribute to his 'steadfast friend'. 'As we were both born in the year of Israel's birth,' he told Sacks, 'I realise that we have of course both reached the official age of retirement. But I do hope yours is going to be a bit more realistic than mine.' He even risked a Jewish joke to a Jewish audience, telling Sacks he sympathised with the difficulties he must have encountered in trying to represent the United Synagogue's sixty-two Orthodox Jewish communities. 'What is it they say? Put ten Jews in a room and you'll quickly have eleven opinions. And to paraphrase Alan Bennett's observation about the Prince of Wales, being the Chief Rabbi is not so much a position as a predicament, so I have every sympathy.'[26]

Sacks had indeed encountered turbulence during his time as Chief Rabbi, not only from the leaders of more liberal forms of Judaism keen to disassociate themselves from the Orthodox strands, but also from members of Orthodox communities who accused Sacks of religious relativism. A passage in his book *The Dignity of Difference* was taken to mean he valued all religions as highly as Judaism. 'If we are to live in close proximity to difference, as in a global age we do, we will need more than a code of rights, more even than mere tolerance,'

Sacks had written. 'We will need to understand that just as the natural environment depends on biodiversity, so the human environment depends on cultural diversity, because no one creed has a monopoly on spiritual truth; no one civilisation encompasses all the spiritual, ethical and artistic expressions of mankind.'[27] Like Charles, in articulating the value of other religions, he was assumed to be moving away from his own. In fact he was making the argument against the idea that 'if faith is what makes us human, then those who do not share my faith are less than fully human'.[28] He was also advocating not for the interchangeability of religions but for their specificity.

This is the Prince's view but it is often conflated with what Richard Chartres terms 'upper-middle-class religion, taking a *bon bouche* from here and there, a bit of Californian Buddhism mixed with a bit of Sufism – a religion which deifies your tastes.' This, says the Bishop, is 'no good at all, unless you commit yourself seriously to a way in God's good time you will be brought to a position where you can befriend all the lovers of God ... You need a way that brings you to a point of unity, poised where you can love without distortions or hidden agendas, you can appreciate. That's absolutely central and anybody who really feels that they have to subject the other to withering negative criticism just shows how little progress they've made on their own way. That's a sign of spiritual immaturity. So I rejoice in the fact that the Prince of Wales loves Islam.'[29]

Visible expressions of that love can be seen in the Prince's many trips to Muslim countries and his fascination with the arts and culture of Islam. The journalist Yasmin Alibhai-Brown, an Ismaili Muslim, committed republican and no fan of Charles, admits to a grudging admiration for his response to Islam and desire to represent British citizenry in all their diversity of belief and heritage. 'There is no doubt that he is as unsettled at being locked into a very narrow Englishness as was Diana. They had much more in common than they knew,' she says. The Princess 'was the first person ever in the

British Establishment to whom to embrace difference was completely natural. She wasn't following policies, she wasn't trying to be good, and she wasn't trying to be kind … [The Prince] responds to this kind of unsettledness inside of him too.' That means, says Alibhai-Brown, that 'there are aspects to his character which continue something important, especially at a time when England is becoming so little England with UKIP and so on. There are very few people who are not cowed by that, so that you don't speak about other cultures in this warm way. Or study them or say they have things to teach us. So credit. I don't want him to be King. I want a revolution, I want them all to go and live in one small palace somewhere, like the Indian Maharajas did after independence. But credit.'[30]

Alibhai-Brown heard Charles speak at the 2006 launch of the Jameel Gallery at the Victoria and Albert Museum. 'It was the most extraordinary speech on Islam, its aesthetics, its values; he seemed absolutely to have studied that and actually feels a real affinity to much of it.' She has also visited the Prince's School of Traditional Arts, an offshoot of Keith Critchlow's Visual Islamic and Traditional Arts programme. 'It was astonishing. Young people were coming from all over the world including from the Arab countries to be trained in the tile work, in the ceiling work, in how to make fountains, but more importantly how to understand the aesthetics of abstraction and all the kind of Islamic shapes.'[31] In 2006, the Prince exported this expertise to a country that used to be rich in it. The Turquoise Mountain foundation in Kabul aims to revive Afghanistan's traditional crafts and regenerate a historic quarter of the city. It took the Prince until 2010 to persuade security chiefs to let him visit his brainchild in person; on the same trip he also dropped in to show support for British troops in Helmand, at a forward operating base, at Lashkar Gah task-force headquarters and at Camp Bastion, where, unlike his son Harry, he enjoyed the flurry his presence created.

His main British vehicle for interfacing with Islam is the Oxford

Centre for Islamic Studies. He has been, in the words of its director, Farhan Nizami, 'a very active patron', enabling the institution to attract a range of speakers as varied as the St James's Palace guest list: from the icon of reconciliation, Nelson Mandela, to avatars of more repressive regimes such as Saudi Arabia's Foreign Minister Saud Al-Faisal who told the audience that 'Saudi Arabia is thrust towards assuming a position of influence and authority to maintain the moral tradition and the purity of Islam'.[32]

Charles delivered his 1993 'Islam and the West' speech under the auspices of the Centre, returning in 2010 to issue a challenge to the Muslim world to reconnect to the environmentalism that he believes inherent in Islam. Nizami describes this interpretation of Islam as 'an eye opener to me. It was not me leading him; he encouraged us to start thinking about those ideas and what Islam has to say.'[33] The Prince's charities run an annual summer school with the Centre, the Young Muslim Leadership Programme, that aims to foster under-standing and links between Muslim communities in Britain and other communities and key institutions.

Like its patron, the Centre is no stranger to controversy. Work started on its permanent building, next to Magdalen College, in 2002; it overshot its target opening date of 2004 by a decade, amid budget shortfalls and planning squabbles. Not everyone welcomed its minaret among Oxford's dreaming spires, not least because its location risks fostering the impression that it is an Oxford University college and not, as billed on its website, 'a recognised independent centre of the University of Oxford', an educational charity that works with the University but is a separate entity. Richard Gombrich, Professor Emeritus of Sanskrit at Oxford University's Faculty of Oriental Studies, complained that 'there is a widespread misapprehension that [the Centre] is part of Oxford. Awkward is putting it mildly. Universities aren't the kind of places that build mosques'.[34]

The Centre's funding has also raised questions that sharpened after 2011 revelations about Colonel Muammar Gaddafi's largesse to the London School of Economics triggered the resignation of the LSE's director Sir Howard Davies. The Centre had not taken Libyan money but its backers have included several Saudi sources including King Fahd and, back in 1989, the bin Laden family who stumped up £150,000. A report by the Centre for Social Cohesion queried the link between donations and influence in British educational institutions, on the basis that big donations left recipients on the hook and therefore less likely to maintain proper academic independence. The report singled out the speech by Saudi Arabia's Al-Faisal at the Oxford Centre for Islamic Studies as an example of how such obligations might play out. It also criticised the Centre's selection of trustees past and present for including religious conservatives such as Abdullah Omar Nasseef, a professor at King Abdul Aziz University in Jeddah and former Secretary General of the World Muslim League closely identified with Salafist or Wahhabi Islam.[35] 'We are interested in all trends and all aspects of Muslim culture and civilisation and place great emphasis on the encouragement of international academic dialogue,' says Nizami.[36]

Charles's traditionalist inclinations mean that he respects some expressions of Islam that many people, within Islam and without, will never accept. There is a moment near the beginning of the *Harmony* film when the Prince speaks over lyrical music and a montage of idyllic footage. 'There is still a chance, just, that we can turn the tide and restore what we have lost. Also that we can hand on to our children and their grandchildren a world that is just as fit to live in and one that is able to go on sustaining those that follow them,' he says. 'We have this extraordinary ability to be connected to the inner patterns of Nature which is really what we call the spiritual, because there is an urgent, crying need to reconnect with that relationship again, with the things that are actually sacred.' The images accompanying the last phrase are a Buddhist temple in Lhasa, an indigenous tribesman in a feathered headdress, a Christian church and the portico to an Islamic building, in front of which stands a woman in a niqab and abaya. Only her hands and eyes are visible. All four images seem to be presented as equally valid symbols of connection to what Charles might term 'timeless' tradition and through that tradition, the natural and spiritual worlds.

An insider says that the Prince disagrees with France and Belgium's bans on covering the face in public places, designed to prevent the wearing of niqabs and burkas. Charles sees these laws as an infringement of human rights, worrying that bans criminalise the wearer rather than challenging the custom. Yet it's far from clear if Charles believes such a challenge appropriate or desirable in any case. The aspects of the Prince's ideology that are most unsettling to liberals give him influence in corners others could never reach, enhancing his abilities as a bridge builder, the insider adds.

Perhaps so, but conversely the gap between the Prince and some of the Crown's liberally minded subjects may never be bridged, for all that they share many of his concerns and impulses.

Chapter 15

Happy and Notorious

A moment in Canada speaks to the nature of the relationship between the Prince and his Duchess. On the first full day of the trip, the royal convoy has split into two, with Charles going to Halifax Public Gardens to perform one of the standard gestures of royalty, 'planting' a sapling by ceremonially dumping a scoop of soil. In 1939, King George VI carried out the same symbolic act at the base of one of the trees that now towers over his grandson. Camilla has been chauffeured to a rougher part of Halifax, to speak to women who have escaped abusive partners with the help of a charity called Alice Housing.

The schedule carefully plotted by Canadian officials and royal aides envisages the Prince making quick work of his tree-planting and going on to Seaport Farmer's Market to tour the stalls before reuniting with his wife for the first of several displays of Scottish dancing Nova Scotia lays on for them. But Charles always runs late. During a walkabout in the park, he stops and speaks to everybody, doesn't just say hello and move down the line but is drawn into conversations, inevitably delaying his segment of the convoy. Camilla, though she engages with people – and at this stop listens intently to difficult stories of spousal violence – tends to keep to the timings she has been given. As a result, she arrives at the covered farmer's market ahead of her husband and takes the opportunity to shelter, briefly, in a side room, recharging the batteries that in people not raised to royal life easily run low during long days of glad-handing.

After ten minutes, she feels refreshed enough to be a Duchess once again and she embarks on her own tour of the market stalls. Charles, unaware that Camilla has beaten him to this destination, makes his own royal progress along the aisles. He feels rough – he will generously share British cold germs with the peoples of Canada on this trip – but nevertheless he again becomes absorbed in the royal job, talking to stallholders, sampling their jams and cakes and cordials. He doesn't spot his wife until their parties converge. As he catches sight of Camilla, he stops, surprised, and then another expression transfigures his pallid face: joy. 'Oh,' he says, enchanted. 'You.'

Hold onto that image. It's not easy to do so amid a clamour of competing pictures and multiple narratives, many of them sulphurous. That is not to say the other versions of Charles and Camilla are all without merit. The Rashomon effect – the way one reality observed by different individuals may produce equally valid, yet apparently contradictory, histories – has proved especially potent in their case.

It doesn't help that any truths about a couple whose love for each other destroyed their first marriages lie buried beneath a man-made lithosphere of nonsense. Many of the most preposterous stories emanate from sources thousands of miles from their protagonists. The First Amendment of the US Constitution protects the right of individuals to express themselves through publication and dissemination of information, ideas and opinions without interference, constraint or prosecution by the government. This noblest of clauses has spawned the strangest of phenomena – the country's supermarket tabloids, sensationalist magazines that are even odder than the stories they purport to cover. They occasionally break real news. The *National Enquirer* ran the Squidgygate transcript before the British media dared to do so. Supermarket tabloids have also published photographs of heaven, reported alien invasions, and declared Elvis alive almost as often as they've announced the Duchess of Cambridge's pregnancy. Diana conspiracies are a perennial. Among 2014 headlines which the *Globe* designed to grab attention at the checkout was this, in March: 'DIANA'S KILLER HIDING IN RUSSIA — HAND HIM OVER, WILLIAM RAGES'.

A glimmer of internal logic illuminated the tall tale. Russia had refused to surrender Edward Snowden to the US authorities, so surely would refrain from sending Diana's assassin for trial in England — should such a person exist. Prince William was furious, as well he might be. There was no love lost between the Russian President and the British royals, the tabloid stated with accidental prescience. (Less than two months later, Charles's critical commentary on Putin's Crimea adventures would make world headlines.)

By July, the *Globe* had devised a fresh and even further-fetched angle on the conspiracy: 'CAMILLA SHOCKS KATE: CHARLES MURDERED DIANA — AND I'M NEXT!' A cover flash provided a clue to the Prince's supposed motive: '$350M DIVORCE TURNS UGLY'. This followed up on an issue earlier the same month that claimed the Queen had ordered him to divorce Camilla. The same issue revealed: 'POPE FRANCIS IS DYING'.

In ages past, the majority of people fortunate enough to live in democracies retained some faith in the authorities to tell the truth. Everybody read magazines like the *Globe* understanding that this was entertainment, not news. As recently as 2007 that led to a real scoop going unremarked for months. In October of that year, the *National Enquirer* revealed that Democratic presidential hopeful John Edwards, married for thirty years and with his wife Elizabeth suffering from incurable cancer, had been dallying with a member of his campaign staff. Mainstream news outlets resolutely ignored the story, as the supermarket tabloid continued to delve, publishing a photograph of Edwards's inamorata, Rielle Hunter, pregnant. It wasn't until August

2008, long after he dropped out of the race for the Democratic nomination, that Edwards admitted his affair and not until 2010 that he
acknowledged paternity of Hunter's daughter.

It's a safe bet that if the *Enquirer* had broken the story just a few
years later, it would have gone viral whether or not mainstream
outlets picked it up, tweeted and Facebooked and Storyfyed and transformed into BuzzFeed-style lists on innumerable infotainment
websites: '10 Pictures of John Edwards Looking Shifty'; '5 Signs That
Say Tot *Is* Disgraced Former Senator's Daughter'. A similar fate
awaits all clickbait content these days, whatever its derivation.
Consumers trust nothing and everything, increasingly unable to
distinguish virtual junk food from something more nourishing. So it
is that an immeasurable but significant contingent of the burgeoning
global population assumes Charles to be heading for the divorce
courts for a second time, possibly at the bidding of the Queen, or
refraining from doing so only because Camilla holds dirt on the royals
(another popular Internet meme).

Does it matter that a prince who mistrusts the legacy of the
Enlightenment should suffer under an encroaching Endarkenment?
Certainly not as much as the Endarkenment itself matters, but its
miasma does help to obscure what Charles does and why, especially
in combination with mainstream coverage, itself riven by old
allegiances and half-forgotten resentments. As for Camilla, if the
punishment for her adultery in an earlier century might have seen
her immobilised in stocks for passers-by to scoff at and spit on, her
latter-day humiliation has been no less public and almost as brutal.

From the moment of her exposure as the Prince's illicit lover, the
British press held her up not just for scorn but for ridicule. 'Trundling
a trolley round Sainsbury's yesterday, [Camilla] hardly looked like a
woman at the centre of a royal love scandal,' reported the *Daily
Mirror* in 1993.[1] But as Camilla faced the world for the first time in
weeks, she did supply the answer to a frequently posed question:

'What DOES Prince Charles see in her? In her outsized headscarf and unfussy clothes, she was a dead ringer for HM ... His Mum.' Here's an excerpt from the *Daily Express* of the same period: 'Women in particular, who tend for some extraordinary reason to be much more bitchy than men in assessing female attributes, have been astounded at the thought that Prince Charles would choose the equine-faced Camilla over the fashion plate Diana, unless it had something to do with his passion for horses.'[2] The barrage of articles reported public disapproval and reinforced it. An oft-quoted story that Camilla had been pelted with bread rolls in a supermarket car park by angry supporters of Diana seems to have been pure invention. In Clarence House there is a suspicion that a Camilla lookalike was hired to stage this and other stunts.

Camilla endured her notoriety in silence. 'People say she's tough,' says Lucia Santa Cruz. 'She's not tough. She's amazingly strong, which is different. She is a solid person. She had a very good family background. She's got very good parents, she's got a sister that she's close to. She has the strength that people from very, very solid families tend to have, and she's very resilient. She is very dignified, which in a way made all this so much worse for her. It was the worst kind of public bullying. [There was] nothing she could do to get out of her situation. She never opened her mouth; she never defended herself.'[3]

She did get some help. Mark Bolland, on the Prince's staff from 1996 until his less-than-happy departure in 2002, worked after Diana's death to gain acceptance for the royal mistress. One strand of the strategy saw Charles and Camilla begin to appear together instead of always sidestepping cameras. Their January 1999 unveiling, on the steps of the Ritz hotel after the fiftieth birthday party of Camilla's sister Annabel Elliot, attracted 'up to 200 photographers and journalists ... to witness the occasion, having set up 60 ladders lined three-deep in anticipation outside the hotel', the BBC reported.

'Television satellite vans were parked in side streets alongside the London hotel, and bright TV lights illuminated the scene. Alongside the media throng was a crowd of members of the public several hundred strong.'[4] Their first public kiss – a peck on the cheek – took place at another birthday party, marking the fifteenth year of the National Osteoporosis Society in June 2001.

The second strategic strand proved more controversial within the palace system. Other members of the Windsor family suspected Bolland of having leaked negative stories about them in order to make Charles look better by comparison. It's an allegation Bolland appeared to accept in a 2005 interview. 'It was all about Camilla,' he told Sholto Byrnes of the *Independent*. 'All about the refusal of the Queen and Buckingham Palace to take the relationship seriously and assist the prince in reaching a conclusion. That underpinned everything.'

'It seems extraordinary for royal servants to be briefing against other members of the reigning family,' Byrnes writes. 'The team that was there probably cared too much and got too emotional about it at times,' concedes Bolland. 'We got in a sort of Prince of Wales bunker within the House of Windsor. But to an extent that reflected him.'[5] Bolland has been gone for more than a decade but the bunker mentality and the edge of competition between rival courts survives. He may have helped to intensify it, but Bolland didn't create it. It's at least in part the legacy of how hard Charles had to struggle as a young man to shake off the dead hand of Buckingham Palace.

In the same interview, Bolland looks forward to the wedding of Charles and Camilla the following month. 'The credits are running on the movie I was a part of,' he says, as if the marriage certificate had the power to kill controversy around the relationship.[6] Instead, the certificate issued by Windsor's Superintendent Registrar, Clair Williams, itself became a source of controversy, proof and symbol of the first civil marriage in the royal family.

———

Charles and Camilla plighted their troth on 9 April 2005, a day later than originally planned. The death of Pope John Paul II on 2 April necessitated the short-notice change when the Prince agreed to stand in for the Queen at the funeral in Rome. Segments of the media reported this as a sign from above that the union was jinxed.

Though technically Princess of Wales since the marriage, Camilla has abjured the title and its unhappy resonances. Nevertheless, divorce rumours have circulated pretty much from the first day of the royal honeymoon at Birkhall, given credence by publications that unlike America's supermarket tabloids consider themselves journals of record and by journalists with histories of procuring real royal scoops. Diana was so fond of the *Daily Mail*'s Richard Kay that she gave him substantial insights into her life; her trust was repaid after her death, when Kay declined to write a tell-all biography. 'I was very close to her and I felt that one of the reasons I never wrote a book was that she'd got a raw deal. Mostly by people who worked for her or were her friends. And they all rushed to get their memoirs out as quickly as possible and I always felt my great difficulty would be not what to put into a book but what to leave out,' he says.[7] In 2010, five years into the Prince's second marriage, Kay and his colleague Geoffrey Levy published a long piece entitled 'Why Charles and Camilla are now leading such separate lives'.

Their article described 'a very strange marriage' made under duress, in anticipation of the Prince's accession. In this version of events, not marrying Camilla represented a greater barrier to Charles's eventual kingship than marrying her, but neither partner wanted to do it. It is not an interpretation the journalist Michael Jones or the Archbishop of Canterbury's frequent correspondent Frederick Phipps would share, and some accounts suggest a different reality. The night the engagement was announced Camilla was 'excited like a young girl', says Robin Boles, the Chief Executive of In Kind Direct, one of the Prince's organisations which redistributes surplus goods from companies to charities.[8]

Kay and Levy wrote that Charles and Camilla's staff routinely clashed. The couple's habits clashed too, the Prince's 'obsessional neatness' offended by the Duchess's 'renowned domestic untidiness'. An 'aged dowager who has known Camilla all her life' provided a pithy commentary: 'When a woman's been a man's mistress for thirty years and then marries him, the relationship is bound to change. They still love each other, I have no doubt of that, but life as a married couple is difficult for two such independent spirits, who have always enjoyed the physical aspects of life. There's a certain electricity about sex between lovers which is bound to dissipate after several years of marriage.'

A 'seasoned royal aide' gave another possible reason for the supposed chill in the heir: 'Camilla absolutely adores having her grandchildren around her and is always talking about them, but Charles simply cannot stand the noise and mess that small children make.' As a result, the authors explained, the Prince preferred splendid isolation in his own houses, while the Duchess entertained her grand-children at Ray Mill, her bolt-hole in Wiltshire since she divorced Andrew Parker Bowles in 1995. Adding to the disaffection, the Duchess apparently resented her royal duties. 'For now,' the article concluded, 'theirs is not a marriage in actual "difficulties", because it is an arrangement that both appear to be content with. And yet – who would ever have imagined that the older woman for whom a crown prince dumped a young and beautiful wife now chooses to spend so much time away from him in a world of her own?'[9]

The authors were wise to hedge. By April 2014, with the couple nine years married and the Prince's delight in his own grandson palpable, Kay and Levy wrote a second long article on the state of the relationship. 'From "that wicked woman" to Her Majesty's secret weapon' described Camilla's 'remorseless' and 'inexorable royal progress', adding that she seemed 'to have settled comfortably into the royal role that arrived late in life'. There is a negative: Camilla's ascendancy in the Queen's affections has created new friction. 'Edward is furious that Sophie now has to curtsey to Camilla … Through all this, the former *maitresse en titre* glides effortlessly beside the Prince of Wales, soothing his brow one moment, cajoling him the next. If she is eventually crowned Queen Camilla, will it be his triumph, or hers?'[10]

'The thrust of the [first] piece, that their relationship works when they are not on top of each other, still holds true,' emails Kay. 'Camilla does prefer being at Ray Mill with her grandchildren around her while the Prince likes the familiarity of Highgrove, where he prefers to work without being disturbed by noisy stepgrandchildren … On their relationship, if anything it seems now that they somehow strengthened the union between them.'[11]

This is the Rashomon effect in action. From some angles, the time Camilla and Charles spend apart is easily interpreted as a symptom of dysfunction. From others, it's a sign of stability, in the relationship and the psyches of both parties to it. The Prince will never be carefree but he has worked out the ingredients he needs to maintain an even keel: Camilla, his family, his gardens, his faith, his sanctuaries and – possibly even above all – his work. When I asked him the standard feature writer's question: 'What gives you joy?', he embarked on a long answer about being able to put back together again and heal things that have otherwise been abandoned or allowed to become derelict or destroyed. His aide Kristina Kyriacou, with evident amusement, prompted him: 'Your grandson, sir.' He laughed and happily proffered a more traditional – and entirely heartfelt – answer: 'Having a wonderful wife. And of course now a grandson.'[12] 'All his friends have been on our knees saying: "Won't you just slow down?"' says Emma Thompson. 'I now think it would be very bad for him. I think he'd unravel in some way.'[13]

Camilla, too, needs the space to pursue her own interests. 'She's got much more of a world of her own than people suspect,' says

Lucia Santa Cruz. 'She's very happy on her own. She's an amazing reader; she's very well read. Every time I discover a new author and I say: "Have you read –?" she's read them all. Very difficult to give her a book. She loves what she calls pottering in the garden so she's very happy on her own and that means she's got a lot of internal life. Which I think also is her protection. She could flit off and be on her own, by herself and happy. She loves being in her house on her own.'[14]

Together, the Prince and Camilla belie the reports of friction. They share secret jokes, mirror each other's body language (though Camilla has yet to adopt the Windsor habit of holding her hands behind her back). 'She's terrific, so down-to-earth, so good for him,' says Patrick Holden.[15] Ben Elliot reckons this cuts both ways: the Prince is good for his aunt. 'He really loves her. They're so affectionate to each other. Some couples when they've been together that long ...' Elliot trails off, then continues. 'He's so sweet to her.'[16]

There are long-standing niggles. Camilla likes plain food, grilled fish, steamed vegetables. Charles has a taste for suet puddings and game. There are potentially more explosive issues. Camilla doesn't entirely buy into the princely philosophy, and sometimes challenges his views, but if other people disagree with him, that's another matter. 'She is entirely loyal to his likes and dislikes,' says Lucia Santa Cruz. 'We argue about organics, the solution to world problems, the extent of ecology versus the needs of huge populations and she will always say: "But he is right about this."'[17]

A Clarence House insider credits Camilla with giving the Prince his most secure line yet to planet earth: 'She's a caring and considerate mother and she's never lost sight of the importance of family, the importance of having them close and keeping them around. That keeps her grounded and that gives her a practicality that perhaps she might otherwise forget. It gives her an anchor. I'm always surprised at how savvy she is ... It's clear she's not in a bubble.'

The couple has developed an effective working partnership too, often appearing as a double act, Camilla the amiable Ernie Wise to the Prince's wisecracking but more combustible Eric Morecambe. She has acquired the usual range of respectable royal involvements, as patron or president, from animal charities, garden trusts, veterans' associations and the Girl's Brigade in Scotland to Maggie's Cancer Caring Centre, hospices and hospitals, opera societies and orchestras. Some patronages, such as the Charleston Trust, are 'arty, literary, she loves that. Ditchling museum again something very arty, it touches the rather bookish side of her nature,' says Amanda Macmanus, one of Camilla's two part-time Assistant Private Secretaries and a woman who appears as jolly as the Duchess herself.[18]

Camilla's good humour cloaks the resilience Santa Cruz describes that enabled her to withstand the backlash against her role in the break-up of the Prince's first marriage. In 1995, at the height of the backlash, the then Mrs Parker Bowles agreed to become the patron of the National Osteoporosis Society after seeing her mother die from the condition that crumbles bones. 'We watched in horror as she quite literally shrank before our eyes,' Camilla recalled later. 'My mother's GP was kind and sympathetic, but he was able to do little to alleviate the pain she was in.'[19] The charity's CEO took a gamble that at the time seemed risky: that Camilla's association would bring the right kind of attention to the brand.

More recently the Duchess has also quietly developed a range of campaigning interests distinct from those of her husband, grappling with issues that in palace terms could seem edgy. She promotes credit unions – non-profit financial cooperatives – seeking to draw attention to the problems of debt and rip-off loans. Since its inception Camilla has shown support for the Southbank Centre's WOW – Women of the World festival – and in 2015 became its patron. At a reception to mark this step in February of that year, she hailed the work of campaigners against the practice of female genital mutilation, and of organisations supporting victims of domestic violence. 'She believes the monarchy is there to create progress and she's prepared to bring subjects to the fore' says Jude Kelly, the Artistic Director of the Southbank Centre and creator of WOW.[20]

From a privileged background, but an earthy one, tempered by the flames of contempt, the Duchess is no shrinking violet. This book had just come out and though well aware of the controversy it engendered, she came straight over to me. 'They think you're about to throw your drink over me,' I said as photographers converged. 'I'm far too sensible for that,' she replied, laughing. At another WOW reception, she spotted her friend Australian novelist Kathy Lette manoeuvring herself through the crowd on crutches. 'What did you do to yourself?' Camilla asked. 'I fell off my toy boy,' Lette replied. Camilla roared.

Her behaviour could rarely be described as queenly, yet as Richard Kay and Geoffrey Levy hinted, the assumption in Clarence House as in Buckingham Palace and in wider royal circles is that Camilla will one day sit enthroned alongside her King not as 'Princess Consort' – the designation mooted by aides during the early days of her rehabilitation – but as Queen. Nobody doubts this is what Charles wants. 'I think she's very good for him,' says Robin Boles. 'She should be Queen. There's nothing in the law that stops her from being Queen. I'd put my money on it.'[21]

That isn't quite the sure thing it looks. People who meet Camilla generally warm to her. She has authenticity, as Nicholas Soames explains with his characteristic exuberance. 'There's not one bit of side to the Duchess of Cornwall. She's what-you-see-is-what-you-get. She's what my father would have called "a bloody good egg". She's terrific, she's great, and people respond to that. What they most respond to is people being themselves. She's just a really good girl, good-natured, she likes people. Exactly like the Prince's grandmother was, who grew up in grand surroundings and was good with what the press, in their patronising way, are pleased to call "ordinary people".'[22] The problem is that most of those 'ordinary people' haven't met Camilla, and many of them remember her predecessor.

Opinion polls may be moving in favour of Charles. A May 2013 poll showed that a narrow majority expects him to make a good king. There is diminishing support for the idea of the crown passing straight to William. But the same poll revealed Camilla as the only member of the royal family judged to have made a negative contribution to the monarchy; 46 per cent of respondents argued that she should be relegated to consort status.[23] Another poll in April 2015 echoed these findings, with 55 per cent against the idea of Queen Camilla.

During the infamous Camillagate phone call, Charles told his then lover: 'I'm so proud of you.' 'Don't be silly. I've never achieved anything,' Camilla demurred. He insisted, she protested. Then he uttered a line often construed as proof of his self-absorption: 'Your greatest achievement is to love me.' 'Oh darling,' she said, 'easier than falling off a chair.' His next sentence gives an insight into their reality at the time: 'You suffer all these indignities and tortures and calumnies.' 'Oh darling,' she replied. 'Don't be so silly. I'd suffer anything for you. That's love. It's the strength of love.'

Loving Charles continues to be an achievement, a test of strength that she keeps winning. For the Prince her victories couldn't be more important, and not only because he has known what love means for more than four decades. 'He's absolutely a whole other person now. He was desperately unhappy. He's not any more,' says Emma Thompson.[24]

Always look on the bright side of life. The Prince of Wails has proven himself conspicuously bad at following this advice, but twice cameras have captured him intoning it. In Jonathan Dimbleby's 1994 documentary, a tentative Charles affects to join in as the rock musician Phil Collins leads a chorus of young jobless. 'When you're chewing on life's gristle / Don't grumble, give a whistle / And this'll help things turn out for the best / And always look on the bright side of life!' The lyrics gained an unexpected poignancy in the mouths of Prince's Trust clients and a Prince at a low ebb.

Written by Eric Idle, the song originally garnished the final sequence of *Monty Python's Life of Brian* in which the hero, a reluctant Jewish messiah in Roman-occupied Judea, is crucified. As Brian hangs amid rows of prisoners condemned to die in the same way, Idle, splayed on an adjacent cross, begins to sing and soon everybody takes up the refrain. Protestors accused the film of blasphemy at its 1979 release and launched pickets. Other jurisdictions banned it altogether. Aberystwyth – the town in Wales where Charles spent a lonely university term – took thirty years to lift its prohibition.

On 12 November 2008, during the final year of Aberystwyth's ban, Idle again performed the ditty, clad in a white tutu and feathered headdress, emerging from a gaggle of ballerinas during an excerpt from *Swan Lake*. His appearance marked the finale to *We Are Most Amused*, a London gala in aid of the Prince's Trust and celebrating its founder's imminent sixtieth birthday. Once again the cameras sought out Charles in the audience and this time found him cantillating with gusto.

Much had changed since his last singalong with the Prince's Trust fourteen years earlier. The song had gained a new audience and some additional lyrics as part of *Spamalot*, a hit musical loosely based on another movie by the Pythons, *Monty Python and the Holy Grail.* The Annual Greenhouse Gas Index had registered an increase of as much as 30 per cent. Humans had reproduced in unprecedented volumes, adding 1.1 billion to the global population. Britain alone had provided Her Majesty with 4 million new subjects, swelling to a population of 61 million. Digital technology had taken hold throughout Her Realms and far beyond, laying waste some industries and creating others, changing how people communicated and the nature of their communications. World wealth had risen but some of it was illusory.

The once mighty Lehman Brothers filed for bankruptcy less than two months before the gala. Trust in most institutions was failing. The monarchy and its heir, by contrast, were undergoing something of a renaissance. Flanked on one side by Camilla, now HRH the Duchess of Cornwall and his dearest wife, and on the other by his younger son Harry, Charles radiated cheer, convulsing with laughter at words Idle unexpectedly inserted into this special rendition. 'If *Spamalot* is hot and you like it or p'raps not / A bunch of knights in search of holy grails / When you're sixty years of age and your mum won't leave the stage / It's good to know that you're still Prince of Wales!'

In his seventh decade, Charles still pursues his grails. His mum remains on the stage but he knows that the moment of her exit is drawing inexorably closer. That is not a prospect he relishes since any coronation must follow a funeral. 'Always look on the bright side of death,' Idle continued. 'Just before you draw your terminal breath / For life's a piece of shit, when you look at it / Life's a laugh and death's a joke it's true / You'll see it's all a show. Leave 'em laughing as you go / Just remember that the last laugh is on you.'

The Prince will never be able to treat mortality with such insouciance, his mother's, his own, anybody's. It's tricky enough to look on the bright side of life. But with Camilla at his right hand and Harry at his left, William happily married and with a son and heir of his own, Charles's world is more benign than he has ever known it.

Chapter 16

Kings to Come

When Charles leads a tour of his psyche, it's best to bring wellingtons or borrow a pair from the storeroom at the side entrance to Dumfries House. Even on clement days – and in this neck of East Ayrshire the weather systems cycle as suddenly as the princely moods – the going can get boggy. In other respects a considerate host, the Prince waits for no man and no woman in Louboutins either. One of his guests realises her spindly heels won't survive the terrain and returns to the Palladian mansion. The rest of the party sloshes on, at the clip set by the royal mountain goat. Most are younger than he is, but only his estate manager Oliver Middlemiss easily keeps pace. At his back, Charles hears time's winged chariot. Before him lie deserted fields, crumbling outbuildings, vast eternities of potential to change lives, in practical, measurable ways and also in a less tangible sense, by reconnecting people to Nature and the past. If *Harmony* is Charles's manifesto, the Dumfries estate has become its physical manifestation, a map of his soul complete with funny little gazebos.

Among the guests exploring these twisting pathways is the group of 'Bond villains' – wealthy donors and potential donors to the Prince's charities – who on the previous evening joined the Prince at Dumfries House for a meal of Walled Garden Pea and Broad Bean Risotto with a Soft Poached Hen's Egg, Pan-Seared Wild Sea Bass, Pomme Écrasé and Hand-Picked Dumfries House Vegetables (exactly the sort of dish Camilla enjoys) and Autumn Plum Crumble with Vanilla Custard (more Charles's thing), served with Puligny-Montrachet Les Meix Olivier Leflaive 2010, Sarget de Gruaud Larose Saint-Julien 2006 and Laurent Perrier Rosé. At the end of this repast, a piper, in full ceremonial uniform – kilt, tunic, sporran, full plaid and a feather bonnet – marched twice around the long oval table, playing a medley of traditional Scottish music that included the 'Skye Boat Song', the story of Bonnie Prince Charlie, 'the lad that's born to be king'.

Conversations ranged widely at pre-dinner drinks in the Tapestry Room, during the meal, and over *digestifs* and coffee in the North Drawing Room. Should anyone have asked about the concept behind the ongoing project to renovate the stately home and transform its grounds, Charles, Camilla and Fiona Lees, Chief Executive of East Ayrshire council, were on hand to explain, along with key members of the Dumfries House Trust including its Chief Executive Michael Fawcett. The plan – inevitably – is to establish a virtuous circle, by saving the timeless – if period-specific – glories of Dumfries House, luring tourists to the estate and the wider area, and in so doing helping to fund the restoration and maintenance of the one and the revival of the other.

The most important surviving early work of architect Robert Adam, Dumfries House was built between 1754 and 1759 for the widower William Crighton-Dalrymple, the 5th Earl of Dumfries, who hoped it would persuade a particularly nubile young woman to marry him. She spurned his advances even though the Earl kitted out his love nest with a stupendous four-poster bed and matching furniture made by a fashionable cabinetmaker of the day, Thomas Chippendale. The lovelorn aristocrat married a cousin instead, dying without an heir eight years after moving in. The house went on to witness further sore disappointments as well as heady excitements. Successive owners splurged care and money, in the nineteenth century installing the first generation of the fully flushable mod cons Britons like to call 'thrones' (pioneered by another famous Thomas C., Thomas Crapper) and adding a wing to the building. The resources to pay for such luxuries came courtesy of the Industrial Revolution. The Butes owned a large chunk of the South Wales Coalfield and leased out mineral rights; the 2nd Marquess of Bute took out a loan against Dumfries House to invest in building docks at Cardiff, a gamble that for years paid handsomely, swelling family coffers and eventually funding construction of a bigger family seat, Mount Stuart on the Isle of Bute, only to rebound when the 7th Marquess, racing driver Johnny Dumfries, found himself with a bill for death duties on both properties.

In April 2007, he put Dumfries House and its estate on the market and planned separately to auction the contents. He secured Mount Stuart by opening it to the public and had hoped the National Trust for Scotland would take on Dumfries House, but the Trust, strapped for cash, declined. A local property developer, a former miner called John Campbell, made an offer, envisaging turning Robert Adams's graceful structure into a spa hotel. The Chippendales stood shrouded in bubble wrap ready for the journey to Christie's salesrooms in London. Then Charles intervened.

This was a characteristic intervention, triggered by passion and instinct, an idea in search of a practicable framework, unfunded, unformulated, seemingly unfeasible, controversial and also visionary. His starting point was the conviction that the house and furniture must not be separated but should be preserved intact and ensemble for the nation. Without having visited the property and lacking the money to match Campbell's offer much less top it, he swiftly convened a consortium that lodged the winning bid of £45 million, including a £20 million loan secured against his charitable foundation and based on the assumed development value of a corner of the estate earmarked for a Poundbury-style housing enclave called Knockroon. Campbell, who had taken a Caribbean cruise with his family, knew nothing of these fevered moves and assumed he was in with a good chance. 'I phoned the solicitor saying: "How did we go?" He replied: "You didn't get it and you'll never guess who did,"' says Campbell, sitting in the bar of the Dumfries Arms, his twenty-six-bed hotel in Cumnock, a short drive from the Dumfries estate.

Being gazumped by a Prince – who knew none of the details of any rival bids – has its compensations, Campbell says. Cumnock is a down-at-heel town in an area laid waste by the closure of all of its deep mines and most of its opencast operations. Charles's involvement in Dumfries House brings reservations to the Dumfries Arms every week and sees the whole hotel booked solid for about twenty nights a year. Campbell modernised the property over a two-year period from 2009 to 2011. 'My accountant asked me why I was spending £2 million on a refurbishment in Cumnock,' says Campbell. 'I told him: "Prince Charles has moved in so it can't be bad."'[1]

Yet by many standards, things aren't just bad; they appear hopeless. A drive through the environs reveals a broken ecosystem. Houses and businesses are shuttered. Indented patches of ground mark the graves of schools and homes that have been pulled down rather than left to dangerous dereliction. A staircase leads up an empty hillside.

At the opening of the newly restored walled garden on the Dumfries estate in July 2014, the Prince gave a brief speech. 'As anyone who saw this garden before work started will know, the challenge posed in restoring the site has been considerable. It's always nice to have statistics, so, since 2011, the project has required 47,000 handmade bricks, 37,000 concrete blocks, 9,500 tonnes of hardcore for paths, 5,000 tonnes of soil, one mile of coping stones and four miles of vine wire,' he said.[2] He omitted sharper statistics: five zones of Auchinleck and Cumnock are among the poorest in the whole of Scotland; 18 per cent of people in the area are officially rated as deprived; soaring unemployment is slowed only by shrinking populations.[3] Against these figures, he might have invoked the fifty full-time and twenty part-time jobs created in the house and grounds or the courses in trades and crafts, free to participants, run on the Dumfries estate that are designed to help the long-term unemployed into work, such as Get Into Hospitality, five weeks of intensive training in the Dumfries House kitchens. Some 70 per cent of alumni head straight into paid work. Sarah-Jane Clark, twenty-three, from nearby Kilmarnock, had been jobless for almost eighteen months before she enrolled. 'I wasn't too sure about the cooking side. Once I got a shot in the kitchen I knew ... It was the first time I felt confident in a job,' she says.[4] She's now employed as an apprentice chef and planning a career in catering.

The Prince – who switches to another of his many titles, Duke of Rothesay, when in Scotland – has summoned several of his charities to see what they can do in and for the surrounding area. One of the first schemes involves the renovation of the town hall in New Cumnock, a conurbation even harder hit by the downturn than its older namesake. The revamped building will offer meeting spaces, IT suites, a stage, arts and crafts rooms; nothing lavish in some contexts but a significant bonus for a place far more used to closures than openings. Gette Fulton, a local resident and one of the directors of New Cumnock's most unexpected facility, an outdoor public swimming pool (it operates for just three months a year), says Charles's arrival in the area has lifted spirits. She is impressed by the Knockroon development. 'Have you been in the houses there? It just shows what can be done ... People are going to say the area is up-and-coming.' Fulton first visited the Dumfries estate recently; previous lairds built walls to keep out commoners. 'We were discouraged from going,' she says.[5] Charles is building to attract visitors, not to repel them, and to establish outposts of benign influence in the community.

This is the strange, compelling geography he lays out for his Bond villains: a work-in-progress he doesn't expect to see completed in his lifetime; an arboretum that at this muddy early stage of its existence looks like a slough of despond but actually represents his optimism; capsules of many of his charities and initiatives; a mini Poundbury; an outdoor centre imparting Gordonstounian principles of rugged communal problem-solving; workshops where young men and women learn crafts that have already been deployed on the estate to build rustic follies. School parties roam the kitchen garden, children too urban to have ever seen a vegetable in its natural state are encouraged to get their hands dirty. At the centre of everything sits a perfect exemplar of eighteenth-century architecture and a unique collection of furniture, cherished again.

These are small groynes set against prevailing tides, but they make a difference to people watching helpless as livelihoods and communities are swept away. None of this would be possible without donations from people like David Brownlow, one of the dinner guests, as impeccable as any Bond villain but like Charles keen to talk about good works rather than plotting the downfall of the planet. Brownlow, who is British and a self-made recruitment tycoon, reckons he has contributed around £3.5 million and given an additional three or four days a month of his time to secure Dumfries House since the Prince first met him and wooed him into supporting his charities in 2005. His largesse helped to dig the Dumfries project out of an early crisis, when land prices, and confidence, dropped as the banking crisis unfolded. Knockroon appeared stillborn and has been slow to disprove doubters, though the families living in its white-rendered homes seem as contented as Poundbury's residents. Critics accused the Prince of endangering his charitable empire through his recklessness. Yet by the autumn of 2011, the loan had been paid off and soon cafés, a restaurant and a bed and breakfast on the estate had added fresh revenue streams. Still, these are small beer against the costs of the project and of Charles's wider and deeper ambitions.

So Charles continues to tap wealthy individuals and potential corporate donors, aiming not only to entice funds for individual facilities but also to create an endowment that will generate regular income in years to come. Similar efforts are under way in relation to any of the Prince's charities and initiatives likely to struggle in a future that will deprive them of their founder's attention by elevating him to a higher place, be it the throne or the afterlife which his faith – his Anglican faith – reassures him he will find. In the financial year ending 2014, his charities raised £131 million in private and corporate donations in addition to their income from public sources and endowments.

'He's on a constant fund-raiser, constant,' says Ben Elliot, who has gained an appreciation of what such efforts involve since setting up his own charity, the Quintessentially Foundation. Elliot came to the September 2013 Dumfries House dinner bringing a member of the Polish aristocracy who was curious to see whether the model the Prince is pioneering might translate to his family's own estates. '[The Prince] has got so many things he cares about that this machine, whether it's Dumfries House or any one of his other projects, takes enormous energy to feed.'[6]

But the machine also feeds the Prince and in July 2014 brought him emotional sustenance from a rare quarter indeed. The Queen and the Duke of Edinburgh travelled to the Dumfries estate to attend the opening of the walled garden. Throughout Charles's life, his mother has conferred on him medals, orders and titles with a generosity that she would never think appropriate to match in sappy sentiment. This time, he was able to return the favour, naming the garden in her honour. Moreover, if the Duke has previously seemed unimpressed by some of his son's achievements, on this occasion he mirrored the weather system that settled over East Ayrshire for the key hours of the visit: dry, a little gusty, but warm.

Fiona Lees accompanied the royals as they toured the estate. 'Thousands of people are benefiting from HRH's work … we could not ask for a better hand up for regeneration and there cannot be a better example of heritage led regeneration,' she emailed later. 'A light has been shone on our communities and they are bursting with pride.'[7] So, on that day, was the Prince.

Asbestos. GM foods. A question about whether he sees echoes in Tony Blair's 'Stakeholder Society' or in David Cameron's minor reworking, the elusive 'Big Society', of the kind of community involvement he has championed for years sets Charles on a different tack, listing technologies developed to provide solutions that have created problems instead. As is often the case, at least half of his assertions are incontrovertibly right; the other half could easily be debated until the genetically modified dairy cows come home. 'What I'm saying is you have to look at things, each one, and not imagine it's the quick fix these things appear to be,' he says.[8] The left corner of his mouth veers downwards.

The time frames of a prince – especially one who has spent more than sixty years in constitutional limbo – are not those of ordinary humanity and certainly not of politicians. He commits to projects such as Dumfries that stretch into the unforeseeable long term and believes in formulae that have proven their worth over centuries, even millennia, the golden mean in architecture, natural designs observed and reverse-engineered by biomimeticists, traditional breeds of cattle and, of course, sheep. He trusts to the value of painstaking group problem-solving, the benefits of convening different constellations of people to reason slowly through options, try out ideas and sometimes fail, gaining from the process as well as from its ultimate success. This is a technique he learned at Gordonstoun and has incorporated into many of the programmes run by the Prince's Trust and his other charities. Participants on team-building exercises at the Tamar Manoukian Outdoor Centre on the Dumfries estate work together to fill with water a pipe riddled with thirteen holes in order to float a rubber duck to the top and retrieve a message attached to it.

Sometimes it's a note of congratulations. Often, it's just a clue about what to tackle next.

In April 2013 William and Kate attended the opening of the Centre, named after a member of the prominent Armenian family that funded it. 'Make it brief,' William told his father as Charles cleared his throat to give a speech. He spoke in jest but with Kate carrying the weight of their unborn child and a sharp bite to the spring air, this wouldn't have been the best moment for one of Charles's more discursive efforts.

William anyway tends to be as clipped as his father is expansive. He has given a few interviews in which his emotions break through; answering questions about his mother and once visibly choking as he watched footage of a rhino injured by poachers and bleeding to death. The segment was filmed soon after George's birth, for a documentary aimed at raising awareness of the plight of endangered wildlife. 'The last few weeks for me have been a very different emotional experience – something I never thought I would feel for myself,' said the new father. 'I find, even though it's only been a short period, that a lot of things affect me now – when I see a clip like that there's so much emotion and so much feeling wrapped up into conservation and environment. It's just so powerful. You'd think something that big and that's been around so long, would have worked out a way to avoid being caught and persecuted, but they really don't. I do feel anger, but I also feel really great hope that we will overcome this as a human race. The more we raise the issue and the more education there is … I wouldn't be here right now if I didn't think there was a chance it could be successful. Poaching is now probably the worst I've ever known it, but I am not the kind of guy to give up.'[9]

In that moment he sounded like his father, albeit without the same level of verbal dexterity or leavening humour. For the most part William reveals little to journalists, radiating a contempt for the increasingly endangered species at least as heartfelt as his concern for rhinos. The royal rat pack assumes this must be because William blames the press for his mother's death, forgetting that he surely remembers enough of his boyhood to blame the press for what it did to her life. Yet William's terseness is also a function of a process Charles himself went through. In defining himself against his parents, Charles became the man he is. In defining himself against his father, William has become more like his royal grandmother, closed and cautious, comfortable with actions rather than words, Saffy to the Prince's Edina.

William has also become his own man. Until comparatively recently, Clarence House advisers clung to a vision of transition that would see Charles pass his charitable empire to his sons when he assumed the Crown. The Prince's Trust would simply move its apostrophe one space to the right. 'It would be nice to see the continuum,' says a palace insider. But neither of 'the boys', as the thirty-something William and Harry are still known among palace staff, shows an inclination to get involved with the Trust or to take on the rest of the sprawl. They dutifully turn up for Prince's Trust events or occasions such as the opening of the outdoors centre at Dumfries House, and joined their father at a February 2014 conservation conference, but otherwise they are focused on their own careers, establishing their own organisations and demonstrating their independence in other ways too.

This sometimes means they make their own mistakes. The conservation conference was overshadowed by revelations that the boys were newly returned from a hunting trip in Spain. They hadn't slaughtered endangered creatures, just wild boar and stag, but the juxtaposition of killing and conference wasn't ideal. Kensington Palace aides were caught on the hop. The boys had not informed them of their plans and if they had, says a source, 'we'd have advised them not to go and they'd have ignored us'. The Princes' determination to plough their own furrows recalls the young Charles. The furrows, however, are distinct.

In July 2015, William embarked on an experiment that sees the second in line to the throne trying to hold down a civilian job, as an air-ambulance pilot, while continuing to carry out royal duties. He is donating his salary to charity, illustrating the larger anomaly of a royal seeking a slice of normal life. Kate, meanwhile, started flying solo in her own way. She was supposed to undertake her first overseas engagement without William in September 2014, a trip to Malta, but William stood in for his wife after severe morning sickness temporarily clipped her wings. She gave birth to Princess Charlotte in May 2015.

The previous autumn Harry celebrated his thirtieth birthday in the afterglow of the Invictus Games, a sporting competition for injured service personnel from thirteen nations that he staged at London's former Olympic Park. Newspaper coverage was benign. The British tabloids like Harry – for now. 'He's the *Sun* readers' favourite royal,' says the newspaper's royal photographer Arthur Edwards. 'They think he's like them and that's the highest compliment. He's a larrikin.'[10] A celebrity wheelchair rugby match at the Invictus Games featured Harry, his first cousin Zara and her husband, Mike Tindall, a recently retired professional rugby player, raising the spectre of *The Grand Knockout Tournament* and a previous generation's pratfalls only to banish it again. The Games provided a platform for the disabled competitors rather than the cavortings of royals. Yet the event's success doesn't solve Harry's larger existential conundrum any more than his current tabloid popularity will shield him against a future narrative of redundancy, as one of the spares not the heir. (Since the birth of his nephew and niece, Harry stands at only fifth in line to the throne.)

Nor has Harry yet solved the problem of how to find a partner who is grounded and sane, yet not so sane that the prospect of life on Planet Windsor sends her into retreat. It took his brother almost a decade and a public rupture with Kate before he felt secure in taking the decision to marry. It took his father far longer to find contentment. Diana never did.

That history still shapes her sons' decisions. 'William seems to have chosen to live up in Norfolk [as his country retreat], and yet his father has spent so long building [Highgrove] that I'm sure he would love one of his sons to inherit. It's a father's expression of immortality,' says an insider. 'It embraces his commitment to sustainable farming and to the world of the botanical, the natural world, and then he's got his Islamic garden there so it's an expression of his interests.'

Highgrove also carries echoes of a difficult past. This is the place where the boys spent some of their best times and the most confusing. Ill-equipped as Charles was to cope with his first marriage or its collapse or the sudden challenge of bringing up children whose resentment at his rejection of their mother had now been layered with grief and more anger at her death, he made a good job of the last of these. At Diana's funeral, her brother delivered a eulogy that included a barely disguised swipe at royal parenting skills. 'I pledge that we, your blood family, will do all we can to continue the imaginative way in which you were steering these two exceptional young men so that their souls are not simply immersed by duty and tradition but can sing openly as you planned,' said Earl Spencer. The Prince's biographer Anthony Holden judged that Diana's influence had already been erased when, less than three months after her death, Harry stood alongside his father at a charity concert in South Africa attended by Nelson Mandela and featuring the Spice Girls. In balmy temperatures, listening to pop, Harry, aged thirteen, wore a suit and tie.

There is no question that Charles raised his sons to an awareness of duty and tradition – and an appreciation for a well-cut suit, though the boys tend to prefer single- to double-breasted – but he nurtured them too. He has always been keen to give them, in place of the tough love favoured by his own parents, something more enveloping; he determined with Diana that they should be as protected from the public gaze as possible and spend as much time with their parents as possible, and when the time came would not attend Gordonstoun but Eton, right on the doorstep of Windsor. He resisted the temptation to denigrate Diana while she lived and afterwards encouraged the boys to think and talk about her and maintain contact with her friends. The relationships between father and sons are not without stresses and complexities but they are stronger as a result. Unsurprisingly, these bonds are most easily visible in a shared sense of humour, says Ben Elliot, 'them ridiculing him, him ridiculing them, that joshing that often goes with good relationships. Not just about a lack of hair or those kinds of things. I've seen with his younger son, them almost just like frolicking with one another in a really lovely way.'[11] 'They are so, so loving,' says Emma Thompson.[12]

When he married and started a family, William shifted the dynamic, presenting the idealised family unit that used to be monarchy's speciality. Yet in appearing to secure the future of the Windsor dynasty, a potential future King happily married to a Queen and already blessed with an heir (and a spare on the way), unblemished by scandals, unburdened by failures, the Cambridges have attained a popularity that threatens to undermine the first in line to the throne. 'People admire the Queen so much because she's impeccable – she shows no emotion – and they also say Prince William is a modern royal, but somehow Prince Charles is in the middle and gets criticised from both sides,' says Patrick Holden. 'But in his own way he's also defining the new role of the monarchy and, in my opinion, doing it brilliantly well.'[13]

Holden says the media narrative of princely jealousies is overdone. He has heard Charles comment ruefully on his sons' and daughter-in-law's ability to draw crowds and headlines but has witnessed far more often the Prince's boundless pride in the younger generation. He is always learning from his children, the Prince remarks during pre-dinner conversation at Dumfries House. He is constantly amazed by what they know about the world – and what he doesn't. In return, he has tried to do as the Queen Mother did for him, introducing them to arts and culture, at any rate those corners of art and culture that resonate for him.

He also takes an obvious pleasure in instructing his boys in the stagecraft necessary to carry off royal ceremonial. 'The role is a role and it's something that has to be played to the hilt all the time,' says Emma Thompson.[14] The metaphor is apt, if somewhat alarming. In September 2013, Charles and his elder son spent hours closeted at Birkhall practising how to conduct investitures ahead of William's debut doing it for real, to ensure William avoided inflicting injury when touching a sword on the shoulders of those receiving knighthoods.

As father and son rehearsed, Camilla and Kate enjoyed the tranquillity of the Balmoral estate, at least during the periods George left it unpunctuated. His birth has drawn a close family closer. The boys not only accept Camilla but are affectionate towards her, seeing how much she lifts their father's spirits. Diana has not been forgotten but she no longer divides and conquers. 'HRH said something in connection with his grandson the other day which I thought was incredibly revealing, about how the most important thing is to have a heart that's open,' says Patrick Holden.[15]

Hearts are open. Harmony reigns. The question remains: will the Prince, his elder son after him, and, after William, George? Part of the answer lies beyond royal control, in social and economic developments that may enhance the residual value of the monarchy or shred it. But a larger responsibility for their fate lies with the royals themselves and in particular with the next sovereign. The Queen has kept the throne safe if not warm. Should her son live long enough to succeed her, he is unlikely to live long enough to secure his legacy through the kind of slow, careful change management that served his mother so well. His greatest challenge will be to stand for continuity while redefining the monarchy, remaking it in his own image while buttressing it for his heirs. He has already embarked on that project, unrolling a potential new model of kingship that melds the ceremonial aspects of the role with a much more active beneficence than the old formula of charitable patronage.

After touring the Dumfries estate with his Bond villains, the Prince returns to the house for a private meeting with Fiona Lees, the Chief Executive of East Ayrshire council, also attended by Kristina Kyriacou. In a small upstairs sitting room the three hunch together, strategising ways to deal with the most urgent problems confronting the area, stimulating a sluggish economy and dealing with the abandoned opencast mines that litter the landscape, filling with contaminated water. 'We need people to help us think about this,' says Lees. The Prince agrees. 'If you get a whole lot of people in one room, they make connections. Much of the time this never happens, in some extraordinary way,' he says.[16]

Conclusion

Until philosophers are kings, or the kings and princes of this
world have the spirit and power of philosophy, and political
greatness and wisdom meet in one, and those commoner natures
who pursue either to the exclusion of the other are compelled
to stand aside, cities will never have rest from their evils – nor
the human race, as I believe – and then only will this our state
have a possibility of life and behold the light of day.

Plato, *Republic*

In April 2014, a broadcaster asked me to participate in a surreal
exercise, recording an interview as part of a pre-prepared obituary
to run if the Prince should die without being so courteous as to give
news organisations prior notice of the event. In an upstairs room of
a London pub called the Peasant – the producers chose the location
without intended irony – I answered questions posed by a journalist,
designed to help me sum up Charles and his impact. I found it tricky
to do this in sound bites and even at the luxury of book length, it
has been a struggle to draw a balanced assessment. So much is written
and said about the Prince, but so much is also distorted for one reason

or another. This book should hopefully have highlighted those reasons and stripped away some of the distortions. As I predicted at the time, its publication was also taken as licence to create fresh mischaracterisations and caricatures of its subject.

That Charles is the victim of such distortions does not exonerate him and his extended court from a share of the responsibility for them. He is always making connections – between people and ideas, the past, present and future, the material and the spiritual, golden threads that bind. This is one of his greatest talents. What he doesn't always spot are key connections between what he does, or what is done in his name, and how this impacts perceptions.

One frequent charge against the Prince, that he does too little, is obviously untrue. Another – that if he were not doing the things he does, as activist and charitable entrepreneur, other such entrepreneurs would fill the breach – seemed increasingly dubious as I delved into the detail and scope of his activities. The Prince's Trust and his other charities and initiatives are near-perfect reflections of the Prince. He has been misrepresented and misunderstood, in ways that have been anatomised in this book. But not infrequently when Charles gets a bad press, it's because he deserves it or an aspect of his organisation warrants it, or because people harbour legitimate disagreements that they cannot directly debate with him or easily voice except by attempting to make as much noise as he does.

Courtiers too often tell him what they think he wants to hear rather than what he needs to hear. He isn't always given the opportunity to understand the full dynamics of a situation. He is surrounded by individuals who will try to hearten him, and sometimes to gain favour by playing princely trigger points that everybody in palace circles knows how to locate. Charles has long been a Defender of Faith – faith in Nature and perennial wisdoms as well as Christianity – and thus will never accept alternative philosophies or movements such as Modernism that to him appear as kryptonite. He doesn't grasp that many of the people he has run up against over the years are as passionate as he is, as driven and well-meaning as he is.

There is no point in arguing that he should jettison the belief system he has spent a lifetime constructing. He would no more be capable of doing that than I, an atheist, can subscribe to that belief system. I may not be fully in harmony with *Harmony*, but I have witnessed positive outcomes of the princely philosophy, the virtuous circles Charles is capable of creating. He sometimes sparks vicious cycles too, and in drawing to a conclusion, I will aim to highlight ways in which he might guard against that tendency in future, for his own benefit and the benefit of the institution he represents.

I do so not as a monarchist but as a pragmatist. I believe all humans are born equal except for the natives of Planet Windsor, who arrive in the world at a huge disadvantage to the rest of us, burdened with expectation and duty. If I were designing a country from scratch, it would be a republic. I was born into such a country, but for most of my life I have lived in the United Kingdom of Great Britain and Northern Ireland, and have come over the years not only to appreciate the public service that some – not all – royals perform, and the pageantry – and comedy – they supply, but also to understand the upheaval their replacement would represent. Monarchy doesn't make sense but the system still, mostly, works quite well. 'If you chuck away too many things,' says the Prince, 'you end up discovering there was value in them.'[1]

Republicans are convinced that the point of transition from the Queen to her son – if and when this comes – will be the moment of maximum danger to the Crown. They are not wrong. But some British republicans also argue that the transition from Crown to elected head of state could be quick and painless, a matter of crossing out 'Her Majesty the Queen' or, far more likely, 'His Majesty the King' and writing in 'President'. The overseas Realms already have inbuilt structures to deputise for the non-resident sovereign. Their national identities are not so intricately interwoven with the Windsor brand. Despite the William and Kate effect, it is possible that Australia or Jamaica or New Zealand may begin to disentangle themselves from the hereditary system after the Queen has died, perhaps even before that. The Commonwealth faces questions in the longer term not only about its titular head but its purpose.

If Britain begins to unwind its constitutional settlement, the process will surely be messier. 'If you get rid of the Crown, you have to write a new constitution,' says Graham Smith of UK campaign group Republic. 'The key point of the constitution is that the people are sovereign and all power starts with them so if the constitution doesn't assign powers to the sovereign then it has to stay with the people. We could say, look, there are certain powers which were with the Crown which are now with government, certain powers which are now with Parliament, some powers are now with the head of state and everything else is just not there. You can have it however you want it.'[2]

I remain sceptical about this. Big constitutional changes are difficult and lengthy and absorb energies that may be better deployed elsewhere. They also risk unintended consequences so must be thoroughly thought through and minutely plotted. There are, as the Prince observes, no quick fixes. The reason Westminster politicians continue to squabble about how to reform the House of Lords – and since Scotland's referendum, about how to devolve more powers across the UK – is not only that vested interests have impeded progress. It is that in replacing self-evidently flawed systems such as an upper chamber stocked with the beneficiaries of naked political patronage and still (ye gods) with a rump of hereditary peers, entitled by accident of birth to make, revise and reject laws, the architects of reform instead threaten to introduce self-evidently flawed replacements.

The current House of Lords, for all its weaknesses, complements the House of Commons. Its members need not seek election and so their time horizons are extended. They are more independent of party affiliations and bring a wider range of experiences to bear than MPs. 'The thing about being here for life is that you are not so bound to your party,' says Labour peer Tony Berkeley. 'Because over a time of thirty years some people are here, each party changes its policies. They all do. And the older people say hang on you're all doing it wrong and they have ways of expressing their view, they don't vote so often. They abstain. Or they speak their minds a bit more.'[3]

Fully or partly elected alternatives risk eroding these useful differences. Representative democracies are precious things but not every one of their constituent parts must always entail direct elections for the systems to be truly democratic.

At Republic's annual general meeting in May 2014, Graham Smith quoted from the final speech made by Tony Benn ahead of his retirement as a Labour MP. Benn renounced his hereditary peerage to sit in the Commons and returned to the reasons for his decision in his parliamentary valedictory, listing five questions for any governing institution: 'What power have you got? Where did you get it from? In whose interests do you exercise it? To whom are you accountable? And how can we get rid of you?' Benn concluded: 'If you cannot get rid of the people who govern you, you do not live in a democratic system.'[4] The current House of Lords is not directly accountable to voters but it is subject to reform and even abolition as and when MPs coalesce around a workable plan. What the debates at Republic's AGM fail to acknowledge is that the monarchy is in a similar position, even if the sovereign is consulted on legislation and would be expected to provide the last signature on any law abolishing the throne. If that day comes, no Windsor monarch is likely to withhold his or her signature or barricade the palace gates.

Delegates paid £4 to attend the AGM. Another £3 purchased a pamphlet called *How to Win the Argument* that makes strong points about the essential ridiculousness of a monarchy in the twenty-first century but glosses over the complexity of any process to replace the Crown and of its potential for disruption, psychological as well as practical, the danger of creating another vacuum in an age of vacuity. In rejecting the idea of the monarchy as a focus for national unity or reassurance through periods of change, the pamphlet sidesteps the question of how the country would handle this particular change.

That may in part reflect the nature of Republic's own support base. The AGM drew a crowd of sixty to seventy people who would not look out of place at a Temenos lecture. That is to say, most participants appeared to be well-heeled, well-spoken and grey-haired, white, English. They drank tea and debated gently. A delegate called Cliff Cottrill regretted that his attempt to organise a get-together of like-minded folk in a Birmingham pub had enjoyed limited success. 'Two people turned up and one of them was my son,' he said. Everyone chimed in with ideas for doing better next time. These are the nicest and politest of Roundheads.

What they are not is representative of the many strains of Britain struggling to carve out places and identities on a crowded archipelago. Smith says later that the AGM has not been properly representative of his organisation either. '[Republic] has become much more diverse … If you look at our protests, it's much younger. If you look at our campaign teams, most of those are under forty. By a long way. I've just turned forty and I'm one of the older people involved actively and when I started I was the youngest by about forty years so it has changed a lot.'[5]

Smith has been spearheading that transformation since 2005, when a bequest from a supporter enabled Republic to employ a full-time director. He has grown the organisation to around 4,500 members paying an annual subscription of £8 with a further 30,000 signed up to receive free information through the website. Clever campaigns around the wedding of William and Kate and ahead of the birth of baby George under the slogan 'BORN EQUAL' have gained Smith and Republic a higher media profile. Now the focus is on the royal activist whom republican activists judge the weakest link, with the aim, says Smith, of 'pre-empting the succession. The key moment is if we can create a groundswell of opinion against Charles saying: "This guy is a problem" over a very short period of time.'

He doesn't really hold out hope of stopping the coronation but expects King Charles to make the argument for republicans once installed on the throne. 'People couldn't imagine David Cameron being Prime Minister until he was. And I think the same will happen with Charles and the other thing that will come is: "Well, hang on a minute, we've just changed our head of state and I didn't get a vote." And that's quite a big thing as well and I think that people kind of talk in theoretical terms saying: "Well, we don't need to vote for them," but when they've actually seen it change in front of their eyes without ever being asked that might change the way people feel about it.'[6]

The secret to galvanising opposition against the monarchy, Smith says, is to get people angry. He thinks the presumed future King will annoy the hell out of his subjects. Here are some thoughts about how Charles could make himself more loved than loathed.

Niccolò Machiavelli, Renaissance Italy's most celebrated political philosopher, declared that sheep and royalty don't mix. In his famous treatise *The Prince*, he tells the story of Emperor Maximinus, who earned the disdain of his subjects by keeping flocks. The cautionary tale is unlikely to chime with a twenty-first-century, sheep-promoting Prince, but Machiavelli also offers more apposite advice. 'It makes him contemptible when he is considered fickle, frivolous, effeminate, mean-spirited, irresolute, from all of which a prince should guard himself as from a rock; and he should endeavour to show in his actions greatness, courage, gravity and fortitude; and in his private dealings with his subjects let him show that his judgments are irrevocable, and maintain himself in such reputation that no one can hope either to deceive him or get round him,' he wrote.[7] Apart from the injunction against effeminacy, this must be as timeless a piece of wisdom as any perennialist prince could hope to follow.

There's another nugget the heir to the throne might usefully take on board: Machiavelli counsels princes to keep their servants and soldiers in check. The ranks of Charles's servants and soldiers – his courtiers and the ground forces implementing his vision through his charities and initiatives – include some of the most talented and dedicated individuals I've ever met, as passionate about the Boss as he is in his activism. The more he is criticised, the more they band together in a protective ring, lowering their lances at the outside world – which in their view includes the other royal courts. This tendency has been reinforced as Buckingham Palace attempts to lead a restructuring to prepare the monarchy for the transition that actuaries looking at the Queen's age and the longevity of her mother might predict still to be ten or twenty years away. A regency may be more imminent.

In either case, this is a time to prepare, to listen and learn with an openness that a siege mentality impedes. The Prince must ensure that everybody working for him brings him bad news as well as good and never seeks to slay perceived dragons on his behalf. The firebreathers may just have a point which the Knight of the Realms would benefit from hearing. If not, he's skilled enough at wielding his own sword, and if anything rather too ready to use it.

There is widespread irritation in Clarence House at some of the efforts to root around in the Prince's affairs. Aides suspect that the declared motive of such missions – a push for more transparency and accountability – masks a desire to get rid of the monarchy, or at least its heir. The *Guardian*'s former editor Alan Rusbridger made no bones about his republican agenda. Investigations by other news organisations more often look to a smaller prize: a scoop. The opacity of the royal palaces means even small details carry a journalistic value.

'It is riveting how much inventiveness exists. People create scenarios and write scripts for strange almost-plays, I find, which bear no relation to reality, no relation to the way I view things or do things or think about things,' Charles complained to Jonathan Dimbleby more than twenty years ago. 'Everyone is saying there's a right to know everything. I don't agree. There isn't a right to know at all.'[8] Even back then, before Edward Snowden but after Andrew Morton – and supposing the Prince hadn't been unburdening himself to a biographer as part of a project he himself had initiated – the Prince's yen for greater privacy was never likely to be fulfilled. Daylight had started to permeate the Windsor courts in ways that damaged the monarchy, strengthening the aversion of 'that Dracula family' to sunshine when they might have benefited from unlocking some of the shutters before others prised them open.

This is not to suggest that the royals should pander to the revised definition of public interest as anything and everything that interests the public. The Windsors are entitled to conduct their personal lives in private. Nor is this an argument for every conversation and communication being automatically subject to scrutiny. There are missions the Prince undertakes and conversations he holds, for example during his Middle East trips, that would be compromised if conducted in the full gaze of the world. It is harder to see why his aides should resist legitimate journalistic inquiries or their master should enjoy a higher level of protection under Freedom of Information laws than a government Minister. Bagehot's dictum about the mystery of monarchy no longer applies in Snowdonia. Its mystery causes strife. Around the same time that Clarence House rushed to try to cast doubt on this book, the BBC finally broadcast a two-part documentary about royal media management, *Reinventing the Royals*, that was delayed by royal media managers, and the Prince's legal team braced against a final decision on his black spider memos. It all sharpened a sense that Charles is light averse.

The decision of the Supreme Court to allow publication of the princely memos requested by the *Guardian* suggested, as Clarence House sources had maintained, that he had little to hide. They gave insight into his obsessions, but contained only a few passages that could be said to overstep the ill-defined boundaries of his role. If he does feel inclined to lobby for political change, he could certainly do worse than asking the government to look at bringing the rules relating to his correspondence under the Freedom of Information Act in line with those covering other public officials and bodies. Far better to let in daylight upon such magic as there is, which after all can be more impressive up close, as the Prince's Trust alumnus Dynamo frequently demonstrates.

A palace insider argues that the royal households cannot be the advocates of public policy on disclosure precisely because they are not subject to the turnover of political generations. The Queen has been stoically doing her job for more than sixty years. A release of documents from earlier stages of her reign might not properly account for the fact that she and the people who have worked for her, the issues and processes that have passed by her over the years, have themselves evolved. That argument might hold true for the retrospective release of letters and memos. There's little sign that Prince Philip has imbibed the rules of political correctness or grappled with the issues that underlie them but his son has done a better job of moving with the times, sometimes falling behind but just as often jumping ahead of them.

Charles now has another opportunity to show leadership, in redrawing and clarifying the boundaries between the private and public spheres of palace life. His views on most things are already in the public domain, laid out in *Harmony* and in his collected speeches. His courtiers gain nothing in downplaying these views or concealing his philosophy. The quality most prized in this trust-free era is authenticity.

The Prince might do well to offer up more access to the work he does – whether royal work or charitable work, especially as the two blend and merge. He might even consider beginning not only to speak for himself but to answer for himself. He leaves it to aides such as his Principal Private Secretary to present his Annual Review and to make his case to the House of Commons Public Accounts Committee. Yet, as I have seen at first hand, Charles can be the most fluent and persuasive of advocates for his own causes.

He should also take an open-minded look at what Tony Berkeley is doing. Berkeley – a rare creature, both a life peer and a hereditary; his full title is Anthony Fitzhardinge Gueterbock, 18th Baron Berkeley and Baron Gueterbock – in 2011 introduced a Private Member's Bill on marine legislation, only to receive a letter from the clerk in the House of Lords bill office: 'Dear Lord Berkeley, The marine navigation bill that you introduced on 5 July would affect the Prince of Wales's interests and so will require the Prince of Wales's consent for its consideration by parliament ... The government whips office in the Lords and the parliamentary branch of the Department of Transport are aware of what is required.'[9] An arcane constitutional convention gives Charles a veto over any proposed legislation deemed to impact on 'the hereditary revenues, personal property or other interests' of the Duchy of Cornwall and given the wide-ranging nature of its business, that is potentially quite a considerable power. What is less obvious is whether he has ever used it to block or amend a bill. That information remains confidential under the same convention.

Understanding the Duchy isn't easy. It operates like a corporation but isn't taxed like one. 'If it looks like a duck and quacks like a duck, and swims like a duck you sort of assume it's a duck,' said Nick Smith, Labour MP for the Welsh constituency of Blaenau Gwent, at a July 2013 hearing of the House of Commons Public Accounts Committee.

'Given the Duchy of Cornwall looks and behaves like a corporation with income from complex investments and quacks like a corporation with a council including the great and good from banking, on the face of it many of my constituents would say the Duchy should pay corporation tax and capital gains tax. Aren't my constituents being reasonable?'[10]

No, said the Prince's then Principal Private Secretary William Nye, one of three witnesses to appear. 'The Duchy is a very unusual organisation. It is a private estate; it is not a corporation. It is a private estate in many respects like other private estates, but in one or two respects not like a private estate. Some of the things that you have highlighted, Mr Smith, still do not make it a corporation. There is a council. It is an advisory council that advises the Duke of Cornwall ... Essentially it is a set of properties that belong to the Duke of Cornwall. The fact that it is a large set of properties and is worth a lot of money does not, per se, make it a corporation. The memorandum of understanding [on royal taxation, agreed in 1993] establishes that it is not a corporation and not subject to corporation tax.'

The Public Accounts Committee had already attempted – and failed – in an April 2005 hearing to get to grips with Prince Charles's tax status and the nitty-gritty of the Duchy. Again it floundered, even after Nye essayed another definition of the Duchy. 'It is a bit like a trust in some respects, although it is not formally, legally speaking, a trust. It is a little bit like a family business in some respects, but it is not solely a business. It is an estate, which has a sort of entail in it, although it is a slightly complex entail. It has aspects of social enterprise, in that although it is commercial, it is able to take a long-term stewardship view of what is in the interests of the Duchy overall, meaning the assets for the Duke [of Cornwall] and future dukes, and of the communities and the tenants. To that extent, it has aspects of social enterprise.'

As the hearing drew to a close, Richard Bacon, Conservative MP for South Norfolk, made a final stab at comprehension. 'If it looks like a private ducal estate set up to provide an income to the heir to the throne, and it quacks like a private ducal estate set up to provide an income to the heir to the throne, can one assume that it might just possibly be a private ducal estate set up to provide an income to the heir to the throne?' 'I think that must be possible,' deadpanned Nye.[11] Britain's unwritten constitutional arrangements, built on precedents and conventions that may have been easily graspable in earlier times, can now seem wilfully obscure.

The committee called for changes to drag the Duchy into the twenty-first century. 'Greater transparency is needed,' said its 2013 report. 'The Duchy enjoys an exemption from paying tax even though it engages in a range of commercial activities. This tax exemption may give it an unfair advantage over its competitors who do pay corporation and capital gains tax.'[12] Its recommendations show no signs of being adopted and that means the fact of the Duchy and the privilege it represents continues to overshadow some of the extraordinary things it has enabled Charles to do.

Berkeley responded to the letter by introducing another Private Member's Bill into the House of Lords intended to iron out inconsistencies between the Prince's status under British law and the position of other subjects of Her Majesty, and to make the system more easily understandable as well as bringing the Duchy in line with the other entities with which it competes commercially. Berkeley says he knows the bill needs further work and anyway has no chance of becoming law without government backing, but he is using the process to generate debate. 'What I'd really like to see is the Duchy making these changes voluntarily,' he explains. 'Either a government does it or the Duchy will have to do it proactively to get the laws changed.'

A fellow peer who spoke to Charles during a shooting party told Berkeley that the Prince had asked: 'Is this man Berkeley a nutter?'

Berkeley certainly seems sensible enough and, as it happens, he isn't a closet republican. 'I want a transparent and smaller monarchy,' he says.[13]

It will always be better for the Windsors to initiate reform rather than to have reform imposed. The small numbers of avowed republicans in Parliament belies the speed with which sentiment could turn. Misty patriotism – and that is all that sustains many parliamentarians' support for the monarchy – would evaporate in the heat of sustained public rage.

The most obvious locus of public neuralgia, especially at a time of economic uncertainty and straitened budgets, is around the expense of maintaining royals in their palaces, their carriages, on walkabouts, in helicopters, on their private train. Even for those who believe monarchy still matters, the contribution royalty makes must always be balanced against debits.

The £255,000 bill for flying Charles to Nelson Mandela's funeral and back in December 2013 – a figure released in the annex to Buckingham Palace's Annual Report and Accounts 2013–14 along with other journeys costing more than £10,000 in that period – looks venal if you assume the Prince might have used ordinary scheduled airlines for the journey. His aides insisted at the press conference for his own Annual Review that the short notice and complexity of getting to Qunu in Kwazulu Natal made private charters the only practicable option. Staffers who made the journey say he was not travelling in style. My own overseas jaunts with royals, including the May 2014 trip with Charles and Camilla to Canada, have not been luxurious. The nose section of the Canadian Air Force jet contained a cramped private cabin but everyone apart from the royal couple rode in conditions familiar to economy-class fliers – in the 1980s. (Journalists and photographers reimbursed the Canadian government C$1,800 apiece for this no-frills transport.)

Aides maintain that security in part dictates the manner of royal travel and swells the size of retinues. Convoys expensively deploy skilled police drivers to recce the routes in advance as well as moving the retinues around once the visit begins. Charles and Camilla travel with valets, assistants, a hairdresser and extensive wardrobes as part of the pageantry of such visits, to project majesty and protect dignity.

There are nevertheless clear arguments for finding ways to project majesty and protect dignity more cheaply. In 1994, a high-water mark of royal turbulence, John Major decided that the forty-one-year-old royal yacht *Britannia* should not be recommissioned when the next major repair bill fell due. Like the royals, the yacht presented an image of Britain to the world; like the royals, that image was becoming increasingly dilapidated. 'You had to judge whether it was worth spending fifty million pounds on it or, to be more accurate, whether it would have been a good idea to spend fifty million pounds on it in the middle of a deep recession, with a public mood deeply aggrieved,' he says.[14] During the 1997 election campaign, the Conservatives pledged a replacement for *Britannia*. Labour won power and swiftly scrapped the yacht instead, consigning the vessel to a new life in Edinburgh as a tourist attraction. The stoical Queen was seen to shed tears at the decommissioning ceremony. She may have cause to weep over the royal train after Britain next goes to the polls: as expensive as if it ran on gilded rails, the nine-carriage train is an obvious target for any incoming government keen on finding quick savings. The Public Accounts Committee has already recommended that it be scrapped. In 2014 Buckingham Palace told the committee that the train will stay in service 'for as long as the rolling stock is working, which it believes will be for another five to ten years. However, it has not yet developed alternative options or a replacement to a royal train, which it considers provides safe and secure transport, particularly for overnight travel to early-morning royal engagements.'[15]

The Prince's aides make a similar point, insisting this form of travel is better value for money than the cost of individual journeys suggests; Charles uses the train not to undertake solo travel but as a mobile hotel and conference facility. A former Cabinet minister enthuses that the train, like the monarchy itself, is an asset, a touch eccentric but ineffably British. To many people, though, the Prince, in taking the train, simply appears on the wrong track. A two-day trip to York and Harrogate added £23,219 to his travel bill in July 2013; a regional tour of Worcester the previous month cost £19,578. His sons, by contrast, have not only both opted for commercial flights for private travel but in May 2014 Harry arrived in Estonia on budget airline EasyJet for a two-day official visit to the country and in December William caught the US Airways shuttle from New York to Washington to meet President Obama at the White House.

Many of his opponents assume Charles stands for the status quo. In fact he already purposes to make some significant changes. As King, he intends to preside over a monarchy that is, as Lord Berkeley hopes, smaller.

For all that the Prince is more inclined to conserve than cut, for all that he dislikes the pain of rationalising and restructuring, he is also focused on distant horizons. His activism is aimed at benefiting populations not yet born. In performing his royal role, he has not only formulated a model for his own potential kingship but is intent on securing the monarchy for the future. He knows that he and his kith must continue to adapt to survive and that part of this process must involve streamlining the Windsor family firm by pasturing older and more marginal − or problematic − members. He is also pondering ways better to preserve the heritage of royal residences and retain their capacity as venues for state occasions while opening them up, to more public access and for other uses.

None of this will happen during the reign of the Queen, who has always commanded her son's allegiance, or the lifetime of her consort, who still inspires his love, fear and respect in equal measure. But after the coronation of the new King – conducted by the Archbishop of Canterbury and with a form of words that reflects the value the sovereign places on all faiths, whether or not this is directly signalled by a change to the coronation oath – his siblings, nieces, nephews and cousins are likely to recede further into the background. At the court of King Charles III and Queen Camilla, immediate family will be easily adequate in skills and numbers to fulfil the toe-scrunching aspects of the royal job, smiling through presentations and speeches, pinning medals, cutting ribbons, cracking bottles against the hulls of ships, exchanging pleasantries, on an endless shuttle through Britain and the Realms.

The King's Trust can expect to continue to benefit from its founder's input, even if his time to raise funds or present achievement awards to graduates of Trust programmes is more limited. Most of his charities and initiatives will survive in some form; a few are likely to struggle and fade.

Charles will never be neutral just as he will never be party political. For better or for worse – in my final analysis, more often for better than for worse – the Prince is a man with a mission, a knight on a quest. His overarching goals – saving his adopted planet and the monarchy – underpin pretty much everything he does and are sometimes at odds with each other. He accepts that he will not be able to campaign from the throne room as he has campaigned from its antechamber, but if he no longer speaks up quite so often, or intervenes quite so vigorously, he'll have his weekly audiences with the Prime Minister instead. Whether he uses those audiences to lobby for additional reforms of the monarchy and health-giving transparencies will depend on his ability to emulate his mother, not by being like her, but by keeping Planet Windsor in close orbit to earth.

If he never becomes King, he has already achieved a substantial legacy and left a huge trail. In researching this book I have waded through morasses of material – books, clippings, pamphlets, documents. I've pored over pretty much everything he's written that's in the public domain and every speech he's delivered that I could get my hands on. I've perused black spiders that have been published and some that haven't. I have interviewed many people who have been party to multiple stages or segments of Charles's highly variegated life, seeking to look beyond the competing claims of his proponents and his critics, while listening intently to both, fragmented camps. I have observed him as closely as he and Clarence House have permitted, and in doing so come to admire his achievements, to regret the missteps that undermine them, and to shake my head over parts of his philosophy. I agree with some of his views, recoil from others. I have laughed with him and, not infrequently, at him, and almost every day stifled snickering at situations that brewed up around him. His planet is the funniest place I have ever visited, and the strangest. I like the Prince. I feel sorry for the child he once was. I am gladdened that in resolving the tensions of his personal life, Charles appears to be coming closer to reconciling the different strains and duties of his position, closer to seizing the grail he most often describes but has rarely glimpsed: harmony.

He and his aides are understandably frustrated that some of the best things he does go unrecognised. This book has shone light into those corners, but also caught in its beam some things that Clarence House preferred to keep in darkness. Reactions to the book focused attention on the latter but happily people read books as well as newspapers. My aim throughout has been to portray the Prince fairly and accurately. I have also done my best to clarify the transactional relationship between monarch and subjects so that these subjects can better judge whether they're getting enough out of the transaction and how the calculation might alter – because it would alter – under King Charles III. Two years of trailing the Prince – and they have been long years; 'I can't wait to stop thinking about you,' I once told the bemused focus of my attentions – have increased my appreciation for the positives he has brought to his role and my understanding of how he might invest the monarchy with fresh meaning. But research has also heightened my awareness of existing negatives and how this process could go wrong.

Like Don Quixote and Hamlet, the Prince faces tangible opponents but also just as frequently tangles with shadows and spectres. A frivolling Prince would never have fought so many battles, polarised opinion or roused such passions. The man who would be King of Hearts has never been able to take the path of least resistance. 'I like to think that it's no accident that a man who feels such a profound sense of service and stewardship should be in his position on our planet at this time,' says Patrick Holden. 'He's a visionary, he's a remarkable human being.'[16] 'The thing that I would say about him is that he's genuine,' says Fiona Reynolds. 'It's all felt in a really deep way and I think that's the thing that above all I admire. Heavens, if he'd wanted an easy life he wouldn't have gone the route he has, but because he cares so passionately he's backed these sometimes very unpopular causes, but done so out of genuine conviction.'[17] 'I would much rather have a monarch who is concerned and interested and tries to do something to help people than someone who is completely disinterested and simply deals with ceremonial and doesn't care,' says John Major.[18] Emma Thompson gives a trenchant summation: 'All of the movements that he's spearheaded and supported for years that have slowly become more mainstream are an example of how difficult it is for the press in this country to support anything the royal family does that isn't being nice to children or small furry animals. He wouldn't have had any shit from the press if he had been looking after donkeys or dogs.'[19]

Prince Charles hasn't done much for donkeys or dogs. Some professions will say he hasn't done much for them either; indeed, that he has actively harmed them. There will always be critics who take him for a parasite, an eccentric, a plant whisperer. He knows what he's trying to achieve but it's hard enough to make his aims understood, much less to capture his grails. 'It's everybody else's grandchildren I've been bothering about,' he says, sadly. 'But the trouble is if you take that long a view, people don't always know what you're on about.'[20]

Acknowledgements

It is said that two Eds are better than one and I cannot but agree. *Charles: The Heart of a King* has been shepherded by the two best Eds in the publishing business: my agent Ed Victor and Ed Faulkner, Ebury's deputy publisher, who commissioned the book. Many thanks to everyone who worked on the project, whether at the imprint WH Allen or within the wider Penguin Random House ecosystem, most especially to Elen Jones and also to Shona Abhyankar and Rae Shirvington. A big, but carefully punctuated, hurrah to copy-editor Mary Chamberlain.

Hannah McGrath proved to be not only an indefatigable researcher but also an invaluable sounding board. Friends and colleagues gave me all sorts of useful tips and in several cases surprised me by revealing hitherto unsuspected connections to royalty.

Writing is an antisocial process and I am lucky that my husband, parents, step-parents, sisters, stepsisters, elective sisters, nephew, godchildren and delightful friends continue to tolerate me. Sara Burns coaxed me out for regular walks. Nicola Jennings spurred me on by regularly updating me on the progress of her own doctoral thesis – reminding me how many hundreds of thousands of words she had banked before I even started – and then invited me to join her in France on a writing break. I finished my first draft under her roof, a little before she handed in her own manuscript.

Acknowledgements

Michael Elliott makes a cameo appearance in these pages, at a lunch with the Prince. Mike and I have known each other since meeting at the *Economist* in the 1980s. Later, as *TIME*'s Deputy Managing Editor, he urged me to keep pushing Clarence House for access to Charles. Several other *TIME* editors played key roles in nursing the 2013 cover story that led to this book, in particular the brilliant and lovely Jim Frederick, who died suddenly in July 2014 at only forty-two. Another death, in April 2014, of an elective family member who was just twenty-five years old, and like Jim a supernova, for a few days made me question whether to stop writing and pay more attention to the people I love. Instead the process enabled me to forget, for hours at a time. Now I would like to remember. I have no garden in which to erect shrines, as the Prince does. These few words must serve.

There are many people at Clarence House, Buckingham Palace and Kensington Palace, working for Charles's charities and among his friends, staff and acquaintances – even some of his 'Bond villains' – to whom I owe a debt of gratitude. All tolerated me hanging around and bugging them with questions over a long period of time. Some are named in the text; others chose to remain anonymous – perhaps wisely, as it turned out. Getting to know these people was one of the most enjoyable byproducts of researching this biography.

Of course, if Prince Charles were not such an endlessly fascinating character there would be no book. My final and biggest thanks, therefore, go to him. This is not an authorised biography – there was never any lack of clarity on that point, on either side – but I could not have written it if he had pulled up the drawbridge.

Finally, an apology to my crestfallen goddaughter: I'm sorry this book is about *the* Prince, not Prince. Next time.

Endnotes

AUTHOR'S NOTE

1. 'Prince Charles lawyers to examine "unhelpful" book' by Gordon Rayner, *Daily Telegraph*, 1 February 2015
2. 'Prince understands the role of monarch', letter to the editor by William Nye, *Times*, 3 February 2015
3. 'Charles: The Heart of a King by Catherine Mayer' by Will Self, *Guardian*, 12 February 2015
4. 'Prince Charles in no hurry to become king' – *TIME* magazine, by Estelle Shirbon, Reuters, 25 October 2013
5. 'Prince Charles fears becoming king will be like "Prison"', by Natalie Evans, *Mirror*, 25 October 2013
6. 'Prince Charles "Prison" Claim Denied', BBC website, 25 October 2013
7. 'Heart of a King', by Catherine Mayer, *TIME*, issue date 4 November 2013 (online and on news-stands October 2013)
8. 'Exclusive: Prince Charles, Born to be King But Aiming Higher', by Catherine Mayer, time.com, 24 October 2013
9. Author's interview with Emma Thompson, 16 September 2013
10. 'Pictured: The encounter that plunged Charles into a global storm when he compared Putin to Hitler in conversation with Jewish refugee' by Rebecca English, *Daily Mail*, 24 May 2014
11. *On Royalty* by Jeremy Paxman, Chapter 12: 'The End of the Line?', Viking, 2006
12. Author's interview with Clive Alderton, 17 September 2013
13. Author's interview with Elizabeth Buchanan, central London, 5 March 2014
14. 'Royals jet off into a storm of protest as they leave George at home during Maldives getaway' by Valerie Elliott, *Daily Mail*, 8 March 2014
15. Email from Katie O'Donovan, 1 April 2014

16. Email from Amol Rajan, 7 May 2014
17. Author's interview with Alan Rusbridger, *Guardian* office, central London, 31 March 2014
18. *Cumberland Evening Times*, 22 August 1962
19. *Charles: A Biography*, by Anthony Holden, Bantam Press, a division of Transworld Publishers, 1998, copyright Anthony Holden
20. *Charles: A Biography*, by Anthony Holden, Weidenfeld & Nicolson, 1988, copyright Anthony Holden 1988

INTRODUCTION

1. Diana's interview with Martin Bashir for *Panorama*, first broadcast BBC1, 20 November 1995
2. Author's interview with The Hon. Timothy Knatchbull, west London, 18 February 2014
3. Author's interview with Emma Sparham, 7 August 2013
4. Author's interview with Ben Elliot, central London, 27 May 2014
5. Author's interview with Ian Skelly, central London, 16 April 2014
6. Author's interview with Chief Rabbi Jonathan Sacks, north London, 20 August 2013
7. Author's conversation with the Prince of Wales, Birkhall, Scotland, 26 September 2013
8. Author's interview with Lucia Santa Cruz, 25 March 2014
9. Author's interview with Chief Rabbi Jonathan Sacks, north London, 20 August 2013
10. Author's conversation with the Prince of Wales, Birkhall, Scotland, 26 September 2013
11. Author's interview with Emma Thompson, 16 September 2013
12. On-the-record briefing, St James's Palace, 25 June 2014
13. *De Kostprijs van de Monarchie in Europa* by Professor Dr Herman Matthijs, University of Ghent and Free University of Brussels, April 2012
14. 'Is There a God?' by Bertrand Russell, *Collected Papers of Bertrand Russell*, Vol. 11: Last Philosophical Testament, 1943–68. Edited by John Slater and Peter Köllner, Routledge 1997
15. From the Prince's website, http://www.princeofwales.gov.uk/the-prince-of-wales/promoting-and-protecting/raising-issues
16. *Harmony: A New Way of Looking at Our World* by the Prince of Wales with Tony Juniper and Ian Skelly, Blue Door, HarperCollins 2010, copyright A. G. Carrick Ltd 2010
17. 'Charles: The Private Man, the Public Role', documentary presented and co-produced by Jonathan Dimbleby for ITV, first screened 30 June 1994
18. *Harmony: A Vision for Our Future* by the Prince of Wales, Harper,

HarperCollins 2010

19. Author's interview with Patrick Holden, central London, 6 August 2013
20. Author's interview with Emma Thompson, 16 September 2013
21. *The Madness of George III* by Alan Bennett, Faber and Faber 1995
22. CVM/Don Anderson poll, March 2012
23. 'Key: NZ becoming a republic "inevitable"', by Simon Wong, 3 News Online, 8 April 2014
24. Ipsos-MORI Almanac 2012
25. British Social Attitudes 30, NatCen Social Research 2013
26. AAP Newswire, 16 April 2014
27. Letter to the editor of *The Times*, from Gerald Vinestock in Lancaster, published 17 April 2014
28. *The Diamond Queen*, BBC 1, Episode 1, written and presented by Andrew Marr, first broadcast 6 February 2012
29. Author's conversation with the Prince of Wales, Birkhall, Scotland, 26 September 2013
30. Interview with Prince Andrew by J. F. O. McAllister and Catherine Mayer for *TIME*, 2006
31. 'The Prince of Wales: Up Close', documentary, presented by Trevor McDonald, first screened on ITV, 16 May 2006
32. Office of National Statistics. Poverty calculated as living below 60% of median incomes before housing costs
33. 'The Prince of Wales: Up Close', documentary, presented by Trevor McDonald, first screened on ITV, 16 May 2006
34. 'Why the Royals Miss Diana' by Michael Elliott, *TIME*, 17 November 2002
35. Author's interview with Elizabeth Buchanan, central London, 5 March 2014
36. *The English Constitution*, by Walter Bagehot, Book No. III (*The Monarchy*), 1867
37. Author's conversation with the Prince of Wales, Birkhall, Scotland, 26 September 2013
38. Author's interview with Elizabeth Buchanan, central London, 5 March 2014

CHAPTER 1: HIS LIFE IN A DAY

1. Author's interview with Julia Cleverdon, Clarence House, 25 July 2013
2. Author's interview with The Hon. Timothy Knatchbull, west London, 18 February 2014
3. Author's conversation with the Prince of Wales, Birkhall, Scotland, 26 September 2013
4. 'Prince Charles: wind farms are horrendous' by Andrew Alderson, *Sunday Telegraph*, 8 August 2004
5. Memo to Oliver Everett quoted in *The Prince of Wales: A Biography* by

Jonathan Dimbleby, Chapter 13, Little Brown & Company 1994

6. Author's interview with Elizabeth Buchanan, central London, 5 March 2014

7. From the Prince's own website as at May 2014: http://www.princeofwales. gov.uk/the-prince-of-wales/royal-duties

8. Letter from Sir Michael Peat to *Dispatches*, Channel 4, 5 March 2007

9. *In Private in Public*, presented by Alastair Burnet, produced by Stewart Purvis for ITV, 1986

10. *The Changing Anatomy of Britain* by Anthony Sampson, Chapter 1: 'Monarchy: the Surviving Tribe', Book Club Associates, 1982

11. *Elizabeth R: A Year in the Life of the Queen*, directed and produced by Edward Mirzoeff, BBC, first broadcast 6 February 1992

12. *In Private in Public*, presented by Alastair Burnet, produced by Stewart Purvis for ITV, 1986

13. Author's interview with Patrick Holden, central London, 6 August 2013

14. 'Prince Charles's Duchy Originals in multi-million pound deal with Waitrose' by Andrew Pierce, *Daily Telegraph*, 10 September 2009

15. Author's interview with Elizabeth Buchanan, central London, 5 March 2014

16. Author's interview with Fiona Reynolds, central London, 29 May 2014

17. *The Prince of Wales: A Biography* by Jonathan Dimbleby, Chapter 22, Little Brown & Company 1994

18. Author's conversation with the Prince of Wales, Birkhall, Scotland, 26 September 2013

19. Author's interview with Clive Alderton, 17 September 2013

20. Author's interview with Emma Thompson, 16 September 2013

21. *The Changing Anatomy of Britain* by Anthony Sampson, Chapter 1: 'Monarchy: the Surviving Tribe', Book Club Associates 1982

22. Quoted by an aide

23. *The Prince of Wales: A Biography* by Jonathan Dimbleby, Chapter 20, Little Brown & Company 1994

24. Author's interview with Sir John Major, south London, 23 October 2014

25. Speech by the Prince of Wales at the Prince's Accounting for Sustainability Forum, 12 December 2013

26. Speech by the Prince of Wales at the Prince's Charities Investor Engagement Event, 27 June 2013

27. Speech by the Prince of Wales to Lincolnshire Young Farmers Club, Riseholme Agricultural College, 29 November 2011

28. *Harmony: A New Way of Looking at Our World* by the Prince of Wales with Tony Juniper and Ian Skelly, Blue Door, HarperCollins 2010, copyright A. G. Carrick Ltd 2010

29. *The Prince of Wales: A Biography* by Jonathan Dimbleby, Chapter 3, Little Brown & Company 1994
30. Author's conversation with the Prince of Wales, Birkhall, Scotland, 26 September 2013
31. Author's interview with Emma Thompson, 16 September 2013

CHAPTER 2: MOTHER LOAD

1. Author's interview with Sir John Major, south London, 23 October 2014
2. *The Monarchy and the Constitution* by Vernon Bogdanor, Chapter 4: 'The Appointment of a Prime Minister', Oxford University Press 1995
3. Author's interview with Sir John Major, south London, 23 October 2014
4. 'Election 2010: The Queen could write herself out of the script' by Graham Smith, *Guardian*, 4 May 2010
5. 'The Cabinet Manual: A guide to laws, conventions and rules on the operation of government', 1st edition October 2011
6. Author's interview with Sir John Major, south London, 23 October 2014
7. Ibid.
8. 'Nigel Farage attacked over Romanians "slur"', BBC Online, 18 May 2014
9. Author's interview with the Bishop of London, the Old Deanery, 23 April 2014
10. Episode 1, *The Diamond Queen*, written and presented by Andrew Marr, BBC, first broadcast 6 February 2012
11. 'Lockerbie begins burial after Flight 103 service' by Robert Barr, Associated Press, 5 January 1989
12. *The Changing Anatomy of Britain* by Anthony Sampson, Chapter 1: 'Monarchy: the Surviving Tribe', Book Club Associates 1982
13. *Charles: A Biography* by Anthony Holden, Chapter 2: 'No, Not You Dear', Bantam Press, a division of Transworld Publishers 1998
14. Author's interview with Prince Andrew, Beijing, April 2004
15. *Elizabeth R: A Year in the Life of the Queen*, directed and produced by Edward Mirzoeff, BBC, first broadcast 6 February 1992
16. *Queen Elizabeth, the Queen Mother: The Official Biography* by William Shawcross, Chapter 13: 'The Queen at War', Macmillan 2009
17. *A Jubilee Tribute to the Queen by the Prince of Wales*, BBC, first broadcast 1 June 2012
18. Author's interview with Sir John Major, south London, 23 October 2014
19. The Queen, speech at Guildhall, 24 November 1992
20. Hansard, House of Commons, 7 December 1992
21. 'Palace tours "inhuman"', BBC Online, 27 March 2000
22. 'Queen's treasurer accused of "shocking complacency" over crumbling palaces by MPs' by Gordon Rayner, *Daily Telegraph*, 14 October 2013

23. *Elizabeth R: A Year in the Life of the Queen*, directed and produced by Edward Mirzoeff, BBC, first broadcast 6 February 1992

24. *The Queen: Elizabeth II and the Monarchy*, Diamond Jubilee Edition, by Ben Pimlott, Chapter 1, Harper Press, originally published 1996

25. 'Hacking trial: Police "told to leave Queen's nuts"', BBC Online, 12 December 2013

26. *The Life and Reign of Elizabeth II* by Robert Lacey, Free Press 2002

27. Interview recorded in 2011 for *The Diamond Queen*, BBC 1, written and presented by Andrew Marr, first broadcast 6 February 2012

28. *Mountbatten: the Official Biography* by Philip Ziegler, Chapter 24: 'Post-Surrender Tasks', Collins 1985

29. Ibid.

30. *School Ties* by William Boyd, Introduction, Penguin 1985

31. *English Progressive Schools* by Robert Skidelsky, Harmondsworth, Penguin 1969

32. *The Duke: Portrait of Prince Philip*, presented by Trevor McDonald, Back2Back Productions for ITV, first broadcast 12 May 2008

33. Ibid.

34. *The Prince of Wales: A Biography* by Jonathan Dimbleby, Chapter 20, Little Brown & Company 1994

35. Author's interview with The Hon. Timothy Knatchbull, west London, 18 February 2014

36. Ibid.

37. Ibid.

38. *From a Clear Blue Sky* by Timothy Knatchbull. Hutchinson 2009

39. Author's interview with The Hon. Timothy Knatchbull, west London, 18 February 2014

CHAPTER 3: A PRINCE AMONG MEN

1. Author's conversation with the Prince of Wales, Birkhall, Scotland, 26 September 2013

2. 'Birkhall, Balmoral Estate, Aberdeenshire' by Alan Titchmarsh, *Country Life*, 14 November 2013

3. 'Charles designs "healing garden"' by John Vidal, *Guardian*, 16 May 2002

4. 'Birkhall, Balmoral Estate, Aberdeenshire' by Alan Titchmarsh, *Country Life*, 14 November 2013

5. Author's interview with the Bishop of London, the Old Deanery, 23 April 2014

6. Author's conversation with the Prince of Wales, Birkhall, Scotland, 26 September 2013

7. *Plato's Republic* translated by Benjamin Jowett, the Internet Classics Archive

8. *The Prince of Wales: A Biography* by Jonathan Dimbleby, Chapter 5, Little Brown & Company 1994

9. Anonymous pupil quoted in *Charles: the Untold Story* by Ross Benson, Chapter 3, St Martin's Press 1993

10. *Kurt Hahn – An Efficacious Educator*, translation of *Kurt Hahn – ein wirkungsmächtiger Pädagoge*, Aus: Pädagogisches Handeln, Wissenschaft und Praxis im Dialog 5 (2001), Heft 2, S. 65–76

11. Address by Dr Kurt Hahn at the Annual Meeting of the Outward Bound Trust, 20 July 1960

12. Author's conversation with the Prince of Wales, Birkhall, Scotland, 26 September 2013

13. BBC Radio 4, 1 March 1969

14. *The David Frost Show*, Episode 1, Series 1, Group W Productions, first broadcast 7 July 1969

15. Author's interview with Lucia Santa Cruz, 25 March 2014

16. Author's interview with The Hon. Timothy Knatchbull, west London, 18 February 2014

17. *Queen Elizabeth: the Queen Mother: the Official Biography* by William Shawcross, Chapter 23: 'Poetry and Pain 1981–1999', Macmillan 2009

18. Author's interview with Sir Nicholas Soames, Portcullis House, 11 February 2014

19. Quoted in *Mountbatten: the Official Biography* by Philip Ziegler, Chapter 51: 'The Shop-steward of Royalty', Collins 1985

20. Ibid., letter from Mountbatten to the Prince, 21 April 1979

21. *The Prince of Wales: A Biography* by Jonathan Dimbleby, Chapter 14, Little Brown & Company 1994

22. Author's interview with Emma Thompson, 16 September 2013

23. Author's interview with the Bishop of London, the Old Deanery, 23 April 2014

24. Author's interview with Elizabeth Buchanan, central London, 5 March 2014

25. Author's interview with Andrew Wright, Clarence House, 2 August 2013

26. Author's interview with Clive Alderton, 17 September 2013

27. *King's Counsellor: Abdication and War: the diaries of Sir Alan Lascelles* by Sir Alan Lascelles with Duff Hart-Davis, Weidenfeld & Nicolson 2006

28. 'Edward Goes His Own Way' by Lee Aitken, *People*, 26 January 1987

29. *The Prince of Wales: A Biography* by Jonathan Dimbleby, Chapter 12, Little Brown & Company 1994

30. *Andrew: the Playboy Prince* by Andrew Morton and Mick Seamark, Chapter 1: 'Andymania', Corgi 1983

31. Author's interview with Prince Andrew, Beijing, April 2004

32. 'US Embassy cables: Prince Andrew rails against France, the SFO and the *Guardian*', *Guardian*, 29 November 2010

33. Author's interview with Sir Nicholas Soames, Portcullis House, 11 February 2014
34. 'Word by word, Sophie digs herself deeper into trouble' by Gaby Hinsliff and Burhan Wazir', *Observer*, 8 April 2001
35. 'It's a royal cock-up' by Andy Beckett, *Guardian*, 5 March 2002
36. *The Grand Knockout Tournament*, BBC North West, Knockout Ltd, first screened 12 August 1987
37. 'Was this the day when royalty lost the plot?' by Ivan Waterman and Daniel Roseman, *Independent*, 21 April 1996

CHAPTER 4: THE KNAVE OF HEARTS

1. Author's interview with Sir Nicholas Soames, Portcullis House, 11 February 2014
2. Ibid.
3. Letter from Mountbatten to the Prince, dated 14 February 1974, quoted in *Mountbatten: the official biography* by Philip Ziegler, Chapter 51, Collins 1985
4. *The Prince of Wales: A Biography* by Jonathan Dimbleby, Chapter 12, Little Brown & Company 1994
5. Author's interview with Lucia Santa Cruz, 25 March 2014
6. Entry in the Prince's naval journals, dated 25 March 1974, quoted in *The Prince of Wales: A Biography* by Jonathan Dimbleby, Chapter 12, Little Brown & Company 1994
7. Letter from Mountbatten to the Prince, dated 14 February 1974, quoted in *Mountbatten: the official biography* by Philip Ziegler, Chapter 51, Collins 1985
8. 'Camillagate' transcript, thought to have been recorded 18 December 1989
9. Author's interview with Lucia Santa Cruz, 25 March 2014
10. Author's interview with Emma Thompson, 16 September 2013
11. Author's interview with Lucia Santa Cruz, 25 March 2014
12. 'Interview with Diana Spencer and the Prince of Wales' by Angela Rippon and Andrew Gardner, first broadcast by the BBC and ITN 28 July 1981
13. *Diana: Her True Story – In Her Own Words* by Andrew Morton, Michael O'Mara Books 1997
14. Author's interview with Lucia Santa Cruz, 25 March 2014
15. Author's interview with The Hon. Timothy Knatchbull, west London, 18 February 2014
16. *Robert Runcie: The Reluctant Archbishop* by Humphrey Carpenter, Chapter 12: 'What the Job Is', Hodder & Stoughton 1996
17. Ibid.
18. *The Little Princesses* by Marion Crawford, Chapter 6: 'The Outbreak of War', St Martin's Press 2003

19. *More Fool Me: A Memoir* by Stephen Fry, Penguin 2014
20. '*Diana – Her Story*: The Book that Changed Everything', documentary, Sky Arts, first broadcast 23 September 2012
21. *Diana, Story of a Princess* by Tim Clayton and Phil Craig, Chapter 10: 'Secret Squirrel', Coronet, Hodder & Stoughton 2001
22. 'Squidgygate' transcript, thought to have been recorded 31 December 1989
23. 'Camillagate' transcript, thought to have been recorded 18 December 1989
24. Review of Press Self-Regulation by Sir David Calcutt QC, cm 2135, HMSO, presented to Parliament by the Secretary of State for the Department of National Heritage, January 1993
25. 'Squidgygate' transcript, thought to have been recorded 31 December 1989
26. Author's interview with Anthony Holden, central London, 17 April 2014
27. *Diana – Her Story: The Book That Changed Everything*, documentary, Sky Arts, first broadcast 23 September 2012
28. *Princess Diana: Behind the Panorama Interview*, documentary, BBC, first broadcast 8 November 2005
29. Author's interview with Jonathan Dimbleby, London, 28 March 2014
30. Ibid.
31. Email from Jonathan Dimbleby, 15 November 2014 *Diana: Story of a Princess* by Tim Clayton and Phil Craig, Chapter 6: 'Mood Swings', Coronet, Hodder & Stoughton 2001
32. Author's interview with the Bishop of London, the Old Deanery, 23 April 2014
33. *Panorama*, BBC, first broadcast 20 November 1995
34. Author's interview with Sir Nicholas Soames, Portcullis House, 11 February 2014
35. *King Charles III* by Mike Bartlett, Act 3, Scene 4, Nick Hern Books 2014
36. 'Princess dismisses bulimia reports with joke', *Scottish Herald*, 5 November 1993
37. *Panorama*, BBC, first broadcast 20 November 1995
38. Author's interview with Emma Thompson, 16 September 2013
39. 'Diana "took Charles to cleaners" in divorce, says his banker', by Chris Logan and Andrew Alderson, *Sunday Telegraph*, 25 July 2004
40. 'Minister denies row over Diana', *Scottish Herald*, 5 March 1997
41. Author's interview with Sir Nicholas Soames, Portcullis House, 11 February 2014

CHAPTER 5: 'WOLF HALL'

1. Author's interview with Andrew Wright, Clarence House, 2 August 2013
2. Author's interview with Elizabeth Buchanan, central London, 5 March 2014

Endnotes

3. Author's telephone interview with Amelia Fawcett, 25 September 2013

4. 'Report to His Royal Highness the Prince of Wales' by Sir Michael Peat and Edmund Lawson QC, 13 March 2003

5. 'Royals deny rumours about Prince Charles' by David Leigh, *Guardian*, 7 November 2003

6. 'Prince Charles "set to sue" Palace aide over scandal' by Andrew Alderson, *Sunday Telegraph*, 9 November 2003

7. 'Blackadder bites back' by Mary Riddell, *British Journalism Review*, Volume 15, No. 2, 2004

8. 'Charles' school comments defended', BBC Online, 18 November 2004

9. 'Prince hits back in memo row', *Daily Mail*, 23 November 2004

10. 'Has the puppet-master of St James's finally pulled one string too many?' by Peter Foster, *Daily Telegraph*, 1 December 2001

11. 'Blackadder bites back' by Mary Riddell, *British Journalism Review*, Volume 15, No. 2, 2004

12. Edited extracts from Prince Charles's travel journal, *Daily Telegraph*, 23 February 2006

13. Mark Bolland's witness statement in full, statement dated 18 January 2006, published in the *Guardian* 22 February 2006

14. Ibid.

15. 'Camilla and the blonde private secretary who's paid the price for being too close to Prince Charles' by Richard Kay and Geoffrey Levy, *Daily Mail*, 13 June 2008

16. Author's interview with Elizabeth Buchanan, central London, 5 March 2014

17. Author's interview with Emma Thompson, 16 September 2013

18. *Storyteller: the Many Lives of Laurens van der Post* by J. D. F. Jones, Chapter 37: 'My Prince', Scribner 2001

19. Ibid.

20. *In Plain Sight: The Life and Lies of Jimmy Savile* by Dan Davies, Chapter 37: 'It's Obscene', Quercus Editions 2014

21. Ibid., Chapter 45: 'Am I Saved?'

22. Ibid., Chapter 23: 'Nostalgic Memories'

23. Email from Dan Davies, 14 April 2014

24. *In Plain Sight: The Life and Lies of Jimmy Savile* by Dan Davies, Chapter 54: 'Runners Are Junkies', Quercus Editions 2014

25. 'Squidgygate' transcript, thought to have been recorded 31 December 1989

26. *The Palace Diaries: Twelve Years with HRH Prince Charles* by Sarah Goodall and Nicholas Monson, Chapter 3: 'Food & Weight', Mainstream Publishing 2006

27. *Jimmy Savile: The Power to Abuse*, *Panorama*, BBC, first broadcast 2 June 2014

28. *Queen and Country*, documentary series written and presented by William Shawcross, BBC, first broadcast 1 May 2002

29. Author's interview with Sir Nicholas Soames, Portcullis House, 11 February 2014

30. 'Magic? Charles can't work a light switch' by Suzanne Moore, *Mail on Sunday*, 16 March 2003

31. 'Diana inquest: Queen ordered palace to be swept for bugs over spy fears', *Mail* Online, 12 February 2008

32. 'Tories blocked royal phone-tapping probe' by Richard Palmer, *Daily Express*, 13 February 2008

33. *Fayed: The Unauthorized Biography* by Tom Bower, Chapter 17: 'The Last Blonde', Macmillan 1998

34. 'Nazi Philip wanted Diana dead, Fayed tells inquest' by Louise Radnofsky and agencies, *Guardian*, 18 February 2008

CHAPTER 6: A MATTER OF TRUST

1. Reuters report by Paul Bloding, 7 May 1975

2. John Rea-Price, Director of Social Services in Islington, quoted in *25 Years of the Prince's Trust* by Adam Nicolson, The Prince's Trust 2001

3. Author's interview with Jon Snow, central London, 21 March 2014

4. *Crisis? What Crisis? Britain in the 1970s* by Alwyn W. Turner, Aurum Press 2008

5. Enoch Powell, speech to a Conservative association in Birmingham, 20 April 1968

6. Letter to Lord Mountbatten, 16 February 1967, quoted in *The Prince of Wales: A Biography* by Jonathan Dimbleby, Chapter 7, Little Brown & Company 1994

7. Author's conversation with the Prince of Wales, Birkhall, Scotland, 26 September 2013

8. The Prince of Wales quoted in *25 Years of the Prince's Trust* by Adam Nicolson, The Prince's Trust 2001

9. Author's interview with Sir William Castell, Wellcome Trust, London, 19 March 2004

10. Author's interview with Sir Nicholas Soames, Portcullis House, 11 February 2014

11. 'Sheila Ferguson's Cinderella story' by Jennifer Shelton, *Cambridge News*, 16 December 2011

12. Author's interview with Martina Milburn, Prince's Trust headquarters, 30 July 2013

13. Author's interview with Sir William Castell, Wellcome Trust, London, 19 March 2004

14. Author's interview with Julia Cleverdon, Clarence House, 25 July 2013

15. 'The ace in the pack' by Hattie Collins, *Guardian*, 1 April 2006

16. Author's interview with James Sommerville, 6 August 2013
17. Author's interview with Sir Charles Dunstone, 17 March 2014
18. John Pervin quoted in *25 Years of the Prince's Trust* by Adam Nicolson, 2001
19. Author's interview with Tom Shebbeare, central London, 9 July 2014
20. Author's interview with Shaun McPherson, 26 March 2014
21. Ibid.
22. Ibid.
23. Author's interview with Martina Milburn, Prince's Trust headquarters, 30 July 2013
24. Ibid.
25. Prince of Wales quoted in the *International Herald Tribune*, 18 November 1978

CHAPTER 7: LONG TO RAIN OVER US

1. 'UK storms are divine retribution for gay marriage laws, says UKIP councillor', *Guardian* Online, 18 January 2014
2. 'Difficult choices, as the flood waters rise' by Chris Smith, *Sunday Telegraph*, 2 February 2014
3. Author's conversation with the Prince of Wales, Birkhall, Scotland, 26 September 2013
4. '21 Pictures of Politicians in Wellies Staring at Floods' by Jim Waterson, BuzzFeed, 11 February 2014
5. 'Prince Charles upstages Cameron, from his wooden throne in flooded Somerset' by Jonathan Jones, *Guardian*, 5 February 2014
6. 'The lessons I learned from the report on the summer riots' by Theresa May, *Mail on Sunday*, 18 December 2011
7. 'London riots: Charles and Camilla hear victims' tales', BBC Online, 17 August 2011
8. Author's interview with David Lammy, Tottenham, 5 April 2014
9. 'Pride of Britain Awards 2011: Gina Moffatt named Prince's Trust Young Achiever for turning her life around', *Mirror* Online, 3 October 2011
10. Author's interview with David Lammy, Tottenham, 5 April 2014
11. 'Secret meeting unites republican MPs' by Nicholas Watt, *Guardian*, 24 January 2002
12. 'Republicans provoke Labour' by Craig Woodhouse', *Evening Standard*, 17 February 2012
13. 'King Charles doomed' by Paul Flynn, his own blog: 'Read My Day', 18 December 2009
14. Author's interview with Sir John Major, south London, 23 October 2014
15. Author's interview with Sir Nicholas Soames, Portcullis House, 11 February 2014

16. Author's interview with Emma Thompson, 16 September 2013

17. *The Blair Years: Extracts from the Alastair Campbell Diaries*, edited by Alastair Campbell and Richard Stott, Hutchinson 2007; and 'Alastair Campbell diaries: Secret war between Tony Blair and Prince Charles' (extracts from second volume of diaries); published in the *Guardian*, 1 July 2011

18. 'Alastair Campbell diaries: Secret war between Tony Blair and Prince Charles' (extracts from second volume of diaries), published in the *Guardian*, 1 July 2011

19. 'Prince sparks GM food row', BBC Online, 1 June 1999

20. Quoted in *The Royal Activist*, documentary presented by Elinor Goodman, BBC Radio 4, first broadcast 29 June 2014

21. 'Wills and Kate plan Chinese charm offensive to repair damage of Prince Charles's "appalling old waxworks" jibe' by Corey Charlton, *Mail on Sunday*, 31 August 2014

22. Author's interview with Sir William Castell; Wellcome Trust, London; 19 March 2004

23. 'Tony Blair defends "helpful" Prince Charles after diary reveals tensions' by Nicholas Watt, *Guardian*, 4 July 2011

24. From the Prince's own website, as of May 2014: http://www.princeofwales. gov.uk/the-prince-of-wales/promoting-and-protecting/raising-issues

25. *Charles at 60: the Passionate Prince*, documentary, BBC1, first broadcast 12 November 2008

26. Author's interview with Alan Rusbridger, *Guardian* offices, 31 March 2014

27. Ibid.

28. 'I've got something to say', interview with Tony Blair by Martin Kettle, *Guardian*, 1 September 2010

29. *A Journey* by Tony Blair, Chapter 17: '2005: TB/GB', Arrow Books, 2011

30. Exercise of the executive override under Section 53 of the Freedom of Information Act 2000: statement of reasons, Evans v (1) Information Commissioner (2) seven Government Departments [2012] UKUT 313 (AAC), Organisation: Attorney General's Office, 16 October 2012, Minister: The Rt Hon Dominic Grieve QC MP

31. British Social Attitudes 30, NatCen Social Research 2013

32. Blackadder, Clive Goodman column, *News of the World*, 6 November 2005

33. 'Fury after he ogled lapdancer's boobs' by Clive Goodman and Neville Thurlbeck, *News of the World*, 9 April 2006

34. 'Met Police loaned horse to Rebekah Brooks' by Vikram Dodd, *Guardian*, 29 February 2012

35. Levenson Inquiry, Seminar 3: Supporting a free press and high standards – Approaches to Regulation, 12 October 2011; 'The future for self regula- tion?', presentation by Paul Dacre

36. *Unlawful Killing*, directed and presented by Keith Allen, Sphinx Entertainment, Allied Stars and Associated Rediffusion Television, 2011
37. British Social Attitudes 30, NatCen Social Research 2013
38. 'Prince Charles "black spider" memos reveal lobbying of Tony Blair', by Robert Booth and Matthew Taylor, *Guardian*, 13 May 2015

CHAPTER 8: ARCHITECTURE OF CONTROVERSY

1. Author's conversation with the Prince of Wales, Birkhall, Scotland, 26 September 2013
2. Author's interview with Peter Ahrends, north London, 2 May 2014
3. Author's conversation with the Prince of Wales, Birkhall, Scotland, 26 September 2013
4. From Foreword by HRH the Prince of Wales to *The Hidden Geometry of Flowers* by Keith Critchlow, Floris Books 2011
5. 'Prince of the City: Charles Takes on London's Architects' by John Taylor, *New York Magazine*, 19 March 1990
6. A speech by HRH the Prince of Wales at the 150th anniversary of the Royal Institute of British Architects (RIBA), Royal Gala Evening at Hampton Court Palace, 17 May 1984
7. Ibid.
8. Author's interview with Peter Ahrends, north London, 2 May 2014
9. 'New wing vindicates Prince Charles' by Thomas Hine, *Philadelphia Inquirer*, 10 July 1991
10. A speech by HRH the Prince of Wales at the Corporation of London Planning and Communication Committee's Annual Dinner, Mansion House, London, 1 December 1987
11. 'Prince of Wales's emotional Chelsea Barracks letter revealed' by Stephen Adams, *Daily Telegraph*, 24 June 2010
12. 'Exclusive: Prince Charles on the Environment, the Monarchy, His Family, and Islam', *Vanity Fair* (abstract of Bob Colacello profile), 6 October 2010
13. Author's interview with Dominic Richards and Hank Dittmar, central London, 21 August 2013
14. 'Prince Charles's meddling in planning "unconstitutional", says Richard Rogers' by Robert Booth, *Guardian*, 15 June 2009
15. Author's conversation with the Prince of Wales, Birkhall, Scotland, 26 September 2013
16. Author's telephone interview with Ewen Miller, 10 September 2013
17. Ibid.
18. Ibid.
19. 'Liverpool Ferry Terminal wins Carbuncle Cup 2009' by Amanda Baillieu, *Building Design*, 28 August 2009

20. *A Vision of Britain: A Personal View of Architecture* by HRH the Prince of Wales, Conclusion, Doubleday, Transworld, copyright A. G. Carrick Ltd 1989

21. Ibid., Introduction

22. Author's interview with Dominic Richards and Hank Dittmar, central London, 21 August 2013

23. 'Liverpool Ferry Terminal wins Carbuncle Cup 2009' by Amanda Baillieu, *Building Design*, 28 August 2009

24. 'Prince Charles's Poundbury fire station is a daft mess' by Justin McGuirk, *Guardian*, 31 March 2009

25. *The Prince of Wales: A Biography* by Jonathan Dimbleby, Chapter 23, Little Brown & Company 1994

26. 'Poundbury houses at St John's Way by Francis Roberts Architects' by Oliver Wainright, *Building Design*, 4 July 2012

27. Author's interview with Ewen Miller, 10 September 2013

28. Author's conversation with the Prince of Wales, Birkhall, Scotland, 26 September 2013

29. *Disney's World* by Leonard Moseley, Chapter 22: 'The Wounded Bear', Stein and Day 1985

30. Author's interview with John Ivall, 26 June 2014

31. Author's interview with The Hon. Timothy Knatchbull, west London, 18 February 2014

32. Ibid.

33. Author's interviews with Highbury Gardens residents, 18 September 2013

34. 'Charles: We need homes for young Londoners' by Jonathan Prynn, *Evening Standard*, 26 March 2014

35. *The Spicer Diaries* by Michael Spicer, Chapter 9: 'Margaret Thatcher – her downfall', Thomas Dunne Books, St Martin's Press 2012

CHAPTER 9: THE KNIGHT OF THE REALMS

1. 'Royal flashback: Princess Di charms Canada', report from 1983 republished in *Toronto Star*, 29 June 2011

2. *De Kostprijs van de Monarchie in Europa* by Professor Dr Herman Matthijs, University of Ghent and Free University of Brussels, April 2012

3. Author's interview with Shelly Glover, Winnipeg, 21 May 2014

4. 'Marianne Ferguson née Echt, Polish Immigrant *Andania*, February 20, 1939', *Tales from My Home Town, Danzig*, written 1942, Canadian Museum of Immigration at Pier 21

5. '"Putin is behaving just like Hitler", says Charles. Prince's controversial verdict on Russian leader's invasion of Ukraine' by Rebecca English, *Daily Mail*, 20 May 2014

6. 'Vladimir Putin condemns Prince Charles's "Nazi" remarks', BBC Online, 24 May 2014
7. Author's interview with Dominic Richards and Hank Dittmar, central London, 21 August 2013
8. Author's interview with Amelia Fawcett, 25 September 2013
9. *In the Ring* by Don McKinnon, Chapter 2: 'A Gracious Presence', Elliott and Thompson Ltd 2013
10. Quoted in *The Royal Activist*, documentary presented by Elinor Goodman, BBC Radio 4, first broadcast 29 June 2014
11. Speech by Commonwealth Secretary General Kamalesh Sharma, Commonwealth Day Reception, Marlborough House, London, 11 March 2013
12. 'Prince George boosts popularity of the monarchy in Canada (provided Charles isn't king): poll', by Josh Vissier, *National Post*, 25 July 2013
13. *Confessions of a Not-So-Secret Agent* by Harry M. Miller with Peter Holder, Hachette Australia 2009
14. *Of Presidents, Prime Ministers and Princes* by Anthony Holden, Weidenfeld & Nicolson 1984
15. Letter to Nicholas Soames, 4 February 1988, quoted in *The Prince of Wales: A Biography* by Jonathan Dimbleby, Chapter 21, Little Brown & Company 1994
16. A speech by the Prince of Wales at the Australia Day Reception, Darling Harbour, Sydney, Australia, 28 January 1994
17. Email from Greg Baker, 2 June 2014
18. Author's telephone interview with Joelle Foster, 19 June 2014
19. 'Does one look like a glasshole in these? Prince of Wales tries out Google Glass as he visits Canada's "innovation alley"' by Mark Prigg, *Mail* Online, published 21 May 2014, updated 22 May 2014

CHAPTER 10: A FOREIGN ASSET

1. 'Islam and the West', a speech by HRH the Prince of Wales, the Sheldonian Theatre, Oxford, 27 October 1993
2. Author's interview with Farhan Nizami, central London, 22 August 2013
3. 'Islam and the West', a speech by HRH the Prince of Wales, the Sheldonian Theatre, Oxford, 27 October 1993
4. Email from Farhan Nizami, 8 August 2014
5. 'Charles of Arabia: The British Monarchy, Saudi Arabia, and 9/11' by Richard Freeman and William F. Wertz, Jr., *Executive Intelligence Review*, Volume 41, Number 21, May 23, 2014
6. Exchange on Stormfront dated 3 September 2008

7. *Saudi Babylon: Torture, Corruption and Cover-Up Inside the House of Saud* by Mark Hollingsworth with Sandy Mitchell, Chapter Two: 'Caught in Al-Qaeda's Wave of Terror', Mainstream Publishing 2005

8. '"My feud with Salman Rushdie is all in the past," says John le Carré' by Jack Malvern, *The Times*, 12 November 2012

9. Martin Amis quoted in 'A Fundamental Fight' by Paul Elie, *Vanity Fair*, May 2014

10. Author's interview with Lucia Santa Cruz, 25 March 2014

11. 'Prince Charles, the Islamic dissident' by Brian Whitaker, *Guardian*, 27 March 2006

12. A speech by the Prince of Wales at the Imam Muhammad bin Saud University, Riyadh, Saudi Arabia, 25 March 2006

13. 'Prince Charles, the Islamic dissident' by Brian Whitaker, *Guardian*, 27 March 2006

14. George Galloway, Comment, Press TV, 20 February 2014

15. 'Galloway denies Saddam "fawning"', BBC Online, 16 November 2004

16. 'The future British king, Saudi princes, and a secret arms deal' by Richard Norton-Taylor, *Guardian*, 24 February 2014

17. Author's interview with Farhan Nizami, central London, 22 August 2013

18. http://www.yerevanmylove.com

19. Author's interview with Vahan Hovhanessian, Armenian Consulate, Kensington, 25 February 2014

20. '"Dissident" Charles snubbed Chinese banquet: court', by Kate Holton, Reuters, 21 February 2006

21. Author's interview with Thubten Samdup, north London, 27 March 2014

22. 'Shall I leave you two chaps to it then? Duchess of Cornwall on the sidelines as the Dalai Lama chats and hold hands with his "best friend" Prince Charles' by Jill Reilly, *Daily Mail*, 20 June 2012

23. The Prince to Geoffrey Howe, 1 February 1989, quoted in *The Prince of Wales: A Biography* by Jonathan Dimbleby, Chapter 20, Little Brown & Company 1994

24. A speech by HRH the Prince of Wales at the opening of the Build a Better Britain Exhibition, the Business Design Centre, Islington, London, 27 April 1989

25. '*Jetzt bin ich hier, jetzt reicht's mir*', *Der Spiegel*, 22 August 1988

26. Author's interview with William Blacker, 26 February 2014

27. Ibid.

28. Author's interview with Dominic Richards, central London, 21 August 2013

29. *Charles: The Private Man, the Public Role*, documentary presented and co-produced by Jonathan Dimbleby for ITV, first screened 30 June 1994

30. 'Soggy Prince Charles blames excessive security for hitting his chances of seeing wild elephants in India' by Vicky Smith, *Mirror*, 12 November 2014

31. http://www.touringromania.com/tours/long-tours/live-like-a-king-prince-of-wales-favorite-places-in-romania-private-tour-8-days.html

32. *Wild Carpathia*, Episode 1, presented by Charlie Ottley, Travel Channel, first broadcast 8 November 2011

33. Author's interview with Craig Turp, 2 July 2014

34. 'Prince Charles & Romania' by Craig Turp, *Bucharest Life*, 16 May 2011

35. Author's interview with Justin Mundy and Jeremy Staniforth, Clarence House, 11 March 2014

36. Ibid.

37. Author's interview with William Blacker, 26 February 2014

38. Author's interview with Justin Mundy and Jeremy Staniforth, Clarence House, 11 March 2014

39. Author's interview with Craig Turp, 2 July 2014

40. 'Charles' school comments defended', BBC Online, 18 November 2004

CHAPTER 11: HARMONIES AND DISHARMONIES

1. *Harmony: A New Way of Looking at Our World*, the Prince of Wales with Tony Juniper and Ian Skelly, Blue Door, HarperCollins 2010, copyright A. G. Carrick Ltd 2010

2. Author's interview with Ian Skelly, central London, 16 April 2014

3. Ibid.

4. http://www.psta.org.uk/research/publications/keithcritchlow/

5. Foreword to *The Hidden Geometry of Flowers: Living Rhythms, Form and Number* by Keith Critchlow, Floris Books, 2011

6. 'The Empire and the world rejoice' by own correspondent and AAP' *Melbourne Argus*, 16 November 1948

7. Author's interview with Peder Anker, 18 March 2014

8. *The Works of John Dryden*, Volume 4 (of 18), *Almanzor and Almahide, Marriage-a-la-Mode, The Assignation* by John Dryden, Project Gutenberg eBook of 1808 edition, released March 2005. Play first performed 1670

9. *1575 Essays* by Michel de Montaigne, IV: 'Of Cannibals', translated by Charles Cotton

10. *Emile* by Jean-Jacques Rousseau, Book I: 'Birth to Age 5', Online Literature

11. *Harmony: A New Way of Looking at Our World*, the Prince of Wales with Tony Juniper and Ian Skelly, Blue Door, HarperCollins 2010, copyright A. G. Carrick Ltd 2010

12. Author's interview with Peder Anker, 18 March 2014

13. A speech by the Prince of Wales at the Foreign Press Association Media Awards, Sheraton Park Lane Hotel, London, 25 November 2008

14. 'Romanians: Never happier than when doing back-breaking work', *Bucharest Life*, www.bucharestlife.net, 20 October 2010

15. A speech by the Prince of Wales at the Foreign Press Association Media Awards, Sheraton Park Lane Hotel, London, 25 November 2008
16. Discussion session at Aspen Ideas festival; Linda Tischler interviews Julie Bergman Sender, Stuart Sender and Jay Harman, 1 July 2013
17. *Harmony: A New Way of Looking at Our World*, the Prince of Wales with Tony Juniper and Ian Skelly, Blue Door, HarperCollins 2010, copyright A. G. Carrick Ltd 2010
18. Author's interview with Peder Anker, 18 March 2014
19. *Venture to the Interior* by Laurens van der Post, Chapter 19, Vintage Classics 2002, first published 1952
20. Interview with Prince Philip by Victoria Finlay for the Alliance of Religions and Conservation, July 2003
21. 'Portrait of a marriage' by Gyles Brandreth, *Sunday Telegraph*, 5 September 2004
22. Quoted in *Imperial Ecology: Environmental Order in the British Empire, 1895–1945* by Peder Anker, Harvard University Press, copyright 2001 President and Fellows of Harvard College
23. Author's interview with Steward Pickett, 20 March 2014
24. *Holism and Evolution* by General the Rt Hon. J. C. Smuts, Macmillan & Co., second edition 1927
25. World Bank 2013
26. Author's interview with Sir William Castell, Wellcome Trust, London, 19 March 2004

CHAPTER 12: ARE THERE ALTERNATIVES?

27. Author's interview with Edzard Ernst, Suffolk, 3 March 2014
28. Quoted in *Essays in the History of Therapeutics* edited by William F. Bynum and Vivian Nutton, Editions Rodopi, 1991
29. http://www.drmali.com/
30. Author's interview with Edzard Ernst, Suffolk, 3 March 2014
31. *Harmony: A New Way of Looking at Our World* by the Prince of Wales with Tony Juniper and Ian Skelly, Blue Door, HarperCollins 2010, copyright A. G. Carrick Ltd 2010
32. Ibid.
33. Email from Malachy O'Rourke, 3 July 2014
34. Email from Professor Giorgios Mitsis, 8 July 2014
35. A speech by the Prince of Wales, 'Complementary Medicine', the British Medical Association, London, 14 December 1982
36. Ibid.
37. Christopher Smallwood's report on integrated health, press release issued by Clarence House, 16 October 2005

38. Author's interview with Edzard Ernst, Suffolk, 3 March 2014
39. Letter from Sir Michael Peat to Professor Steve Smith, Vice Chancellor of Exeter University, 22 September 2005, quoted in *Scientist in Wonderland: A Memoir of Looking for Truth and Finding Trouble*, unedited manuscript
40. '"Make-believe and outright quackery" – expert's verdict on prince's detox potion' by Sarah Boseley, *Guardian*, 11 March 2009
41. Email from Michael Dixon, 10 August 2014
42. Author's interview with Michael Dixon, National Liberal Club, Westminster, London, 30 April 2004
43. Website for College Surgery, Devon: http://www.collegesurgery.org.uk/
44. Author's interview with Michael Dixon, National Liberal Club, Westminster, London, 30 April 2004
45. Ibid.
46. Ibid.
47. Ibid.
48. *The Great Plague* by Stephen Porter, Chapter 2: 'The Great Plague in London', Amberley Publishing 2009
49. Author's interview with Michael Dixon, National Liberal Club, Westminster, London, 30 April 2004
50. http://www.pennybrohncancercare.org/
51. Author's interview with Elizabeth Buchanan, central London, 5 March 2014
52. Foreword to *Fighting Spirit: The stories of women in the Bristol breast cancer survey* edited by Heather Goodare, Scarlet Press, collection copyright Heather Goodare 1996
53. Quoted in *The Royal Activist*, BBC Radio 4, first broadcast 29 June 2014
54. 'How Prince Charles disrespects his constitutional role' by Edzard Ernst, http://edzardernst.com/, 30 June 2014
55. Author's interview with Ian Skelly, central London, 16 April 2014

CHAPTER 13: KING SAVE THE GOD

1. Quoted in *The Servant Problem: the Home Life of a Global Economy* by Rosie Cox, Chapter 5: 'The new "upstairs, downstairs"', I. B. Tauris & Co. 2006
2. 'Campbell interrupted Blair as he spoke of his faith: "We don't do God"' by Colin Brown, *Sunday Telegraph*, 4 May 2003
3. 'Our next prime minister?' by Nicholas Watt and Patrick Wintour, *Guardian*, 16 July 2008
4. 'My faith in the Church of England' by David Cameron, *Church Times*, 16 April 2014
5. Author's interview with Jonathan Dimbleby, north London, 28 March 2014
6. *Charles: The Private Man, the Public Role*, documentary presented and co-produced by Jonathan Dimbleby for ITV, first screened 30 June 1994

7. Quoted in *The Prince of Wales: A Biography* by Jonathan Dimbleby, Chapter 26, Little Brown & Company 1994
8. Ibid.
9. Author's interview with Jonathan Dimbleby, north London, 28 March 2014
10. *Robert Runcie: The Reluctant Archbishop* by Humphrey Carpenter, Chapter 12: 'What the Job Is', Hodder & Stoughton 1996
11. Tribute by the Prince as patron of the Prayer Book Society for the 2012 celebration of the 350th anniversary of the Book of Common Prayer
12. *Robert Runcie: The Reluctant Archbishop* by Humphrey Carpenter, Chapter 12: 'What the Job Is', Hodder & Stoughton 1996
13. Author's interview with the Bishop of London, the Old Deanery, 23 April 2014
14. *Robert Runcie: The Reluctant Archbishop* by Humphrey Carpenter, Chapter 11: 'Now Your Troubles Start', Hodder & Stoughton 1996
15. 'Richard Chartres, the formidable bishop leading Lady Thatcher's funeral' by Peter Walker, *Guardian*, 16 April 2013
16. 'Bishop of London Richard Chartres on bankers, Occupy and Justin Welby' by Martin Vander Weyer, *Spectator*, 11 May 2013
17. 'A working life: the Bishop' by Anna Tims, *Guardian*, 19 August 2011
18. Author's conversation with the Prince of Wales, Birkhall, Scotland, 26 September 2013
19. Author's interview with the Bishop of London, the Old Deanery, 23 April 2014
20. Ibid.
21. Interview for this book conducted by Hannah McGrath, 15 July 2014
22. Letter from Frederick Phipps of Shrewsbury to the Queen, 15 March 2014
23. Letter from Andrew Nunn to Frederick Phipps, 31 May 2013
24. Interview for this book conducted by Hannah McGrath, 15 July 2014
25. 'The Church, Charles and Camilla' by Jane Little, BBC Online, 10 February 2005
26. 'Lord Chancellor's statement in full', BBC Online, 23 February 2005
27. Submission by Michael F. Jones to the ICO, 23 November 2008
28. Freedom of Information Act 2000 (Section 50), Decision Notice, Public Authority – the Ministry of Justice, Complainant – Michael Jones, 31 March 2010

CHAPTER 14: SACRED SPACES

1. Author's interview with Ian Skelly, central London, 16 April 2014
2. *Storyteller: the Many Lives of Laurens van der Post* by J. D. F. Jones, Chapter 37: 'My Prince', Scribner 2001

Endnotes

3. Letter to Arianna Huffingon, 23 April 1996, ibid.

4. Obituary of Kathleen Raine by Janet Watts, *Guardian* Books, 8 July 2003

5. *No End to Snowdrops: A Biography of Kathleen Raine* by Philippa Bernard, Chapter 11: 'Temenos', Shepheard-Walwyn 2009

6. Quoted in *Radical Prince: The Practical Vision of the Prince of Wales* by David Lorimer, Chapter 4: 'A Sense of the Sacred', Floris Books 2003

7. http://www.temenosacademy.org/temenos_home.html

8. *No End to Snowdrops: A Biography of Kathleen Raine* by Philippa Bernard, Chapter 12: 'India', Shepheard-Walwyn 2009

9. Ibid.

10. Author's interview with Ian Skelly, central London, 16 April 2014

11. Video message from the Prince of Wales, recorded for Temenos Conference at St Hilda's College, Oxford, 13–15 September 2013

12. 'Seeds of Doubt: An activist's controversial crusade against genetically modified crops' by Michael Specter, *New York Magazine*, 25 August 2014

13. *Harmony: A New Way of Looking at Our World* by the Prince of Wales with Tony Juniper and Ian Skelly, Blue Door, HarperCollins 2010, copyright A. G. Carrick Ltd 2010

14. *Against the Modern World: Traditionalism and the Secret Intellectual History of the Twentieth Century* by Mark Sedgwick, Chapter 1: 'Traditionalism', Oxford University Press 2004

15. *Harmony: A New Way of Looking at Our World* by the Prince of Wales with Tony Juniper and Ian Skelly, Blue Door, HarperCollins 2010, copyright A. G. Carrick Ltd 2010

16. 'Sacred Web Conference contemplates the role of religion in a secular age' by Jenny Uechi, *Vancouver Observer*, 27 April 2014

17. *Against the Modern World: Traditionalism and the Secret Intellectual History of the Twentieth Century* by Mark Sedgwick, Chapter 11: 'Europe after 1968', Oxford University Press 2004

18. *Harmony: A New Way of Looking at Our World* by the Prince of Wales with Tony Juniper and Ian Skelly, Blue Door, HarperCollins 2010, copyright A. G. Carrick Ltd 2010

19. Religion in England and Wales, 2011 Census, Key Statistics for Local Authorities in England and Wales, Office for National Statistics, released 11 December 2012

20. 'Prince of Wales "abused and ridiculed" over his attempts to promote interfaith dialogue' by Gordon Rayner, *Daily Telegraph*, 6 April 2011

21. 'Black worshippers keep the faith' by Cindi John, BBC Online, 1 August 2005

22. A speech by the Prince of Wales during a visit to Jesus House Church to celebrate the work of black-majority churches, Brent Cross, London, 14 November 2007

23. Author's interview with the Bishop of London, the Old Deanery, 23 April

2014

24. Author's interview with Chief Rabbi Jonathan Sacks, north London, 20 August 2013

25. Ibid.

26. A speech by the Prince of Wales at the tribute dinner in honour of the Chief Rabbi, 24 June 2013

27. *The Dignity of Difference: How to Avoid the Clash of Civilisations* by Jonathan Sacks, Chapter 3: 'Exorcising the Ghost of Plato', Continuum Books 2002

28. Ibid.

29. Author's interview with the Bishop of London, the Old Deanery, 23 April 2014

30. Author's interview with Yasmin Alibhai-Brown, west London, 1 April 2014

31. Ibid.

32. *A Degree of Influence: The funding of strategically important subjects in UK universities* by Robin Simcox, the Centre for Social Cohesion, 2009

33. Author's interview with Farhan Nizami, central London, 22 August 2013

34. 'Dreaming spires face minaret eclipse', *Times* Higher Education, 7 July 1997

35. *A Degree of Influence: The funding of strategically important subjects in UK universities* by Robin Simcox, the Centre for Social Cohesion 2009

36. Email from Farhan Nizami, 8 August 2014

CHAPTER 15: HAPPY AND NOTORIOUS

1. 'It's Camilla, looking just like One's mum' by Harry Arnold, *Daily Mirror*, 6 March 1993

2. 'Why Camilla has such a hold on Charles' by Heather McGlone and Rosemary Carpenter, *Daily Express*, 16 January 1993

3. Author's interview with Lucia Santa Cruz, 25 March 2014

4. 'Charles and Camilla go public', BBC Online, 29 January 1999

5. 'Mark Bolland: Marital aide' by Sholto Byrnes, *Independent*, 30 March 2005

6. Ibid.

7. Author's interview with Anthony Holden and Richard Kay, central London, 17 April 2014

8. Author's interview with Robin Boles; In Kind Direct headquarters, 21 August 2013

9. 'Why Charles and Camilla are now living such separate lives' by Richard Kay and Geoffrey Levy, *Daily Mail*, 29 June 2010

10. 'From "that wicked woman" to Her Majesty's secret weapon: Camilla's the only one who stops Charles sulking about Kate and George's popularity' by Richard Kay and Geoffrey Levy, *Daily Mail*, 18 April 2014

11. Email from Richard Kay, 22 July 2014

12. Author's conversation with the Prince of Wales, Birkhall, Scotland, 26

September 2013

13. Author's interview with Emma Thompson, 16 September 2013
14. Author's interview with Lucia Santa Cruz, 25 March 2014
15. Author's interview with Patrick Holden, central London, 6 August 2013
16. Author's interview with Ben Elliot, central London, 27 May 2014
17. Author's interview with Lucia Santa Cruz, 25 March 2014
18. Author's interview with Amanda Macmanus, Clarence House, 9 April 2014
19. 'Camilla's dearest cause' by Emma Soames, *Daily Telegraph*, 20 November 2006
20. 'Duchess of Cornwall supports efforts to end female genital mutilation', Press Association, 27 February 2014
21. Author's interview with Robin Boles, central London, 21 August 2013
22. Author's interview with Sir Nicholas Soames, Portcullis House, 11 February 2014
23. YouGov / *Sunday Times* survey, sample size: 1945 GB Adults, fieldwork: 9–10 May 2013
24. Author's interview with Emma Thompson, 16 September 2013

CHAPTER 16: KINGS TO COME

1. Author's interview with John Campbell, Cumnock, 20 January 2014
2. A speech by the Prince of Wales at the opening of the Queen Elizabeth Garden, Dumfries House, 2 July 2014
3. Scottish Index of Multiple Deprivation 2012
4. Author's interview with Sarah-Jane Clark, Dumfries estate, 21 January 2014
5. Author's interview with Gette Fulton, Cumnock, 20 January 2014
6. Author's interview with Ben Elliot, central London, 27 May 2014
7. Email from Fiona Lees, 7 July 2014
8. Author's conversation with the Prince of Wales, Birkhall, Scotland, 26 September 2013
9. 'Prince William on why conservation and Africa are burning passions he was born to pass on' by Jane Treays, *Radio Times*, 15 September 2013
10. Conversation with author during Canada tour, May 2014
11. Author's interview with Ben Elliot, central London, 27 May 2014
12. Author's interview with Emma Thompson, 16 September 2013
13. Author's interview with Patrick Holden, central London, 6 August 2013
14. Author's interview with Emma Thompson, 16 September 2013
15. Author's interview with Patrick Holden, central London, 6 August 2013
16. Meeting with the Prince of Wales, Fiona Lees and Kristina Kyriacou, 13 September 2013

CONCLUSION

1. Author's conversation with the Prince of Wales, Birkhall, Scotland, 26 September 2013

2. Author's interview with Graham Smith, central London, 29 May 2014

3. Author's interview with Lord Berkeley, House of Lords, 3 April 2014

4. Hansard Debates for the House of Commons, 22 March 2001

5. Author's interview with Graham Smith, central London, 29 May 2014

6. Ibid.

7. *The Prince* by Niccolo Machiavelli, Chapter 19: 'That One Should Avoid Being Despised and Hated', first distributed 1513, first published 1532, Wankeep Publishing 2013

8. *Charles: The Private Man, the Public Role*, documentary presented and co-produced by Jonathan Dimbleby for ITV, first screened 30 June 1994

9. 'Prince of Wales: a private individual's effective veto over public legislation' by Robert Booth, *Guardian*, 30 October 2011

10. Public Accounts Committee – Minutes of Evidence / HC 475

11. Ibid.

12. House of Commons Committee of Public Accounts, The Duchy of Cornwall, HC 2013–2014

13. Author's interview with Lord Berkeley, House of Lords, 3 April 2014

14. Author's interview with Sir John Major, south London, 23 October 2014

15. House of Commons Committee of Public Accounts, The Sovereign Grant, Thirty-ninth Report of Session 2013–14, January 2014

16. Author's interview with Patrick Holden, central London, 6 August 2013

17. Author's interview with Fiona Reynolds, central London, 29 May 2014

18. Author's interview with Sir John Major, south London, 23 October 2014

19. Author's interview with Emma Thompson, 16 September 2013

20. Author's conversation with the Prince of Wales, Birkhall, Scotland, 26 September 2013

Selected Bibliography

Anker, Peder, *Imperial Ecology: Environmental Order in the British Empire, 1895–1945* (Harvard University Press, London, 2001)

Arbiter, Dickie, *On Duty with the Queen* (Blink Publishing, London, 2014)

Bartlett, Mike, *King Charles III* (Nick Hern Books, London, 2014)

Bedell Smith, Sally, *Diana: The life of a troubled princess* (Aurum Press Ltd, London, 1999)

—Bedell Smith, Sally, *Elizabeth the Queen: The life of a modern monarch* (Random House, 2012)

—Bedell Smith, Sally, *Elizabeth the Queen: The woman behind the throne* (Penguin Books, 2012)

Benson, Ross, *Charles: The untold story* (St. Martin's Press, New York, 1993)

Bernard, Philippa, *No End to Snowdrops* (Shepheard-Walwyn Ltd, London, 2009)

Blair, Tony, *My Vision of a Young Country* (Fourth Estate, London, 1996)

Bogdanor, Vernon, *The Monarchy and the Constitution* (Clarendon Press, Oxford, 1995)

Bower, Tom, *Fayed: The unauthorised biography* (Macmillan, London, 1998)

Boyd, William, *School Ties* (Penguin Books, London, 1985)

Bradford, Sarah, *Diana* (Penguin Books, London, 2007)

—Bradford, Sarah, *Queen Elizabeth II: Her life in our times* (Viking, London, 2012)

Brandreth, Gyles, *Breaking the Code: Westminster diaries* (Orion Publishing, London, 2000)

—Brandreth, Gyles, *Charles & Camilla* (Arrow Books, London, 2006)

Brown, Tina, *The Diana Chronicles* (Century, London, 2007)

Burden, Peter, *News of the World? Fake sheiks and royal trappings* (Eye Books, London, 2008)

Burrell, Paul, *A Royal Duty* (Penguin Books, London, 2004)

Campbell, Alastair, *Diaries Volume One: Prelude to power* (Arrow, London, 2011)

—Campbell, Alastair, *Diaries Volume Two: Power and the people* (Arrow, London, 2011)

—Campbell, Alastair, *Diaries Volume Three: Power and responsibility* (Arrow, London, 2012)

Cannadine, David, *Class in Britain* (Penguin Books, London, 2000)

Carpenter, Humphrey, *Robert Runcie: The reluctant archbishop* (Hodder & Stoughton Ltd, London, 1996)

Clayton, Tim and Craig, Phil (eds), *Diana: Story of a princess* (Hodder & Stoughton Ltd, London, 2001)

Cohen, David, *Diana: Death of a goddess* (Arrow, London, 2005)

Cohen, Nick, *You Can't Read this Book* (Fourth Estate, London, 2012)

Colley, Linda, *Acts of Union and Disunion* (Profile Books, London, 2014)

Crawford, Marion, *The Little Princesses* (Orion Publishing, London, 2012)

Critchlow, Keith, *The Hidden Geometry of Flowers: Living rhythms, form and number* (Floris Books, London, 2011)

Cunningham, Hugh, *The Invention of Childhood* (BBC Digital, London, 2012)

Cywinski, Sara, *Kate: Style princess* (John Blake Publishing Ltd, London, 2011)

Davenport-Hines, Richard, *An English Affair: Sex, class and power in the age of Profumo* (HarperPress, London, 2013)

Davies, Dan, *In Plain Sight: The life and lies of Jimmy Savile* (Quercus, London, 2014)

Davies, Nick, *Flat Earth News* (Vintage Books, London, 2009)

—Davies, Nick, *Hack Attack* (Chatto & Windus, London, 2014)

Dimbleby, Jonathan, *The Prince of Wales: A biography* (Little, Brown & Company, London, 1994)

Doyle, William, *The French Revolution: A very short introduction* (Oxford University Press, Oxford, 2001)

Duffel, Nick, *The Making of Them: The British attitude to children and the boarding school system* (Lone Arrow Press, London, 2000)

Goodall, Sarah and Monson, Nicholas (eds), *The Palace Diaries: Twelve years with HRH Prince Charles* (Mainstream Digital, London, 2012)

Gottlieb, Anthony, *The Dream of Reason* (Penguin, London, 2000)

Hardman, Robert, *Our Queen* (Hutchinson, London, 2011)

Heywood, Colin, *A History of Childhood* (Polity, Cambridge, 2001)

Hoey, Brian, *Mountbatten: The private story* (CB Creative Books, London, 2013)

Holden, Anthony, *Prince Charles: A biography* (Atheneum, New York, 1979)

—Holden, Anthony, *Of Presidents, Prime Ministers & Princes: A decade in Fleet Street* (Weidenfeld & Nicolson, London, 1984)

—Holden, Anthony, *A Princely Marriage: Charles and Diana, the first ten years* (Bantam Press, London, 1991)

—Holden, Anthony, *Charles: A biography* (Bantam Press, London, 1998)

Hollingsworth, Mark and Mitchell, Sandy (eds), *Saudi Babylon: Torture, corruption and cover-up inside the House of Saud* (Mainstream Digital, London, 2012)

HRH The Prince of Wales, *A Vision of Britain: A personal view of architecture* (Doubleday, London, 1989)

—HRH The Prince of Wales, *The Old Man of Lochnagar* (Picture Puffin, London, 1991)

—HRH The Prince of Wales, *Harmony: A vision for our future* (HarperCollins, London, 2010)

—HRH The Prince of Wales, eds Juniper, Tony and Skelly, Ian, *Harmony: A new way of looking at our World* (Blue Door, London, 2010)

Hutchins, Chris and Thompson, Peter (eds), *Diana's Nightmare: The family* (Christopher Hutchins Ltd, London, 2011)

Hutton, Will, *Them and Us: Changing Britain, why we need a fairer society* (Little, Brown & Company, London, 2010)

Jephson, Patrick, *Portraits of a Princess: Travels with Diana* (Sidgwick & Jackson Ltd, London, 2004)

Jobson, Robert, *William and Kate: The love story* (John Blake Publishing Ltd, London, 2010)

Jones, J. D. F., *Storyteller: The many lives of Laurens van der Post* (Scribner, London, 2002)

Joseph, Claudia, *Kate: The making of a princess* (Mainstream Publishing, London, 2010)

Jung, Carl, *Man and his Symbols* (Pan Books Ltd, London, 1978)

Junor, Penny, Prince Harry: *Brother, Soldier, Son* (Hodder & Stoughton, London, 2014)

Kear, Adrian and Steinberg, Deborah Lynn, *Mourning Diana: Nation, culture, and the performance of grief* (Routledge, London, 1999)

Kelley, Kitty, *The Royals* (Warner Books, New York, 1997)

Knatchbull, Timothy, *From a Clear Blue Sky* (Hutchinson, London, 2009)

Knevitt, Charles, *One's Life: A cartoon biography of HRH The Prince of Wales* (Michael Joseph, London, 1988)

—Knevitt, Charles, *From Pecksniff to the Prince of Wales: 150 years of* Punch *on architecture, planning and development, 1841–1991* (Polymath Publishing, London, 1991)

Lacey, Robert, *A Brief Life of the Queen* (Gerald Duckworth & Co. Ltd, London, 2012)

Lang, Andrew, *Pickle the Spy: Or, the incognito of Prince Charles* (Public Domain, London, 2012)

Levine, Tom, *Die Windsors* (Campus Verlag, Frankfurt Am Mein, 2005)

Lorimer, David, *Radical Prince: The practical vision of the Prince of Wales* (Floris Books, Edinburgh, 2004)

Machiavelli, Niccolo, *The Prince* (Waxkeep Publishing, London, 2013)

MacMillan, Margaret, *The War that Ended Peace: How Europe abandoned peace for the First World War* (Profile Books, London, 2013)

Marr, Andrew, *The Diamond Queen* (Macmillan, London, 2011)

—Marr, Andrew, *The Real Elizabeth: An intimate portrait of Queen Elizabeth II* (Henry Holt & Company, New York, 2012)

Mayer, Catherine, *The Royal Family: Britain's resilient monarchy celebrates Elizabeth II's 60-year reign* (Time Books, New York, 2012)

Mckinnon, Don, *In the Ring: A Commonwealth memoir* (Elliot and Thompson Ltd, London, 2013)

Morton, Andrew, *Diana: Her true story* (Simon & Schuster Books, London, 1992)

—Morton, Andrew, *William and Catherine: Their lives, their wedding* (Michael O'Mara Books, London, 2011)

Paxman, Jeremy, *On Royalty* (Penguin Books, London, 2007)

Peat, Sir Michael and Lawson, Edmund QC (eds), *Report to His Royal Highness the Prince of Wales* (published 13 March, 2003)

Pimlott, Ben, *The Queen: A biography of Elizabeth II* (HarperCollins, London, 1996)

—Pimlott, Ben, *The Queen: Elizabeth II and the monarchy* (HarperPress, London, 2012)

Price, Lance, *Where Power Lies* (Simon & Schuster, London, 2010)

Republic Campaign Ltd, *How to Win the Argument: Challenging common arguments made in favour of the monarchy* (Republic, London, 2010)

—Republic Campaign Ltd, *60 Inglorious Years: A provocative reassessment of the Queen's Record* (Republic, 2012)

Richards, Jeffrey; Wilson, Scott and Woodhead, Linda (eds), *Diana: The making of a media saint* (I. B. Tauris & Co., London, 1999)

Routledge, Paul, *Gordon Brown: The biography* (Simon & Schuster, London, 1998)

Sampson, Anthony, *The Changing Anatomy of Britain* (Book Club Associates, London, 1982)

Sedgwick, Mark J., *Against the Modern World: Traditionalism and the secret intellectual history of the twentieth century* (Oxford University Press, Oxford, 2004)

Shawcross, William, *Queen Elizabeth: The Queen Mother* (Macmillan Publishers, London, 2009)

Singh, Simon and Ernst, Edzard, *Trick or Treatment?* (Transworld Publishers, London, 2008)

Snell, Kate, *Diana: Her last love* (Granada Media, London, 2013)

Spicer, Michael, *The Spicer Diaries* (Thomas Dunne Books, London, 2012)

Starkey, David, *Crown and Country: A history of England through the monarchy* (HarperPress, London, 2010)

Straw, Jack, *Last Man Standing: Memoirs of a political survivor* (Macmillan, London, 2012)

Stubbs, David, *The Prince Charles Letters: A future monarch's correspondence on matters of the utmost concern* (Aurum Press, London, 2011)

Thatcher, Margaret, *The Downing Street Years* (HarperCollins, London, 1993)

Turner, Alwyn W., *Crisis? What Crisis?: Britain in the 1970s* (Aurum Press,

London, 2008)

Turner, Graham, *Elizabeth: The woman and the Queen* (Macmillan Publishers, London, 2002).

Van der Kiste, John, *Childhood at Court 1819–1914* (The History Press, Stroud, 2003)

Voltaire, *Candide* (Boni & Liveright, New York, 1918)

Watson, Tom, and Hickman, Martin, *Dial M for Murdoch* (Penguin Books, London, 2012)

Wharfe, Ken and Jobson, Robert (eds), *Diana: Closely guarded secret* (Michael O'Mara Books Ltd, 2003)

Whittle, Peter, *Monarchy Matters* (The Social Affairs Unit, London, 2011)

Wilson, Christopher, *A Greater Love: Prince Charles's twenty-year affair with Camilla Parker Bowles* (Headline Publishing, London, 1995)

—Wilson, Christopher, *The Windsor Knot: Charles, Camilla and the legacy of Diana* (Pinnacle Publishing, London, 2002)

Wright, Peter, *Spycatcher* (Viking Penguin, London, 1987)

Ziegler, Philip, *Mountbatten* (Collins, London, 1985)

Index

Index